FRONTISPIECE TO THE FIRST BOOK OF CONSTITUTIONS,
1723

THE CONCISE HISTORY OF FREEMASONRY

ROBERT FREKE GOULD

Revised by

FREDERICK J. W. CROWE

Illustrated

"The curious subject of Freemasonry has
unfortunately been treated only by panegyrists
or calumniators, both equally mendacious."
— HENRY HALLAM

"History, to be above evasion or dispute,
must stand on documents, not on opinions."
— LORD ACTON

DOVER PUBLICATIONS, INC.
Mineola, New York

Bibliographical Note

This Dover edition, first published in 2007, is an unabridged republication
of the Second (Revised) Edition of the work originally published in 1920 by
Gale & Polden Limited, London. The book was first published in 1903.

International Standard Book Number: 0-486-45603-X

Manufactured in the United States of America
Dover Publications, Inc., 31 East 2nd Street, Mineola, N.Y. 11501

PREFACE

*I must here claim your attention the more, because before you
I freely express my opinion as the best. My difficulty here is in
each case to place the things before you in their right light, or in
that light of which I am convinced it is the true one; but I hope I
shall succeed, if you will give me your undivided attention.*—B. G.
NIEBUHR: *Lectures on Ancient History.*

SINCE the publication of my original *History of Freemasonry,*
the first half-volume of which appeared in 1882 and the last in
1887, there has been a demand for an abridged edition, or for
a History of the Society conducted on the same lines, but in
a more compendious form.

In the meantime, moreover, the boundaries of the historic
domain embraced in my own Work have been greatly enlarged,
by the successful investigations of many distinguished contemporaries, and by the organized labours of the QUATUOR
CORONATI Lodge.

Learned books have been written on English, Irish, Scottish,
German, American, and Canadian Freemasonry; and valuable
monographs on the Manuscript Constitutions or written traditions of the Society, the *old* and *new* degrees of the Fraternity,
the customs of the German "Steinmetzen" and the French
"Companions," the Masons' Company of London, Masons'
Marks, the Religion of Freemasonry, and the Engraved, Printed,
and Manuscript Lists of the English Lodges.

The *Transactions* of the QUATUOR CORONATI Lodge are a
perennial fount of information, and among the Essays of enduring
value to be found there may be named the highly instructive
papers on *Masons' Marks, Masters' Lodges, The Proper Names
of Masonic Tradition* (a Philological Study), and *The Companionage*—by the late Professor HAYTER LEWIS and Mr. JOHN
LANE, the Rev. C. J. BALL, and Mr. W. H. RYLANDS
respectively—all of which may be said to have at once become

the leading authorities on the subjects to which they relate.
Nor can I leave unnoticed the interesting contributions of Mr.
W. J. HUGHAN and Dr. W. BEGEMANN, who have fully maintained their pre-eminence as expositors of the Old Scrolls of
the Fraternity.

In the preparation of the present volume, therefore, my
object has been to reconsider those portions of the original
Work which have been criticized by careful writers since its
publication, to illustrate and elucidate some passages which
were imperfectly or obscurely treated, to incorporate the results
of the latest discoveries, and to acknowledge with candour my
own mistakes.

In the execution of this design the whole subject-matter has
been entirely re-cast, re-written and brought up to date.

To use the words of Professor S. E. THOROLD ROGERS (in the
preface to his *Historical Gleanings*), "I have not undergirded
my pages with a single note," but evidential references to
authorities cited *for the first time* will be found within parentheses
in the text. For a large number of the authorities, however,
on which I have relied, the reader is referred to my original
History of Freemasonry, which contains fuller particulars of the
progress of the Craft in the various countries of the world than
are to be met with in any other work; while in the present volume
will be found a succinct account of Masonry in all its stages,
together with the fruits of the most recent research.

The first Chapter contains the leading theories with regard
to the origin of Freemasonry. In each of the four succeeding
Chapters will be found a sketch more or less connected with
the immediate subject-matter, of the history of British Freemasonry during the period preceding the era of Grand Lodges.

The second Chapter (which has been twice re-written) embraces a subject which has always had a particular interest
for architectural writers, whether members or not of our own
Society. In its preparation I derived much assistance from the
late Mr. WYATT PAPWORTH, who was not a Freemason, and
the fuller draft from which the present sketch is abridged received the cordial approval of the late Professor HAYTER
LEWIS, my fellow Past Master in the QUATUOR CORONATI Lodge.

I am greatly indebted moreover, to the Masonic collection of the former friend, kindly presented to me by Mrs. WYATT PAPWORTH, which ranges over a long series of years, and embraces almost every topic connected either nearly or remotely with the Masons' Art.

In the third Chapter there are some new speculations with respect to the problem of the Masonic Assembly; and in connection therewith I must not omit to record the obligation I am under to Mr. JOHN BILSON for tracings of the Yorkshire Forests as existing in the time of Edward I. The fourth Chapter embodies several recent discoveries, including noteworthy entries in the records of the Masons' Company of London, and in the Paston Letters, together with the account of a Speech delivered at Dublin in 1688, which attests the existence of a system of Speculative Masonry at the Irish capital during and prior to that year. In the fifth Chapter Dr. BEGEMANN rendered me an essential service, which is elsewhere acknowledged; and I have also to thank Mr. W. H. RYLANDS, who kindly figured for me the plates of Masons' Marks. A sufficiently exhaustive study of the written traditions of the Society having been given in this Chapter, the idea I had entertained (p. 146) of presenting a further classification of the Masonic Constitutions has been abandoned.

Chapter VI contains a Digression on the early Symbolism of the Craft, for which a foundation was laid in the fourth half-volume of my *History of Freemasonry*—published in 1885—where I show that *two* degrees, and not *three*, were referred to by Dr. ANDERSON as existing in 1723. Of Old Regulation XIII, in the *Constitutions* of that year, it may be remarked that the *number* of degrees to which it points as being practised at the time was as little understood in those days as (at any date prior to 1885) in our own, and to the general ignorance on this subject by the Craft at large was probably due the evolution of an additional degree, in order to conform with an imaginary tri-gradal system which was supposed to be recognized by the Grand Lodge. Of this there is collateral evidence in the famous Speech of FRANCIS DRAKE, Junior Grand Warden, at York, delivered *after* the publication of ANDERSON's *Con-*

stitutions. He mentions, in 1726, *three* degrees, which, however, were certainly unknown (or not practised) at York, in that year and much later, as we learn from the records of his Grand Lodge. In this Chapter, indeed, as well as in the next one (VII), many points are discussed in which my views are not in harmony with those of other writers. But, to adopt the words of Mr. FREDERIC HARRISON, in his lecture on *The Meaning of History*, "if opposite opinions are not noticed they have still been weighed. If I have spoken of many still debated topics almost as though they were decided, it is only because in such a plan as this any sort of controversy is out of place, not that I forget or slight all that has been urged on the other side. But discussion, like research, must have an end somewhere, and the great need now is not to increase but to use our stores of historical learning. After all, the only real answer to any theory of history, professing to be complete and not manifestly inconsistent, is the production of a counter theory at once more complete and consistent."

For the particulars relating to the "Ulster Schism" in Irish Masonry I am indebted to Dr. CHETWODE CRAWLEY.

In the preparation of Chapter VIII I was greatly assisted by Dr. W. BEGEMANN (Sweden—Norway—Denmark); CARL WIEBE, Grand Master of Hamburg (Germany—France); LADISLAS A. DE MALCZOVICH (Austria—Hungary); and the late J. P. VAILLANT (Holland).

Chapter X covers a wide field. The commentary, however, of the NESTOR of American Masonry, Past Grand Master JOSIAH H. DRUMMOND, of Maine, on my own history of the Craft in the United States, has smoothed many difficulties from my path; and the historiographer of the Grand Lodge of Canada, Past Grand Master JOHN ROSS ROBERTSON, has kindly furnished me with a *précis* of the progress of Masonry in the "Dominion."

The subject of Lodges in Regiments and Ships of War has been very fully treated by me in a separate Work—*Military Lodges, or Freemasonry under Arms* (Gale and Polden, Ltd., 1899).

Throughout the entire volume, it is essential to add, I have received the invaluable assistance of my friend, Mr. WILLIAM

JAMES HUGHAN, to whom also I am greatly indebted (as on the previous occasion when the larger "History" was passing through the press), for his kindness in reading the proofs. I must likewise acknowledge the unvarying courtesy of Mr. HENRY SADLER, Sub-Librarian of the Grand Lodge of England, whenever I have had occasion to consult the printed and manuscript volumes of which he is the custodian.

Many speculations, both curious and entertaining, have been advanced by contemporary Masonic writers, but their consideration lies far outside the scope of the present Work. For example (to borrow from the excellent manual of MM. LANGLOIS and SEIGNOBOS), "we meet with declarations like the following: 'I have been long familiar with the documents of this period and this class. I have an impression that such and such conclusions, which I cannot prove, are true.' Of two things, one: either the author can give the reasons for his impression, and then we can judge them, or he cannot give them, and we may assume that he has none of serious value" (*Introd. to the Study of History*, translated by G. G. Berry).

The name of the Laird of Auchinleck (1600) was *John*, and not *James* Boswell, as inadvertently shown on p. 184. A similar mistake occurs on p. 321, where for *James* should be read *Charles* Ratcliffe. Any other misprints that are detected will be found on a separate page.

> "And this, gentle reader, I hartelie protest,
> Where erroure hath happened, I wisshe it redrest."

R. F. GOULD.

WOKING,
September, 1903.

PREFACE TO THE REVISED EDITION

AT the request of the Publishers, I have brought the *Concise History* up to date, and made certain alterations in the body of the Work. The alterations are mostly in the way of condensing the matter of the earlier chapters, which was often in danger of becoming tedious and irrelevant, but the principal change I have made is to re-write the first part of Chapter VII. Since Mr. Sadler made his most valuable researches in the archives of Grand Lodge and elsewhere, it has become clear to all students of our history that his view of the Irish origin of the Grand Lodge of the Ancients is the correct one, and I feel sure I shall be supported by all lovers of truth in the changes I have made.

In regard to the "Higher" or "Additional" degrees, the notices of them are so meagre and so scattered that I have thought it advisable to add Chapter VIIA, giving a compact summary of the degrees usually worked in Europe and America and the Dominions and Colonies.

My thanks are due to the BOARD OF GENERAL PURPOSES for their kind permission to reproduce the Grant of Arms, and other documents in the Grand Lodge Library; to the Grand Secretary Mr. P. COLVILLE SMITH, and Dr. HAMMOND the Grand Librarian, for valuable assistance; also Mr. H. H. SADLER for permission to copy the plate of English and Irish Grand Lodge seals from his father's book, *Masonic Facts and Fictions*.

I trust the bringing up to date of the statistics and other information will render the book as serviceable to present-day readers as it has been to others in the past.

FRED. J. W. CROWE.

S. PETER'S HOUSE, CHICHESTER.
  June, 1920.

CONTENTS

CHAPTER I

PAGE

INTRODUCTORY — THE ANCIENT MYSTERIES — THE ESSENES—THE ROMAN COLLEGES—THE CULDEES —THE VEHM-GERICHTE—THE STEINMETZEN—THE FRENCH CORPS D'ÉTAT—THE COMPANIONAGE—THE ROSICRUCIANS 1

CHAPTER II

MEDIÆVAL OPERATIVE MASONRY 57

CHAPTER III

THE ENGLISH LAWS OF THE MIDDLE AGES AND THE FREEMASONS 80

CHAPTER IV

THE STORY OF THE GUILD 96

CHAPTER V

THE LEGEND OF THE CRAFT—THE QUATUOR CORONATI, OR FOUR CROWNED MARTYRS—MASONS' MARKS ... 125

CHAPTER VI

THE EARLY SCOTTISH CRAFT—GRAND LODGES—THE EPOCH OF TRANSITION—A DIGRESSION ON DEGREES —FREEMASONRY IN THE BRITISH ISLES 170

CHAPTER VII

PAGE

THE GREAT DIVISION IN ENGLISH MASONRY—THE
LATER HISTORIES OF THE GRAND LODGES OF ENG-
LAND, SCOTLAND, AND IRELAND 252

CHAPTER VIIA

A CONCISE NOTICE OF THE ADDITIONAL DEGREES USUALLY
WORKED 269

CHAPTER VIII

FREEMASONRY IN EUROPE 277

CHAPTER IX

ASIA—THE EAST INDIA ISLANDS—THE FAR EAST—ASIA
MINOR—AFRICA—THE WEST INDIES—CENTRAL AND
SOUTH AMERICA 317

CHAPTER X

THE UNITED STATES OF AMERICA—CANADA AND NEW-
FOUNDLAND—AUSTRALASIA—OCEANIA 332

APPENDIX

GRANT OF ARMS TO THE UNITED GRAND LODGE OF
ENGLAND 351
INDEX 356

LIST OF ILLUSTRATIONS

FRONTISPIECE TO THE FIRST BOOK OF CONSTITUTIONS,
1723 ... ... *Frontispiece*

Facing page

CONDUITE DE COMPAGNONS DU DEVOIR 32

GRANT OF ARMS TO THE UNITED GRAND LODGE OF
ENGLAND 64

PORTRAIT OF THE FAMOUS ANTIQUARY, ELIAS ASH-
MOLE 114

ORIGINAL SUMMONS OF THE OLD "GRAND LODGE
OF ALL ENGLAND," AT YORK 122

ILLUMINATED HEADING OF THE "HADDON" MS. 125

THE OLDEST extant WARRANT IN THE WORLD (1731) ... 190

PORTRAIT OF ANTHONY SAYER, FIRST GRAND MASTER... 201

THE "GOOSE AND GRIDIRON" TAVERN 203

ANCIENT SUMMONS OF A LODGE AT NUREMBERG 239

OLD CERTIFICATE OF THE "ANCIENTS" GRAND LODGE,
DATE, 1805 250

PLATE OF SEALS FOR COMPARISON 254

ANCIENT FRENCH COMMEMORATIVE ENGRAVING, DATED
1789 277

FREDERICK THE GREAT 282

MARSHAL BLUCHER AS MASTER OF A LODGE 292

PORTRAIT OF GENERAL WASHINGTON 332

THE CONCISE
HISTORY OF FREEMASONRY

CHAPTER I

INTRODUCTORY

*What signifies it, for instance, that we attribute letters to
Cadmus, or trace oracles to Zoroaster, or the Cabbala to Moses,
the Eleusinian Mysteries to Orpheus, or Freemasonry to Noah;
whilst we are profoundly ignorant of the nature and true beginning of any one of these things?*—ANON.

WHO the early Freemasons really were, and whence they
came, may afford a tempting theme for inquiry to the
speculative antiquary. But it is enveloped in obscurity,
and lies far outside the domain of authentic history. In
proceeding retrogressively, and attempting to trace the
origin of the Society, when we reach the fourteenth century
the genealogical proofs are exhausted. Still, from the
documentary evidence which has carried us thus far, we
shall at least be justified in assuming that the Masonry
practised in the Lodges of that period was of no recent
institution. Beyond this conclusion, nothing further can
be confidently laid down with regard to the more remote
past of the sodality. Certain possibilities are, indeed,
suggested by the evidence, and to these attention will
again be directed; but as my own inferences may be found
to differ in some material respects from those of other
writers, it will be best if a short summary is first proceeded
with of the leading theories of Masonic origin that have
seemed tenable to our *literati*.

A few explanatory words may, however, place the method
of treatment I am about to adopt in a clearer light before
the reader.

Freemasonry has exercised a remarkable influence over all other oath-bound societies for a long period. What that period is cannot be absolutely, though it may be approximately, determined. The second quarter of the eighteenth century constitutes a sort of zone that will illustrate my meaning. About the year 1725 Freemasonry was beginning to be widely known, and about the year 1750 it had become thoroughly so. If, therefore, we can trace the customs of any oath-bound societies as they existed, let us say before 1725, there is strong probability, amounting almost to certainty, that such were in no way influenced or affected by Freemasonry. But directly that line is passed, and we are introduced to usages which prevailed at any later date, the suspicion will arise that the influence of our own Craft may have made itself felt, and it will resolve itself into a mere question of degree, becoming extensive or the reverse, according to the evidence dating earlier or later in that century. As we pass, moreover, from the eighteenth to the nineteenth century, what was previously suspicion will merge into strong probability or more. Evidence of customs now existing by no means proves that they are of very old standing. If the ceremonial of the Craft to a certain extent finds a parallel in the present observances of the Druses and the Ansariyeh —that is to say, if the writers, by whom we are so informed, have not been misled by resemblances more or less fanciful and imaginary—then I believe that these sectaries of Mount Lebanon adopted some of the practices of the Freemasons. The same may be said with respect to the rites of many other secret societies of current date—for example, the Begtaschi of Turkey, and the Yesidis of Armenia and Asia Minor. Though I must not pass over in silence an alternative supposition, namely, what has been called "the doctrine of chance coincidences," which may possibly be held to apply in some of the cases I have already cited, and certainly appears to myself to fully account for the great bulk of stories that are related of so-called "Masonic signs" having been exchanged by travellers with Arabs, Abyssinians, Dervishes, North American Indians, Australian natives, and the various tribes of Africa.

Examples of older types of such associations may be found in the Soofees of Persia; in the Komosô of Japan (now extinct), who challenged one another by signs; and very possibly in the leading secret societies of China, which claim to have existed for several centuries, and admit their members with ceremonies approximating more or less closely to our own.

The late Sir Chaloner Alabaster, who was not only one of our most respected sinologues, but also an indefatigable student of Freemasonry, tells us:—"Going then to the records we possess of the earliest historic times in China, I find clear evidence of the existence of a mystic faith expressed in allegorical form, and illustrated, as with us, by symbols. The secrets of this faith were orally transmitted, the chiefs alone pretending to have full knowledge of them. I find, moreover, that in these earliest ages this faith took a Masonic form, the secrets being recorded in symbol buildings like the Tabernacle Moses put up in the desert, and the Temple his successor, Solomon, built in Jerusalem; that the various offices in the hierarchy of this religion were distinguished by the symbolic jewels held by them during their term of office, and that, as with us, at the rites of their religion they wore leather aprons, such as have come down to us, marked with the insignia of their rank. I find in the earliest works that have come down to us . . . the compasses and the square used as the symbol of right conduct. The man who had the compasses and square, and regulated his life thereby, being then, as now, considered to possess the secrets and to carry out the principles of true propriety. Finally, I find one of the most ancient names by which the Deity is spoken of in China is that of the First Builder, or, as Masons say, "the Great Architect of the Universe."

According to the same authority, "the Mysteries of this ancient Faith have now become lost, or at best obscured, though attempts at a revival may be traced in the proceedings of existing brotherhoods, whose various rituals and signs are supposed to be in some measure founded on ancient rites and symbols which have been handed down from the earliest ages."

The extracts from the oldest of the Chinese classics which refer to the symbolism of the mason's art might be greatly multiplied, but a sufficiency has been adduced to warrant the assumption that among a very ancient people, and long prior to the Christian era, there was a moralization of the implements of the mason's trade, together with a symbolical teaching which in course of time became lost or obscured.

THE ANCIENT MYSTERIES

There is nothing definite which points to the country wherein the Mysteries were first introduced. The most ancient, indeed, are generally supposed to have been those of Isis and Osiris, in Egypt and the most widely diffused the Orphic, the Bacchic or Dionysiac, the Eleusinian, the Samothracian, the Cabiric, and the Mithraic. The Eleusinian, which enjoyed a pre-eminence in Greece, were celebrated annually at the festival of Ceres at Eleusis. Initiates were first of all admitted into the lesser Eleusinia, after which they bore the title of Mystæ, and, having served a probation of twelve months, a second oath of secrecy was imposed upon them, and they were led into the innermost sanctuary of the temple, where they were allowed to see what it was not proper for any but the Epoptæ to behold.

Of the Mysteries, indeed, as existing in different countries, it may be said that they were distinguished by varying forms, while it is equally certain that there was a great similarity between them all. The ceremonies of initiation were invariably funereal in their character. They celebrated the death and the resurrection of some cherished being, either the object of esteem as a hero, or of devotion as a god.

The conformity between death and initiation is strikingly exemplified in a passage preserved by Stobæus from an ancient record, and runs thus:—"The mind is affected and agitated in death, just as it is in initiation into the Great Mysteries; the first stage is nothing but errors and uncertainties, labourings, wanderings, and darkness. And now, arrived on the verge of death and initiation, everything wears a dreadful aspect; it is all horror, trembling, and affrightment. But this scene once over, a miraculous and divine light displays itself . . . perfect and initiated, they are free; and crowned and triumphant, they walk up and down in the regions of the blessed.

"The light exhibited in the Eleusinian Mysteries, *i.e.*, in the true initiations, as is plainly to be gathered from the sense of the Ancients, was the Light of Life which these could kindle and fortify, and the total drama was divine."

> . . . Thy piercing sight
> Beholds in paths oblique a sacred light.
> Whose plenteous rays *in darkness most profound,*
> Thy steps directed and illumined round.
> While from your eyes you shake the gloom of night,
> The glorious prospect bursts upon your sight.

As recently summed up, the result of modern researches appears to be that the worship of the One God was the basis on which the vast amount of Pagan Mythology was ultimately formed, and that the splendour of the beams of the Sun rising in the East was idealized as the visible representation of the Deity; whilst the West, in which its glory disappeared, was considered as an emblem of the regions of death.

It is doubtless true that the later, or corrupted, Mysteries became greatly contaminated and debased, but this ought not to lessen our esteem for the original institution, to which the subsequent orgies were diametrically opposed. It is sufficiently clear that those initiated into the earlier or pure Mysteries were taught to believe not only in Providence, but in a future state.

There was undoubtedly a secret hanging about these

celebrations, both Ethnic and Christian, which no record
has entirely divulged. It would also seem that, as time
went on, new elements were added to the Mysteries which
were originally foreign to them. The development of
philosophy, and more especially the intercourse with Egypt
and the East, appear to have exercised a considerable influence on their character.

The Greeks borrowed extensively from the Egyptians
and Persians, whose temples were visited by nearly every
philosopher of note.

The Egyptian, or Hermetic Art, was by the Greeks
called Theurgy, and it was practised to a great extent at
Eleusis, and more or less in all the temples of their gods.

Philosophy, according to Strabo, was the object of the
Eleusinian rites, and without the initiations of Bacchus and
Ceres he considers the most important branch of human
knowledge would never have been attained.

In all forms of the Ancient Mysteries signs of recognition
were communicated to the initiated. Thus, in describing
the action of one of the votaries of the Mysteries of Isis,
Apuleius (*Metamorph.*) says: "He walked gently, with a
hesitating step, the ankle of the left foot being a little bent,
in order that he might afford me some sign by which I
might recognize him." And in another work (*Apologia*)
by the same writer, there is an almost identical allusion
to the practice of initiates communicating with one another
by means of signs—a custom of which a further illustration
is given by Plautus in his *Miles Gloriosus*, where the words
occur:—

"Give me the sign, if you are one of these votaries."

None of the Ancient Mysteries afford a more interesting
subject for Masonic research than those of Mithras—the
Sun-god or Persian Apollo—who is generally represented
as a beautiful youth dressed in Phrygian attire, pressing
with his knee upon an ox, into whose neck he plunges a
knife.

From the Mithraic monuments in the collections at the
Louvre and the British Museum, it may reasonably be

concluded that the immortality of the soul was one of the doctrines taught by the worshippers of the Sun-god. The neophyte, at one part of the ceremony, was made to personate a corpse, whose restoration to life dramatically represented the resurrection.

Sir Charles Warren, in his review of my *Military Lodges*, wishing to point out that, in the Army, Masonry banishes class and even rank distinctions, without in the least endangering discipline, quotes instances where subalterns, and even non-commissioned officers, have controlled Lodges in which superior officers were sitting as ordinary members.

Is it not strange, says Count Goblet D'Alviella (after citing the above), that there are cases exactly parallel in the Mithraic Mysteries under the old Romans? It is a well-known fact that these Mysteries offer striking analogies with much that is found in Freemasonry: their celebration in grottoes or covered halls, which symbolized the Universe, and which in dimensions, disposition, and decoration, presented a strict counterpart to our Lodges; their division in seven degrees conferred by initiatory rites wonderfully like our own; their method of teaching, through the same astronomic symbolism, the highest truths then known in Philosophy and Morals; their mystic bond of secrecy, toleration, equality, and brotherly love.

Professor Franz Cumont, having devoted the last ten years to the study of this worship, has just published a most trustworthy and powerful book (*Textes et Doc. rel. aux Mysteres de Mithra*). Not only does he confirm the alleged similarities, but he also presents new ones. For instance, he shows that it was not uncommon for a non-commissioned officer, or even a simple soldier, to preside over ceremonies where legates and *clarissimi* played a subordinate part, in accordance with their respective degrees in the Mysteries.

Their discipline established not only a strict equality among their members, in spite of all outside social distinctions, but also a bond of real brotherhood and of mutual help. Their successive initiations favoured emulation, gave the neophytes something to look for, and also flattered the vanity of those who were fond of high-sounding titles. Finally, their prospect of revelations, deeper and deeper at every stage, fostered a hope to reach a supreme goal—the absolute wisdom whose secret was supposed to have been brought from the East.

How came it then to pass that this sudden rise was followed by a still more rapid fall? Our author explains that by excluding the women from their worship they parted with an element of propagandism which the Christian faith knew how to utilize. Thus the Mysteries of Mithras were doomed to disappear before the Mysteries of Christ. But their doctrine was not entirely lost; it survived among the Manichæans and other heretics who strove, until the close of the Middle Ages, to reconcile Zoroastrianism with Christianity.

THE ESSENES

The three chief Jewish sects appear to have been the Hellenists, the Maccabeans, and the Chassidim. The last-named were the Puritans among the post-Babylonian Jews, but in process of time, their principles becoming too narrow, they split up into two divisions, the *Essenes*, who strictly adhered to the old customs and devoted themselves to a retired life, while the less austere party (to which the Pharisees belonged) retained the title of *Chassidim*.

The references to the Essenes by ancient authors are brief and unsatisfactory. We learn, however, that before the acceptance of a candidate, a solemn obligation was entered into by him that he would suffer death rather than reveal the secrets of the brotherhood; that two members of this singular sect, on meeting for the first time, at once recognized each other by means of signs; and that it was the general practice of the fraternity to philosophize on most things in symbols.

The Essenes are first mentioned as a distinct sect in the time of Jonathan the Maccabean, about 160 years before Christ. Our Saviour has been supposed, by many writers, to have been an Essene, because, while repeatedly denouncing the errors of the other sects, He has nowhere uttered a word of censure against the Essenes. John the Baptist was described by our Lord as having attained the highest degree of Essene purity (*Matt.* xi, 14), and much of the Sermon on the Mount is expressed in the phraseology of the sect.

They had a common treasury, and from this the wants of the whole community were supplied, so that they had all things in common. There were no distinctions among them. The only gradation of rank that existed was derived from the degrees or orders into which the members were divided, and this depended on holiness alone. They got up before sunrise, and, before entering upon the business of the day, prayed together with their faces turned towards the East. At the fifth hour the morning labour terminated, and, in solemn silence, the brethren partook of a common meal.

As the majority lived in celibacy, the ranks of the brotherhood were only kept up by the admission of proselytes from the other sects. The candidate, or aspirant, was required to pass through a novitiate of two stages, the first of which lasted for a year. After this probation he passed into the second stage, and was called an *approacher*. Two years were then allowed to elapse, and the aspirant, if his conduct met with approval, became an *associate* (or full member of the brotherhood), and was allowed to partake of the common meal.

There was a third rank or degree, called *disciple* or *companion*, in which there was a still closer union. Those who were admitted into this highest grade received a threefold rule for the conduct of their life—Love of God, of Virtue, and of Mankind—and they were bound by a solemn oath to practise charity, maintain truth, and to conceal the secrets of the society.

It is reasonable to assume that the principal doctrines and practices of the Essenes must have assimilated many foreign elements, and the opinion that they borrowed largely from the "old Oriental, Parsee, and Chaldean notions," may be said to have been very commonly accepted.

In a remarkable book—*The Three Oldest Documents of the Freemasons*, which, notwithstanding its errors, is one of the most learned works ever written on the early history of our Society—Dr. Krause argues that the customs and doctrines of the Craft were inherited from the Culdees, and in the usages of the latter he finds numerous points of agreement with those of the Essenes and the Roman *Collegia*.

A still bolder hypothesis has been advanced by Mr. Herbert, in his *Britannia after the Romans*. According to this writer, when the Essenes were driven from what he imagines to have been their ancient cœnobium at Engaddi by Zoar, England became the new Engaddi, and the seat of the chief Essene Lodge.

Passing over this fanciful supposition, we shall hardly err if we attribute what similarity there may be found to exist between the customs of the Essenes, the School of Pythagoras, and the Freemasons, to the spirit of brotherhood which has prevailed in all ages throughout the civilized world. The characteristics of any fraternity—all of whose members are engaged in the same pursuit and votaries of the same creed—will, on a close view appear to be brotherly love, charity, and that secrecy which gives them their exclusiveness. Hence, between all societies, ancient or modern, which are united by a fraternal tie, these "remarkable coincidences" will be found to exist.

THE ROMAN COLLEGES

Many learned works and a variety of existing inscriptions furnish conclusive evidence of the survival of the *Collegia* until the "Decline and Fall" of Imperial Rome. To each of the Roman Legions there was attached a college or corporation of artificers, which served with it throughout its campaigns, and whose mission it often was to plant on foreign soil the seeds of Roman civilization, and to teach the principles of Roman art.

When Britain was subdued by the Romans, the legions that went there took with them, of course, their colleges of artificers. After a time, however, owing to the decay of the Empire, Britain was abandoned, and the natives, together with the Romans who had settled among them, were left to defend the country from the attacks of the barbarians.

The Roman colonists also possessed their colleges. Mr. Coote observes, "No sooner was the Roman conquest of Britain begun, and a *modicum* of territory was obtained, than we find a *collegium* in our own *civitas Regnorum*—a *collegium fabrorum*" (*The Romans of Britain*). This statement rests on the authority of a tablet which was discovered at Chichester (or *Regnum*) in 1723, recording the erection of a temple to Neptune and Minerva. There is other sculptured evidence of the existence of this corporation, which probably embraced the masons, carpenters, and the professors of many other arts and trades. But the Chichester inscription is the most famous, because of its recital that this temple, to two purely Italian Deities, was erected by the order of a British Prince, Tiberius Claudius Cogidubnus, who appears to have accepted the dignity of a *legatus* while continuing to assert his own title of *rex*. That many points of resemblance will be found between what is actually known of the *Collegia* and the customs of the building corporations of later date, is free from doubt. Indeed, the opinion has been advanced that the coincidences which exist cannot be attributed to imitation or mere copying, but fully demonstrate the absolute identity of the guild of England with the *collegium* of Rome and of Roman Britain.

The craft guilds do not come into notice before the Norman Conquest, yet, on the other hand, they show themselves very shortly afterwards, and there seems no good reason for denying them any previous existence. The actual derivation of any of the three forms of guild can only, however, be regarded as a pure matter of conjecture. From one point of view the guild bears a strong likeness to the family tie of the Germans; from another, it assumes

the appearance of a sort of bail; while from a third it
closely resembles the association of which a sketch is now
being presented, *i.e.*, the *collegium* (or *corpus*) of the Romans.

These associations sometimes consisted of religious
bodies, and at others of official persons, of corporations
the members of which followed a common occupation,
and of sodalities which closely resembled our modern
clubs.

Among the general features by which the colleges were
distinguished we find the following:—under the Empire
and before it, they were corporations composed of men
voluntarily bound together for a common lawful purpose.

The number of *sodales* or *collegæ* who composed the
college could not be less than three, and it might be any
larger number.

Each college had its appropriate officers, a Master,
decuriones (in whom may be traced a certain similarity
to the wardens of a Lodge), a secretary, and treasurer.

The *collegæ* (or companions) had a common chest and,
a *curia* (or meeting house) where the whole sodality assembled at their general meetings and to feast. This habit of
dining together must also have necessarily involved the
custom of a free interchange of thought. Free thought,
therefore, found in the colleges a refuge and a home. However the law might restrict the meetings, and attempt to
regulate the formal conferences of the members, it never
affected (any more than the "Constitutions" of the Freemasons) to interfere with what occurred at the social
board.

Candidates were required to take a solemn obligation
prior to their admission, and the *sodales* supported their
poor brethren.

It is, indeed, asserted by authorities of weight that the
members did not, like the Freemasons, exchange the title
of "Brother," but, if we believe Mr. Coote, "the *sodales*
called and regarded themselves as *fratres*," a point which
he seems to have made perfectly clear in the work to which
I have previously referred.

It is stated—though only by Masonic writers—that the colleges held secret meetings, in which the business transacted was the initiation of neophytes into the Fraternity, and of mystical and esoteric instructions to their apprentices and journeymen. We also learn, through the same channel, that the colleges of workmen made a symbolic use of the implements of their art or profession.

On various grounds, therefore, the speculation has been advanced that in the form, the organization, the method of government, and the customs of the Roman colleges, there is an analogy between these ancient corporations and the modern Masonic Lodges which is evidently more than accidental.

THE CULDEES

When St. Augustine came to Britain in the sixth century, for the purpose of converting the natives to Christianity, he found the country already occupied by a body of priests and their disciples, who were distinguished for the pure and simple apostolical religion which they professed. These were the Culdees, and though the actual name does not appear until the eighth century, so long as the monks of the Celtic Church were the only clergy in the country, it is plain that no special epithet was needed to point them out.

They were virtually merged in the Roman Church after the close of the twelfth century, though traces of their existence are to be found at a much later date. Their origin is lost in obscurity. It has been supposed by some authorities that they came from Phœnicia, while by others it has been asserted that they accompanied the Roman legions to Britain. Their chief seat appears to have been at Iona, where (according to a third conjecture) St. Columba, the founder of the sect, proceeding from Ireland with twelve brethren—A.D. 563—established their principal monastery.

It is quite clear, indeed, that Iona was not the original any more than it was the only seat of the Culdees. There were ministers of religion called by that name in North and South Britain, in Ireland, and in Wales.

The Culdees were the officiating clergy of the Cathedral Church of St. Peter's at York in 936, and their prayers were invoked by King Athelstan, in that year, on behalf of himself and his expedition against the Scotch. Returning victorious from his campaign, the King publicly offered up thanks in St. Peter's Church, and he granted the *Colidei* and their successors a thrave of corn from every plough-land in the diocese of York, in order that they might be able for all time to extend relief to the poor, to exercise the duties of hospitality, and to continue to perform the works of piety so well discharged by them in the past.

According to the "Legend of the Craft," the mightiest warrior who ever sat upon the throne of Saxon England, like the Saviour of Christendom, Charles Martel, and other military patrons of the Craft of earlier date, loved Masons well; but his son, Edwin, loved them better still, and procured for them from the King, his father, a charter, or commission, to hold every year an Assembly, and Edwin himself held an Assembly at York.

Athelstan, indeed, had no son, at least in the Royal line, but the Manuscript Constitutions of our Society are very strikingly in accord with regard to Edwin being a patron and York the traditional centre of early English Free-masonry.

Anachronisms, however, are plentiful in all legendary narratives, and that the Edwin of Masonic tradition was the first Christian King of Northumbria is a suggestion which has much to recommend it.

The written traditions of the Freemasons will be considered in a later chapter, but, in passing from the subject, the thought may be expressed that the name and fame of each of those great soldiers, St. Edwin, King and Martyr, and our "Glorious Athelstan," continue to be preserved in the "Legend of the Craft."

It has been maintained that a connection existed between the Roman Collegia and the Culdees, and the latter are said to have organized, as a part of their system, corporations of builders, while, on the other hand, it has been contended that they rarely, if ever, figured as architects or constructors, but were chiefly occupied in educating mankind by imparting a knowledge of those pure principles which they taught in their Lodges.

THE VEHM-GERICHTE, OR FEHM-GERICHTE

The Vehmic tribunals were the secret criminal courts of Westphalia in the Middle Ages. The reception of the chiefs and free judges was of a most imposing character, and, for many reasons, these courts have been considered to possess many points common to Freemasonry. There were curious forms of initiation, a system of enigmatical phrases, and a use of signs and symbols of recognition. The Emperor was the head of the institution, and next to him came the free counts, after whom were the free judges and the assessors or counsellors.

Initiation could only take place on the "red earth," *i.e.*, within the limits of the ancient Duchy of Westphalia. The candidate appeared bare-headed, and took a solemn oath. He then received the password, together with the modes of recognition, whereby he would be able to discover his fellow-members. The sign is described to have been made by placing, when at table, the points of the knives in their own direction, and the hafts away from them. Three separate degrees of mystic receptions are mentioned in one of the Vehmic Codes. The punishment of a member who betrayed any of the secrets of the association was very severe. His tongue was torn out by the roots, and he was hung on a tree seven feet higher than any felon.

The courts were opened by a colloquy between the officials, and if any stranger was found to be present his life paid forfeit for his temerity.

During the fourteenth and fifteenth centuries the power of the Vehm-Gerichte was at its height; after that its influence rapidly waned, and while secret meetings continued to be held, they were shorn of any real authority. The institution is said to have lingered, at least in name, until finally suppressed by decree of Jerome Bonaparte in 1811.

THE STONEMASONS (STEINMETZEN) OF GERMANY

From the sixth to the twelfth century, by which latter date most of the monasteries were completed, they may be regarded as the earliest school of Masonry, and the cradle of architecture in Germany. They did not, however, contribute in any way towards the organization of the stonemasons. For the origin of this sodality we must look to the trade guilds, which, beginning in the towns in the tenth century, or earlier, gradually increased in number and importance, until, in the twelfth, they had extended throughout the greater part of Germany. The charter of the twenty-three fishers, in Worms, was sanctioned by Bishop Adelbert, A.D. 1106. Another was granted by the Emperor Lothaire II to the clothmakers of Quedlimburg in 1134. But there can be no doubt that, as in England, guilds were frequently in existence for long periods before it was considered necessary to obtain any written authority for their proceedings.

The power wielded by these associations went on increasing, but at the Diet of Worms in 1231 it experienced a check, as so many complaints were made of the trade guilds of the towns that King Henry summarily dissolved all such societies, without any exception, then existing in the German cities—which decree was confirmed by the Emperor in 1232. This decree, however, was never carried into effect, although again confirmed by the Emperor Rudolf of Hapsburg in 1275, and the guilds were shortly afterwards fully reinstated—by the same monarch—in their former privileges.

In the German towns of the Middle Ages there were two classes. One, the patrician class, represented by the burghers' guild; the other, and lower class, by the craft guild. But, about the close of the fourteenth century, the latter had everywhere either seized the government of the towns from the hands of the former, or at least obtained a share in it by the side of the burghers' guild.

The next movement was initiated by the masters, who gradually excluded the workmen from their meetings. This took place in all guilds, the stonemasons alone forming an exception, but not a lasting one, as the same custom, though probably not until the end of the seventeenth century, eventually became a feature of their system. The workmen (journeymen), therefore, founded guilds or fraternities of their own, sometimes electing officers of their own body, at others from among the masters. The works written about these societies are very numerous, and in many instances the accounts given of them will assist us in forming an opinion of the usages of the stonemasons, which, though closely akin to those of the other craft guilds, nevertheless, in particular matters, differed from them all.

It is possible that somewhere about the twelfth century the skilled masons of the monasteries amalgamated with the craft builders in the towns, and together formed the society afterwards known throughout Germany as the *Steinmetzen.*

By German writers the exodus from the convents is placed at about this date, but as they ordinarily attribute the origin of the *trade* association to the cloister builders, any previously existing guilds of stonemasons are able to be dispensed with altogether. But in the twelfth century the stonemasons are certainly met with as a distinct fraternity, and the evidence points in the direction of their having had their origin neither in the cities nor the convents exclusively, but, with greater probability, in both concurrently.

All trades were inclined to subdivide themselves, and this custom was adopted by the *Spinnewetter*, which originally comprised all the building trades; a branch of this corporation—the masons—further split up into minor ramifications, and we find these offshoots taking the names of *Steinmetzen* (stonemasons), *Steinhauer* (stonecutters), and *Maurer* (masons, rough masons, bricklayers, etc.). It is with the first-named of these, the stonemasons, that we are now concerned, and whose later history, as revealed by their own records, will next be proceeded with.

At this point it will be convenient if three dates are borne in mind—the years 1459, 1462, and 1563, in each of which a Code (or set) of Statutes was enacted, and these, examined collectively, will carry us a good way towards a full comprehension of the inner life and organization of the *Steinmetzen*.

The Statutes referred to might with equal propriety be described as Laws or Regulations, but to avoid ambiguity they will be separately classified as the Strasburg Constitutions of 1459, the Torgau Ordinances of 1462, and the Brother Book of 1563.

The Constitutions of 1459 recite that, the Masters and Fellows having held meetings at Speyer, Strasburg, and Ratisbon, Jost Dotzinger, of Worms, Master of the buildings at Strasburg Cathedral—and his successors for ever—was acknowledged as chief judge (*oberster Rychter*) of the fraternity. But in the next clause—enacted at Ratisbon in 1459, and at Speyer in 1463—the Masters of Work at Cologne and Vienna were each recognized as occupying a similar position in his own district. Lower down still, a fourth chief judge is named as wielding authority—over the entire Swiss Confederation—at Bern. Then follow the names of six persons who agreed to these laws on April 9th, 1464, and of twenty-one others by whom they were subscribed "four weeks after Easter," 1459.

These Constitutions present a very good picture of the stonemasons at that stage of their career, and of the association, in its general aspect, as it must have existed for a century or more before. After this period all disputes were rendered less probable by the formation of a general guild or fraternity, and four Chief Lodges to which all differences were to be referred. Of these Head Lodges, that at Strasburg was unquestionably the chief.

The Code of 1459, with probably some slight alterations in particular regulations, continued in force until 1563. In the latter year a revision took place at two meetings, held at Bale and Strasburg respectively. According to the later Code, Thuringia, Saxony, and Frankfort disappear from the rule of Strasburg. These territories, it is believed, had been constituted into a separate province, under a fifth Head Lodge at Dresden. As will presently appear, the stonemasons of the new province held an assembly of their own and passed a set of Ordinances in 1462.

The Brother Book of 1563 is the latest Code of Laws relating to the German stonemasons that has come down to us. It was printed in folio form and a copy sent to every Lodge of importance, the master of which was willing to join the fraternity. We may assume that it continued to regulate the trade until quite recent times, leaving out of sight for the present the supremacy of the Strasburg Chief Lodge, which came to an end, at least nominally, with the cession to France of Alsace-Lorraine. But something is still required, in the nature of documentary evidence, to enable us to survey the inner life of the German mediæval Lodges, and this we fortunately meet with in the Torgau Ordinances, enacted in 1462. From the preamble it may be gathered that the Strasburg masters had sent a copy of their Constitutions (1459) to the Lodges in North Germany. The signatures to the Code of 1459 show that these were not represented at Ratisbon and Strasburg, although the territory in which they were comprised was placed in subjection to the latter city. The North German masters, however, yielded submission to the Code (or Constitutions) of 1459, and put their seal on the work by the issue of Ordinances for the use of their own Lodges, which they expressly declare to be merely explanatory of the Strasburg Code, and to be based on ancient landmarks instituted by the "Holy Crowned Martyrs, to the honour and praise of the Holy Trinity and Mary the Queen of Heaven." The Constitutions of 1459 also contain a devout invocation of the names of the "Father, Son, and Holy

Ghost; of our gracious Mother Mary; and of her blessed servants, the Holy Four Crowned Martyrs of everlasting memory." (*Quatuor Coronati.*)

Viewed as mere trade regulations, all these Statutes or Regulations—1459, 1462, and 1563—were probably only confirmations of previously existing customs; but the *fraternity* was quite a new departure, the preamble of the 1459 Code expressly stating that the "Masters and Fellows at Speyer, Strasburg, and Ratisbon, *renewed* and *revised* these ancient usages, and kindly and affably *agreed upon* these Statutes and *fraternity*." Of this, additional proof could be afforded, and from the wording of the "Constitutions" of 1563 it may be inferred that even after the lapse of more than a century there were masters who had not joined the fraternity.

The stonemasons, like all other crafts, were divided into three classes—masters, fellows, and apprentices, the last named not being admitted to the brotherhood. Of this, however, the master remained a member and owed his position in it, as presiding judge, to the fact of his also being the master of work. In other crafts the masters and journeymen each formed fraternities of their own. The journeymen associations were presided over in some cases by a master of the locality, and in others by one (or more) of the journeymen themselves, who then took the title of *Alt-gesell* (old-fellow). In both instances, however, the president was elected by vote, and in the former the master was admitted rather as a representative of his class than as an officer, the proceedings always being conducted by the *Alt-gesell*, with whom the master sat as a kind of assessor.

It must not be assumed that this distinction was intentional, and that the stonemasons deliberately set up a custom of their own, differing from the ordinary practice of the other craft guilds. In none of the towns could there have been any great scarcity of rough masons, but the stonemason masters in many of them must have been few; possibly only two, one at the head of the Cathedral building staff, and the other in the permanent service of the municipality. Each would employ a number of "fellows," but the total would be insufficient for the formation of two fraternities. Masters and workmen were therefore obliged to remain together, and each master would naturally preside over the proceedings of his own workshop or Lodge. His office, therefore, never became elective, and probably the stonemason fraternities are scarcely to be distinguished from those of other crafts except by this characteristic.

An apprentice was indentured for five years, but, as a necessary preliminary, he was required to prove that he was of legitimate birth. The contract with his master was executed and cancelled in the presence of the entire Lodge. The period of five years, though rigorously insisted upon in the Ordinances of 1462, was neither before nor after that date universal in its operation.

A doubtful point occurs in the Statutes of 1563, where a distinction is drawn between a rough and an art apprentice, and the latter expression (*Kunst diener*) appears in several of the clauses. The explanation, however, I am unable to supply.

Having duly served his time, the passed apprentice was declared free of the craft, and acquired the title of "fellow" (*gesell*). His admission into the craft took place in the Lodge, and some of the formalities which attended his reception may be pointed out.

A serious promise was required that he would be true to the craft, that he would not vary his distinctive mark, and that he would not improperly disclose the secrets that were about to be revealed to him. The methods of greeting (*gruss*), and it may be of hand-clasping (*schenck*), were then entrusted to his keeping. But the evidence is far from being conclusive that the stonemasons were in possession of a grip. Except in a solitary (and doubtful) instance, the word *schenck*, which is constantly met with in the Statutes, invariably refers to the pledge feast, at which, in apparently all trades, toasts were drunk (or pledged) with much ceremony and precision. Still, as the most trusted German authorities assure us that a grip is

used by Steinmetzen of the present day, it is possible that
one may also have existed in a period of time more or less
remote from our own.

On being declared free of his trade, the passed apprentice
became a journeyman, and was ready to enter upon his
travels, the extent and duration of which varied in the
different trades.

Whether there was anything in the nature of what we
are now in the habit of calling a "ceremony" at the admission (or affiliation) of new members is uncertain. Nothing
is said of one in any existing records of the stonemasons,
but this is by no means decisive of the point at issue, as such
ceremonies were undoubtedly in vogue among the journeymen fraternities of other trades.

Usually the president called the meeting to order by a
blow of his hammer, and silence was enforced. The method
of opening and closing the proceedings was in dialogue form.
Subscriptions were paid, and other business transacted.

Three formal inquiries were made (by the locksmiths)
before a meeting was closed.

In many of the crafts the candidate went through a
ceremony of a more or less symbolical character. A journeyman joiner, at his reception, was called "rough wood,"
and after it "smooth wood." The proceedings terminated with a lecture. In the case of the locksmiths,
a key was turned round three times in the mouth of the
candidate.

That a ceremony of some kind was practised by the
Steinmetzen is highly probable, though no proof is forthcoming; while, on the other hand, it is quite open to conjecture that the signature of a stonemason in the Brother
Book, together with the payment of dues, completed the
formulary of his affiliation.

There was no *sign*, and greater importance was attached
to the proper delivery of the ceremonious formula of saluta-
tion, or *greeting*, than to the communication of either *grip*
or *word*. The last named is only referred to in the Ordinances of the Masons of Halberstadt, as laid before their

reigning prince in 1693:—"A master shall enjoin a work-man whom he has passed according to the custom of the craft, that he shall keep enclosed in his heart, on peril of his soul's salvation, that which has been entrusted to him 'of words' (*an worten*), and by no means make the same known to anybody but an honest Mason, under pain of losing his handicraft."

The Torgau Ordinances direct that "The master shall knock with three blows, the warden with two consecu-tively, and one for announcements at morning, noon, and eve, as is the old usage of the land" (§ 28). It would appear that warden, parlierer, and *pallirer* were merely different names for the same office.

Returning to the "Constitutions" of 1459—the tie of brotherhood, upon which I have already enlarged, was created in that year. The Lodges were independent of each other, but groups of them owed fealty to a District Lodge. A number of the latter were, in turn, subordinate to a Provincial Lodge, and the whole system reached an apex in the supremacy of the Chief Lodge at Strasburg.

Every individual Lodge was a distinct court of justice, and above the Lodges came the courts of the districts, at the head of which were masters to whose care copies of the Brother Book had been committed. These were the masters at the head of permanent building works and, conjointly with their fellow masters of like degree, they were enjoined to rule and govern the craft, and, if necessary, to convoke a general assembly of the neighbourhood. There were annual courts, and only when the business could not be decided by these tribunals were appeals allowed. The Brother Book could not be either copied or lent, but was read every year to the fellows in the Lodge. From the District courts there was (under certain condi-tions) a right of appeal to the Provincial masters at Stras-burg, Cologne, Vienna, Zurich, and (apparently) Dresden. The highest tribunal of all, and the supreme court of judica-ture for the entire union (or system), was at Strasburg.

The "mysteries" of the mason's trade, which it was

the object of the various "Ordinances" enacted from time to time to strictly safeguard, were, without doubt, the elaborate carving of stone, and the preparation of plans and designs, in neither of which class of work was the skilled craftsman allowed to instruct anyone, unless he had joined the association through the only lawful channel.

Stieglitz, in his *Early German Architecture*, gives an illustration of two famous pillars—Jachin and Boaz—as they now exist in the Cathedral of Würsburg, one of the oldest cities of Germany, and formerly the capital of Franconia. They were originally situated, like the brazen columns of King Solomon's Temple, on either side of the porch, Jachin on the right, and Boaz on the left, but at the present time their relative positions are reversed and they stand in the body of the Cathedral. Their shafts are not of the ordinary cylindrical form, but are composed of clustered pillars, curiously interlaced. Stieglitz says that they were intended to bear a symbolic reference to the fraternity, which is revealed to the initiated in their peculiar proportions, in the ingenious construction and combination of the shafts and capitals, as well as by the names (Jachin and Boaz) sculptured on the abacus.

The foundation stone of the *Steinmetz* origin of Freemasonry was laid by a French writer, the Abbé Grandidier, in 1779. The theory attracted no attention for many years, but ultimately found favour in Germany, and its general acceptance at one time, both in this country and America, may be attributed to the English translation of Findel's History of our Society. The delusion, I believe, has long ceased to exist, and in parting with the subject, it may be remarked, that while there was a great outward similarity between the usages of the *Steinmetzen* and the *Freemasons*, no sort of connection between the two associations was ever set up as an article of belief until 1779. At that date the Freemasonry of England had found a home in Germany for nearly half a century, and there would be a great initial difficulty in our crediting that the two institutions had flourished side by side for all that long period without intermingling, even were it possible for us to believe that the marvellous stories related of the *Steinmetzen* by Schneider, Heideloff, Fallou, and other German writers, rested on any basis of well attested fact.

THE CRAFT GUILDS (CORPS D'ETAT) OF FRANCE

The design of the present and the following sections is to present the reader with an outline of the rise and fall of the craft guilds of France, and to weave into a connected narrative, from the fragments of evidence I have been able to collect, a brief account of their remarkable off-shoot, the Companionage.

Clovis, the founder of the French monarchy, in the year 486 began his career of victory, at Soissons, by defeating Siagrius, the ruler of what then remained of Roman Gaul. Thus ended the Imperial authority, but not of necessity the Imperial civilization. Rome was a power preeminently military; yet what is her history but the most remarkable instance of a political development and progress? More than any power, she was able to accommodate and expand her institutions according to the circumstances of successive ages, extending her municipal privileges to the conquered cities, yielding herself to the literature of Greece, and admitting into her bosom the rites of Egypt and Phrygia.

In the cities there seems to have been at once formed, on the departure of the legions, a sort of municipal government. The elected officers of the various trades, together with the superior clergy, constituted a council. It is certain that down to the death of Pépin, the first of the Carlovingian dynasty, in 768, the French cities were virtual republics, and that the existence of craft guilds may be dated back to a very remote period.

The literature on this subject is of a very extensive character, but the generality of French authorities are of opinion that the weight of evidence is in favour of the guilds and communes of mediæval France having been the direct descendants of the Roman corporations.

Under the Carlovingian kings there was centralization, and with the rise of the feudal system the municipalities lost much of their independence; but in the thirteenth century they had recovered most of their privileges, though obliged to exercise them in strict subordination to the royal authority.

It must be carefully borne in mind, however, that until comparatively recent times France was never a homogeneous state; consequently, no general sketch of the rise and progress of craft guilds can be expected to portray more than the leading features of these institutions, or by any means to exhibit the modifications which might be looked for in the north, where the German influence was predominant, or perhaps with even greater reason in Normandy, which at a later period than in other districts was over-run by the barbarians.

In Paris the officials of a single (though enormous) guild, the Hanse, controlled the entire municipality. This association we first meet with under the title of *Marchands de l'eau de Paris*, and to a great extent it enjoyed a monopoly of the commerce of the Seine. The duties of mayor of the city were performed by its leading official, who was styled Provost of the Merchants, until late in the thirteenth century. There is evidence to show that this guild was in existence prior to 1121, and particular privileges granted to it in that year by the reigning monarch were confirmed by his successors in 1170 and 1192.

Subsequently it took the name of the *Marchands* or *Six Corps de Paris*, but the building and other trades of the metropolis, not included among these six bodies, must have gradually sprung into existence very much in the same way as those of the provincial cities.

Under Louis IX, in 1258, Etienne Boileau became the Provost of Paris, and the municipal government of the city, together with the supervision of the trade and craft guilds, passed into his hands. The Provost, however, of the *Marchands* still retained his jurisdiction over the *Six Corps de Paris* (goldsmiths, cloth-workers, furriers, grocers, hatters, and mercers), and, to some extent, over the commerce of the Seine. The powers, indeed, were taken away from him in 1383, and vested in the Provost of Paris; an attempt being also made at the same time to suppress the trade fraternities and even the municipality itself. But the efforts of Charles VI in this direction were unsuccessful. The guilds continued to exist, and the municipality again met with legal recognition in 1411. Eventually the office of Provost of Merchants was revived and the whole of his former jurisdiction restored to him; the Provost of Paris disappeared from the scene, and the authority of the *Six Corps* continued in force until the closing years of the eighteenth century.

In the year 1258, Etienne Boileau, the Provost of Paris, collected the rules and regulations affecting the various trades of that city, and digested them into manuscript form under the title of "Reglements sur Les Arts et Métiers de Paris," and by royal authority they were ordained to be the law to which all guilds or mechanical occupations in Paris should be thenceforth subjected. The usages of a hundred craft guilds were tabulated in this book. The exercise of any trade or craft was restricted to those who had served as apprentices, and had been received as masters. Anciently, and in particular trades, the apprentice passed at once to the status of master on being duly qualified. But the *Livre des Métiers*, while it permits the master to have as many assistants as he desires, expressly stipulates that the secrets of the trade must not be communicated to them; and also that the apprentice who had duly served his time should be sworn on the holy writings not to reveal them.

The necessity must have at length arisen for the institution of a new grade, intermediate between those of apprentice and master, and that of journeyman was established.

Into this position the apprentice who had attained his freedom then passed, and was indifferently styled

compagnon, aide, valet, varlet, or garçon. Travelling was
not strictly enjoined; but the journeyman usually became
a wayfarer for a time, and worked his way as he proceeded
on his "Tour of France." Out of this custom must have
originated the Companionage, a singular institution, of
which a description will be given in the next section.

A necessary preliminary to the attainment of a mastership was the achievement of a masterpiece, the nature of
which was in all cases decided by a committee of the masters.
The test selected was usually such as to involve great
labour and expense, but without successfully passing through
the ordeal the young workman could not fully exercise
his trade. There was, indeed, a "lesser masterpiece,"
with respect to which the conditions were much relaxed;
but when these were surmounted the aspirant only
became what was called "a perpetual companion,"
a rank (or status) of which I can elsewhere find no trace,
and, while permitted to work without the intervention of
a master in his own apartment, he was debarred from either
keeping a shop or engaging assistants in his business.
These restrictions did not, however, apply to the relatives
of masters, who were not required to pass through the grades
of apprentice and journeyman, and the execution of a masterpiece by whom was dispensed with. In certain trades
the masterpiece was distinctly patrimonial, but jealously
restricted to candidates in the male line of succession.

The forms of reception at the admission of new masters
were of a varied character. In the generality of instances
they appear to have been received with something in the
nature of a ceremony, and the proceedings were enlivened
by good-humoured merriment, and occasionally by bur-
lesque. For example, at the reception of a millstone maker,
a feast was prepared, and while the masters were carousing
below, the candidate was led to an attic *above*, his con-
ductor being the latest accepted master, who was armed with
a broomstick. There then followed a succession of loud
and long-continued screams, just as if someone was being
beaten to death.

By the *Livre des Métiers* the stonemasons, masons, plasterers, and mortarers are placed under the banner of St. Blaise. There are other writings which disclose the fact that ranged under the same banner were the millstone makers, tylers, and quarry workers.

Moving on parallel lines with, and often intersecting the craft guilds, were the *fraternities*, which appear under many names, chiefly as variants of the term *confrérie* (confraternity), and sometimes (in each particular instance) as *le cierge* ("the candle")-or *la caritat* (the "charity"). The guild and the fraternity were separate institutions, although frequently composed of the same members. Sometimes also a plurality of fraternities was to be found in a single craft, while at others several crafts were associated in one fraternity. Like the social guilds of England, the leading objects of the fraternities were the assembly of the members on fixed occasions, devotional exercises, conviviality, charity, and relief to poor or distressed brethren and their families. Apprentices and journeymen were ineligible for membership, though required to contribute to the treasury of the society. The latter, however, were assisted from the funds of these institutions when on their travels through France. The talisman of the crafts was a banner, and that of the fraternities a wax candle.

In France, as in Germany, the principal object of the craft guilds was to secure their members in the independent, unimpaired, and regular earning of their daily bread. But when in the former country these bodies, like the earlier English guilds for the maintenance of justice (of which a good illustration is afforded by the *Judicia Civitatis Lundoniæ*, reduced to writing in the time of King Athelstan), were legally recognized as special associations for the regulation of their trades, a new characteristic—namely, their function as a police authority—was added to those by which they had previously been distinguished.

The French masters, at fixed periods, elected from their own number certain persons who, under various names, of which *prud'hommes* may be cited as a frequent type, presided

at all meetings of the craft, possessed many powers
of petty justice, and were expected to bring any infraction
of the rules of a trade to the cognizance of their provost or
head. To these assessors (wardens or inspectors) was entrusted the common seal of the craft. But with hardly an
exception every workman possessed his private mark,
which he was obliged to place upon his work.

The code says, "The masons and plasterers owe the
watch duty," and in the next article (*i.e.*, XXII), "The
mortarers are free of watch duty, and all stonemasons
since the time of Charles Martel, as the wardens (*preudomes*)
have heard say from father to son."

It is evident from the foregoing, that so far back as the
thirteenth century there was a traditional belief that certain exceptional privileges had been granted by Charles
Martel to the stonemasons. The circumstance, therefore,
should be accorded its due weight, as in the Legend of the
British Craft the "Saviour of Christendom" is also
described as a great patron of operative masonry.

This community of tradition, which pervaded the minds
of the mediæval masons in Gaul and Britain, is a remarkable fact, and the influence it suggests will be further considered in my account of the Companionage.

At Montpellier the words *fai la piera* (does stonework)
follow the name of a workman in a document of 1201, and
maistre de piera, that of a "Master Mason," in a manuscript of 1244. "About the beginning of the seventeenth
century," says Samuel Ware in the *Archæologia* (xvii, 83),
"the art *de la coupe des pierres* was still held a secret, and
the possessors of this mystery were called the *Cotterie*."
As will appear in the next section, the term seems to have
been regarded with much favour by the stonemasons.

Efforts to suppress the *confréries* were made by Simon,
Count de Montfort, in 1212, and by Philippe le Bel in 1308.
A series of more stringent enactments, corresponding in
great measure with our own "Statutes of Labourers," and
arising from the same cause—the ravages of the "Black
Death," which affected every class of artisan—were issued
by royal authority in 1350.

THE COMPANIONAGE, OR LES COMPAGNONS DU TOUR
DE FRANCE

The "Companionage" (*Compagnonnage*) is a comprehensive term, and comprises the three fellowships formed
by the French journeymen (or apprentices who had served
their time) for the purpose of affording them assistance
while making what was called the "Tour of France."

The Companions (*Compagnons*) recognize three principal
founders, Solomon, Maître Jacques, and Maître (or Père)
Soubise, and each of these legendary patrons is alleged
to have left behind him a *devoir* (*i.e.*, a Rule, like St. Benedict's; a code; or the constituents of a Rite, or Sodality)
for the guidance of his disciples. The companionage is,
therefore, composed of three distinct associations, the Sons
(*enfants*) of Solomon, of Maître Jacques, and of Maître (or
Père) Soubise. The first two were originally (or anciently)
composed of stonemasons, and the last-named of carpenters only. But at some unknown date the Sons of
Solomon admitted the joiners and locksmiths into their
fraternity; the Sons of Maître Jacques followed their
example, and this society eventually comprised the members
of nearly all trades, while the ranks of the Sons of Maître
Soubise were strengthened by the adhesion of the plasterers
and tylers. It may be added that at a recent period some
of the carpenters seceded from the system of Soubise, and
claimed to form a fourth corps under the banner of Solomon,
but they are not recognized as such by the other three.

The dates of origin of the three divisions of the companionage are generally supposed to agree with the order
in which they have been described above, and it is freely
conceded by the companions of the remaining sub-divisions
that in point of antiquity the stonemasons of the Sons of
Solomon are entitled to take the highest rank of all. The
masons (to be carefully distinguished from the stonemasons)
and a few other crafts have never been included in the companionage.

Journeymen of all religious persuasions are freely admitted

into the system of Solomon, but a profession of Roman
Catholicism is required from candidates in those of Jacques
and Soubise.

In every French town with which a *devoir* was associated,
the travelling journeymen found a house of call. These
villes du devoir, or towns of the Tour of France, are situated
for the most part in the South. In other centres of population, called "bastard towns," where there was no *devoir*,
the companion also met with assistance, though on a reduced
scale.

It has been already mentioned that some of the trades
owned a divided fealty, the stonemasons, joiners, and
locksmiths being arrayed under the banners of Solomon
and Jacques, the carpenters under those of Solomon and
Soubise, and the remaining trades which form a part of the
companionage being comprised within the system of Maître
Jacques. Each craft, however, in the three families constitutes a separate and independent fraternity, and is often
at open variance with one or more of the remaining corps
under the same banner. But they all present a united
front to a common enemy; for example, the societies of
one *devoir* are in a chronic state of discord with those of
the other two. Sometimes, also, there is a difference on
a larger scale, and if all of the three families are drawn
into it, the Sons of Solomon find themselves confronted
by a union of the various corps under the combined banners
of Jacques and Soubise.

Among the joiners—*enfants de Salomon*—as we learn
from Agricol Perdiguier in his *Livre du Compagnonnage*,
the Ordinances were first of all read to the candidate,
after which he attained his first step, that of affiliation. The remaining "steps" were those of "accepted,"
"finished," and "initiated" companion. From the circumstance that newly-admitted members were enjoined to
"keep secret the forms of initiation and the methods of
recognition," it may be inferred that each of these "steps"
or degrees was attended with a ceremony.

Of the stonemasons (*enfants de Salomon*), the informa-

CONDUITE DE COMPAGNONS DU DEVOIR

(From Clavel's *Histoire Pittoresque de la Franche Maçonnerie*)

tion forthcoming is very scanty; it is known, however, that the affiliates were styled "young men," and that the rank of companion was attained at a single step.

The titles of aspirants and upper companions were peculiar to the system of Maître Jacques, and companions and foxes to that of Maître Soubise. Among all the fraternities there was a belief in an alleged connection of the stonemasons with Hiram, and white gloves were always worn, in certain of the corps, by way of disclaiming the complicity of their members with regard to the circumstances of his decease.

Canes, long or short, and generally metal-tipped, were carried by all companions, who likewise wore the colours of their particular societies, consisting of silk ribbons of varying hue. These staves and ribbons often changed owners, as after one of their desperate encounters the conquering companion bore them off as trophies of the fray. The square and compasses were emblems in general use.

There were regular officers of each fraternity, and every sub-division (or degree) of it, in all the towns composing the Tour of France.

As with the *Steinmetzen*, each French craft had its own house of call, and the inmates were accosted in the same way—father, mother, brother, sister—but the house itself was styled, in France, *La mère* (the mother). We are told that in the journeymen fraternity of both Germany and France "there were the same ceremonies on entering the inn, and that a neglect of these formalities was severely punished."

A *sobriquet* was selected by every companion on his admission (or initiation), by means of which it would be indicated to what corps he belonged.

The title of *Compagnons du devoir* was common to all affiliated journeymen, but that of *Compagnons du devoir de liberté* (or, shortly, *Compagnons de liberté*) was specially assumed by the Sons of Solomon. In the most ancient corps of each family, or system, there were further distinctions. For example, the stonemasons of Solomon take the name of "Foreign Companions," on the ground that they were strangers in Judea; while the stonemasons of Jacques and the carpenters of Soubise assume that of "Passing Companions," for the reason that they never contemplated being other than temporary sojourners when at Jerusalem.

It may be added, with respect to the same corps, that among themselves the stonemasons of Solomon are known as "Wolves," those of Maître Jacques as "Were-Wolves," and the carpenters (S. of S.) as "Good Fellows" (*Bons Drilles*).

The term *gavots*, denoting the natives of a mountainous country, is applied to the joiners and locksmiths (*enfants de Salomon*). In the systems of Jacques and Soubise, the members of all corps, except that of the stonemasons, are called *chiens* and *dévorants*, the former expression arising out of a singular tradition which ascribes the discovery of Hiram's remains to the instinct of some dogs. The latter, apparently, is a corruption of *devoirants*, meaning the members of a *devoir*.

The custom of howling, which, as Brand tells us in his *Popular Antiquities*, has been in general use at funerals from very early times, is practised extensively, and in other cases than at the interment of one of their own number, by the companions.

It is stated that on these occasions particular words are muttered in such a way as to be only intelligible to members of the corps. The habit, however, has not found favour with the stonemasons.

In addressing each other, the terms used are *coterie* by the stonemasons, and *pays* by the other crafts, with the addition in either case of the companion's nickname (when known) in the place of his lawful patronymic.

When two companions met on their travels, one addressed the other with the *topage*, or challenge, being a formula of words, the conventional reply to which would indicate that the other was a member of the same *devoir*. If such was the case, friendly greetings ensued; but if from the colloquy it was evident that they belonged to rival associations, a war of words, commonly ending in a stand-up fight, was the result.

The death of one of the combatants was a frequent occurrence, and these encounters were often conducted on a much larger scale, with hosts of companions on either side.

The *topage*, as a general practice, only finds acceptance in the systems of Jacques and Soubise, but the stonemasons of Solomon, sometimes, though rarely, "tope" with the members of their own trade in the other division of the companionage.

The causes of feud were infinite, and though a hollow peace was preserved, in the main, between the stonemasons of the two *devoirs* at Paris, they continued to be open enemies in the provinces.

The benefits derived by the travelling journeyman were of a very substantial character. He was lodged, fed, and obtained other work or credit.

The journeyman, on resuming his Tour of France, was escorted beyond the limits of the town, and to speed him on his way songs were sung by the other companions, who marched in procession; before the final leave-taking occurred, there was usually a "ceremony," but the exact nature of it has not been disclosed.

Annually, each craft has its grand assembly, which takes place on the day of its tutelary saint, who is presumed, of course, to have been a worthy member of the same trade. The stonemasons, indeed, form an exception to the general rule, as they commemorate the Ascension Day.

At the death of a companion his funeral is conducted with much solemnity. A circle is formed round the grave, the mourners kneel on one knee, a prayer is offered up, the coffin is lowered, and then follows the *guilbrette*.

The ceremony of the *accolade* or *guilbrette* is thus performed. Two of the companions step on to the four quarters of a pair of crossed staves, each clasps the other by the right hand, they whisper in one another's ear, remain folded for a moment in each other's arms, and retire. This is done by all the companions in turn, after which they again kneel, say a further prayer, and with three motions sprinkle earth on the grave.

In certain instances a covering is placed over the grave, and from a companion who descends beneath it are heard sounds of lamentation and regret. At this particular moment something takes place at the funeral of a carpenter of Soubise, which, as we learn from Perdiguier, he was not allowed to reveal.

It is possible that this veiled rite comprised some modification of the *guilbrette*, and the opportunity seems a fitting one to remark that unless the method of joining hands in this embrace (*accolade*) was performed in any special manner, there is no evidence that will justify our belief in the existence of a grip.

It has been shown that the stonemasons and three other crafts (the joiners, locksmiths, and carpenters) paid a dual fealty; but in towns where the influence of one of the three systems had long been firmly established, any invasion of territory by the members of rival *devoirs* rarely took place. This monopoly, however, was sometimes acquired by success in a trial of skill between the champions of opposing families. The victory was decided by a comparison of the two masterpieces, and the winning side obtained an exclusive occupation of the city.

A contest of this kind took place between the two corps of stonemasons, at Lyons, in 1726. The losers, followers of Jacques, accordingly left the city, but a century later they returned and a sanguinary encounter occurred, in which the Sons of Solomon were the victors. Yet this did not end the matter. The winners strove to drive the enemy still farther back, and another bloody battle was the result.

The most remarkable of all these conflicts occurred in 1730, the scene of action being the plains of La Crau, in Provence.

The belligerents were the *Enfants de Salomon* on the one side, and the allied forces of Maître Jacques and Soubise on the other. Fire-arms were freely used, and victory hung for a long time in the balance. The number of combatants "killed in action" and mortally wounded was very great, and the active intervention of the military power alone brought this pitched battle to a close.

It is customary, except among the Sons of Solomon, for members, on attaining the status of master, to retire from the companionage.

The legendary history of the companionage begins with the Temple of Solomon. The stonemasons (S. of S.), called *Compagnons Etrangers*, and *Loups*, together with the joiners and locksmiths of the *Devoir de Liberté*, called *Gavots*, say that the Wise King gave them a *devoir*, and united them fraternally in the precincts of the Temple, the work of their hands.

The stonemasons (S. of J.), called *Loups-Garous*, with the joiners and locksmiths *du Devoir*, called *Dévorants*, also assert that they issued from the Temple, and that Maître Jacques—an overseer under King Solomon—founded them. The carpenters, *Compagnons Passant* or *Bons Drilles*, claim a similar connection with the Temple, as the last group; and also that Maître (or Père) Soubise—famous in carpentry—was their founder.

The legend of the Sons of Solomon is of a very fragmentary character, although the stonemasons of that division are generally recognized as the most ancient of the companions.

After the *Enfants de Salomon*, the next in order of precedence are the followers of Maître Jacques, the most prominent figure in the legendary history, and the fable of whose career was probably the only written tradition of the society which Perdiguier had before him when compiling the first edition (1839) of his *Livre du Compagnonnage*.

From the fullest and most complete story of this traditionary founder of the companionage, as presented for the

first time by Mr. W. H. Rylands in the English tongue
(1888), I extract the following:—

Maître Jacques a stone-cutter, at the age of fifteen, left
the South of France and travelled into Greece, where he
became famous as a sculptor and architect. His steps
were next directed to Egypt, and afterwards to Jerusalem,
where he became one of the chief masters of King Solomon,
and a colleague of Hiram. After the completion of the
Temple, Maître Jacques and Maître Soubise set out on their
return to Gaul. They had vowed to remain together, but
jealousy impelled the latter to leave his friend, and to form
a separate band of disciples. Jacques disembarked at
Marseilles and Soubise at Bordeaux.

An attempt to assassinate Maître Jacques was made by
the rival faction, but he took refuge in a marsh, the reeds
of which protected him from his assailants. He then retired to St. Beaume, and shortly afterwards one of his
disciples betrayed him with a kiss. Five ruffians fell upon
him and inflicted five deadly wounds. His disciples arrived
in time to receive his last *adieux*. He gave them the kiss
of peace, which he charged them to pass on to future companions as coming from their father. His death occurred
in his forty-seventh year, and with his last breath he for-
gave his assassins. On his person was found a little *reed*
(*jonc*), which he carried about him in memory of his adventure in the marsh, and it has since been adopted as an
emblem by the companions.

Whether Soubise was privy to the murder is unknown.
He shed tears on the tomb, and ordered a pursuit of the
assassins, which removed a portion of the suspicion which
attached to him.

As for the betrayer, in the agony of his remorse he cast
himself into a well, which the companions filled up with
stones.

The schism in the society is said by one writer to have
taken place at Arles, A.D. 800. There is also a tradition
which makes the Companionage *du Devoir* take birth at
Orleans, and that of the *Devoir de Liberté* at Chartres, the

theory being advanced that, in the thirteenth or fourteenth century, between the workmen of these towns—engaged on the cathedrals—an enmity arose, which led to their forming two societies under rival *Maîtres* or conductors.

A variation of the Orleans legend states that "those dissenting from the original foundation of the two associations were taken under the protection of Jacques de Molay, Grand Master of the Templars; that the Templars introduced mystic forms into France, Solomon and his temple figuring in their ceremonies; and that Jacques de Molay summoned the dissentient companions and formed them into three new associations."

In 1803 delegates assembled in conference from every town of the *Tour de France*. It was felt that many of the old customs were unsuitable to the age, and that the association itself required to be remodelled in various ways. One of the delegates was a Freemason, and his proposal that a superior class—the *troisième ordre*—of *initiés* should be introduced was adopted.

This new degree—*initiés* or *troisième ordre*—though abolished in 1843, did not at once disappear, and for quite forty years exercised an influence over the companionage, which, within that period—if not before—must have received a distinct tinge from Freemasonry.

It will doubtless have been observed, that many of my remarks are expressed in the past tense, but the picture I have drawn of the companionage must be understood to date in the main from about the year 1840, and there cannot be a doubt that with the extension of railways, much of the *raison d'être* for the existence of such an association has disappeared.

Any real insight into the ceremonies peculiar to the systems of Solomon and Soubise is withheld from us, but a glimpse has been afforded of those practised by certain of the corps under the banner of Maître Jacques.

Some of the customs at the reception of new members were revealed in 1651, and others at a slightly later date, the trades among which they were in vogue being the saddlers, shoemakers, tailors, cutlers, and hatters. The forms varied slightly, but the leading types were a mock baptism, the bestowal of a new name, and the communication of a watch-word (*mot de guerre*), which was to be kept secret. The "Story of the First Three Companions" was related at the admission of a journeyman tailor.

An account of the ceremonies of the "Free Carpenters" of France was contributed to *Ars Quatuor Coronatorum*, vol. xxvii, p. 5, by F. J. W. Crowe; also of the "Fendeurs" in vol. xxii.

It also appeared on record that many of the usages which are met with in more recent times were practised in one (and doubtless all) of the chief divisions of the companionage. For example, the custom of calling the tavern (or house of call) the "Mother"; and the habit of "forming everywhere an offensive league against the young men of their trade who are not of their cabal; beating, maltreating, and soliciting them to enter into their society."

A long string of questions on the above practices was addressed to the Doctors of the Sorbonne, and they were adjudged by them to "combine the sins of sacrilege, impurity, and blasphemy against the mysteries of our religion."

From some "Observations" on the "impieties" of the companions, and the "Resolutions" of the learned doctors "of the Sacred Faculty of Theology at Paris," I extract the following:—"What more enormous sacrilege than to counterfeit the ceremonies of baptism, than to abuse the sacred words."

The document under contribution (1651) is a lengthy one, and, in parting from it, I shall only remark that the last count of the indictment may possibly have referred to the use of scriptural names, as passwords, by the companions.

It nowhere appears when the masters, as a class, ceased to be members of the companionage. They belonged to it in 1651, and their retirement probably took place soon after the practices of the companions were forbidden, under pain of excommunication, by the Archbishop of Toulouse in that year.

The existence of at least two great divisions of the association—those of Solomon and Jacques—is carried back by lapidary evidence to 1640; and that there was also a third, at the same (and a far earlier) date, may be inferred, not alone from the legend of the "First Three Companions," which figures in the revelations of 1651, but also on other grounds.

For example, we should do well to bear in mind the use of obsolete and long-forgotten words by the companions, such as *Gavots, Gavotages, Gabords, Bons-Drilles, Topage, Tope, Guilbrette,* all of which indicate a far-stretching and unknown history.

The precise extent to which the legends of the companionage, as existing in 1840, received a colouring from the Freemasonry of an antecedent period cannot, of course, be even approximately determined.

But the question must be examined as a whole. And conceding to the fullest the conclusions that may be drawn with regard to the combined influence of Freemasonry and other causes upon the companionage of 1840, let us go back for a couple of centuries and carefully scrutinize the evidence which has already been presented under that date.

A companion tailor, at his admission, was taught the *History of the First Three Companions,* relating, there cannot be a doubt, to the lives or actions of *some* three supposed originals or founders. If these were *not* Solomon, Jacques, and Soubise, there must have been three *previous* leaders or head-men, who acted as their precursors, and have since dropped out of the story—a supposition wholly unworthy of serious refutation.

It has been noticed that the revelations of the seventeenth century were confined to the followers of Maître Jacques. Also, that no disclosures of their secrets were made by the stonemasons (*Compagnons Passant,* or *Loups-Garous*) of that family. From the revelations, however,

of the saddlers, tailors, cutlers, and hatters, it is evident
that the form of reception was not of a uniform character,
and the inference will be permissible, that a further diversity
would be apparent if the practice of the stonemasons
(*du Devoir*) on such occasions had been similarly laid
bare.

So with the mysteries peculiar to the followers—at that
time—of Solomon and Soubise, and from the stonemasons
of Jacques to those of Solomon (*Compagnons Etrangers* or
Loups), will be my next step. The latter (*Compagnons de
Liberté*) are recognized by the other divisions as being certainly the oldest branch, if not the parent stem, of the
companionage. This traditional acceptance of their priority
of origin will carry great weight, and the more so when
found to agree, as it does, with the dictates of common sense,
that a society able to take Solomon as its founder must
rank first. That no legend of Solomon, corresponding in
length with that of Maître Jacques, has been preserved,
or rather *revealed*, is to be regretted. But we may assume
with confidence that in the "History of the First Three
Companions" (1648-55), the leading figure of all must
have been the chief founder of the companionage. How
long before the year 1840 the legend of Hiram (or Adon-
hiram) had obtained currency among the stonemasons of
the division (*Compagnons de Liberté*) must remain a matter
for speculation. Not, indeed, that I wish to blot out the
words of Perdiguier (*Livre du C.*, ii, 80), who observes:—
"As to this history of Hiram's, I look upon it in the light
of a Masonic invention, introduced into the companionage
by persons initiated into both of these secret societies."
But however this may be, and it should be borne in mind
that Perdiguier was neither a Freemason nor a stonemason
of Solomon, the fact confronts us that the Legend he refers
to was current among the *Compagnons de Liberté* in 1839-41;
and as it is improbable, not to say impossible, that this
corps was wholly without a legend at the beginning of the
present century, I find a difficulty in believing that it was
suddenly discarded—to make room for the Hiramic myth—

at the instance of some companions who also happened to be Freemasons.

Perdiguier, indeed, elsewhere (i, 61) informs us, "that the joiners of Maître Jacques wear white gloves, because, as they say, they did not steep their hands in the blood of Hiram." Also, *apropos* of *chien*, a title bestowed on all the Companions *du Devoir*, he says, "It is believed by some to be derived from the fact that it was a dog which discovered the place where the body of Hiram, architect of the Temple, lay under the rubbish, after which all the companions who separated from the murderers of Hiram were called *chiens* or dogs."

If we read from the above, from the same writer (i, 45), "That the name *étrangers* came from the fact that almost all the stonemasons employed at the Temple were not of Judea, but of Tyre and the neighbouring countries, and that the society consisted of these alone in ancient times," then we find in the legend of the murder of Hiram, the blame resting, according to the followers of Jacques and Soubise, with the *Enfants de Salomon*; the actual crime, moreover, being laid at the door of the particular section who were strangers, and had come from the country where Solomon obtained the services of Hiram, who lost his life, therefore, at the hands of his own countrymen. Thus the filiation of the legend is traced from the most ancient segment of the companionage, the stonemasons of Solomon, otherwise called Companions *Etrangers*, or *de Liberté*, and *Loups*.

It is probable in the main that when the companionage was condemned by the Church, greater prominence, or possibly an entirely new *rôle*, was given to Maître Jacques in the legendary history, with the object of silencing the imputation of blasphemy, to which some of the companions had rendered themselves liable.

Soubise has been described as a Benedictine monk, but the name is evidently French, having been borne by a well-known and noble family. There was a Charles de Rohan, Prince of Soubise, whose brother, the Cardinal of that name, really was *a* Père Soubise.

A collection of the various legends existing in the different *devoirs* is still among the *desiderata* of Masonic literature. Several of them are traceable only in very scattered references, and it is a task of much nicety to hit upon even a plausible conjecture with respect to their complete forms.

The texts of the Maître Jacques and Orleans legends would seem to be of undeniably late origin. Portions of the story in either case may be (and apparently are) *old*, but the legends themselves have come down to us in *new* vehicles of transmission.

Of the Hiramic legend there is no text whatever, merely "scattered references," and whether, in 1839-41, it was of ancient or comparatively modern date, is a point on which opinion may possibly be divided.

The Mysteries of Egypt and Greece—in a form more or less resembling their originals—were practised by the Romans in Gaul; Roman institutions survived in Gaul after the departure of the Romans; Roman corporations and colleges gradually developed into French *corps d'état*, trade guilds, etc.; these last were the parents of the companionage. The debased (or corrupted) Mysteries continued to exist in Gaul long after the departure of the Romans and the introduction of Christianity; our knowledge of these, or of the ceremonies of the companions, is not extensive, but it is sufficient to prove that between them there are points of resemblance.

THE ROSICRUCIANS

"The true origin of the Rosicrucian Fraternity," says Mr. Waite, "has been food for incessant conjecture. Romance, which accredited its adepts with all the superhuman attributes which have ever been imagined by alchemist, kabbalist, and retailer of magical traditions, has been at work on this problem, and has variously interpreted the mystery. Persons of excessive credulity, and addicted to the largest views, have represented it as an order of preternatural antiquity, and its principles as the origin of every theological system. They are seen in the solar-mythologies and in phallic worship; their symbolism has permeated East and West alike; it is in Hindustan to-day as it was in Egypt, Greece, and Scandinavia at various epochs of the past." (*The Occult Sciences*, 207.) The same writer tells us (in a subsequent work) that "the Rosicrucian theorists may be broadly divided into three bands: I. Those who believe that the history of Christian Rosen-kreuz is true in fact, and that the society originated in the manner recounted in the 'Fama Fraternitatis'; II. Those who regard both the society and its founder as purely mythical, and consider with Liebnitz '*que tout ce que l'on a dit des Frères de la Croix de la Rose, est une pure invention de quelque personne ingenieuse*'; III. Those who, without accepting the historical truth of the story of Rosencreutz, believe in the existence of the Rosicrucians as a secret society, which drew attention to the fact of its existence by a singular and attractive fiction." (*Real History of the Rosicrucians*, 217.)

Towards the close of the sixteenth century, cabalism, theosophy, and alchemy had spread over the whole of Western Europe, and more especially Germany. This result had been mainly brought about by the writings of PARACELSUS (whose works had secured him a vast popular audience), and among the things that excited deep interest was a prophecy of his to the effect that soon after the death of the Emperor Rudolph II—who was himself deeply infected with the prevailing mania—there would be found three treasures which had never been revealed before. Accordingly, shortly after his decease, about 1612-14, occasion was taken to publish three whimsical pieces or bagatelles.

The first was the *Universal Reformation of the Whole Wide World*, a tale not altogether devoid of humour, which appears to have been borrowed, if indeed not translated verbatim, from the Italian of Boccalini. The second was the *Fama Fraternitatis; or, a Discovery of the Fraternity of the Most Meritorious Order of the Rosy Cross*; and the third its supplement, the *Confessio; or, the Confession of the Rosicrucian Fraternity, addressed to the Learned in Europe.*

Whatever success the first of these *jeux d'esprit* may have had in its day, has long been forgotten, and it is now only interesting as having been a precursor of the far more celebrated *Fama*, from which I abridge the following:—

In the fourteenth century, Christian Rosenkreuz, a German noble, went on a pilgrimage to the Holy Land. From Damascus he proceeded to Damcar, where he was welcomed by the Wise Men, who instructed him in the occult sciences. After three years he departed for Egypt, and thence proceeded to Fez, where he tarried two years, and under the tuition of new masters, became familiar with the secrets of the Invisible World. His reception in Spain, whither he next repaired, was not a favourable one, and the same neglect awaited him in other countries. Returning to Germany, he pondered over many things, particularly his knowledge of the great art of transmutation, and of the method of prolonging life. These and other marvels he considered ought not to be lost, and at the expiration of five years he sent to the cloister where he was brought up, for three brethren, with whose aid was begun the Fraternity of the *Rosie Cross.*

The four members invented a magical language and writing, a large dictionary replete with sublime wisdom, and also the first part of the *Book M.* But their labours increasing, together with the number of their sick, and a new building, the House of the Holy Spirit, being finished, the society was enlarged, making the total number eight, all of vowed virginity; and by their joint efforts was collected a book (or volume) of all that which man can desire, wish, or hope for. It was then agreed to separate, but six rules were first of all enacted—that the members should cure the sick, practise gratuitously, and follow no other calling; that they should wear no distinctive dress; that they should meet annually at the House of the Fraternity, or explain the cause of absence; that each brother should select some worthy person to be his successor; that the letters *R.C.* were to be their seal, mark, and character; and that the fraternity should remain secret for one hundred years.

Only five, however, went away at once, two always remaining with Father Christian Rosenkreuz, who, after many years, having finished his labours, gave up his initiated spirit to God; not that his strength failed him, but because he was tired of life. The place of his interment remained unknown for the space of one hundred and twenty years, but a great and profitable discovery was made by the adepts of the third generation. This was a secret door, upon which was written in great letters—

"POST CXX ANNOS PATEBO."
(After one hundred and twenty years I shall appear.)

The door guarded the entrance to a heptagonal vault (constructed somewhat after the fashion of the Mithraic Cave), lighted by an artificial sun, and in various repositories were found the secrets of the fraternity, together with many curious inscriptions and magical instruments. On removing the altar and a brass plate beneath it, there came to view the body of the founder in a perfect state of preservation.

The *Fama Fraternitatis* concluded by inviting the scholars of Europe to test the pretensions, and join the ranks of a fraternity, that was in possession of a thousand secrets, of which the art of gold-making was the least.

This pamphlet caused a great excitement, which was heightened, after the lapse of a twelvemonth, by the publication of the *Confessio*, which again appealed to the learned in Europe, offering them the privilege of initiation, and gradual instruction in the weighty secrets of the Society.

A fourth treatise, *The Chymical Marriage of Christian Rosenkreuz*, must be briefly referred to. It was first published in 1616, but is alleged (on very slender authority) to have existed in manuscript as early as 1601. The author was JOHANN VALENTINE ANDREA, a learned theologian, in whose undoubtedly authentic writings and in the Rosicrucian Manifestoes of 1614-15, there is, says Arnold, in his *History of the Church*, such an identity of literary style as to make it quite clear that the *Fama Fraternitatis*, the *Confessio*, and the *Chymical Marriage*, must have been the offspring of a single mind.

Grave doubt, however, has recently been cast upon the Andrean theory by Mr. Waite; but, as he rightly says, the chief point—*i.e.*, the argument from the identity of literary style—can only be adequately treated by a German. The votaries of Rosicrucian literature, therefore, will be glad to know that the series will shortly be enriched by a volume from the pen of Dr. Begemann, in which he hopes to show to the satisfaction of his readers that no other than JOHANN VALENTINE ANDREA could possibly have been the author of the *Fama* and *Confessio*. The armorial bearings of Andrea's family were a St. Andrew's Cross and four Roses, and this has also lent colour to the theory which associates the issue of the Rosicrucian Manifestoes of 1614 and 1615 with his name. But the interpretation of the Rose Cross Symbol is as difficult of solution as that of the actual history of the "Brethren" who bore it as their badge.

According to some authorities, the name is composed of *ros*, dew, and *crux*, a cross; *crux* is supposed mystically to represent LVX, or light, because the figure of a cross exhibits the three letters of that word; and light, in the opinion of the Rosicrucians, produces gold; whilst dew, *ros*, with the (modern) alchemists, was a powerful solvent. Others have considered the rose as an emblem of secrecy— hence, *sub rosa*—and the cross as signifying the solemnity of the oath by which the vow of secrecy was ratified. A purely religious explanation of the symbol is given by ROBERT FLUDD, who asserts it to mean "the cross sprinkled with the rosy blood of Christ."

The Rosicrucian Manifestoes found an immediate defender in an English physician, ROBERT FLUDD (1574-1637), whose first published work appeared in 1616, about which time he was visited by MICHAEL MAIER. Besides his own name, he wrote under the pseudonyms of "ROBERTUS DE FLUCTIBUS," "ALITOPHILUS," and "JOACHIM FRIZIUS."

Of this remarkable man, Mr. Waite observes, "The central figure of Rosicrucian literature is ROBERTUS DE FLUCTIBUS, the great English philosopher of the seventeenth century: a man of immense erudition, of exalted mind, and, to judge by his writings, of extreme personal sanctity." FLUDD's works were extensively read throughout Europe, and one of the profoundest scholars of our own country, the illustrious SELDEN, highly appreciated the volumes and their author.

A Manifesto, of which there are at least four different versions, was affixed to the walls of Paris in 1623. It professed to emanate from the deputies of the Brethren of the Rosy Cross, who, sojourning, visible and invisible, in that city, taught every science.

An equally mysterious announcement was made in London in 1626, in the form of an offer from the Ambassador of the "President of the Society of the Rosy Cross," that if Charles I would follow his advice, the royal coffers should be enriched to the extent of three millions sterling, and the King himself instructed how to suppress the Pope, to advance his own religion over all Christendom, and to convert the Jews and Turks to the Christian faith.

A little later (1638), Henry Adamson, a Master of Arts, and a citizen of Perth, published his *Muses' Threnodie*, a well-known metrical account of the "Fair City" and its neighbourhood. In the third muse he gaily sings:—

> For we are Brethren of the Rosie Cross,
> We have the Mason word and second sight.

From which may be inferred, not only that the light of Masonry was burning brightly in Perth at that time, but also that among the "brethren" of the craft there were some at least who claimed to be members of a brotherhood of Rosicrucians.

ELIAS ASHMOLE, "the eminent philosopherm, chemist, and antiquary," as he is styled by his fullest biographer, was made a Freemason in 1646. Among his Hermetic works is the *Way to Bliss* (1658), a treatise in prose on the Philosopher's Stone, and it is a popular theory that he was a connecting link between Freemasonry and the votaries of Alchemy and Astrology.

I shall next proceed to the year 1652, at which date was published the first English translation of the *"Fama"* and *"Confessio Fraternitatis."* The translator was THOMAS VAUGHAN, of whom Wood says, in his *Athenae Oxoniensis:*— "He was a great chymist, a noted son of the fire, an experimental philosopher, and a zealous brother of the Rosie-Crucian fraternity." VAUGHAN was greatly assisted in the prosecution of his chemical studies by SIR ROBERT MORAY, the first president of the Royal Society. Of the latter, Wood tells us:—"He was a single man, an abhorrer of women, a most renowned chymist, a great patron of the Rosie-Crucians, and an excellent mathematician." SIR ROBERT MORAY was also a Freemason, and the somewhat singular circumstances under which he was initiated will be related in a subsequent chapter.

The author of the *Athenae Oxoniensis* also informs us that in 1659, PETER STHAEL, of Strasburg, "the noted chemist and Rosicrucian, who was a Lutheran and a great hater of women," began a series of lectures at Oxford, and that among his pupils were John Locke, the distinguished philosopher, and Mr. (afterwards Sir) Christopher Wren.

It will be an easy transition if I next pass to the widely spread belief that, in some shape or form, the Rosicrucians —including in this term the Fraternity, strictly so-called, together with all votaries of the Hermetic art (or alchemistical philosophers)—have aided in the development or evolution of Freemasonry.

To begin with the Rosicrucian *Fraternity*; in 1782, CHRISTOPH FREIDRICH NICOLAI, a learned bookseller of Berlin, advanced a singular hypothesis—viz., that English Freemasonry had its origin in the *New Atlantis* of LORD BACON, who himself was much influenced by the writings of ANDREÄ, the founder of the Rosicrucian sect, and of

FLUDD, his English disciple. The "Baconian" apologue bore fruit in the shape of the Royal Society, and of an Hermetical and Rosicrucian fraternity, consisting of ASH-MOLE and others, who sought to arrive at truth by the study of alchemy and astrology. The latter was established at Warrington in 1646, and afterwards, in order to conceal their mysterious designs, the members were admitted into the Masons' Company, with the result that, as freemen of London, they took the name of Freemasons and adopted as symbols the implements of the Masons' craft.

Another German writer, Professor JOHANN GOTTLIEB BUHLE, attempted to prove, first of all in Latin (1803) and subsequently in his native language (1804), that the Rosicrucian *Fraternity* was founded really quite accidentally by ANDREÄ—that FLUDD, becoming enamoured of its doctrines, took it up in earnest, and in consequence the sect, which never assumed any definite form abroad, became organized in England under the new name of Freemasonry. Accordingly, the first formal and solemn Lodge of Free-masons—the name (or title) itself being then publicly made known—was held in Masons' Hall, London, in 1646. It was into this Lodge that Ashmole was admitted.

The theories of NICOLAI and BUHLE are dead and I am not going to raise their melancholy ghosts, but the pages of the latter, who was a professor at Göttingen University, where so many letters were addressed after the publication of the *Fama* and *Confessio*, afford even yet the only informa-tion, at first hand, which is available with respect to much of the earliest written history of the Rosicrucians. An abridgment of his essay was published by De Quincey in the *London Magazine* (vol. ix) and reprinted in the collected works of that writer (vol. xvi, *Suspiria de Profundis*).

The entries in ASHMOLE's *Diary*, recording his having been "made a Free Mason at Warrington," in 1646, and his subsequent attendance at a Lodge in "Masons' Hall, London," in 1682, will be referred to with some fulness in a later chapter; but before entirely parting with the subject in the present one, there remain to be considered

the speculations of one of the most learned Freemasons
that ever existed—the late ALBERT PIKE—from whose
letters to myself I extract the following:—

"ASHMOLE had *some* inducement that led him to seek
admission into Masonry—some object to attain, some
purpose to carry out. Even his utter silence as to the
objects, nature, customs, and work of the Institution is
significant. There was something *in* the Institution that
made it seem to him worth his while to join it, *and what
was in it then may have been in it centuries before.* He is even
more reticent about it than HERODOTUS was about the
Mysteries of the Egyptian Priests.

"I have been for some time collecting the old Hermetic
and Alchemical works in order to find out what Masonry
came into possession of from them. I have ascertained
with certainty that the square and compasses, the triangle,
the oblong square, the three Grand Masters, the idea embodied in the substitute word, the Sun, Moon, and Master
of the Lodge, and others [were included in the number].

"The symbols that I have spoken of as Hermetic may
have been *borrowed* by Hermeticism, but all the same it
had them, and I do not know where they were used, outside
of Hermeticism, until they appeared in Masonry.

"I think that the Philosophers, becoming Free-Masons,
introduced into Masonry its symbolism—secret, except
among themselves—in the Middle Ages, and not after the
decline of operative Masonry began.

"Whoever endowed Masonry with these particular
symbols they were Hermetic symbols; and I know what
they meant to the Hermetic writers, French, German, and
English. I should think it most likely that ASHMOLE became
a Mason because others who were Hermeticists had become
Masons before him."

The Rev. A. F. A. WOODFORD was similarly of opinion—
"That the importance of Hermeticism, in respect of a true
History of Freemasonry, is very great." In the view of
this writer, the primeval and religious lore, which, according
to our inclinations, we may describe as theosophy or philo-

sophy, mysticism or ineffable science, was preserved originally in the Mysteries and found an outcome in alchemy,
astrology, the mysterious learning, the *apporreta* of the East,
which is repeated in the Hebraic Cabala.

His general conclusions are:—

"Hermeticism is probably a channel in which the remains
of archaic mysteries and mystical knowledge lingered through
successive ages.

"Freemasonry, in all probability, has received a portion
of its newer symbolical formulæ and emblematic types from
the societies of Hermeticism.

"At various points of contact, Freemasonry and Hermeticism have aided, sheltered, and protected each other, and
it is not at all unlikely that the true secret of the preservation
of a system of Masonic initiation, and ceremonial, and
teaching, and mysterious life through so many centuries,
is to be attributed to the twofold influence of the legends
of the ancient guilds, and the influence of a contemporary
Hermeticism."

It will be seen that both WOODFORD and PIKE agree in
claiming for the Hermetic philosophers a *prior* possession
of much of the symbolism which is *now* the property of the
Freemasons. Some of the emblems have been already
mentioned, which are relied upon as connecting Masonry
with the science of the mystics, and to those named by PIKE
I shall add the following which were cited by WOODFORD
in the final lecture—*Freemasonry and Hermeticism*—that
preceded his untimely decease:—"The rule and plumb-
rule, the perfect ashlar, the two pillars, the circle within the
parallel lines, the point within a circle, and the sacred delta.
The Pentalpha, or five-pointed star, which Pythagoras is
asserted to have taken from Egypt to Crotona and adopted
as the mystic symbol of his fraternity. Lastly, there is
the Hexapha, or Hexalpha, otherwise called Solomon's Seal
or the Shield of David; this was the great symbol of Hermeticism, and, besides being a high Masonic emblem, was
also a Masonic mark, used all over the East in mediæval
times, as well as a mystical, tribal, and religious mark."

It is certainly true that many symbols *now* in the possession of the Freemasons are proved to have been extensively
used by the Hermetic Philosophers, but whether the former
body derived them from the latter, and, if so, at what period,
are points which, in the absence of positive evidence, it is
impossible to decide.

Here, however, let me revert to the words of ALBERT
PIKE, who says of ASHMOLE that there must have been
something in Masonry which induced him to join the
Institution, "and what was in it then may have been in
it centuries before."

The *Autobiography* of a later antiquary, the Rev. WILLIAM
STUKELEY, M.D., records that in January, 1721—"His
curiosity led him to be initiated into the mysterys of Masonry,
suspecting it to be the remains of the mysterys of the an-
tients." It is possible, and indeed highly probable, that
ASHMOLE was influenced by very similar feelings, which he
satisfied in the same way.

STUKELEY's admission into the Craft occurred shortly
after the formation of the Grand Lodge of England, the
earliest of governing Masonic bodies, in 1717, and a slight
pause will now be made before I resume and conclude my
account of the Rosicrucians.

Before, however, proceeding with some brief remarks on
the era of Grand Lodges, let me, in order to be better understood, make use of a comparison. Unlike that of other
nations, the civilization of Egypt presents a continuous
deterioration from the earliest ages to the latest. The
farther we go back the more consummate is the art, the
more complete the command of mechanical processes and
appliances. In other words, the civilization of Egypt must
have culminated before the very earliest dawn of its recorded
history. If Egypt is not altogether exceptional and ab-
normal, the use of the mechanical methods employed by
the Pyramid builders points to an antecedent civilization
of which the extent in time becomes literally incalculable,
while it seems to become more and more inexplicable the
more its real character is investigated and brought to light.

In the same way, there cannot be a doubt that the symbolism of Masonry, to a considerable portion of which, even at this day, no meaning can be assigned which is entirely satisfactory to an intelligent mind, must "have culminated before the earliest dawn of its recorded history." Also, that it underwent a gradual process of decay, which was arrested, but only at the point we now have it, by passing under the control of the Grand Lodge of England in 1717.

In other words, the meaning of a great part of our Masonic symbolism has been forgotten, and it may be laid down with confidence that this partial obliteration of its import *must* have taken place before the era of Grand Lodges. The grounds on which this conclusion is based will form the subject of a separate study, but if we assume the symbolism (or ceremonial) of Masonry to be older than the year 1717, there is practically no limit whatever of age that can be assigned to it. *After* the formation of a Grand Lodge there was centralization; *before* it there was none. Each Lodge then met by inherent right, and even if we go so far as to admit the possibility of new and strange practices being introduced into any one of them, there was no higher body by whose authority these innovations could have been imposed on the other Lodges.

It is, therefore, very far from being an arbitrary hypothesis that the symbolism we possess has come down to us, in all its main features, from very early times, and that it originated during the splendour of Mediæval Operative Masonry, and not in its decline. I am therefore of opinion that if Freemasonry is in any way indebted to Hermeticism for its symbolism, the period in which the Saracenic learning found its way into England is the epoch wherein we must look for its occurrence.

I shall next present a striking passage from an anonymous work, entitled *A Suggestive Inquiry concerning the Hermetic Mystery*, which appeared in 1850, but was shortly afterwards withdrawn from circulation for reasons that remain unknown:—

"Modern Science has hitherto thrown no light on the Wisdom of Antiquity . . . the ancients were not enlightened on the *à priori* ground alone, but the same power of Wisdom was confirmed in many surpassing effects of spiritual chemistry, and in the asserted miracle of the Philosopher's Stone. With this theosophic doctrine of Wisdom the tradition of Alchemy runs hand in hand. It was this which inspired ALBERTUS MAGNUS, AQUINAS, ROGER BACON, the fiery LULLY, FICINUS, PICUS DE MIRANDOLA, SPINOZA, REUCHLIN, CORNELIUS AGRIPPA, and all the subsequent Paracelsian school. It was this which, under another title, PLATO celebrates as the most efficacious of all arts, calling it Theurgy and the worship of the gods; this PYTHAGORAS practised in his school, and the Chaldaic Oracles openly proclaim, announcing the efficacy of material rites in procuring divine assimilation; these the Alexandrian Platonists continuously pursued in their Mysteries, which PROCLUS, PLOTINUS, JAMBLICUS, and SYNESIUS have explained in their records, tracing the same to the most remote antiquity in Egypt, as being the prime source and sanctuary of the Hermetic art."

CHAPTER II

MEDLÆVAL OPERATIVE MASONRY

Some have ascribed the principal ecclesiastical structures to the fraternity of Freemasons—depositaries of a concealed and traditional science. There is probably some ground for this opinion; and the earlier archives of that mysterious association if they existed, might illustrate the progress of Gothic architecture, and perhaps reveal its origin.

HENRY HALLAM

UPON no subject of antiquity have so many discordant opinions been maintained as upon the origin of what is called Gothic Architecture. John Evelyn appears to have brought the term Gothic into use in this country (1697), and he was followed by Sir Christopher Wren, whose authority gave currency to the phrase, and led to its employment by the majority of those who wrote on the subject during the eighteenth century. But Wren, though he used the word Gothic, did not consider it as expressive of the origin of the mode of building which it designated; for he ascribes the invention to the Saracens, from whom, as he conceived, it was adopted by the Crusaders of the West.

According to the editors of the *Parentalia or Memoirs of the Family of the Wrens*:—

"He [Sir Christopher] was of opinion that what we now call *Gothick* ought properly and truly to be named the *Saracenick Architecture refined by the Christians*. The Holy War gave the Christians who had been there an Idea of the Saracen Works, which were afterwards imitated by them in the West. The *Italians* (among which were yet some *Greek* Refugees), and with them *French*, *German*, and *Flemings*, joined into a Fraternity of Architects, procuring

57

Papal Bulls for their Encouragement and particular Privileges; they stiled themselves Freemasons, and ranged from one Nation to another, as they found Churches to be built (for very many in those Ages were everywhere in Building, through Piety or Emulation). Their Government was regular, and where they fixed near the Building in Hand, they made a Camp of Huts. A Surveyor govern'd in chief; every tenth man was called a Warden, and overlooked each nine." Hence has arisen the familiar story of a Fraternity of Architects, travelling with Papal Bulls, and styling themselves Freemasons, which for upwards of a century held possession of our encyclopædias. Yet, even if we go so far as to believe that Wren really said all that has been put into his mouth by the editors of the *Parentalia*—a point on which I shall again touch—it will be well to bear in mind that this legend or tradition derived its chief authority from the popular delusion that the great architect had been for many years the "Grand Master" of our Society.

The curious statement that Papal Bulls were granted to the early Freemasons will be more fully examined at a later stage. The influence of the "Monks," who were only a portion of the clergy, has, I think, been greatly exaggerated. Nevertheless, it was a prevalent theory that the nations of Western Europe were thrown into a stupor towards the end of the tenth century, believing the end of the world to be at hand. That when the dreaded year A.D. 1000 came and went harmlessly, and the world was still intact, the nations awakened from their stupor, and, animated by the most fervent piety, everywhere commenced building Churches, Abbeys, and Cathedrals, under the guidance of the monks, who, being a cosmopolitan body, were under one head and worked with one aim in every country; that these monks trained a body of men, a kind of lay brethren, to build for them, called Freemasons; and that these, like their masters (or superior brethren), were also cosmopolitan, and hence that the churches and other ecclesiastical structures were everywhere erected with a wonderful similarity of design.

The influence of the Crusades upon the architecture both of the East and West has been carefully summed up by my late friend and fellow Past-Master in the "Quatuor Coronati" Lodge, Professor T. Hayter Lewis, in the following words, which, with his sanction and full approval, are reproduced in the present work:—

"The Norman and Anglo-Saxon style appears to have been perfected, and to have had its head-quarters, in the North of France; and, although Romanesque architecture on the Rhine has many features in common with the Norman, the latter stands out clearly and distinctly from it.

"At or about the middle of the twelfth century, signs of a change became apparent in the general forms of the style, giving to them lighter proportions, less pronounced Norman details, and, above all, a rapid change from the round to the pointed arch; these changes taking place not only in France, but also in England and other countries, the name of the style, thus altered, being well-known as Transitional. At that time Palestine was in the hands of the Crusaders (who came chiefly from the various provinces of France), who entered Jerusalem in 1099, and were not expelled from it until 1187. This period embraces the greater part of that of the Normans and the Transition in Britain.

"The Crusaders were in possession of Jerusalem for little more than three-quarters of a century, but the amount of work which they did in that time all over Palestine was enormous, and the influence which that work received from Eastern civilization was great and lasting. Every part of the country bears witness to the gigantic energy of the Western nations, great forts, churches, and hostelries being built as if to last for ever. Palestine must have been as thickly covered with churches as England is now—so mighty was the living force of the Western world 700 years ago. I feel no doubt that trained architects, masters of the works, and leading Masons were sent from the great religious orders in Europe. But the actual manual labour must have devolved, to a large extent, upon the native population— part Christian, part Moslem—accustomed to work under

the influence of the Persians, whose capital, Bagdad, was
the centre of Eastern art from the ninth to the thirteenth
century.

"These native workmen must have been, at first, altogether in subjection to the Crusaders; but many of them
would, in course of time, rise higher on the scale of work,
and so gradually influence, in various ways, the Western
art of their masters. That they actually did so influence
it I fully believe, more especially in the important use of
the Pointed arch, which, owing to the same Eastern influence, had been already introduced in Southern France.

"Towards the end of the twelfth century the Crusaders'
hold on Palestine became very insecure. In 1187, Jerusalem was captured by Saladin, and the Christians were
soon after expelled from nearly the whole of Palestine,
though Antioch was not taken until 1268, nor Acre until
1291. This expulsion was not a merely nominal one, but
applied to every Christian who would not turn Mussulman
or remain a captive. Thus there must have been forced
into Germany, France, and Britain, thousands of skilled
men accustomed to work under the guidance of the monastic
orders, and under vows or oaths, more or less strict.

"After the expulsion from Jerusalem, a great change
occurred in the architecture of Europe. Up to that time,
France and England had gone fairly hand in hand in architecture, but soon afterwards they went somewhat different
ways. In our own country we see the rise of our beautiful
Early English Style—one as peculiar in its ornamental
details as was the later Perpendicular."

The same high authority, however, carefully states: —
"I have not the slightest wish to suggest that our beautiful
Early English work was the result of Eastern influence, for
in none of the Crusaders' work in Palestine which I have
seen can I find definite traces of our lovely ornamentation
or other details. All that I suggest is, that by that influence
the Norman Style was gradually lightened in detail, its
round arches raised to the Pointed form, and its Masons'
Marks and tooling obtained."

"I absolutely refuse to believe," continues Professor Hayter Lewis, "that so great a change as that from the Norman to the Pointed Style, made in so short a time, was the result of gradual development; nor can I believe that it was the result of any partnership of minds, be they monks or laics, monasteries or guilds. No great work in the world was ever done yet which had not some great mind to start it. Whether the seclusion of the Cloister or the Guild shall ever surrender this identity to us, one may fairly doubt. But I do believe that a study of the marks which the Masons of old have left us—a study so much in its infancy that it owes its origin only to the late George Godwin—may ultimately lead us to the knowledge of the place from which came the influence of the master mind."

Mr. Fergusson, however, tells us, "No individual has, so far as we know, ever invented a new style in any part of the world. No one can even be named who, during the prevalence of a true style of art, materially advanced its progress, or by his individual exertion did much to help it forward. . . . In Architecture, the merit of one admirable building, or of a high state of national art, is not due to one or to a few master minds, but to the aggregation of experience, the mass of intellectual exertion, which alone can achieve any practically great result. Whenever we see any work of man truly worthy of admiration, we may be quite sure that the credit of it is not due to an individual, but to thousands working together through a long series of years." (*Hist. of Arch.*, i, 44; ii, 128.)

The subject of Masons' marks will again claim our attention, and before passing away from Palestine and the East, I shall merely remark that Gothic architecture was not properly naturalized in the Golden period of the Crusades; and that there is an essential difference between the Gothic and the Saracenic Styles, as shown (among other things) by the absence of domes in the former, and of heights in the latter. There can be no doubt, however, that through the influence of the Crusades a new fervour of study sprang up in the West from its contact with the more civilized

East. Travellers, like Athelard, of Bath, brought back the
first rudiments of physical and mathematical science from
the schools of Bagdad or Cordova; and if "Masonry" was
formerly called "Geometry," as we are told in the Manuscript Constitutions (or written traditions) of our Society,
then the merit of having introduced it into England must
be assigned to the scholar and philosopher of Bath.

One reason why the true Gothic sprang up almost simultaneously in France and England was that at that time
the frontiers of the two Kingdoms were almost conterminous
from one end of France to the other.

The Early Pointed Style is simple and severe in its proportions, and the period of its duration, roundly speaking,
was from the end of the twelfth to the end of the fourteenth
century. The Pointed Style of England was formed in a
peculiar and independent manner. The Single Pointed
Style of the earliest period was known by the name of
Early English, of which the finest specimens are the west
front and nave of Wells Cathedral, built by Joscelin Trot-
man, the bishop of that See.

The Middle or Perfect Pointed, known in England as the
Decorated Style, is considered as that in which Gothic
architecture attained its climax. Among its *chefs-d'œuvre*
are the Presbytery of Lincoln, with which it is said no fault
has ever been found; Lichfield Cathedral (chiefly within
this period), the only church in this country possessing three
spires, and the only genuine example of an English apse;
the choirs of Bristol and Carlisle; the larger portion of York
Minster; and what is, perhaps, the most beautiful feature
in the whole range of Gothic architecture, the famous
octagon of Alan de Walsingham at Ely.

It may be here observed, as showing to how great an
extent our mediæval churches display local peculiarities of
style, and what little ground there is for believing in one
universal consensus, that almost every county in England
has its distinct architectural features. The northern and
the eastern shires are each a class apart. The existence of
local schools may be plainly traced in Devon, Somerset,

Cornwall, and Northamptonshire, while in Gloucestershire there would appear to have been a kind of architectural college, in which theory was properly blended with practice. Of the churches, indeed, of the early Middle Ages, it was observed by Mr. G. E. Street:—"I could have told you how they may be classified into groups, speaking to us of the skill and genius of individual architects, each in his own district or diocese." It is probable that every cathedral possessed its own Lodge of Masons, and to quote from Sir Gilbert Scott:—"The point of the necessity of gangs of skilful workmen accustomed to work together has not been sufficiently attended to. The fables of the Freemasons have produced a natural reaction, and the degree of truth which there is in these traditions has consequently been overlooked. Each of our great cathedrals had a gang of workmen attached to it in regular pay."

The last phase of Gothic architecture is constituted by the English Perpendicular Style, and the Flamboyant Style of the Continent. It lasted from the end of the fourteenth to the middle of the sixteenth century.

Fan Tracery, a beautiful form of vaulting, which is only found in England, is said to constitute the veritable "swan-song" of Gothic architecture. It is a leading characteristic of the Perpendicular (or Tudor) Style, and appears to have been invented by a local school of masons at Gloucester.

In the earliest examples, such as the cloisters at Gloucester Cathedral, these great fans, with their wide-stretching circular outline, spring apparently from a narrow pier shaft on each side, and meet in the centre. At Peterborough the size of the fans is increased, but at King's College Chapel, Cambridge, and the later St. George's at Windsor, there was a return to the arrangement at Gloucester, although the shape of the fans was altered.

But mediæval architecture had long been decaying. The Reformation struck its death blow, and when the Royal Chapel of St. George's, Windsor; King's College, Cambridge; Henry the Seventh's, Westminster; and other exquisite fan-roofed buildings were completed, the true Gothic of England passed away "in a blaze of glory" under the Tudors.

But it never quite died out, although its traditions (to which I shall hereafter more particularly refer), together with its constructive principles and processes, were well-nigh forgotten. Traces of the old style may yet be distinguished in the long series of buildings which are intermediate in date between the decline of Gothic architecture at the close of the Perpendicular period, and the dawn of the revival under Batty Langley and Horace Walpole.

The architecture of Scotland has a style which is peculiarly its own. Except Melrose, there is nothing at all resembling the English Perpendicular, but there are frequent traces of Flamboyant, which is explained by the long connection with France. Deeply interesting are the ruins of the Abbeys of Kelso (1128), Melrose (1136), and Kilwinning (1140), but the fable which makes the last named the cradle of Scottish Freemasonry must be reserved for separate treatment. Roslin, the gem of the whole Scottish series, is unlike any other structure in either North or South Britain. The designer was evidently a foreign architect, and it appears on record that masons and other workmen were collected by Sir William St. Clair from all parts. In the chapel there is a fine fluted column, to which a legend is attached. The master mason is said to have gone to Rome, and finding on his return that he had been surpassed by his apprentice, slew him with a hammer. The story has been associated with an early and unhistorical phase of Freemasonry, of which art or science in Scotland the hereditary Grand Mastership was traditionally vested in the St. Clair family. A similar legend is current at Strasburg and Rouen, and possibly in all three cases it had an origin in fact.

At the present day, the idea of there having been, in the early part of the thirteenth century, *Colleges of Masons* in every country of Europe, which received the blessing

TO ALL AND SINGULAR

GRANT OF ARMS TO THE UNITED GRAND LODGE OF
ENGLAND FROM HERALDS' COLLEGE, 1919
Reproduced by permission of the Board of General Purposes
(See Appendix)

of the Holy See, under an injunction of dedicating their skill to the erection of ecclesiastical buildings, may be dismissed as chimerical. Though I must not forget that, according to the well known and highly imaginative *Historical Essay on Architecture* (1835) of Mr. Hope—who greatly expands the meaning of two passages in the works of Muratori—a body of travelling architects, who wandered over Europe during the Middle Ages, received the appellation of *Magistri Comacini*, or *Masters of Como*, a title which became generic to all those of the profession. The idea has been revived by a recent writer, who believes that these *Magistri Comacini* were a survival of the Roman Collegia, that they settled in Como, and were afterwards employed by the Lombard Kings, under whose patronage they developed into a powerful and highly organized guild, with a dominant influence on the whole architecture of the Middle Ages (*The Cathedral Builders*). But, even if such a theory had any probability, it would be far from clearing up certain obscurities in the history of mediæval architecture, as the author suggests would be the case. Interchanges of influence were not uncommon, but the works of local schools present far too marked an individuality to render it possible that they could owe much (if anything) to the influence of any central guild. The question therefore arises, who were the men by whom the stately buildings of the Middle Ages were erected ?

The Fabric Rolls of York Minster show that "Orders for the Masons and Workmen" were issued in 1352:— "The first and second masons, who are called masters of the same, and the carpenters, shall make oath that they cause the ancient customs underwritten to be faithfully observed. In summer they are to begin to work immediately after sunrise until the ringing of the bell of the Virgin Mary; then to breakfast in the fabric lodge (*logium fabricæ*) then one of the masters shall knock upon the door of the lodge, and forthwith all are to return to work until noon; Between April and August, after dinner, they shall sleep in the lodge, then work until the first bell for vespers ;

then sit to drink till the end of the third bell, and return to work so long as they can see by daylight. In winter they are to begin work at daybreak, and continue as before till noon, dine, and return to work till daylight is over. On Vigils and on Saturdays they are to work until noon."

These rules continued in force until 1370, when they were superseded by others of a like character, but expressed in the vernacular idiom. The duties to be performed in the "*loge*" remained very much the same as before, and the regulations conclude:—"Ande, alswa, it es ordayned yt na masoun sall be receavyde atte wyrke, to ye werk of ye forsayde Kyrke, but he be firste provede a weke or mare opon his well wyrking; and, aftyr yt he es foundyn souffissant of his werke, be receavyde of ye commune assente of ye mayster and ye kepers of ye werk, ande of ye maystyr masoun, and swere upon ye boke yt he sall trewly ande bysyli at his power, for oute any maner gylyry, fayntys, outher desayte, hald and kepe haly all ye poyntes of yis forsaye ordinance."

We learn from the same Fabric Rolls, that there was a duly appointed pledge-day (*pleghdai*), when the workmen swore to observe the orders which the Chapter had ordained for their management. This they were required to do at least once a year. It was usual to find tunics (gowns), aprons, gloves, and clogs, and to give occasional potations and remuneration for extra work. Gloves were given to the carpenters in 1371, and to the setters in 1403. The last named workmen received both aprons and gloves (*naprons et ciroteci*) in 1404.

The Lodge (workshop or residence) is probably referred to under the words *tabulatum domicialem*, as the shed in front of the Abbey Church, St. Alban's, was called in 1200. If not, the entry in 1321 of 2s. 6d. for straw to cover the masons' lodging at Caernarvon, may perhaps be accepted. In 1330, a man at St. Stephen's Chapel, Westminster, had, among other duties, to clean out the lodge. The City (of London) Records show that in 1337 certain stones were removed to the Guildhall from the lodge in the garden.

The York Fabric Rolls refer to the lodge in 1352 and 1370 (as already shown); also in 1399, when a list is given of "the stores in the loge in the cemetery." In 1395, at Westminster Abbey, 15s. 6d. was paid to the "dauber" in respect of the lodge for the masons.

The Manuscript Constitutions (or written traditions) of the Freemasons will form the subject of a separate study, but the earliest writing in which the "Legend of the Craft" has been preserved may be referred to. This, which reflects the charges and customs of the masons' trade as prevailing at the close of the fourteenth century, enjoins in *Articulus quartus* that no bondsman should be made a "prentys," lest he might be reclaimed by his lord, and if taken in the "logge," it would cause trouble; and in *Tercius punctus* that the "prentes,"

> " Hys maystu conwsel he kepe and close,
> And hys felows by hys goode purpose;
> The prevetyse of the chamber telle he no mon,
> Ny yn the logge whatsever they done;
> Whatsever thou heryst, or syste hem do,
> Telle hyt no mon, whersever thou go."
>
> *Regius MS.*

This plainly refers to the concealment of trade mysteries, and an entry of 1405-6, "One runnyng bar for the door of the lodge, 5d.," which is supplied from Exeter, may possibly have a similar meaning. The masons at Catterick Church, in 1421, were to be provided with a "luge" of four rooms; and those engaged to build Walberswick Steeple, 1426, with a "hows" to work, eat, drink, and lay in. A "loygye lathamorum" was attached to Christchurch, Canterbury, in 1429. A "loge" was erected in the cemetery garth at Durham in 1432; and a "warden of the lodge of masons" at York Cathedral is mentioned in 1470.

The "tylying of iiii. lodgys for the fremasons and for the brycke-hewers" is met with under 1553, and lastly, as regards England, in 1542-3, the freemasons employed to build the Coventry Cross were, at their own charge, to procure, find, and make "an house or lodge for masons to work in" during the process of its erection.

In Scotland, the earliest use of the word is associated with the burgh of Aberdeen, where in 1483, we find enumerated the fines payable by the "masownys of the luge," from which they were to be entirely excluded after a third offence. The "work" and "recreatioun" to take place "in the commoun luge," are specified in a statute for the "Maister Masoun of the College Kirk of St. Giles, Edinburgh, 1491." The Indenture, however, "betwix Dunde and its Masoun, A.D. 1536," is particularly interesting, as containing the earliest authentic instance of a Scottish lodge adopting the name of a saint, namely, "Our Lady [*i.e.*, the Virgin Mary's] luge of Dunde." The "masoun craft" falling within the purview of the above statute probably reappear as the "Ludge of Dundie," which was a party to the St. Clair Charter of 1628.

The origin of masonic guilds is wrapped in much obscurity. One—the present Masons' Company of the City of London—certainly existed in 1375, and inferentially at a far earlier date. A fuller account, however, of this body will be given in another place. Two curious coincidences have been connected with the above year (1375). The first, that the earliest copy of the manuscript constitutions (*Regius MS.*) refers to the customs of that period; the second, that the formation of a wonderful society, occasioned by a combination of masons undertaking not to work without an advance of wages, when summoned from several counties by writs of Edward III, to rebuild and enlarge Windsor Castle, under the direction of William of Wykeham, has been placed at the same date. It is said also that these masons agreed on certain signs and tokens by which they might know one another, and render mutual assistance against impressment; and further agreed not to work unless *free*, and on their own terms. Hence they called themselves *Free-Masons*. In the opinion of Mr. Wyatt Papworth "there is probability about much of this, but (he believes) no authority." The same writer adds—"The earliest of such writs of impress in my notes is dated 1333, and one exceptional document is worth mentioning, of about the date 1353, it being a special protection given to the workmen —ten masons, ten carpenters, and their servants—engaged upon the erection of the church at Stratford-on-Avon, until the edifice should be completed."

At Canterbury, in 1429, under Archbishop Chichely, Wm. Molash, the Prior of Christchurch, shows in his accounts that a livery of murray cloth was given to the magister, custos, sixteen lathami, and three apprentices "de la loygye Lathamorum." This may, indeed, have been a guild of masons, but the indications appear to me more consistent with the idea that it was merely a permanent staff of workmen attached to the priory in regular pay. "It is certain," says Mr. Papworth, "that there were fellowships, or guilds of masons, before the middle of the fourteenth century, but whether the one in London had any communication with other guilds then existing in the other corporate towns, or whether there was a supreme guild, which led to a systematic working, is still without elucidation (1887). All the documents have led me to believe that there was not any supreme guild in England, however probable the existence of such a body may appear. Thus the 'orders,' supplied to the masons at work in York Cathedral in 1352, give but a poor notion of there being then in that city anything like a guild or fellowship claiming authority in virtue of a charter, supposed to have been given to it by Athelstan in 926, not only over that city but over all England."

The Masons' Company of London was represented on the Court of Common Council in 1375, and it is also recorded that Regulations for the Trade of Masons were ordained by the Mayor, Alderman, and Sheriffs of London, so early as 1356. On the latter date, twelve of the most experienced members were supposed to inform the Mayor and his assessors as to the customs of the trade, but it is very improbable that the masons should themselves propose that if a mason failed to fulfil his contract certain men of his trade who acted as his sureties should be bound to fulfil his task; or that the masons and carpenters (on a different

occasion) should have volunteered to take oath before the
Mayor and Aldermen of London that they would do their
duty in their trade (*Lib. Cus.* 100).

That there was a guild of masons at Norwich in 1389
may, I think, be safely inferred from certain passages in
Mr. Smith's collection (*Eng. Gilds*, 39, 41).

The gathering together of artisans in the various craft
guilds and fraternities was not always a matter of free will.
If the masons of London had already possessed a guild or
company in 1356, it is scarcely likely that regulations for
the trade would only have been enacted in that year.
Hence I am unable to agree with Mr. Papworth that the
existence of masonic guilds before the middle of the fourteenth century is not open to dispute, though I am entirely
with him in the belief that not only is there an absence of
proof with respect to a supreme guild, but that all the evidence we possess points in quite an opposite direction.

As to the secrets (apart from any possible symbolism)
possessed by the operative masons of the Middle Ages, all
trades even of the present day have their own, and the
very word "mystery," so often used, indicates the jealousy
with which each craft guarded the arcana of its trade. A
high authority tells us—"I am disposed to believe that
just as when one sense is extinguished in any person the
rest are stimulated to preternatural acuteness, so in the
ages with which we are concerned, when literature was so
scanty and the means of occupation so unvaried the single
art which was developed in any notable degree was studied
with such intensity and concentration as to bring about
results which we, in our wider means of thought, study,
and application, find it difficult if not impossible to rival."
There was a double motive with the mediæval masons for
not disclosing their trade secrets, for besides the mystery
which mankind is so prone to affect, they really had something both to learn and conceal; and the principles on which
their style of building was founded were unknown to the
greatest professors of architecture that appeared after the
Reformation.

It has been maintained that the knowledge of the "master law" was not communicated to all workmen even in the Middle Ages, but was strictly guarded as a profound secret possessed only by the most eminent of their number, who were honoured as chief masters. Indeed, Professor Kugler informs us, in his *History of Art,* that a Bishop was murdered at Utrecht by a master mason, because the son of the latter had communicated to him the architectural master secret. The incident is also recorded by a native historian, who places the date at 1099, and states that the prelate had extracted from the young man the mystery (*arcanum magisterium*) of laying the foundation of a church (Beka, *Episcop. Ultraject*).

With the *Wahrzeichen* of the Steinmetzen may be compared the *grotesques* of the early British masons. These symbols or caricatures, though common to sculpture, painting, and carving, are, perhaps, most usual in the carved misereres in conventual churches. The satire which some of them embody is chiefly to be referred to the jealousies of the secular and regular clergy one against the other, and of both against the mendicant friars. The symbols occur in all ages, and in all works of art.

A fox seems to have been a very common device for a friar, who is often represented preaching to geese, thus including the stupidity of those that listen to him in the same device with the craft of the obnoxious friar.

The superintendents of English buildings in the Middle Ages are referred to under numerous designations. Of the term ARCHITECT there was apparently no use, and it seems to have only been introduced into English books about the end of the reign of Queen Elizabeth. In a writ, dated 1199, Elias de Derham is styled INGENIATOR, and allowed ten marcs for repairs of the King's Houses at Westminster. This word, though translated "Architect," may be properly regarded as signifying "Engineer." Elias was a canon of Salisbury, *a prima fundatione rector fuit novæ fabricæ per* 25 *annos; et Robertus cementarius rexit per* 25 *annos.* The connection between the two men, one of whom was *rector* and the other *rexit*, is, however, difficult to comprehend, unless, indeed, the canon was succeeded by the cementarius.

A term in use for several years after the Conquest was SUPERVISOR, which has generally been translated Surveyor or Overseer. But the office, though changed to surveyor in later times, was never equivalent to that of surveyor at the present day; nor had a large number of the ecclesiastics and noblemen who held it any just claim to be considered as the architects of the buildings which were erected under their supervision. In 1356, William of Wykeham, was appointed "Supervisor of the King's Works at Windsor," and the next year his salary was enlarged to two shillings a day, "until he should obtain ecclesiastical preferment." Wykeham was empowered by his first patent *to impress all sorts of artificers*, and to provide stone, timber, and all other materials and carriages. The second patent extended his authority, as, besides the appointment and disposition of all workmen, he was to provide carpenters, masons, and other artificers, stone, timber, etc.; also *to hold leet and other courts*, pleas of trespass and misdemeanours, and to *inquire* of the King's liberties, rights, and all things appertaining thereto.

From the foregoing it has been suggested that the real meaning of the term SUPERVISOR, as used in these and other old records, would be best conveyed to us by the word "Steward," and the authority of Shakespeare has been cited in support of this contention. It may also be remarked that the Court Leet or View of Frankpledge, where every person at the age of twelve years had to swear obedience to the King, was held before the Steward of the Leet. The due observance of this custom by the masons is enjoined in their Manuscript Constitutions, where also we meet with the tradition that "St. Alban was a worthy Knight and Steward of the King's household, and had government of his realm and also of making the Town Walls, and loved masons well."

At Croyland, the MAGISTER OPERUM was the first of the

six greater officers. The SACRISTAN (or sometimes the treasurer) held this post.

Besides the office of MASTER OF THE WORK, those of KEEPER OF THE FABRIC and KEEPER OF THE WORK are occasionally met with in conjunction with it. In Scotland, Sir William Bruce of Balcaskie is mentioned as "His Majesty's Surveyor," and also as "Master of the King's Works," 1670-9. The terms "masoun wrycht" (carpenter) and "maister of wark" occur in the Acts of the Parliaments of Scotland.

A very rare title, that of DIRECTOR or MASTER, was held by Elias de Derham, the King's Ingeniator, already referred to.

In the King's household there was an office for carrying out royal works, and with three exceptions the designation of CLERICUS OPERATIONUM does not appear to have been used by any person in another employment. The earliest Clerk of the Works was appointed in 1241, after which there is a long list of these officers, and on the 12th of July, 1389, Geoffrey Chaucer, the poet, was nominated to the post. About the title of DEVIZOR there is some confusion, but this officer had the same remuneration as a Clerk of the Works.

In the opinion of Wyatt Papworth, "the Master Masons were generally the architects during the mediæval period in England. The Master of the Works may have been so, and probably the Clerk of the Works was also in the latest times."

It is a very noteworthy fact that the master mason, though obtained occasionally on the spot, appears to have been sought for in some distant locality, similarly to the architects of the present day. Among other instances of this practice, a cementarius, named Durandus, employed from 1214 to 1251 upon Rouen Cathedral, is known to have been sent for by, and to have obeyed the summons of, the Abbot of Beaulieu, in Hampshire.

Many of the master masons appear to have amassed wealth, and to have had lands at their disposal. They seem to have insisted upon having comfortable habitations while at work, to say nothing of a gown, furred or otherwise, a practice recorded as early as 1321, and which is known to have been a common claim or reward in the Middle Ages to household retainers. Tunics, aprons, gloves, and clogs, or shoes, were found for the operatives of the secondary and lower classes.

In the *fifteenth century*, the master mason at the building of the last portion of the nave of Westminster Abbey was M. William Colchester, 1400-15, when he was sent in a similar capacity to York Cathedral—"assigned to that fabric by letters patent from the King." In a writ of 1415 are the words, "petras vocatas ragge calces et liberas petras"—here, as *fraunche pere*, or *free stone*, is commonly supposed to mean stone that cut freely, the substitution of *liber* for *fraunche* (unless merely a literal translation), may be held to indicate some connection between the *freemason* and the *freedom* of a trade. Thomas Hyneley, cementarius, contracted for a portion of the cloisters at Durham, 1416. There is a notice of a guild of cementarii in 1422. In 1421 M. John Long was master mason at York, and in 1423 William Waddeswyk was the guardian (warden) or second master mason.

The Fabric Roll of Exeter Cathedral, under the year 1426, shows the following:—

"Johi Harry fremason opanti ibim p septiam . . . 3s.

"Johi Umfray fremason p hanc septiam . . . nl. q. hic recessit."

In 1427, John Wolston (clerk of the works) and John Harry, freemasons, were sent from Exeter to Beere to purchase stone. At St. Albans a tombstone records the death, 1430, of a "Latomus in arte," who was also esquire to Richard II. John Wode, masoun, 1435, contracted to build the tower of the Abbey Church of St. Edmundsbury, "in all mannere of thinges that longe to free masounry"; and, in the same year, William Horwode, freemason, contracted to build Fotheringay Church, "by oversight of masters of the same craft," and "by oversight of master masons of the country." The wages of a "frank mason" are specified in a Statute of 1444-5 (28 Hen. VI, c. xii). A "Serjeaunt of the King's Masonrye" within the realm of England, is exempted in an Act of Resumption, 1464. John Stowell, "ffreemason," 1470, contracted for the frontal of an altar at Wells. It was customary at York for the person next in rank to the master mason to receive that office when it became vacant, and M. William Colchester above named, an outsider, was assaulted and nearly killed by the "stone cutters" who had been placed under his direction. William Hyndeley, however, warden, of the Lodge of Masons in 1472, became master mason in due course. In 1485-88, a freemason made a cross in the church-yard at Wigloft in Lincolnshire. The Statutes of Wells Cathedral record, Oct. 23, 1490, the appointment with a salary, of "W. Atwodde, ffremason, pro suo bono et diligenti servicio in arte sua de ffremasonry." In 1494, William Este, a freemason of Oxford, was engaged on works at Wodestock Hall. In the following year, 1495, a free mason, master carpenter, and rough mason were to take per day 4*d*. with diet, between Easter and Michaelmas; while master masons and master carpenters, taking charge of work, and having under them six men, were to receive 5*d*. (11 Hen. VII, c. xxii). The actual word "freemason" here appears for the first time in the Statutes of the Realm, and whether conveying the same meaning as mason "de franche pere" in the Acts of 1350 and 1360, or as "frank mason" in the Statute of 1444-5, or partaking of the signification of both terms, cannot be positively determined.

In the *sixteenth century*, the term *freemason* becomes more common. John Hylmer and William Vertue, freemasons, 1507, contracted to execute the groined vaulting to the choir of St. George's Chapel, Windsor, for £700; and afterwards, 1512, Vertue assisted William Este to build Corpus Christi College, Oxford, About 1509, Robert Jenyns, Robert Vertue, and John Lobins are called "Ye King's Mr. Masons," when estimating for a tomb for Henry VII. During the erection of Christ Church College. Oxford,

1512-17, the master and overseer of the works were priests; John Adams was freemason, and Thomas Watlington, warden of the carpenters. At King's College Chapel, Cambridge, about 1513, John Wastell, the master mason, with Henry Semesk, one of the wardens of the work, contracted for some of the vaulting. By an indenture of the same date it was stipulated that the former should "kepe continually 60 fre-masons workyng." "Rec. of the good man Stefford, ffremason, for the holle stepyll wt Tymbr, Iron, and Glas, xxxviij*l*," occurs in the records of a London parish, under 1535. John Multon, freemason, had granted to him in 1536, by the prior and convent of Bath, the "office of master of all their works commonly called fremasonry, when it should be vacant." While the Great Hall at Hampton Court was in course of erection, 1531, Multon was master mason at 1*s.* per day; William Reynolds, warden, at 5*s.*; the setters at 3*s.* 6*d.*; and the lodgeman (a curious expression) at 3*s.* 4*d.* per week. In 1537 the existing Masons' Company of London is described as "The Company of ffree Masons," a title it retained until 1656. Thomas Phillips, of Bristol, freemason (and another), contracted, 1543, to rebuild the Coventry Cross for £187 6*s.* 8*d.* A distinction is drawn in the building accounts of Corpus Christi College, Cambridge, 1578, between the "rough" and the "free" masons.

Mason is the word generally used in the Privy Purse expenses of Henry VII and his successor; also master mason at Windsor, and freemason for making images. The latter term, as above noticed, will be found in a statute of 1495. It also occurs in those of 1515 (7 Hen. VIII, c. v) and 1548 (2 and 3 Edw. VI, c. xv). Though in the later Act of 1562-3 (5 Eliz., c. iv) all classes of workmen in the mason's trade are included under "artificers" and "labourers." Thereafter, mason and freemason are terms in constant use down to the present time, which will render unnecessary my doing more than subjoin a few of the later examples that occur in my notes.

A transcript of the certificate of "John Wincester, Master

frie mason, 1581," is given in the Melrose MS. of 1674. But the earliest existing copy of the Legend of the Craft (or Manuscript Constitutions of the masonic body) which contains the word *Freemason*, is the York roll of (about) the year 1600. In older transcripts, or readings, the term used is *true* (or *trew*) *mason*. The grant of incorporation of the Company of Free Masons, Carpenters, Joiners and Slaters of the City of Oxford, is dated October 31, 1604. In 1610, by an order of the Justices of the Peace, "a free mason which can draw his plot, work, and set accordingly, having charge over others," was considered worth 12*d*. a day before Michaelmas, and 10*d*. after it; while a "rough mason which can take charge over others," was worth 10*d*. and 8*d*. during those seasons respectively. The "frie mesones"—meaning, no doubt, the free-men masons—"of Ednr." are referred to in the minutes of the Lodge of Edinburgh, December 27, 1636. The Lodge of Scoon is described in its Charter as "ane frie Lodge," December, 24, 1658. "Lodge" and "Freemasonry" are mentioned in the final "Charge" of Sloane MS. 3,323 (A.D. 1659). Harleian MS. 2,054, of (about) 1660, is headed "The ffree Masons Orders and Constitutions"; while in the same writing, and apparently of the same date, we meet with a form of oath relating to the "words & signes of a free mason." In the Melrose MS. of 1674 (already cited), "frie mason"—which occurs very frequently—is clearly used as synonymous with freeman-mason; and "frie-men" as an equivalent for frie-masons.

It will be seen that the word "freestone," or its equivalent in French or Latin, was employed from the beginning of the thirteenth century (1212), and the conclusion has been drawn that the term "freemason" itself is clearly derived from the mason who worked freestone, in contradistinction to the mason who was occupied in rough work. But it has been shown that the earliest use of the English word "freemason" (at present known to us) is associated with the freedom of a London Company (1376), and it is from a similar (or in part identical) class of persons, and not from the masons who worked freestone, that I imagine the existing term "freemason" to have been inherited.

Three distinct methods, therefore, must be ascribed to the English builders of the Middle Ages. The first, where the designer was the *Cementarius*, or *Latomus*, and in still later times *Freemason*; the second, where the architect, or superintendent, was an ecclesiastic; and the third, where there was a sort of dual control, in which the clergy (or certain representatives of that body), together with their master masons, designed and worked out the plans between them.

With respect to continental Europe, there is in the first place the theory of Viollet le Duc, who considers Clugny to have been the centre and even the controller of civilization in the eleventh century. Other writers of eminence are of a similar opinion, and believe that the original design of the great buildings constructed during the twelfth and thirteenth centuries emanated from the Abbey of Clugny, or from men trained in that monastery.

The usual term in France was "Master of the Works," and is often found on tombs. The figures of the *maîtres des œuvres* (*magistri operum*, etc.) are frequently represented, and always in lay habits, with square and compasses. The tombs of "Maître" Alexandre de Berneval (St. Ouen), and "Maître" Hues Libergier (Rheims) are very beautiful.

The same expression was used in Italy, but out of a long list (127) of Spanish architects (*i.e.*, builders or contractors) collected by Street, he only finds three who were ecclesiastics.

In Germany, as we learn from the Strasburg "Constitutions" of 1459:—"If any master accepts a work in contract, *and makes* a *design for the same* . . . he shall execute it . . . so that nothing be altered."

But the "design" contemplated may, indeed, have only amounted to a specification.

It is, however, sufficiently clear that while in many instances the architects of the great ecclesiastical buildings on the Continent may have been numbered among the clergy, the majority were laymen.

In Italy, after the invasion of the Goths, architecture continued in a depressed state nearly eight hundred years, until, at the close of the fourteenth century, an academy was founded at Florence, which produced many great and noble men of genius who once more restored the art.

The Italian architects certainly existed as a professional class, and the list of the great masters of the art, most of whose names have been preserved, may, perhaps, be said to close with Bernini, who flourished in the seventeenth century.

Comacenus is given as the (late) Latin term for a native or inhabitant of Como, and two laws in the Lombardic code of Rothar mention the *Magistri Comacini* (*ante* 65) as the builders of that period.

Upon the whole, therefore, we shall, I think, be safely warranted in assuming that the symbolism we now possess as Freemasons has come down to us in all its main features from very early times, and that it originated during the splendour of Mediæval Operative Masonry, and not in its decline.

CHAPTER III

THE ENGLISH LAWS OF THE MIDDLE AGES AND THE
FREEMASONS

*At first sight these long rows of statutes and ordinances seem
the coldest things in the world, the most devoid of life. They
are not even mummies or skeletons, they look as if they were nothing
more than the dust of old bones. But we soon grow accustomed
to their language, and, under the apparently cold dust, we end by
finding sparks of life.*—JUSSERAND.

ALTHOUGH the Story of the Guild and Legend of the Craft
will be related in the two following chapters, I must so far
anticipate as to treat of both these subjects within the limits
of the present one.

The oldest Masonic writing we possess—the Regius MS.—
a poem dating from about the first quarter of the fifteenth
century, contains allusions to an assembly frequented by
great lords, the sheriff of the county, the mayor of the city,
knights, squires, and aldermen. Attendance was incumbent
on the masons, who were required to swear allegiance to
the King, and to answer for their defaults, the authority
of the sheriff being held in reserve to punish them if found
contumacious.

Similar injunctions are met with in later manuscripts of
the Society, and have in either instance been very fanci-
fully interpreted by enthusiastic Freemasons—unlearned in
the law. Indeed, so much so as to recall the somewhat
parallel cases of Tertullian and Justin Martyr, who, possessed of equal self-confidence, entered into controversy
with the Jews, and assumed to come to right conclusions,
albeit they were ignorant not only of the language of the
Jews, but of their learning and history.

For the question that most naturally arises—and the solution of which is not to be attained by mere random conjecture, but requires a very patient study of the legal and judicial procedure of the Middle Ages—is whether there was anything in the laws of the land as then (or at any previous time) existing, which would form some foundation in fact for the references that are made in the masonic poem and the Manuscript Constitutions to this "Assembly." A study of the system of Frankpledge, a remarkable feature of the Anglo-Saxon polity—continued and perhaps enlarged by the Norman Kings—which attained its highest development under the Angevin dynasty, might, perhaps, afford a reply.

The Frankpledge or *Frith borh* (*lit.* peace pledge), an institution peculiar to England, was created for the purpose of preserving the public peace, and in order to enforce the obedience of the people to the provisions of the law.

I began this chapter with an allusion to the Legend of the Craft, and the stage has now been reached when the question can be proceeded with: Whether anything can be found in the fabric of English mediæval law, which will form some foundation in fact, for the references that are made in the Regius and Cooke *codices*, and the Manuscript Constitutions of the Society, to an "Assembly"?

All classes of these venerable documents contain a legendary narrative, and, taken as a whole, among the injunctions or "general charges" with which they ordinarily conclude will be found the following:—That every mason must attend the annual assembly provided he resides within a certain distance (usually computed at fifty miles) and has received due warning. Also that any brother who has trespassed against the craft must abide the award of the master and fellows.

In the "Roberts" group, or family, of the Manuscript Constitutions, we meet, however, with some "New Articles," and by one of these (No. 31) it is ordained that the "Society, Company, and ffraternity of ffree Masons shall be governed by one Master and Wardens," to be chosen "att every yearely general assembly." (*G. Lodge MS.*, No. 2.)

But in the *New Book of Constitutions*, compiled for the Grand Lodge of England by Dr. James Anderson in 1738, this "Article" was made to read:—"That the said Fraternity of Free Masons shall be govern'd by one *Grand Master* and as many Wardens as the said Society shall think fit to appoint at every Annual General Assembly."

A belief consequently sprang up that prior to the formation of a grand lodge there was a General Assembly which met once a year and was presided over by a Grand Master.

The influence exercised by the writings of Dr. Anderson is on the wane, but it has not wholly disappeared. Freemasons believe no longer in his mythical Grand Masters, but they cannot abandon their faith in his equally mythical Assemblies.

The point, then, we have to consider, is whether there existed, at any time, General Assemblies of the masons, armed with exceptional powers, such as were granted to the members of no other trade, or whether the theory of a "Masonic Parliament" is to be regarded as a strange and prodigious hypothesis, for which there is no manner of foundation either in history or probability.

There was, indeed, a legal (or lawful) assembly, which all labourers and artificers were bound to attend, in order (*inter alia*) to take the oath of allegiance to the King; but that there was *another assembly*, convoked specially for the masons, and graced by the presence of great lords, the sheriff, mayor, knights, squires, and aldermen, where the same formalities were gone through *for a second time*, is one of those suppositions which are alike foreign to my opinions and incredible to my conceptions.

The masons, as we learn from their "Constitutions," were only obliged to go up to the assembly when they received any warning. But from whom was this warning to proceed? The meeting, if it took place at all, must have been convened by some person or persons, and who could they have been? In other words, there must have existed a sort of official machinery somewhat resembling that of a modern trades union. Yet we are asked to believe, not only in the reality of so remarkable an organization, but also to carry our faith to the extreme point of supposing that the legal writers, commentators, annalists, and antiquarians, from Chief Justiciar Glanvill downwards, together with the vast array of ancient records, have passed over in utter silence the extraordinary privilege thus enjoyed by the masons (and possessed by no other trade), which must have been common knowledge while the custom lasted.

It has, indeed, been suggested that instead of there having been one General Assembly of masons for the whole kingdom, there were several, but this conjecture would appear to be by a long way the less tenable of the two. It seems to me quite incredible that *one* such assembly could have been held yearly (or triennially) without some trustworthy record of the circumstance descending to us, and therefore the holding of a score of them (let us say) in different parts of the country would have been, in my judgment, precisely twenty times as miraculous (if the expression may be allowed to pass) as the alleged custom of meeting in a single body, which I have criticised at greater length.

What the assembly really was, which we find so universally referred to in the written traditions of the Freemasons, is a question that will admit of more than one highly plausible conjecture. The unions of the trades and crafts in the towns met in what were styled "General," of "Common Assemblies," and both these terms occur in the Manuscript Constitutions, though the words "Common Assembly" are very unusual, and we only meet with them in what are known as the "Hope" and "York No. 4" MSS. The suggestion might, therefore, be advanced that the assemblies of which we read in the masonic codes were really those of the associated trades in the town.

But there is another, and, as it seems to me, a preferable

hypothesis. The earliest masonic writings we possess, the "Regius" and "Cooke" MSS., date from the first half of the fifteenth century. In both documents there are allusions to the "Assembly," and in each case the contents of the manuscript have been copied (either in whole or part) from some earlier work. From this alone a higher antiquity than the actual dates of transcription of the two writings may be claimed for their several readings or texts. But whatever may have been present to the mind of the scribe who first committed to writing the alleged injunction of the craft with respect to the assembly, that the period of time to which it should be carried back must be far older than the first half of the fifteenth century, there cannot be a doubt. In the second half of the fourteenth century (passing over the effect of the Statute of Labourers), the actual supervision of trade fell into the hands of the craft guilds, and in the first half there was the great pestilence and the beginning of the Hundred Years' War. The constant depopulation of the country must have seriously damaged the efficiency of the old local courts, and, still ascending the ladder of time, we meet with the influence of the Crusades and the circumstance that the authority of the sheriff, even in the early years of the thirteenth century, was being gradually excluded owing to the purchase of privileges by the towns.

Assuming, however, that the "gathering" of the masons was in reality some assembly of the shire, the *latest* possible date at which it could have occurred would seem to be the opening period of the reign of Edward I, or, let us say, before the passing of the Statute of Winchester in 1285.

Down to the time of Edward I there remained some points in which the sheriff and the county court still reviewed the jurisdiction of the towns. These, however completely organized, could not exclude the itinerant justices, whose court, being the shiremoot, involved the recognition of the sheriff. Descriptions of the county court in full session have been preserved and in the magnates who attended on such occasions may be found a parallel to the "great lords, knight, squires, and alder-men" who are cited as supporting the sheriff of the county and the mayor of the city in the Regius MS. In-deed, if we are not to understand that the latter were giving their attendance at an assembly of the people, law-fully summoned under authority from the Crown, it will be difficult for any one—except a masonic visionary, who prefers dreaming in his study to acquiring wholesome practical knowledge—to believe in the alternative hypo-thesis of their being present at a meeting of a mysterious trades union, convened in some unknown manner, for the purpose of enabling a particular section of the building trades to settle differences connected with their handi-craft.

"The county court in full session," says Dr. Stubbs, "contained all the elements of a local parliament." Similar powers were possessed by the "Semblé," of which we read in the masonic poem or Regius MS.—

> "Suche ordynance as they maken there,
> They schul maynté hyt hol y-fere" (*ll.* 415, 16).

In the same ancient manuscript we are also told—

> "They ordent ther a semblé to be y-holde
> Every yer, whersever they wolde,
> To amende the defautes, yef any where fonde
> Amonge the craft withynne the londe,
> *Uche yer or thrydde yer* hyt schuld be holde" (*ll.* 471, 75).

At this meeting—

> "Ther they schullen ben alle y-swore,
> That longuth to thys craftes lore,
> To kepe these statutes everychon,
> That ben y-ordeynt by Kynge Alderston" (*ll.* 483, 86).

I shall next glean from the Cooke MS., which informs us that "In the tyme of kynge adhelstone, bi his counselle and othere grete lordys, for grete defaute y founde amonge masons, thei ordeyned a certayne reule a mongys hom *on tyme of the yere or in iij. yere,* as nede were to the kynge . . . congregacions scholde be made bi maisters of alle maisters Masons and felaus in the forsayde art" (*ll.* 694—711).

From the two manuscripts may be gathered that once a year or *every three years*, as the King thought fit, assemblies (or congregations) of the masons were to be held.

To the host of commentators on the Regius and Cooke MSS., the reference to triennial meetings of the masons' craft has always proved a stumbling block, and whether my own efforts to remove it will be successful now remains to be ascertained.

I shall depend, however, solely on the laws of the land, as, for the reasons already expressed, I cannot bring my mind round to the belief that there was anything exclusively masonic in the traditionary assemblies, at which (in the Middle Ages) the attendance of all the operative craftsmen was required.

It will be recollected that the Court of *Justice Seat*, the chief court under the Forest Laws, was held every three years, *or when the King thought fit* ; that an exact analogy had been established between the courts of the forest and the shire; and that a special summons (or "warning") was issued by the sheriffs of counties to bring together the shiremoot to meet the itinerant justices or the officers of the forest.

A vast majority of the Manuscript Constitutions, and the whisper of tradition, unitedly assure us that—throughout Britain—York was long regarded as the earliest centre of the building art. In that ancient city all lines of way seem to converge, and it was there (as we learn from the old "Constitutions") that permission was obtained from King Athelstan to hold the first annual assemblies of the craft.

If, therefore, the passages in the Regius and Cooke MSS. really point to the holding of the court of *Justice Seat*, the coincidence is not a little remarkable that the legendary home (and birth-place) of the masonic assembly should have been situated in the immediate adjacency of an extensive area (or zone) within the limits of its jurisdiction.

The period during which a portion of Yorkshire remained subject to the forest laws, I am unable to determine. Royal forests continued to exist in no fewer than twenty-four counties until 1301, in which year the Great Charter and Forest Charter of Henry III were finally confirmed by Edward I. The result seems to have been that large tracts were disforested or withdrawn from the peculiar and stringent jurisdiction of the forest laws.

In the same year (1301), before a full Parliament, an historical narrative showing the supremacy of the English King over Scotland was drawn up. In this appears the familiar story of Athelstan's expedition to the North (*ante* 14), and among other evidences of the divine right inherent in the English Crown, a marvellous sword stroke is brought forward, with which Athelstan, by favour of St. John of Beverley, had hewn a gap in a rock near Dunbar.

Upon the possibility of this fabulous exploit having been present to the minds of those persons by whom the laws, as well as the Legend of the Craft, were first sung or recited, I have elsewhere expressed myself at some length (*Commentary on the Regius MS.*). It is also worthy of reflection, whether the placing by William the Lion, King of Scotland, in 1175, of his spear and shield on the altar of St. Peter's at York, as symbols of his submission to the English King, may not have given the idea or suggestion underlying the alleged miracle a strong local colouring which, together with Edwin's foundation of the Minster and the various incidents connected with Athelstan's famous march against the Scots, have combined to render the old capital of the Deirii the traditionary centre of the latest items of masonic history recited in the (prose) Legend of the Craft.

The circumstance, however, should be accorded its due weight, that triennial assemblies are only referred to in the Regius and Cooke MSS. In all the other "forms" or versions of the Craft Legend and Regulations, the general meeting which the masons were required to attend was an annual one. This suggests the possibility of there having been yet another type of assembly in actual fact, out of which the prevalent delusion of the existence, at some distant and unknown date, of a Parliament composed entirely of members of the masons' trade has been evolved. The real assembly to which such a large fringe of legend has become attached may have been the sheriff's "Turn," and, in considering the hypothesis, it will be best to do so at a period when the authority of that functionary was at its height.

This will take us back to the Assize of Clarendon (1166), when the jurisdiction of the sheriff, or, in other words, his "law-day" or View of Frankpledge, extended over the towns; and before the rise of the manorial and municipal jurisdictions which afterwards intercepted certain classes of persons who had previously flocked to his progress or "Turn." The "General Assembly" of the sheriff was held in each hundred of a county by rotation, and every male above the age of twelve years was under an obligation to attend.

I strongly incline to the opinion that the actual or living "Assembly" referred to in certain passages of the masonic poem or Regius MS., and in the great majority of the Manuscript Constitutions, was the sheriff's "Turn." Every mason, according to the old writings of the craft, had to attend the "Assembly," if within a certain distance and he received any warning.

A general summons was a positive necessity in the case of all those whose presence was obligatory at the "Turn." Nor could it have been at any time an easy task in a large county containing numerous hundreds, to notify every town, village, and hamlet in all of them, when and where the assembly of the shire would be held. These considerations may help in some degree to explain a singular feature of the Manuscript Constitutions, to which attention has already been directed—namely, the radius within which attention was obligatory at the assembly.

The "Articles of Inquiry," which came regularly before every sheriff's Turn, are given in *Fleta*, and may be usefully compared with sundry injunctions in the Regius (*l.* 441) and Cooke (*l.* 931) MSS. Among the "Inquiries" to be made is—"*Whether all on the Roll have come up to the Folk-mote.*"

It is possible, and in my own judgment highly probable, that the apparent discrepancy between the language of the two manuscripts last cited, and that of the later "Constitutions" with respect to the assembly, may be capable of rational explanation.

The Regius and Cooke MSS., as written documents, date from the year about 1425, and after an interval of more than a century and a half we meet with the "Manuscript Constitutions"—properly so called—of which the earliest dated form is the "Grand Lodge" MS. of 1583.

Both classes of documents evidently reflect the proceedings of traditionary assemblies of much earlier dates than those of their own actual transcription. Hence, as it appears to myself, the wording of the Regius and Cooke MSS. may (and probably does) point to a condition of affairs when every artisan—according to the particular code of laws affecting his vicinage—was compelled to attend either the court of the Forest, *or* that of the Shire.

In the "Grand Lodge" (1583) and later MSS., the reference to annual, though *not* to triennial gatherings of the craft, continues to find a place, and from this I think may be deduced, that the proceedings are reflected of lawful assemblies (affecting every labourer and artisan) held after the jurisdiction of the Forest Courts (to quote from a treatise of 1578, which is the standard work in that department of the law) had gone "clean out of knowledge," and before that of the ancient courts of the shire had similarly become obsolete and forgotten.

With a few closing words I shall now pass away from the problem of the assembly. It is possible, of course, that a Legend of the Craft had been handed down from a period antedating the Norman Conquest. The laws of the Frith guild or (in the opinion of many authorities) Frankpledge system were codified by Athelstan, who was, moreover, a great giver of charters. "No period of Anglo-Saxon history was more glorious, or is less known, than the reign of Athelstan; a few simple notices in the Saxon Chronicle, and the old poem which Malmesbury somewhat contemptuously follows, alone remaining, with the exception of *the Great King's Laws*, to throw a scanty light upon the events of this epoch" (Robertson, *Scotland under Early Kings*, ii, 397). The belief, however, will be permissible that the name of Athelstan, by virtue of his laws and charters, became a favourite one as a legendary guild patron.

No English prince before his time had ever possessed so much influence abroad, or so much power at home. The title of "Emperor (*Imperator* and *Basileus*) of Britain" he was the first to adopt, and of the witenagemot of Wessex during his reign, Sir F. Palgrave observes:—"We may suppose that the assembly convened by the Basileus was a *Shire Court* for the District in which it was held; a *Landgemot* for the particular Kingdom; and an *Imperial Witenagemot* for the whole Empire. In such a case there would be three assemblies appearing, at this distance of time, as resolved into one; but which would be perfectly distinguishable by a contemporary." In this connection we shall, perhaps, do well to recollect that (according to Dr. Stubbs), until the shire system was made uniform, it is quite possible that the witenagemots of the heptarchic kingdoms may have continued to exist.

Other examples of a plurality of assemblies, which, under a certain aspect, were "resolved into one," have been known, and to these a parallel may, perhaps, be discerned in the traditional "Gathering" of the masons, which, as described from the conflicting points of view of individual transcribers of the old "Constitutions," has been handed down to us in a somewhat Protean form. Indeed, the custom (or practice) of distinct bodies assembling jointly, as well as severally, may have lingered until much later times. The head meeting day of many guilds and crafts may have often coincided with the law day or leet, at which the annual View of Frankpledge was held. This, however, could only have occurred in the towns, and after the minor court leet of the steward (or bailiff) had been carved out of the sheriff's Turn. The tradition, therefore, of a masonic assembly, as it seems to me, must have had its origin at a much earlier date, and probably not later than the period at which the authority of the sheriff was at its height.

But although there would seem to be no rational foundation for the belief that the English masons of the Middle Ages met in legal (or lawful) assemblies for the transaction of business connected with their handicraft, there is evidence to show that they were in the habit of meeting in illegal (or unlawful) assemblies (congregations or conventicles) for the purpose of defeating the course of legislation, which it will become my next task to review.

On the hopeful prospect which existed before the Black Death, that great pestilence fell like a season of blight, but worse than the pestilence was the Statute of Labourers. "The pestilence," says Dr. Stubbs, "notwithstanding its present miseries, made labour scarce and held out the prospect of better wages; the Statute offered the labourer wages that it was worse than slavery to accept" (*Constit. Hist.*, ii, 454).

At the very beginning of the trouble the attempt made by the Government to fix the rate of wages produced disaffection, which smouldered until, after many threatenings, it broke into flame in 1381.

The STATUTES OF LABOURERS, from which I shall next quote, will be found collected in my *History of Freemasonry* (Chap. VII). In 1439 the wages of "masons (*cementarii*) and all other artificers and workmen," and the price of provisions, were regulated. But this ordinance proving ineffectual, it was made more stringent and enacted as a statute in 1350. The wages of a "master freestone mason (*mestre mason de franche pere*)" were fixed at fourpence a day, which sum was not likely to secure a high standard of artistic skill, and while the statute must to some extent have remained a dead letter, so far as it had any effect at all, it operated to drive the artificer out of the country. "It certainly is significant," remarks an architectural writer, "that Perpendicular forms, which of all that are included under the name of Gothic make the slightest demand on the invention, should have come into vogue at the very moment when the craftsmen of original talent (at no time a numerous class) had almost disappeared."

Wages were again regulated in 1360, and "all alliances and covines of masons and carpenters, and congregations, chapters, ordinances (*tote alliances et Covignes des Maceons et Carpenters, et Congregacions, Chapitres, Ordinances*), and oaths betwixt them made, or to be made, shall be from henceforth void and wholly annulled." This statute (34 Edward III, c. ix) shows that the masons had acted in opposition to the law, and contrary to the tenor of their own rules or "Constitutions."

The poll tax of 1380 gave occasion for the revolutionary rising of 1381. A mystery pervades the organization of the rebellion, but among the leading factors in the problem were the associations formed for the purpose of defeating the Statutes of Labourers, and the existence throughout the land of numbers of mechanics thrown out of employment by the war. But before the 20th of June, 1381, the result had ceased to be dangerous, and on the 23rd the King (Richard II) issued a proclamation forbidding unauthorized gatherings. A similar decree, prohibiting "conventicula, congregationes seu levationes" (*secret assemblies, unlawful associations, or raisings of the populace*), was issued on the 3rd of July.

The Statutes of Labourers were frequently confirmed and augmented, of which a notable instance occurred under Henry IV, in the seventh year of whose reign it was enacted "that in every Leet, once in the year, all the Labourers and Artificers dwelling in the same shall be sworn to serve and take for their service after the form of the Statutes."

The same course of legislation was further extended in 1414, 1423, and 1425, the last-named year bringing us to a remarkable statute—3 Henry VI, c. i—with which should be compared the earlier law of 1360, and the Royal Proclamation of 1381. All three of these mandates or prohibitions were directed against combinations, congregations, and chapters of workmen, and the two statutes (of 1360 and 1425) against workmen in the building trades only.

3 HENRY VI, C. I, A.D. 1425

"Whereas by the yearly Congregations and Confederacies made by the Masons in their general Chapiters assembled (*Generalx Chapitres Assemblez*), the good course and effect of the Statutes of Labourers be openly violated and broken, in subversion of the law, and to the great damage of all the Commons: our said Lord the King willing in this case to provide Remedy, by the advice and assent aforesaid, and at the special Request of the said Commons, hath ordained and established that such Chapiters and Congregations shall not be hereafter holden; and if any such be made, that they cause such Chapiters and Congregations to be assembled and holden, if they thereof be convict, shall be judged for Felons; and that all the other Masons that come to such Chapiters and Congregations be punished by Imprisonment of their Bodies and make Fine and Ransom at the King's Will."

The terms of this Act were first disinterred from the Statute-book by Dr. Plot, in his "Account of the Freemasons" (1686), and have since been regarded as confirming the "Legend of the Craft"—that there was an annual assemblage of the fraternity or, in other words, a periodical meeting of a governing body (or Grand Lodge) of the entire brotherhood. Indeed, by the less credulous school of modern writers, it is relied upon as presenting the *one indisputable fact* which alone prevents the old Craft Legend from being consigned to the region of fable and romance.

Almost identical language, however, with that which occurs in the law of 1425 (3 Hen. VI, c. i) will be found (as already pointed out) in the earlier statute of 1360 (34 Edw. III, c. ix). Nor is it credible for an instant that the workmen, whose *unlawful* conventions it was the object of these statutes to repress, met in precisely the same kind of "general assemblies" as those undoubtedly *authorized gatherings* which are adumbrated in the written traditions (or Manuscript Constitutions) of the masonic craft.

Other links in the chain of statutes relating to combinations, confederacies, and the making of unreasonable ordinances to enhance the wages of labour, were formed in the years 1437, 1503, 1530, and 1536. These Acts, indeed, refer by implication to every class of artisan, but the building trades are not specifically mentioned, and the object of the legislation may, perhaps, be described as a series of efforts to check the increasing abuses of the craft guilds. Moreover, the statutes are too late in point of date to render any assistance in an attempt to "rationalize" the traditionary account of the "Assembly" at which the attendance of all members of the masons' trade was required.

The law passed in the third year of Henry VI (1425) has derived a factitious importance from the statement that the King himself was subsequently admitted into the Society. Of any actual connection, however, between this imbecile monarch and the Freemasons there is no trace, except in one of the texts or versions of the Legend of the Craft—similar, apparently, to that seen by Dr. Plot—and in a singular catechism which first appeared in the *Gentleman's Magazine* of 1753, though it purports to be a reprint of a pamphlet published at Frankfort in 1748. The latter —which contains "Certayne Questyons, with Answeres to the same, concernynge the Mystery of MACONRYE; wryttenne by the hande of Kynge Henrye, the Sixth of the Name"—was at one time generally accepted as an authentic document of the craft. But the view is not shared by modern writers, who regard it as a palpable fraud and wholly unworthy of the critical acumen which has been lavished on its contents.

The word *freemason* is first met with in the statutes under the year 1495, though the same term is possibly signified by *frank-mason*, which occurs in an earlier Act of 1444-5.

The "gevyng and receyvyng of signees and tokens unlaufully," are also referred to in the law of 1495 (II Hen. VII, c. iii). These "signs and tokens" were *not*, however, methods of masonic recognition, as contended by German commentators on the statute, but badges and cognizances.

Upon the uncritical spirit in which the masonic traditions were adopted by successive copyists of the old "Constitutions" as ascertained facts I have dwelt at some length. But we are now able, in some degree, to take the measure of their credulity and to apply severer canons of criticism to the facts themselves which they believed and recorded. "If, therefore, we endeavour to destroy the credit of traditions which have long existed, it is only to put something in their place, inconsistent with them, but of more value. To reduce them to what they really are, lest their authority should render the truth more obscure, and its pursuit more difficult than is necessary; but to use them whenever they seem capable of guiding our researches, and are not irreconcilable with our other conclusions."

CHAPTER IV

THE STORY OF THE GUILD

As regards Guilds, I certainly think that they have been much too confidently attributed to a relatively modern origin. The trading guilds which survive in our own country have undergone every sort of transmutation which can disguise their parentage. They have long since relinquished the occupations which gave them a name. Yet anybody who, with a knowledge of primitive laws and history, examines the internal mechanism and proceedings of a London Company, will see in many parts of them plain traces of the ancient brotherhood of kinsmen, "joint in food, worship, and estate."— SIR HENRY S. MAINE.

ENGLISH guilds (we are told by the late Mr. Toulmin Smith) are older than any Kings of England. As population increased, guilds multiplied; and thus, while the beginnings of the older guilds are lost in the far dimness of time, and remain quite unknown, the beginnings of the later ones took place in methods and with accompanying forms that have been recorded (*Old Crown House*, 28).

Whether, indeed, the peace (*frith*), the social, or the trading guild was first in origin, cannot be positively determined. The trading guild appears in more forms than one—as the guild-merchant, which it is difficult to distinguish from the town corporation, and as the guild of craftsmen. An antiquity, extending at least as far back as the reign of Ethelwolf (856), has been satisfactorily established for the guild merchant. The craft guild has a remoteness of origin less assured, but comes prominently into notice about the middle of the twelfth century. The peace guilds (*frith borh*) can be traced with certainty to the reign of Athelstan, and with reasonable probability to a far earlier date.

The oldest records we possess of the English social (or religious) guilds consist of three statutes, which were apparently drawn up in the beginning of the eleventh century. The title by which these fraternities are ordinarily described, is, however, somewhat misleading, as in numerous instances their assumed character of social (or religious) associations was merely a thin disguise for a craft guild.

The sooner a town became chiefly a commercial place, the sooner did the guild there take the form of a merchant guild. These *gildæ mercatoriæ*, as they were termed, had also the general control of the various classes of artisans, as at first the craft guilds stood in a filial relation to the merchant guild.

Where, however, there was no ancient merchant guild, or its existence had been forgotten, the admission of free men to a share in the duties and privileges of burghership was a part of the business of the leet.

Ultimately, when in either instance the merchant guild had acquired jurisdiction or merged its existence in the *communa* (or corporation), the guild hall became the common hall of the city, and the court of the guild became the judicial assembly of the free men and identical with the leet.

These meetings are sometimes referred to as "General" and at others as "Common Assemblies." Their privileges are perhaps best defined in the customs of Hereford, drawn up in 1383, but which doubtless embody customs of older times. Thus we learn that at the great meetings held at Michaelmas and Easter, to which the whole people were gathered for View of Frankpledge (in other words, at the court leet), the bailiff and steward may command that all those who are not of the liberty should depart from the court, and may afterwards "notice if there are any secrets or business which may concern the state of the city or the citizens thereof" (*Archæol. Jrl.*, xxvii, 464).

According to Mrs. J. R. Green, from about A.D. 1300 "all independent trade jurisdictions in the towns came to

an end, and the crafts were presently forced to conciliate
the local powers according to their measure of art or cun-
ning" (*Town Life in the 15th Century*, ii, 143). "Congregations and confederacies" were jealously watched and
forbidden. No craft fraternity could be formed without
the leave of the municipality, and every warden took his
oath of office before the mayor, at whose bidding, and subject
to whose approval, he had been elected. The rules made by
any trade for its government had no force until approved
by the corporation. Men who offended against the rules of
the trade were brought before the town officers for punishment. Carpenters, masons, plasterers, daubers, tilers, and
paviours had to take whatever wages the law decreed and
to accept the supervision of the municipal rulers, and their
regulations were framed according to the convenience of
the borough (*ibid.*, 148, 152). For example, after the great
storm of 1362, in London it was forbidden to raise the
prices for repairing the citizens' roofs (Riley, *Mem. Lond.*,
308); and the "Ordinances of Worcester" (1467), in their
regulations for the tilers, enjoin that they must "*sett no
parliament amonge them, to make eny of them to be as a maister,*
and alle other tylers to be as his seruant and at his com-
maundement, but that euery tyler be ffree to come and
go to worche wᵗ euery man and citezen, frely, as they may
accorde" (*Eng. Guilds*, 399).

This is the only reference I have met with in any ancient
document to a "parliament" of the building trades, and
had the words italicized been used in a good instead of a
bad sense, they would have been destructive of much (or
all) of the criticism which I have ventured to pass on the
popular theory of a masonic legislature having long existed
in the guise of a *lawful* "Assembly." But, as will be plainly
seen, they refer with the utmost clearness to the class of
unauthorized gatherings, which were otherwise known as
congregations, confederacies, conventicles, and *unlawful*
"Assemblies."

I shall next proceed with the remark, that no evidence
is forthcoming from the Statutes of the Realm, or has any

proof as yet been adduced from any authentic record of this country, that the Freemasons, *as a fraternity of guild*, at any period possessed, or held by patent, any exclusive privileges whatsoever; also, that all we are able to collect from either written or printed sources, of undoubted authority, is of a contrary tendency.

At this point it will be convenient if I attempt to penetrate the forest gloom of mediæval antiquity, by taking up the story of the travelling bodies of Freemasons, fraught with Papal Bulls, by whom all the great buildings of Europe are said to have been erected. The earliest mention of them was penned by John Aubrey, at some time after 1656, in his *Natural History of Wiltshire*, which was printed for the first time in 1847. Of the manuscript work, however, there are two copies; and the latest in point of date (from which I quote) has the following:—

"Sir William Dugdale told me many yeares since, that about Henry the Third's time, the Pope gave a bull or patent to a company of Italian Freemasons, to travell up and down all Europe to build churches. From those are derived the Fraternity of adopted masons. They are known to one another by certain signes and watch words; it continues to this day. They have severall lodges in severall counties for their reception; and when any of them fall into decay, the brotherhood is to relieve him. The manner of their adoption is very formall and with an oath of secrecy."

What we may suppose to have been an amplification of the above was published in Ashmole's posthumous work, the *Antiquities of Berkshire*, which, together with "a short account of the author," saw the light in 1719. We learn from the *Athenæ Oxonienses* of Anthony Wood (iv, 363) that the editor of the work and the writer of the biography was Dr. Richard Rawlinson, who, in referring to Freemasonry, copies very closely from John Aubrey, expanding, however, the authority granted by the Pope into "a Bull, Patent, or Diploma," and the various names by which the "Fraternity" was known, into "Adopted Masons, Accepted Masons, or Free Masons."

In the memoir of Elias Ashmole, which is given in the *Biographia Britannica* (1747), we are told by Dr. Knipe:

"What from Mr. Ashmole's collection I could gather was, that the report of our Society taking rise from a Bull granted by the Pope in the reign of Henry III to some Italian architects, to travel over all Europe to erect chapels, was ill-founded. Such a Bull there was, and those architects were masons. But this Bull, in the opinion of the learned Mr. Ashmole, was confirmative only, and did not by any means create our fraternity, or even establish them in this kingdom."

With these three extracts should be compared the citation I have previously given from the *Parentalia* (*ante*, 57). It is almost certain that the four statements may be traced to a single source. Moreover, if we look closely into the matter, it becomes apparent that not even in a solitary instance has the story of the Bulls been handed down to us in the form of evidence that would satisfy the requirements of a court of law.

The *original* version—in the hand-writing of John Aubrey —is prefaced with the remark, "Sir William Dugdale told me." It is, perhaps, scarcely open to doubt either that Dr. Rawlinson prepared the *Antiquities of Berkshire* (1719) for publication, or that he copied freely from the manuscript of John Aubrey, in his allusions to the Freemasons. But the memoir of the deceased author is followed by no signature, nor does the name of any editor appear on the title page of the posthumous work. Dr. Knipe (*Biog. Brit.*) says, "What from Mr. Ashmole's collection I could gather was "; and lastly, by way of prelude to the belief which has been *ascribed* to the great architect of St. Paul's Cathedral by the editors of the *Parentalia*, we meet with the words—"He [*Wren*] was of opinion."

The story nevertheless, for a long time had its vogue, on the faith of such respectable (though shadowy) authorities, but no other evidence of any kind whatsoever has been adduced in its support.

After the death of Sir Christopher, it was promulgated to

the world by Dr. James Anderson, in his *New Book of Constitutions* (1738), that the great architect had been not only a prominent craftsman, but also one of the (pre-historic) Grand Masters of the Society. There is, indeed, an entire absence of *proof* that Wren was a Freemason at all, and with regard to his alleged Grand-Mastership, it will be sufficient at the present day to remark that he could not well have held, in the seventeenth century, an office which at that time did not exist.

The fable, however, was received with acclamation by successive generations of masonic antiquaries and archæ-ologists, whose enthusiasm seems to have been contagious; of which we have possible examples in the pages of the *Parentalia* and the *Biographia Britannica*, and unequivocal illustrations in many learned works written by members of the architectural profession and others, who were in no way connected with the fraternity.

The climax was reached in the fascinating essay of Mr. Thomas Hope (*ante*, 65), who, building on the old (or assumed) foundations laid by Dugdale, Ashmole, and Wren, completed the superstructure of error by bringing in the Magistri Comacini as the original masonic corporations and depositaries of the Papal Bulls, and thus adding (as it were) an upper story to a pre-existing castle in the air.

"The universal promulgation of the principles, rules, and practice of the Gothic architecture," observes Dr. Milman (1854), "has been accounted for by the existence of a vast guild of Freemasons, or of architects. It is said the centre, the quickening, and governing power was in Rome. Certainly, of all developments of the Papal influence and wisdom, none could be more extraordinary than this summoning into being, this conception, this completion of these marvellous buildings in every part of Latin Christen-dom. But it is fatal to this theory that Rome is the city in which Gothic Architecture has never found a place; even in Italy it has at no time been more than a half-naturalized stranger. It must be supposed that while the Papacy was thus planting the world with Gothic Cathedrals this was but a sort of lofty concession to Trans-Alpine barbarism, while itself adhered to the ancient, venerable, more true and majestic style of ancient Rome. This guild, too, was so secret as to elude all discovery. History, documentary evidence, maintain rigid, inexplicable silence. The theory is not less unnecessary than without support. Each nation, indeed, seems to have worked out its own Gothic with certain general peculiarities. All seem to aim at certain effects, all recognize certain broad principles, but the application of these principles varies infinitely. Sometimes a single building, and sometimes the buildings within a certain district, have their peculiarities. Under a guild, if there had been full freedom for invention, originality, boldness of design, there had been more rigid uniformity, more close adherence to rule in the scientifical and technical parts" (*Hist. of Lat. Christianity*, vi, 587).

The names of other and greater (architectural) authorities have since been arrayed on the same side as that of the learned Dean of St. Paul's; for example, those of the late George Edmund Street (1865) and Wyatt Papworth (1876), the former of whom states:—"The common belief in ubiquitous bodies of Freemasons seems to me to be altogether erroneous"; and the latter, "some will expect from me an account of those travelling bodies of Freemasons who are said to have erected all the great buildings of Europe; nothing more, however, will be said than that I believe they never existed."

With the above, I am fully in accord, though, instead of contenting myself with an expression of my individual opinion on the question of the "Bulls," it has seemed much better to give the reader such necessary information as may enable him (by the aid of further investigation) to form one of his own.

In passing out of the wilderness of conjecture into the region of ascertained fact, it is, however, important to recollect, that while there is a total absence of proof (or, indeed, of probability) that during "Henry the Third's time" the "Colleges of Masons" in every country of Europe received the blessing of the Holy See, it is undoubtedly true that the Papal authority stood at its highest when that feeble monarch succeeded to the throne. Nor was any country so intolerably treated by Gregory IX and his successors as England throughout the ignominious reign of Henry III.

The great age of monasteries in England is stated by Hallam to have been the reigns of Henry I, Stephen, and Henry II (*Middle Ages*, ii, 145). But the period when the activity of the church builders was in its zenith appears to have been "about the time of Henry the Third," or, at all events, during the thirteenth century, when we find —and it gives us some idea of their numbers—that no less than ten cathedrals were in progress simultaneously (Dibdin's *Tour*).

"The master-masons and their brotherhood," observes the Rev. J. Dallaway, "could have been scarcely ever void of employment, as their labours were not always confined to ecclesiastical buildings. They were employed not only in raising castles, but in inventing military stratagems in their formation, and making engines of war: such had the peculiar name of *Ingeniatores* (*ante*, 71). For completing castellated or grand domestic mansions, they were no less in requisition. A very early instance occurs in the reign of Henry III of Paul le Peverer, in his house at Todington in Bedfordshire, and of the numerous artificers whom he had employed " (*Discourses upon Arch.*, 420).

At the time referred to, for other than the textile arts, the smith was a recognized institution in every village. For the building of a church or castle, however, masons and carpenters were imported from a distance, like the stone and shingles and lead with which they worked (*Social Eng.*, i, 465).

In the course of the thirteenth century the great majority of towns obtained rights of self-government. Two master-masons were reconciled before the mayor of London in 1298. Craft guilds existed, but at Norwich they were specially prohibited by a charter of the 40th year of Henry

III. The most ancient of these associations appear to
have been those of the weavers, guilds of which trade
are referred to as existing at Oxford, Huntingdon, and
Lincoln in the Pipe Roll of 31 Henry I. The next in point
of date were the goldsmiths, the fullers, the bakers, the
loriners, and the cordwainders, all of which were in high
repute. But the mediæval masons were a body of men
scattered over the whole country, who travelled hither and
thither as journeymen builders do now in search of work.
Hence they were long unable to establish similar associations to those set up by the other trades. It has been suggested that about the time they borrowed the pointed
arch, they also became acquainted with the Gnostics and
Manichæans (*Quart. Rev.* xxv, 146), from which it has been
further deduced that, owing to their necessarily wandering
habits—for wander they did, though not by any means to
the extent which is generally supposed—they may have been
chosen as emissaries for these sects or societies. But the
statutes, the traditions, and the legends of (or relating to)
the masons of the Middle Ages, in their last stage of existence, are before us, and, whatever may have been loosely
asserted, there is no ground for suspecting them to have
been more than ordinary mediæval guilds, differing, indeed,
from those of other trades, but only from the circumstance
that while the usual trades were local, and the exercise of
them confined to the locality where the tradesman resided,
the builders were, on the contrary, forced to go wherever
any great work was to be executed (Ferguson, *Hist. of Arch.*,
i, 477). Impregnated, indeed, many of the masons of old
doubtless were with the peculiar doctrines of the ages in
which they lived and worked, but (with all due respect for
the learned credulity by which a contrary opinion is upheld)
they were in no way an integral part of some great secret
society which had existed from the beginning of the
world.

In the following century architecture continued to be
the great art of the age, and we have further proof that
the services of the higher class of "master masons," together

with those of their "brotherhoods," were certainly not an exclusive monopoly of the Church. Monasteries and abbeys, indeed, were no longer built, for the taste of the times had changed; but manors, hospitals, castles, schools, and colleges were then erected which modern architects can only feebly imitate (W. Warburton, *Edward III*, 247).

The fourteenth century witnessed the triumph of the craft over the merchant guilds, and in London the former were in full possession of the mastery in the reign of Edward III. Charters were freely granted by this monarch, and the craft guilds thus incorporated became better known as companies, a designation under which they still exist.

The foundation of the Masons' Company of London, in the opinion of Mr. Edward Conder, may be placed at about the year 1220 (*The Hole Crafte and Fellowship of Masons*, 54), and the "Regulations for the Trade of Masons," enacted by the municipal authorities in 1356 (Riley, *Mem. Lond.*, 280), are relied on by the same excellent authority as affording the earliest documentary evidence of the existence of the guild. The first distinct (or unequivocal) notice of the masons of London as a guild or sodality cannot, however, be traced farther back than 1376, of which date there is (among the City records) a list of the companies entitled to send representatives to the Court of Common Council. From the original record we learn that the Masons' Company (at that time represented by four of its members) was otherwise described as the Company of ffree-masons. The existence of a guild of masons at Norwich in 1375 has been referred to on a previous page.

Eventually the towns began to look upon the craft guilds with as much favour as they had formerly shown distrust, and proceeded to multiply their numbers both by creating new fraternities and reorganizing the old ones. Nor was the drawing together of artisans into the later craft fraternities at all times a matter of free will (*ante*, 70). If the trades did not voluntarily associate they were ultimately forced to do so, and at the close of the fifteenth century we find the towns everywhere issuing orders that crafts which had hitherto escaped should be compelled to group themselves into companies (Green, *Town Life*, ii, 155).

The *Gildæ Mercatoriæ* began to decline in the thirteenth century, and in the two following centuries they had practically ceased to exist. Sometimes the old merchant guild became indistinguishably blended with the town, and gave its name to the whole community. Elsewhere its title was in some vague way transferred to the aggregate of the craft guilds, and, indeed, according to Dr. Gross, all guilds of merchants formed after the decline of the *Gildæ Mercatoriæ* in the thirteenth century must be considered as being merely craft unions of the ordinary kind (*Gild Merch.*, i, 129). The fifteenth century, if we are to believe the host of commentators on the Statute 3 Henry VI, c. i (1425), witnessed the downfall of the Freemasons, but the true meaning of that enactment has already been considered with all the fulness at my command. Then came the famous Wars of the Roses, during which period social improvement was suspended. The high and the low suffered alike. Whole families of the great were swept away, massive castles were thrown down, and villages were by hundreds laid in ashes. The *Paston Letters* (1422-1509) may be commented as a mirror of the times, and among them is one which may throw a possible gleam of light on the speculative masonry of an era at once so obscure and so remote.

A missive, which is anonymous and bears no date, but is supposed to have been written in 1464, runs:—

"*To my ryght worshipfull maister and brother, John Paston, this letter be taken.*

"Ryght worshipfull and reverend mayster and brother, with alle my service I recommaunde me on to yow. Please hit onto your grete wysedom to have yn your descrete remembrauns the streite ordre on which we ben professid, and on which ze er bownden to kepe your residens, and specially on this tyme of Crystmas amonggis your confrerys of this holy Ordre, the Temple of Syon; for ynlesse than ze

kepe dewly the poynts of your holy Religion, owr Maister
Thomas Babyngton, maister and soverayn of owr Order
of th'assent of his brythryn ben avysed to awarde azenste
yow ryght sharp and hasty proces to do calle yow to do
your obcervauns, and to obeye the poynts of your Religion,
whice wer on to me grete hevynesse .·. hit drawith fast on
to Cristmas, on which tyme every trewe Crysten man
sholde be merry, jocunde and glad. And sethyns ther is
no place which by lyklyhod of reason ze shulde fynde yn
your hert to be so gladde and yocunde yn as ye sholde be
yn the place of your profession amounggis your holy bry-
theryn; yn which place yn this ceson of the yer hit ys
a custumyd to be alle maner of desport, lyke as hit is nat
unknowe to your wisse descrescion .·. of whos comyng
alle your saide bretheryn wolde be glade and fayn, and yn
especial I, your servaunt and brother .·.

Wrytten yn the Temple of Syon, iij^d day of December,
yn grete hast.

By your Servaunt and brother.

"It is difficult," observes Mr. Gairdner, the latest editor
of the *Paston Letters*, "to assign with confidence either a
date or a meaning to this strangely worded epistle. The
signature itself is a mystery. The Order of the Temple of
Sion is unknown to archæologists, and the place from which
the letter is dated cannot be identified. From the peculiar
device used as a signature, resembling what in heraldry
represents a fountain, Fenn [a previous editor] threw out
a suggestion that Fountaine was the writer's name. For
my part, I am inclined to think it was a mocking letter
addressed to John Paston by one of the prisoners in the
Fleet, where Paston had himself been confined in 1464.
The name of Thomas Babington occurs in Dugdale's *Origines*

Juridiciales, p. 63, as having been elected a reader in the Inner Temple in 22 Henry VII, when he seems to have been an old man."

The same writer further suggests that some of Paston's "late fellow-prisoners, probably members of the Inner or Middle Temple like himself, who had formed themselves into a fancy 'Order of the Temple of Sion,' amused themselves by speculating on the probability that he was not yet clear of the toils of the law, and that he would be obliged to come back and spend Christmas in gaol among the jolly companions whom he had recently deserted" (*Paston Letters*, ii, 170). It may be so, but the explanation is one which is wholly unsatisfactory to my own mind, nor do I see any possible clue to a solution of the mystery, unless it is to be found in the more general existence than has commonly been supposed of a system of speculative masonry in the twilight of the Middle Ages.

It is also a curious circumstance, and whether or not pointing in the same direction deserves at least to be recorded, that by the will of Margaret, "late the wiff of John Paston, Squier, doughter and heire to John Mauteby, Squier" (dated February 4th, 1482), it was enjoined that a form of words corresponding very closely with the motto of the Masons and Freemasons (in later years) should be inscribed upon her tomb. A stone of marble, with "scochens sett at the iiij corners," was to be placed on the grave, "and in myddys of the seid stoon," says the testatrix, "I wull have a scochen sett of Mawtebys armes [*Mauteby's arms*] allone, and under the same thise wordes wretyn,—

In God is my trust." (*Ibid.*, iii, 281.)

The Masons' Company of London is described as the "Hole Crafte and felowship of Masons" in the grant of arms, which it was one of the very first guilds to obtain, in 1472. The latter title, however, was exchanged in 1537 (and possibly at an earlier date) for that of the "Company of ffree Masons," a designation which was retained until 1656 (Conder, *Hole Crafte*, 104).

In the sixteenth century the guild system was evidently in danger of breaking down, and it was necessary to bolster it up by Acts of Parliament, while, at the same time, preventing it from putting excessive hindrances in the way of competition and individual enterprise (*Soc. Eng.*, iii, 121). Upon the statutes which were passed in furtherance of this design it is not, however, my purpose to enlarge. It has, indeed, been suggested that, together with other laws of the previous century, they were enacted to put down the annual assemblies of some companies or guilds, including those of the Freemasons. But, as I have endeavoured to show in the last chapter, the origin of the Legend of the Craft, with its traditionary "Assembly"—supposing it to have had any foundation in actual fact—must be looked for in a period far more remote.

The guilds were suppressed by the Statutes of 37 Henry VIII, c. 4, and 1 Edward VI, c. 14, but virtually their *raison d'être* was restored by that of 5 Eliz., c. 4, commonly called the Statute of Apprentices.

London, indeed, saved her guilds because she was powerful enough to have made a revolution, even against the most absolute Tudor, and would have certainly made it had her great livery companies been swept away. A few other guilds survived, though for the most part, as at Preston, in a condition of picturesque decay.

In the Church of St. Helen, Bishopsgate (London), there is a handsome tomb, and on the south side there is the following inscription:—

"HERE LYETH THE BODIE OF WILLIAM KERWIN OF THIS CITTIE OF LONDON FREE MASON WHOE DEPARTED THIS LYFE THE 26TH DAYE OF DECEMBER ANO 1594."

On the west end are sculptured the arms of the "Hole Crafte and felowship of Masons" (of which Kerwin was a member), as granted in 1472. On a chevron engrailed, between three square castles, a pair of compasses extended; as a crest, the square castle; also (*for the first time*) a motto, "God is ovr Gvide" (W. H. Rylands).

The words, "In the Lord is all our Trust," observes Mr. Conder, are never found before the year 1600, and as a change in the arms of the Masons' Company took place about this date, there is little doubt that with it was associated the later form of the old guild motto.

As we have seen, however, a devout invocation of the Deity, closely resembling the guild motto in its later (known) form, and which may, or may not, have possessed a masonic significance, was inscribed on the tomb of Margaret Paston in 1482.

Masonry in the sixteenth century had passed its meridian, but continued to remain the shadow of itself until the end of the seventeenth. The fluctuations of commerce and population led to the existence of new towns and the decay of some of the old ones, thus tending to break up the ancient guilds (or trade and mechanical fraternities) which had survived the great cataclysm of the Reformation. Moreover, there were great numbers of foreign workmen who settled in England before and during the sixteenth and early part of the seventeenth centuries, bringing with them the trade traditions and usages of the French, German, Flemish, and Dutch artisans, "who, perhaps, joining some of the societies or lodges they found existing in England," may, it has been suggested (but on no other foundation than mere conjecture), have left their mark on the speculative masonry which has descended to our own time.

Evidence, indeed, if not entirely wanting, is nevertheless wholly insufficient to supply more than an occasional glimpse of the way in which the old system of masonry was gradually succeeded, and ultimately supplanted, by the new. The earliest authentic record of a non-operative being a member of a masonic lodge occurs in a minute of the Lodge of Edinburgh, under the date of June the 8th, 1600. John Boswell, the Laird of Auchinleck, was present at the meeting, and, like his operative brethren, he attested the minute by his mark. But that speculative or symbolic flourished side by side with operative masonry, at a much earlier period, may be safely inferred from the solemn declaration of a Presby-

terian synod in 1652, that ministers of that persuasion had
been Freemasons "in the purest tymes of the Kirke," the
reference almost certainly being to the years immediately
following the Reformation of 1560, and without doubt
considerably antedating the introduction of Episcopacy
in 1610.

In the south of Britain, however, it is not until much
later that any distinct proof of the existence of what I
shall venture to characterize as an actual or living *Freemasonry* is afforded us, and this we meet with in connection
with the "Company of ffreemasons" (*now* the Masons'
Company) of London, in the early part of the seventeenth
century.

Most of the records of the Company are missing, but
from an old book of accounts which has been preserved
it is made clear that previously to 1620 and inferentially
from a remote past, certain brethren who were members of
the Company, in conjunction, it is supposed, with others
who were not, met in lodge at Masons' Hall, London, and
were known to the Company as the Accepted Masons.

Seven persons were received into the "Accepcon" (*i.e.*,
the *Acception*) or Lodge in 1620-21, all of whom were already
members of the Company, which is sufficient to prove
that the two bodies were distinct associations, though
of this there is a still more conspicuous illustration in the
case of Nicholas Stone, the King's master mason, who,
though master of the Company in 1633, and again in 1634,
was not enrolled among the "Accepted Masons" of the
Lodge until 1639.

"Unfortunately," observes the historian of the Company, "no books connected with this Acception—*i.e.*, the
Lodge—have been preserved. We can, therefore, only
form our ideas of its working from a few entries scattered
through the accounts. From these it is found that members
of the Company paid 20s. for coming on the Acception,
and strangers 40s. Whether they paid a lodge quarteridge
to the Company's funds it is impossible, in the absence of
the old Quarteridge Book, to state. One matter, however,

is quite certain from the old book of accounts commencing
in 1619, that the payments made by newly accepted masons
were paid into the funds of the Company, that some or all
of this was spent on a banquet and the attendant expenses,
and that any further sum required was *paid out of the ordinary
funds of the Company*, proving that the Company had entire
control of the Lodge and its funds."

The valuable discoveries so recently made by Mr. Conder,
in connection with the Masons' Company, will be again
paid under contribution as I proceed, but in order to pursue
the general narrative as nearly as possible in chronological
sequence, *the first initiation on English soil*, of which any of
the surrounding circumstances have come down to us, will
be next referred to.

A minute of the Lodge of Edinburgh—"At Neucastell
the 20th day off May, 1641"—records the admission of
"Mr. the Right Honerabell Mr. Robert Moray, General
Quartermaster to the Armie of Scotlan."

From this we may conclude that there were members of
the lodge who accompanied the forces of the Covenanters
to Newcastle in 1641, and that it was at the hands of these
militant craftsmen that Sir Robert Moray was made a
Mason.

The next evidence in point of date which relates to an
actual or living Freemasonry in the south is supplied by
the *Diary* of Elias Ashmole, from which I extract the
following:—

"1646—Oct. 16, 4.30 p.m.—I was made a Free Mason
at Warrington, in Lancashire, with Coll. Henry Mainwaring, of Karincham in Cheshire."

The *Diary* also gives "the names of those that were
then of the Lodge," who, as Mr. W. H. Rylands has clearly
shown, were all presumably men of good social position,
without a single operative mason belonging to their number.

From the circumstance that one of the copies of the Manuscript Constitutions (*Sloane*, 3848) was transcribed by an
Edward Sankey on the 16th of October, 1646, the use of
the document has been connected with the initiation of

Ashmole into the mysteries of the craft. A *Richard* Sankey was present in the lodge, whose son *Edward*—as we may infer from the monograph of Mr. Rylands—a young man of four or five and twenty, was apparently alive in October, 1646 (*Freemasonry in the Seventeenth Century*).

It is obvious that symbolical masonry must have existed in Lancashire for some time before the admission of Ashmole and Mainwaring, though how far the pedigree of the lodge in which they were received can be carried back is a point on which, in the absence of further evidence, it is impossible to offer any remark. But we shall be safe in assuming that the ascendancy of speculative over operative masonry must certainly have been established in London from 1619-20, and at Warrington in 1646; while, inferentially, the epochs of transition (in both instances) must be looked for in periods which are far more remote.

In 1655-56 the "Company of ffreemasons" became the "Worshipful Company of Masons," of London.

The following, which I extract from a *Memoir of the Family of Strong*, appeared on a monument at Fairford, Gloucestershire:—

> "Here lyeth the body of VALENTINE STRONG,
> Free Mason,
> He departed this life,
> November . .
> A.D. 1662.

> "Here's one that was an able workman long,
> Who divers houses built, both fair and Strong;
> Though Strong he was, a Stronger came than he,
> And robb'd him of his life and fame, we see:
> Moving an old house a new one for to rear,
> Death met him by the way, and laid him here."

The six sons of this Valentine Strong "were all bred to the mason's trade," and the "Family" will again enter into the narrative as we proceed.

Elias Ashmole accompanied Sir William Dugdale in his visitation of Staffordshire in 1663, about which date it is highly probable that the two heralds and antiquaries exchanged views with respect to the origin of Freemasonry, the substance of which was reproduced by John Aubrey in his "Story of the Bulls." The prevalence of masonic "customs" in his native county (afterwards so graphically depicted by Dr. Plot) could hardly have been unknown to Ashmole, nor can the supposition be regarded as an entirely visionary one, that their general notoriety may have had its share of influence in inducing him, at a still earlier period, to join the ranks of the Freemasons at Warrington in 1646.

Returning to the Masons' Company of London, there are two inventories of its effects, one of which was taken in 1665 and the other in 1676. Among the articles enumerated in both schedules are a copy of the Manuscript Constitutions and a list of the members of the lodge, the former being described as "One book of the Constitutions of the Accepted Masons" (in 1676), and the latter as "The names of the Accepted Masons in a faire enclosed frame with a lock and key" (in 1665).

In the opinion of writers who have made the subject a special study, it is highly probable that this list of Accepted Masons is connected in some way with the "New Articles" cited by Dr. Anderson in his publication of 1738, and which form a distinctive feature of a group or family of the Manuscript Constitutions, as classified by Dr. Begemann, and lettered F in the *Old Charges* of Mr. Hughan. I shall next refer to another form, or version, of the Manuscript Constitutions, known as the "Harleian 2054." It is in the handwriting of the third Randle Holme (1627-99), who, like his father and grandfather, was an heraldic painter, professional genealogist, and acted as Deputy Garter for Cheshire, Shropshire, Lancashire, and North Wales. He was the principal contributor to the "Holme" collection of manuscripts in 260 volumes which, after the death of the fourth Randle Holme, were purchased for (or on behalf of) Robert Harley, first Earl of Oxford. In 1753 they were sold to the British Museum, and are now numbered Harleian MSS. 1920—2180.

PORTRAIT OF THE FAMOUS ANTIQUARY ELIAS ASHMOLE

The transcript referred to (*Harl.* 2054) was apparently made about the year 1665, and of presumably the same date is a rough memorandum, also penned by Randle Holme, which contains the following:—

"There is seu^{r}all word & signes of a free Mason to be revailed to y^u wch as y^u will answ: before God at the great & terrible day of Iudgm^t y^u keep Secret & not to revaile the same to any in the heares of any pson w but to the M^{rs} & fellows of the said Society of free Masons so helpe me God, xt."

Connected with the foregoing, and in the same hand-writing, are other entries, including twenty-six names (and embracing that of Randle Holme himself), which, without a doubt, were those of members of the Chester lodge.

The conditions under which Freemasonry was practised at Warrington in 1646 seem to have been largely repro-duced at Chester in 1665-75. The circumstances in life of seven out of the twenty-six members have not been ascer-tained, but of the remainder four only were of the masons' trade. An equal number were aldermen, and two (including Holme) were gentlemen.

The third Randle Holme was the author of the *Academie of Armorie* (1688), from which I extract the following:— "I cannot but Honor the Felloship of the Masons because of its Antiquity; and the more, as *being a Member of that Society, called Free-Masons.*"

In the same book Randle Holme also states:—"A Fra-ternity, or *Society*, or Brotherhood, or Company are such in a corporation, that are of one and the same trade and occupation who, being joyned together by oath and cove-nant, do follow such orders and rules as are made for the good order, rule, and support of such and every of their occupations."

The Accepted Masons are referred to in the Account and Minute Books of the Masons' Company (London) for 1677, but there is no subsequent mention of them in any records of the fellowship. A side light, however, is thrown on the proceedings of the Acception or Lodge

by the *Diary* of Elias Ashmole, from which I shall again
quote:—

"March, 1682.

"10.—About 5 p.m. I rec^d: a sumons to app^r at a Lodge
to be held the next day, at Masons Hall, London.

"11.—Accordingly I went, & about Noone were admitted
into the Fellowship of Free Masons,

"Sr William Wilson Knight, Capt. Rich: Borthwick,
Mr Will: Woodman, Mr Wm Grey, Mr Samuell Taylour,
& Mr William Wise.

"I was the Senior Fellow among them (it being 35
yeares since I was admitted). There were p^rsent beside
my selfe the Fellowes after named.

"Mr Tho: Wise M^r of the Masons Company this p^rsent
yeare, Mr Thomas Shorthose, Mr Thomas Shadbolt . . .
Wainsford, Esqr, Mr Nich: Young, Mr John Shorthose,
Mr William Hamon, Mr John Thompson, & Mr Will:
Stanton.

"Wee all dyned at the halfe Moone Tavern in Cheap-
side, at a Noble dinner prepaired at the charge of the
New=accepted Masons."

With the exception of Sir William Wilson, Captain
Richard Borthwick, and Elias Ashmole, all those whose
names are recorded in the *Diary* as having been present at
the lodge were members of the Masons' Company.

Thomas Shorthose filled the Master's chair in 1664,
Thomas Shadbolt in 1668, Thomas Wise in 1682, William
Wise in 1703 and William Woodman in 1708.

"From the initiation of Sir William Wilson and Captain
Borthwick," observes Mr. Conder, "we have evidence at
this date that the Lodge of Freemasons held at Masons'
Hall continued to admit those who were not members of
the Company, and it was evidently still possible for 'gentle-
men-Masons' to become members without the obligation
of afterwards joining the Company or taking up the Freedom of the City. In fact, the Lodge had now probably become a more or less distinct body, and was not merely the

private esoteric division of the Masons' Company, as it had been in earlier years."

No later evidence bearing, however remotely, on the continued existence of the lodge at Masons' Hall has come down to us. Whether it passed away with the seventeenth century, or lived for any longer period, can only form the subject of conjecture.

"The one thing certain is that, up to about 1700, the Company and the Society were hand in hand, but *after* that date the connexion appears to have ended, and there is nothing to show that Speculative Masonry had a place in the thoughts of the Company" (*Hole Crafte*, 14).

The armorial bearings of the Company appear to have served as a model for those of all later masonic corporations, whether speculative or operative. They are to be found also on several copies of the Manuscript Constitutions, in certain instances accompanied by the Arms of the City of London, and in others by those of some illustrious family connected with a particular lodge.

The "New Articles," a remarkable feature of the "Roberts" group of the old Constitutions, have been referred to in a previous chapter (III), and of the clause (No. 31) I reproduced (*ante* 81), Mr. Conder says that it might have been drafted direct from the existing rules of the Masons' Company, and he adds: "If by any chance they (the New Articles) are taken from such rules as might perchance have been included in, or added to, the Constitutions of the Masons' Company at a later date, then we can trace the origin of Dr. Anderson's remarks in his Constitutions of 1738 concerning the Grand Lodge, and conclude that, as lodges began to increase in London towards the end of the seventeenth century, these 'New Articles' emanated from the senior lodge—*i.e.*, that connected with the Masons' Company."

In the opinion of Mr. Hughan: "The 'additional' or 'new' articles appear to have been agreed to by some Company or body of Freemasons, having jurisdiction, in one form or other, over a number of lodges, about which at the present time we are absolutely without information, and which seem to have been in part of a speculative character" (*Old Charges*, 124).

Returning to the Masons' Company, Thomas the first and Edward the fifth son of Valentine Strong, Freemason, were members of the London Company, and successively the master masons of St. Paul's, under Sir Christopher Wren. According to the *Memoir of the Family of Strong*, Thomas Strong laid the foundation-stone of St. Paul's Cathedral with his own hand. The lanthorn on the dome was begun about the year 1706, and on the 25th of October, 1708, Edward Strong, senior, laid the last stone upon the same.

Valentine Strong, the father of Wren's two master masons, was in all probability a member of the "Company of Freemasons, Carpenters, Joiners, and Slaters of the City of Oxford," incorporated in 1604.

In this instance, it will be observed that while the members of several trades are united in a guild, the post of honour is given to the Freemasons. They are also named first in a charter granted by the Bishop of Durham, constituting various crafts into a "Comunitie, ffelowshipp, and Company," in 1671. The incorporated body was to "assemble" yearly on "the Feast of St. John Baptist" and elect four wardens, one of whom "must allwaies be a ffree mason, and shall vpon the same day *make freemen and brethren.*"

It is very possible that certain external privileges were possessed by the Masons' Company of London, and among these may have been a more or less acknowledged suzerainty over *all* the *guild* members of that trade (or Free Masons). Great and unusual powers were conferred on the weavers by Henry II. In 1327 Edward III granted a charter to the girdlers of the metropolis, *which took in all the girdlers of the kingdom, ordered them under the same rules,* and set them under the mayors of whatever city they might be in. (Riley, 154). By Edward IV, and later kings, charters were granted to various trade communities, giving them an existence independent of the town.

There were the tailors of Exeter, who, rich, powerful, and well drilled, cherished ambitions beyond the perfecting of the sartorial art. They were permitted by Edward IV to "augment and enlarge" their guild as they chose, and forthwith took into their company "divers crafts other than of themselves, and divers others not inhabitants within the same city"—men, in fact, of every conceivable trade and occupation, *free* brethren who swore to be true and loving brothers of the guild, never to go to law with any of the fraternity, to pay their fines duly during life to the treasure box, and leave a legacy to it at their death (*Town Life*, ii, 174).

I shall next quote from the *Natural History of Staffordshire* (Chap. iii), by Dr. Robert Plot, which was published in 1686:—

§85. "To these add the *Customs* relating to the *County*, whereof they have one, of admitting Men into the *Society* of *Free-Masons*, that in the *moorelands* of this *County* seems to be of greater request, than anywhere else, though I find the *Custom* spread more or less all over the *Nation*; for here I found persons of the most eminent quality, that did not disdain to be of this *Fellowship*. Nor indeed need they, were it of that *Antiquity* and *honor*, that is pretended in a large *parchment volum* they have amongst them, containing the *History* and *Rules* of the craft of *masonry*."

§86. "Into which *Society* when they are admitted, they call a *meeting* (or Lodg as they term it in some places), which must consist at lest of 5 or 6 of the *Ancients* of the *Order*, when the *candidats* present with *gloves*, and so likewise to their *wives*, and entertain with a *collation* according to the Custom of the place: This ended, they proceed to the *admission* of them, which chiefly consists in the communication of certain *secret signes*, whereby they are known to one another all over the *Nation*, by which means they have maintenance whither ever they travel: for if any man appear though altogether unknown that can shew any of these *signes* to a *Fellow* of the *Society*, whom they otherwise call an *accepted mason*, he is obliged presently to come to

him, from what company or place soever he be in, nay,
tho' from the top of a *Steeple* (what hazard or inconvenience
soever he run) to know his pleasure and assist him; *viz.*,
if he want *work* he is bound to find him some; or if he
cannot doe that, to give him *mony*, or otherwise support
him till *work* can be had; which is one of their Articles."

After stigmatizing the Legend of the Craft as false and
incoherent, the doctor goes on to say: "Yet more improbable
is it still, that *Hen.* the 6 and his *Council*, should ever peruse
or approve their *charges* and *manners*, and so confirm
these right Worshipfull *Masters* and *Fellows*, as they
are call'd in the *Scrole*: for in the third of his reigne (when
he could not be 4 years old) I find an *act of Parliament*
quite abolishing this *Society*."

Among the subscribers to the *Natural History of Staffordshire* were Elias Ashmole, Sir William Dugdale, and Sir
Christopher Wren, by all of whom the author was held in
high respect and esteem.

The *Natural History of Wiltshire* (from which I shall next
quote), Dr. Plot was asked by John Aubrey to prepare
for the Press, but as already related, the work remained
in manuscript form until 1847. A rough and a fair copy were
made by the author. From the latter I transcribe the following:—

"Memorandum. This day, May the 18th, being Monday,
1691, after Rogation Sunday is a great convention at St.
Paul's Church of the Fraternity of *adopted masons*, where
Sir Christopher Wren is to be adopted a brother, and Sir
Henry Goodric of the Tower, and divers others. There have
been kings that have been of this sodality."

In the original (or rough) copy of the Aubrey MS., the
words italicized above (*adopted masons*), as first written,
were "*Free*-Masons," but "*Free*" is crossed out, and "*Accepted*" (which in the fair copy becomes "*Adopted*") takes
its place.

The above is the only contemporary evidence which tends
in any way to connect Sir Christpoher Wren with the Freemasons, though after the death of the great architect we

meet with a long array of fabulous statements which declare that he was for many years the Master of a private lodge, and also (though at a period anterior to the existence of that title) the Grand Master of the Fraternity.

The *year*, however, in which, as we learn from Aubrey, the great convention of Free, Accepted, or Adopted Masons was held, may have witnessed some important meeting of the Craft, of which no record has been preserved. In the Engraved List for 1729, the senior lodge is described as "No. 1. Goose and Gridiron, St. Paul's Churchyard. Constituted 1691."

According to Dr. James Anderson, "Particular *Lodges* were not so frequent and most *occasional* in the *South*, except in or near the Places where great Works were carried on. Thus Sir Robert Clayton got an *Occasional* Lodge of his Brother *Masters* to meet at *St. Thomas's Hospital, Southwark*, A.D. 1693, and to advise the Governours about the best Design of rebuilding that Hospital; near which a *stated* Lodge continued long afterwards."

"Besides that and the *old* Lodge of *St. Paul's*, there was another in *Piccadilly* over against *St. James's* Church, one near *Westminster* Abby, another near *Covent-Garden*, one in *Holborn*, one on *Tower-Hill*, and some more that assembled statedly" (*Constitutions*, A.D. 1738).

At the beginning of the eighteenth century we meet with the "Orders to be observed by the Company and Fellowship of Freemasons att a Lodge held at Alnwick, Septr. 29, 1701, being the Gen$^{ll.}$ Head Meeting Day."

Among these "Orders" are: "5th,—Thatt noe mason shall take any Apprentice [but he must] enter him and *give him his charge* within one whole year after"; and "9th,—There shall noe apprentice after he have served seaven years be *admitted* or *accepted* but upon the Feast of St. Michael the Archangell."

The Alnwick Lodge was an essentially operative body, and of speculative or symbolical masonry its records do not disclose a trace, until thirty or more years after the dawn of the era of Grand Lodges in 1717.

In 1704 the Festival of St. John the Evangelist became the General Head-Meeting Day, and, as the frequent entry "made Free Decr 27th" attests, apprentices who had served their time, in conformity with the ninth regulation, were admitted or accepted on that date.

"The Old Lodge at York City" was in a very flourishing condition in 1705, but, in the absence of documentary evidence, its earlier history must remain a matter of conjecture.

An offshoot of this body is probably referred to under the heading of "The names of the Lodg," which is inscribed on a roll of the MS. Constitutions (*York*, No. 4), with the date of October, 1693. But the parent stem doubtless rises to an equal height with that of the known (or living) masonry of the south (1619-20); and it is quite possible that an operative (if not a speculative) ancestor of the "Old Lodge at York" may have existed in the *logium fabricæ*, of the proceedings of which we obtain a glimpse in the Fabric Rolls of 1352 (*ante*, 65).

The York Lodge, however, from at least 1705, was exclusively the home of speculative or symbolical masonry. No minutes of earlier date than 1712 have been preserved, but from that date they extend to and overlap those of the Grand Lodge of England, at London, established in 1717. The greater number of the meetings are described as those of PRIVATE, while a few are referred to as those of GENERAL Lodges. New members were "Sworne and Admitted" or "Admitted and Sworne," and from these words alone can we form any notion of the method of reception. The Lodge itself is indifferently styled the Antient and Honourable Society and Fraternity of Free Masons; the Company of Free Masons; and the Society of Free and Accepted Masons.

There were PRESIDENTS and DEPUTY PRESIDENTS. The former include Sir George Tempest, Bart., 1705; Robert Benson (afterwards Lord Bingley), Lord Mayor, 1707; Sir William Robinson, Bart., 1708; and Sir Walter Hawkesworth, Bart, 1711. Among the latter were George Bowes,

Brother You are desired to meet ther Antient
Society of Free Masons at the Grand Lodge in York
on   the   17   at   o Clock
                                By order of the Grand Master
N of 2   from Yr Faithfull Bror
                                &c

ORIGINAL SUMMONS OF THE OLD "GRAND LODGE OF ALL ENGLAND
AT YORK

1713, and Charles Fairfax, 1716, both of whom were county magnates; also Rear-Admiral Robert Fairfax (brother of the last-named) who, a month after he had been "admitted and sworne into the hon^ble. Society and fraternity of Free-masons" (1713), was elected as Parliamentary representative and, two years later, as Lord Mayor of the City of York.

A "private" Lodge was held at Scarborough on the 10th of July, 1705, "before William Thompson, Esqr. Pr'sident & severall others, brethren ffree Masons," at which six gentlemen "were then admitted into the said ffraternity."

Between the Lodges at York and Scarborough respectively there was probably the relation of maternity and filiation. The former, however, was not always a stationary body, as we are told (on the authority of original records that were existing in 1778) that "there is an Instance of its being holden once (in 1713) out of York, viz., at Bradford in Yorkshire, when 18 Gentlemen of the first families in that Neighbourhood were made Masons."

In the South of England during the same period—*i.e.*, the first and second decades of the eighteenth century—there must also have been a considerable amount of masonic activity, although the proceedings of the lodges have unfortunately not been recorded. This conclusion is based on two of Steele's Essays in the *Tatler*, the first of which appeared June 9th, 1709, and the second May 2nd, 1710. In the former the writer alludes to a set of people who *"have their Signs and Tokens like Free-Masons"*; and in the latter remarks (of certain "idle fellows") "that one who did not know the true cause of their sudden Familiarities, would think *that they had some secret intimation of each other like the Free-Masons."*

It is abundantly clear that, in the foregoing extracts, Steele refers to a well-known and long-established institution, and from his two statements alone (in the absence of any other evidence), it would be safe to assume that in London, *many years prior* to 1709, there had existed a Society possessing *distinct* forms of recognition, the members of which were commonly and generally known as the Free-Masons.

As will be hereinafter shown, traces of speculative masonry in the north of Britain are found in greater abundance and of higher antiquity than in the south; while the recent research of Dr. Chetwode Crawley has clearly established, that in Irish academical circles Freemasonry was well known before the landing of William of Orange at Carrickfergus in 1690.

ILLUMINATED HEADING OF THE "HADDON" MS.
Reproduced by permission of the Board of General Purposes
from the Original in the Grand Lodge Library

CHAPTER V

*We see on our shelves, in handsome Volumes, the Works of
old Authors who lived and wrote before the invention of printing;
but how few of us ask ourselves the questions: Where are the
originals of which these books are the copies? And what authority
have we for the genuineness of the text?*

WILLIAM FORSYTH

*The Four Crowned Martyrs were so called because their names
were not known.—"Breviarium Spirense"* (A.D. 1478).

*Science there
Sat musing; and to those that loved the lore
Pointed, with mystic wand, to truths involved
In geometrical symbols.*

REV. WILLIAM MASON

ALTHOUGH manuscripts containing the legendary history
of the Masonic body have come down to us in great profusion and variety, neither the testimony of history nor the
voice of legend can be relied upon as affording any distinct
clue to the *incunabula* of the Craft mythology.

These ancient writings are described in various ways:
e.g., as the Manuscript (or Masonic) Constitutions, the Constitution of the Craft, the History of Freemasonry, the Story
of the Guild, and the Legend of the Craft. Ordinarily they
consist of three parts: First, the Introductory Prayer,
Declaration, or Invocation; secondly, the History of the
Society—Story of the Guild, or Legend of the Craft—which,
beginning before the Flood, alludes to Euclid, Solomon
(and many other Biblical characters), a "curious Mason"

called Naymus Grecus, who, having assisted at the building of the Temple at Jerusalem, afterwards taught the Science of Masonry to Charles Martel; St. Alban the Proto-Martyr; and generally ends with the era of King Athelstan, or about A.D. 926; and, thirdly, the peculiar statutes and duties, the regulations and observances, which the members of the Masonic trade were bound carefully to uphold and inviolably to maintain.

These documents were used at the reception of candidates for admission. The Legend of the Craft was read over to them, and they then swore on the Holy writings to faithfully observe the statutes and regulations of the Society.

In his well-known work, *The New Book of Constitutions*, published with the "SANCTION" of the Grand Lodge of England, in 1738, Dr. Anderson states:—"THE FREE-MASONS had always a Book in *Manuscript* call'd the *Book of Constitutions* (of which they have several very antient Copies remaining) containing not only their *Charges* and *Regulations*, but also the History of *Architecture* from the Beginning of Time; in order to show the Antiquity and Excellency of the Craft or Art."

Besides these compilations, of which the majority now extant are in roll or scroll form, there are two manuscripts —the Regius and Cooke—of higher antiquity, possessing many characteristics of the Masonic "Constitutions" (properly so-called), and apparently derived in great part from versions or readings of them now lost to us, but which were evidently not used at the reception of new brethren in the same way as the documents in roll or scroll form; and must be classified rather as histories of, or disquisitions upon, Geometry (or Masonry) than as "Constitutions" of the Craft or Society.

Of the ordinary versions of the Masonic Constitutions, the oldest dated form is the "Grand Lodge" MS. No. 1 of the year 1583. The *readings* or *texts*, however, of these documents, as distinguished from the *forms* or *writings* in which they have been preserved, exhibit many discrepancies, whereby some confusion and much disputation have arisen. In their *prima facie* character, indeed, the manuscripts present themselves as so many independent and rival texts of greater or less purity. But, as a matter of fact, they are not independent; by the nature of the case they are all fragments—frequently casual and scattered fragments—of a genealogical tree of transmission, sometimes of vast extent and intricacy.

Leaving the old "Constitutions" (properly so-called), and passing to the next group of documents in the ascending scale, we come in the first instance to the Cooke MS., and, a little higher, reach the Masonic Poem, or Regius MS., after which the genealogical proofs are exhausted.

These two manuscripts, however, afford conclusive evidence of there having been—at the time from which they speak—pre-existing "histories" of Geometry (or Masonry) of much earlier date.

This part of my subject has been anticipated in other passages of the present work, but the written traditions of the Freemasons will now be examined as a whole, and an attempt made to judge of their mutual relations.

A history of the discovery of ancient manuscripts has been frequently mentioned as a work that would prove highly interesting to the scholar and the man of taste; and in such a volume Poggio Bracciolini would merit every encomium which gratitude could supply. The whole lives of Italian scholars in the fifteenth century were devoted to the recovery of manuscripts and the revival of philology. The discovery of an unknown manuscript, says Tiraboschi, was regarded almost as the conquest of a kingdom. Poggio especially distinguished himself by his persevering and successful researches in continental Europe for the manuscripts of the works of ancient authors; and in our own day, for the memorable resurrection of early documents of the English Craft, which has so recently taken place, we are under a similar weight of obligation to William James Hughan, of Torquay.

Thirty or less years ago, not a score of the old written

traditions of the Freemasons were known to exist, whereas at the present time some seventy copies (or forms) of the Manuscript Constitutions have not only been traced but transcribed, and to these must be added nine printed versions (some of which are fragments of unknown originals), together with ten missing documents (referred to, but not traced), making a grand total of eighty-nine, a few being copies (or duplicates) of other existing MSS.

The labours of Mr. Hughan, in this field of research, were shared at the outset by the Rev. A. F. A. Woodford, and in later days by other coadjutors, among whom Dr. Wilhelm Begemann easily takes the first place.

The division of the Manuscript Constitutions into groups or families was long regarded as a golden impossibility by the limited number of students who had alone attempted to penetrate beneath the somewhat forbidding husk of their actual meaning and intent. The task, however, has been happily performed by Dr. Begemann in a manner that leaves very little to be desired, though I must be careful to guard myself from being supposed to admit that the other methods of classification of older date are entirely superseded by the new arrangement.

In the second edition of Hughan's *Old Charges of British Freemasons* will be found particulars of all known copies of these old Constitutions, arranged in families of MSS. The whole subject has also been exhaustively treated, in a series of most interesting articles, contributed by Dr. Begemann to the *Zirkelcorrespondenz* (or official organ), of the National Grand Lodge of German Freemasons, at Berlin.

To the serious detriment, however, of English students, the invaluable commentaries of the latter on the ancient manuscripts of the Craft are (to the generality) either totally lost, or at least partially veiled in the obscurity of a foreign tongue. But a condensed outline (in English) of his German articles has been kindly made for me by the learned doctor, a sketch of whose main thesis (in relation to the inquiry we are pursuing) will next be laid before the reader.

I shall only premise that many of the views held and conclusions drawn by Dr. Begemann are supported by arguments and illustrations, for which space cannot be found in this volume; also, that in the letterpress of the following sketch (for which I am solely responsible), I may have occasionally failed to express my friend's exact meaning with absolute precision in our vernacular idiom.

DR. BEGEMANN ON THE MANUSCRIPT CONSTITUTIONS

I. *The Regius MS., 17 A.I., British Museum.*—This document would seem to have been *transcribed* between the years 1390 and 1415, from an original of slightly earlier date, compiled, say, between 1380 and 1400, in the north of Gloucestershire or Herefordshire, or even possibly in the south of Worcestershire. The manuscript, which is in metrical form, and deals with a variety of topics—though at unequal length—may be divided into eight leading divisions:—

I. The History of Masonry—*i.e.*, its foundation by Euclid in Egypt, and its introduction into England by King Athelstan (*ll.* 1—86);

II. Fifteen Articles (*ll.* 87—260);

III. Fifteen Points (*ll.* 261—470);

IV. An Ordinance (*Alia ordinacio*) about future Assemblies (*ll.* 471—96);

V. *Ars Quatuor Coronatorum* (*ll.* 492—534);

VI. and VI*a*. The Tower of Babylon and King Nabogodonosor—Euclyde, and the teaching by him of the Seven Sciences "wondur wyde" (*ll.* 535—50 and 551—80):

VII. Rules for good behaviour at Church (*ll.* 581—692); and

VIII. A series of recommendations with respect to deportment and etiquette (*ll.* 693—794).

Of the above only I.—IV. are purely Masonic. V. and VI. show a loose connection with Masonry, while VII. and VIII. are not Masonic at all. I.—IV. were doubtless based on some passages in old "Books of Charges," written in prose, and corresponding very closely with what we meet with in the latter part of the Cooke MS., which appears to be a specimen of an old "Book of Charges." If the texts of these two early documents of the British Craft are compared, it will be found that the first 62 lines of the poem cover substantially the same ground as 54 (*ll.* 643—92) of the prose narrative. Then comes a difference between the two versions. According to the poem (*ll.* 63—86), King Athelstan, in order to amend defaults which he found existing among the masons, convoked an Assembly, or kind of Parliament, consisting of Dukes, Earls, Barons, Knights, Squires, Great Burgesses, and others, by whom fifteen Articles and fifteen Points were ordained for the governance of the Craft. In the corresponding lines (698—720) of the Cooke MS., however, we are told that (also for great defaults) King Athelstan, with his councillors and other great lords, "ordeyned a certayne reule," that once a year or in three years congregations should be made by all masons to be examined of the Articles, and to receive their Charge. In the old "Book of Charges," therefore, the previous existence of the Articles is implied, while in the poem we are informed that not only the Articles, but also the Points were enacted by Athelstan and his Assembly. In the nine Articles of the former are to be found, though not quite in an orderly sequence, the first eight and the tenth of the latter, while the ninth of the poem can be traced in lines 715—19 of the Cooke MS. The last five of the fifteen Articles in the older manuscript have not yet been identified in any other written or printed work, and whether they originated in the fertile imagination of the poet, or were copied by him from some "Book of Charges," amplified by Articles that have not come down to us in any other line of transmission, is so obviously a matter of conjecture that its consideration need not be proceeded with. Comparing the fifteen Points of the poem with the nine of the junior codex, the first eight in either document possess a common ancestry. Nos. 9 and 10 of the Regius are not to be found among the

Points of the Cooke MS., but they correspond to some extent with the passages in the prose writing commencing at lines 921 and 930 respectively.

The eleventh Point of the poem is the ninth of the junior codex, and Nos. 12 to 15 of the former (like 9 and 10) have their prototypes in the original writings, from which the concluding portion of the latter (*ll.* 911—51) is derived.

As I have elsewhere shown, the archetype of the "Book of Charges" contained Articles only, hence the versifier, to whom we are indebted for the Regius MS., must have indulged (and not for the first or last time) in what is called poetic licence, when he boldly announced that the fifteen Points were already enacted by Athelstan and his Assembly.

The fourth part of the poem—*Alia ordinacio artis geometriæ*—which, equally with the passage referred to above in the Cooke MS. (*l.* 693 *et seq.*), is based on an older writing, was apparently inserted at this place, in consequence of the versifier having forgotten to do so at the end of the historical part, to which it properly belongs. The opening lines are:—

> They ordent ther a semble to be y-holde
> Every yer, whersever they wolde,
> To amende the defautes, yef any where fonde
> Amonge the craft withynne the londe,
> Uche yer or thrydde yer hyt schuld be holde.
> Yn every place whersever they wolde.

From which it is evident that the Assembly hinted at in the first line by the word *ther* was identical with the Assembly (or Parliament) convoked by Athelstan at an earlier stage of the metrical narrative (*ll.* 63—86), and that the "Ordinance" enacted at that gathering has its analogue in the "certayne reule" in the Cooke MS.

The rhymist next presents us with a personal utterance of King Athelstan in regard to "these statutes everychon" —*i.e.*, the Articles, Points, and *Alia Ordinacio*—which purports to be an expression of the Royal will that they ought to be kept throughout the country, and should be confirmed by later kings.

The fifth part of the poem has the title of *Ars Quatuor Coronatorum*, and glorifies the Four Crowned Martyrs on account of their constancy, referring for fuller particulars of their fate to "the legent of scanctorum," meaning, no doubt, the so-called "Golden Legend" (*Legenda Aurea*) of Jacob a Voragine, which is often cited as *Legenda Sanctorum*.   Neither oral tradition nor any other written authority is relied upon, or at least mentioned by the compiler, and it is well known that the *Quatuor Coronati* never became the patron saints of the English, as they undoubtedly were of the German masons.   It may be supposed, therefore, that the object of the versifier was to place on record some early examples of Christian truth and fortitude among the members of the building art.

The sixth part of the poem opens with an account of the tower of Babylon, erected by "Kyng Nabogodonosor" in order to protect the human race from being entirely destroyed by any future flood.   After which, without any connecting link, Euclid is brought on the scene, and we learn that he commenced in the seven sciences, which are next enumerated, though rather confusedly, the fault— it may well have been—of the transcriber.   Lastly, we meet with—

> These ben the syens seven,
> Whose useth hem wel, he may han heven.

According to the belief of the Middle Ages, the seven sciences were virtually a similar number of steps leading to virtue, and finally to Heaven.

The seventh section of the manuscript is composed of excerpts from many sources, for example the *Lay Folks' Mass Book*, the *Book of Curtesye*, the *Merita Missæ*, and notably from the *Instructions for a Parish Priest*, by John Myrc.

The last-named work was probably written by the author —who was a Canon of Lillieshall in Shropshire—between 1350 and 1390, though the copies preserved are of a later period.   Shropshire—especially in its southern part—is included within the area when the Western-Midland dialects prevailed, and between the dialect of Myrc's *Instructions* and that of the Masonic poems there is a very close similarity, the latter, however, being of rather later date, and inclining a little in a south-easterly direction.

The eighth and final portion of the Regius MS. is taken from another poem, entitled *Urbanitatis*, the original of which must have existed in the fourteenth century. It is also traceable, as a composition, to the Western-Midland district, where, in the fourteenth century, a great many poems were compiled on matters relating to practical life.

In my opinion, the author of the Masonic poem (or Regius MS.), who was a priest or clergyman, intended the whole of it for operative Masons, of whom, perhaps, he was an overseer, in order to give them a higher notion of the excellency of their ancient craft, and at the same time render them worthier of it, by fostering ideas which might result in their becoming more religious and better mannered. The English literature of the fourteenth and two following centuries abounds with versified exhortations and directions in regard to good behaviour, and in many guild ordinances we read of fines being imposed for breaches of decorum or offences against good manners. Whether the Masonic poem was extensively copied and circulated during the fifteenth century, there are no means of determining, and possibly the only transcript made of the original document exists in the solitary copy which has come down to us.

II. "*Additional MS.* 23, 198" (*British Museum*).—This old MS. was first printed in 1861 by Mr. Matthew Cooke, and has since borne his name. The experts at the Museum pronounce it to be of early fifteenth century transcription, but in my own judgment dates from about 1430, and was copied from an older original, compiled either in the last decade of the fourteenth or the first decade of the fifteenth century. Like the Masonic poem, the Cooke MS. came from the Western-Midland district, and the opinion expressed (after an independent investigation) with respect to its original home meets with welcome confirmation in the

Diary of Dr. Stukeley, from an entry in which we learn that what must undoubtedly have been the Cooke MS. was brought to London from the West of England, and produced in the Grand Lodge by Grand Master Payne, on St. John's Day (in summer), 1721.

The manuscript consists of two chief or leading parts, the first of which is a new history of Masonry written by a learned man, probably a priest, and the second, without doubt, a copy of an old "Book of Charges." The entire document extends to 959 lines, and in the *First Chief Part* there are 642, which may be classified as follows:—

I. Introductory remarks (1—35). II. The seven liberal sciences (36—76). III. Origin and worth of Geometry, from which came Masonry (77—158). IV. The children of Lamech: Jabal found Geometry and Masonry, Jubal Music, Tubal Cain Smith's Craft, and Noema Weaver's Craft: Jabal wrote all the sciences on two pillars to protect them from fire or water: and after Noah's flood these pillars were found by Pythagoras and Hermes, who taught and spread the sciences they contained (159—326). V. Nimrod began the tower of Babylon, and taught his workmen, whom he loved and cherished, the Craft of Masonry; he sent his cousin Assur 3,000 Masons, and gave them a Charge (327—417). VI. Abraham knew all the Seven Sciences, and taught Masonry to Euclid, who gave it the name of Geometry: Euclid taught the Egyptians to make walls and ditches and to divide the land into parts: he also instructed the sons of the lords in the Craft of Masonry, and gave them a Charge (418—538). VII. The Israelites learned the Craft of Masonry in Egypt and took it to Palestine, where David and Solomon favoured Masons and gave them Charges (539—75). VIII. *Carolus Secundus* was a Mason before he was King of France; he gave the Masons Charges and ordered them to meet together once a year, in order to be ruled by masters and fellows of all things amiss (576—601). IX. St. Alban, having been converted to Christendom by St. Amphibal, gave the English Masons their first Charges and convenient pay for their travail;

afterwards King Athelstan and his youngest son loved masons well; the latter, who became a mason himself, gave the masons Charges, together with reasonable pay, and purchased a free patent from his father that they should make an assembly when they thought fit (602—642). The new history of Masonry, of which this outline has been presented, was not compiled from oral traditions existing among the masons, but from the Bible and other sources. The Compiler, who was evidently a man of learning, besides the sacred writings, quotes from the *Polychronicon*, Beda, Isidorus, Methodius, and the "Master of Stories." The last named, however, is not the Greek historian Herodotus, who is so often referred to as the "Father of History," but the author of the well-known *Historia Scholastica*, Petrus Comestor, who is styled "Master of Stories" by Trevisa in his English translation of Higden's *Polychronicon*, as well as by Wycliffe in one of his disquisitions.

In many portions of his narrative the compiler is in full agreement with the stream of writers of the Middle Ages, while in others there are passages which cannot be traced to any known source, and were probably the coinage of his own brain. For example, the statement that the two pillars were made by Jabal, and subsequently discovered by Pythagoras, the great clerk, and Hermes, the philosopher; that Solomon's Master Mason was the King's son of Tyre; and that *Carolus Secundus* (meaning "Charles the Bald") was not only a Mason himself, but also a great patron of the Craft. The introduction of Masonry into England is also embellished by the names of some additional protectors—St. Amphibal, St. Alban, and King Athelstan's youngest son. Athelstan, indeed, had no son, but his reputed offspring is said to have become a Mason himself, and to have purchased from his father a free patent for the Craft.

The *Second Chief Part* (lines 643—959) may be thus subdivided:—

I. Euclid taught the sons of great lords, in Egypt, the Science of Geometry, and called it Masonry; the cleverest he ordered to be called masters, and those that were of less ability, fellows; in this manner the art was begun in Egypt, and went from country to country (643—93). II. In the time of King Athelstan Masonry came to England, and because of many defaults among Masons, the King and his Council ordained a certain rule, that they should come together every year, or once in three years, as the King thought necessary, and congregations should be made from province to province of all masters and fellows, and the new masters should be examined of the Articles of Masonry, and they should receive their charge to serve well the lords from whom they took their pay (694—727). III. Nine Articles for the Masters (728—826). IV. Nine Points for Fellows (827—900). V. Various mandates, concerning the congregation, the charging of new men, the inquiry as to breaches of the Articles, and the punishment of rebels against the Statutes (901—59).

On a variety of grounds, which are considered at length in my German essays on the Manuscript Constitutions, it is possible to affirm that the compiler of the Cooke MS. and "author" of the *First Chief Part* simply made use of an existing "Book of Charges," which he added, without alteration of any kind, to his own "history." The divisions into which the *Second Chief Part* naturally falls are five, as given above. The fourth section, containing the nine Points, in my judgment could not have formed an integral portion of the very earliest "Book of Charges" but must have been interpolated at some later (and unknown) date.

III. *The William Watson MS. ("Plot" Family).*—The Masons' Arms, with the motto, "In the Lord is Al our Trust," form an appropriate heading for this roll, which is a connecting link between the Cooke codex and the later (or ordinary) versions of the Manuscript Constitutions.

The W. W. follows the Cooke MS. very closely down to line 601, after which the text is slightly amplified in the junior document (*ll.* 602—42); while the "Book of Charges," contained in the second or concluding portion of the Cooke, gives place in the W. W. to a new set of eight "Generall" and 23 "Singular" Charges.

In the new and enlarged part of the history, which takes the place of lines 602—42 in the Cooke MS., we meet with St. Amphabell, who, laden with Masonic Charges, came from France to England, where he brought St. Alban into Christendom and made him a Christian man. St. Alban was the King's steward, paymaster, and governor of his works. He loved Masons well, and gave them charges "as St. Amphabell had taught him, and they doe but a little differ from ye charges yt be used now at this time."

For these embellishments of the "History of the Craft" the author was indebted, not to oral traditions, but, as he expressly tells us, to "Old Charges" of St. Alban and King Athelstan, and "Stories of England," referring no doubt to the various legends in circulation respecting the British Proto-martyr, from which it can be shown that he copied freely, possibly from Latin or French originals, but with greater probability from the English translation made by Lydgate in 1439.

Athelstan next enters into the narrative and is followed by Edwin, who takes the place of the former's hitherto unnamed "youngest son." The writer apparently knew very little about the historical periods in which these valiant soldiers had flourished. He found, however, in the manuscript he copied from, that Athelstan had a youngest son, so he further embellished the history of Masonry by providing him with a name. He had probably read in Beda's *Historia Ecclesiastica* of Edwin of Northumbria, who erected a church of wood in 627, and began to build one of stone. Nor should the anachronism in making Athelstan and Edwin contemporaries surprise us, as such confusion was very common at the time. Without looking beyond the Craft legend, it will be sufficient to refer to Abraham and Euclid, who are made to figure as teacher and scholar, whereas the former lived about 2,000 years before and the latter about 300 years after Christ. That the Edwin of the junior MS. was the King of Northumbria may also be inferred from the circumstance that, in addition to purchasing a free patent from his father (as set down to the credit of Athelstan's "youngest son" in the older legendary narrative), he orders the Masons to assemble together at *York*, where he was himself. He also commanded them to bring all the old books of the Craft, out of which were "contrived" the charges of the wisest Masons, and that they might be kept and holden, he ordained that such congregation should be called an Assembly and "thus was the Craft of Masonry there grounded and confirmed."

It is quite possible that the compiler had read of the Parliament which was actually held by the Edwin of Saxon history, near York, in 627. But from whatever sources the additions in his narrative were obtained, it is noteworthy that the three new features, *the name of Edwin, the Assembly at York, and the making of new charges from the old books of the Craft*, which distinguish the document under review, are preserved in all subsequent versions (or texts) of the Manuscript Constitutions.

The next passage of importance recites that the charges transcribed in the MS. had been perused and allowed by our late Sovereign, King Henry VI and his Council, which I think must be accepted as a fact, and that it occurred after 1437, when a statute was passed (15 Hen. VI, c. vi) forbidding the passing of new ordinances by guilds and fraternities without the sanction of the public authorities.

The eight "Generall" Charges comprise some of the Points, and the 23 "Singular" Charges certain of the Articles and Points, which are given in the Regius and Cooke MSS.

IV. *The T.W. Tew MS.*—This roll, which is of the seventeenth century and perhaps older than 1680, bears the title of THE BOOK OF MASONS, and forms a link between the Plot Family (of which the William Watson MS. is the leading exemplar) and the bulk of the ordinary versions of the Constitutions.

The final recension must have taken place before the Reformation (1534). A great part of the text follows that of the W. Watson, but many of the particulars given in the last-named manuscript, which the *rédacteur* (or digester) thought could be dispensed with, are omitted in the Tew, though, by way of compensation, he adds a goodly number that seemed to him essential to render the narrative more coherent.

The leading characteristics of this scroll are—I. The statement that Cain killed his brother Abel with an arrow—a legend, the filiation of which may be traced through the Atcheson-Haven MS. to the "Master of Stories," Petrus Comestor, who relates in his notes on Genesis (chap. iv) that Lamech, who had been an archer, accidentally killed Cain (who therefore was not the slayer, but the slain) in a chase; II. Following the W. Watson text, the *two* pillars are discovered by Pythagoras and Hermes— a passage which is totally corrupted in latter readings. For example, in the oldest dated form, the Grand Lodge, No. 1, of 1583, Pythagoras no longer figures in the story, and Hermarines, "aft'ward called Hermes," finds *one* of the two pillars of stone, from which it is clear that the bulk of the younger versions—*i.e.*, later readings or texts— go back, or in other words are derived from a later form, in which Hermarines had taken the place of Pythagoras, and been blended with Hermes. III. The King of Tyre first obtains the name of Hiram, and also the "King's son" (as described in the Cooke and W. Watson) is provided with a name. We now learn that the former "had a son who was called Hyman [*i.e.*, Hiram, or Hyram], and he was Master of Geometry and Chief Master of all Masons, and Governor of all his Carved and Graven Works, and of all Masonry that belonged to the Temple." *This* Hiram's name appears under a great diversity of spellings, in the various copies of the Constitutions, but it is evident that Hiram was the chosen name in the manuscript of origin. IV. We are introduced to a "*curious Mason* that had been at the Making of Solomon's Temple, and came into France, and taught the Craft of Masonry to men of France," who is styled *Mammongretus* and *Memongretus*. But the *t* has plainly been misread for *c*, and that *Grecus* (which we find in the

Grand Lodge and Sloane families, or groups), was the concluding portion of the name, as originally written, may be confidently assumed. The precise form, however, of the first two syllables of the word cannot be restored. It almost certainly began with an *M*, as we may infer from the spelling of the name in other MSS. more closely connected with the Tew version (*Maymus, Marcus, Mamus, Minus*, etc.), and possibly the person whom the scribe had in his mind was *Maimonides—i.e., Moses ben Maimon*, also called *Maimuni*—who died in 1204, *and had written about the Temple at Jerusalem*, the compiler mistaking him for a Greek. V. For Carolus Secundus (in the Cooke and W. W.) we have Carolus and Charles Martill. VI. The old books of the Craft brought to the Assembly at York are now stated to have been written, some in French, some in English, and some in other languages.

V. *The Ordinary Versions.*—While it is abundantly clear that the Tew represents an intermediate *form* between the Plot Family (as represented in the W. Watson MS.) and the later readings (or versions), it is equally evident that there must have been some more connecting links. It is impossible that all the subsequent versions could have derived their origin from the Tew MS. itself. There must have been one or two *revised Tew forms* in order to account for the points of agreement, as well as of non-agreement, which are to be met with in the texts of the later families. The genealogy of the Manuscript Constitutions may be illustrated by the following diagram:—

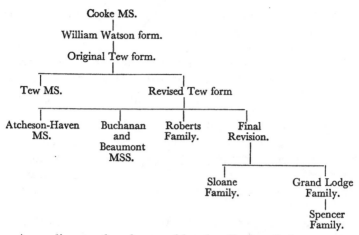

According to the above table, the Cooke of about 1400-1410 is the original form of all the Manuscript Constitutions now extant, with the solitary exception of the Masonic Poem (or Regius MS.), which is *sui generis*, or in other words an errant form peculiar to itself, without any known descendants. From the Cooke came the Plot (or W. Watson) text. Then followed an original Tew version of about 1510-20, of which the existing Tew MS. is a very late transcript. From the former sprang a "Revised Tew," the prototype of some Branches or Families, of which the Atcheson-Haven, the Buchanan and Beaumont MSS., and the Roberts Family are three distinct examples. Furthermore, there was a second or Final Revision of the Tew form, which became the prototype of the Grand Lodge and Sloane (the two chief) Families. Lastly, a somewhat modified wording of the Grand Lodge *Branch* (as represented by the Cama *form*) was used as a model for the Spencer—quite a new Family. It consists of two written and two printed forms. The Manuscripts are the Spencer of A.D. 1726; and the Inigo Jones, which, though bearing the date of 1607, must really have been compiled about 1723-25. The Prints are the Cole and Dodd, of 1729 and 1739 respectively.

The text peculiar to this Family is evidently a modern

compilation, dating, it may be supposed, from about the year 1724. The Spencer is the best representative of the group, for though the Inigo Jones is based on an older original, the reading it presents departs very widely from what we may assume to have been the normal text, and doubtless owes its existence very largely to the imagination of the transcriber.

Among the noteworthy features of this Family are— I. The use of chronological figures, which are never met with in any of the really old manuscripts of the seventeenth century. II. The *modern* term of Free and Accepted Masons, which is first found in the Roberts Print of 1722, and afterwards in Dr. Anderson's "Constitutions" of the following year. This is an irrefutable proof that neither the version peculiar to this Family, nor the Inigo Jones MS. itself, could possibly have been "compiled" at any earlier period. III. The name Hiram Abif, which occurs in this Family *only*, and appears to have been first embodied in the Legend of the Craft by Dr. Anderson, in his "Book of Constitutions," 1723, where, however, he justifies its insertion by a long and argumentative footnote. It is true that in some English Bibles of the sixteenth century —1535 to 1551—we meet with Hiram Abif and Hiram Abi, but these names had dropped out of use, and to the masons of the *seventeenth* century were unknown. Of this there can be no reasonable doubt, and if Hiram Abif had either figured in the ceremonial or the traditions of the Craft at a period anterior to the eighteenth century, the Manuscript Constitutions of corresponding date would not maintain, as they do, such a uniform and unbroken silence with respect to the existence (legendary or otherwise) of such a leading character in the later history and symbolism of the Craft.

In my opinion, the lost original of the Spencer version was not compiled before 1723 or 1724, and I also think that the author of the embellished text was familiar with the writings of Doctors Robert Plot and James Anderson, the Roberts Print, a translation of Josephus, and other comparatively modern works. The genealogy of this Family—premising that its prototype may, with good reason, be assumed to have been, not actually the Cama MS., but an older copy (and variant) of the same original —was probably as follows:—

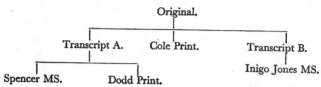

Finally, it may be observed, that in the Spencer family there are numerous variations of the ordinary text, and many *new* historical characters are substituted for the *old* ones. Maimon (or *Naymus*) Grecus, together with Charles Martel, drop entirely out of the narrative, while we learn for the first time that the Emperor Claudius came over with an army, when Aururiagus was King of Britain; also, that the "sumptuous Art of Geometry was professed by Emperors, Kings, Popes, Cardinals, and Princes innumerable, who have all of them left us the permanent Monuments of it in the several Places of their Dominions." We are further told that the science of Masonry (in England) was much decayed until the reign of Ethelbert, who—with two other English Kings, Sibert and Sigebert—has hitherto escaped notice in the written traditions of the Craft.

VI. *The Roberts Family.*—Something has still to be said with respect to a remarkable group of the old "Constitutions," at present consisting of five documents, the Roberts' *Print*, and the Harleian, 1942, Grand Lodge, No. 2, Macnab, and Rawlinson MSS. The framework of the history corresponds with that which is met with in the ordinary version, but the phraseology is peculiar to itself, though possessing points of affinity with the Tew, Atcheson-Haven, Buchanan, and Beaumont texts. The version under examination was evidently a digest or reconstruction of a second or revised Tew form, as outlined above. The Charges are numbered in all of the five copies, the "Generall" and

the "Singular" Charges (on the higher plane), being
united, and forming a total of 26 in the Roberts' Print,
and of 25 (by the omission of No. 15) in the Grand Lodge,
Macnab, and Harleian MSS., while in the Rawlinson the
whole are condensed into 24.

A striking peculiarity of this family is the appearance of
a group of new charges—seven in number. These, in the
Roberts' pedicle, are styled "Additional Orders," and in
the Harleian "New Articles"—the latter omitting one
and numbering the rest from 26 to 31. In the Macnab
they are prefaced by the words, "These articles following
were added here unto since by ye best Mrs. & fellowes,"
and numbered from one to six, three and four having been
blended together by a negligent scribe. In the Grand Lodge
MS. No. 2, which contains 33 general articles (or Charges),
they consist of the last seven (27 to 33), and simply follow
on, without any note or heading, after the first 26. In
the Rawlinson they are not to be found, and whether the
omission was occasioned by their absence from the manuscript of origin, or due to the caprice of the transcriber, it
is impossible to say.

The *Seven* rules are ascribed to the year 1663 in the
Roberts Print, and there is nothing to prevent our believing
that this date was really found in the original document
from which the Print was taken. The Articles are headed,
"Additional Orders and Constitutions made and agreed
upon at a General Assembly held at..............................
on the Eighth Day of December, 1663."

If this date be accepted as that of the *first* making of the
new rules, then the Grand Lodge and Harleian MSS. will
not be older than about the same period—say 1665-70.
The Macnab, it may be observed, is a copy of 1722. The
new Charges (which I take from the Roberts Print) bear
a somewhat modern stamp:—

"1. That no person of what degree soever be accepted
a free mason, unless he shall have a Lodge of five free
Masons at the least, whereof one to be a Master or Warden
of that Limit or Division, wherein such Lodge shall be

kept, and another to be a workman of the Trade of free Masonry.

"2. That no person hereafter shall be accepted a free Mason but such as are of able body, honest parentage, good reputation, and observer of the Laws of the Land.

"3. That no person hereafter, which shall be accepted a free Mason, shall be admitted into any Lodge or Assembly, until he hath brought a Certificate of the time and place of his acception from the Lodge that accepted him unto the Master of that Limit and Division, where such Lodge was kept, which said Master shall enroll the same on parchment in a roll to be kept for that purpose, and give an account of all such acceptions at every general Assembly.

"4. That every person who is now a free Mason shall bring to the Master a note of the time of his acception, to the end the same may be enrolled in such priority of place as the person deserves, and to the end the whole company and fellows may the better know each other.

"5. That for the future the said Society, Company and Fraternity of free Masons shall be regulated and governed by one Master and Assembly and as many Wardens as the said Company shall think fit to choose at every yearly General Assembly.

"6. That no person shall be accepted a free Mason unless he be one and twenty years old or more.

"7. That no person hereafter be accepted a free Mason or know the secrets of the said Society until he shall have first taken the Oath of Secrecy hereafter following."

In succession to these "Additional Orders" (or "New Articles"), the Harleian, Grand Lodge, and Macnab MSS. have ten Charges for Apprentices, but those in the Roberts Print are inserted between the usual Charges and the "Additional Orders." They are missing from the Rawlinson MS. The "Apprentice Charges" are found in other groups or divisions of the old Constitutions, but as given in the Roberts Family they are more original and complete.

So far Dr. Begemann, whose remarkable analysis of
the old documents of the Craft I here bring to a close.
The special features of the Grand Lodge and Sloane—the
two chief Families—I was unable to include in the above
sketch, but these are carefully enumerated in the *Old Charges*
of Mr. Hughan, to which the reader is referred. For easy
reference, however, a nominal roll of all known copies of
the Masonic Constitutions, as tabulated and classified by
Dr. Begemann, is given with the present chapter. Many
essays of enduring value on particular manuscripts are also
to be found among the *Transactions* (and other publications) of the *Quatuor Coronati* Lodge (*Ars Quatuor Coronatorum*).

It is not, indeed, within the scope of a *Concise History*,
meant especially for general readers, to enter into the
details and merits of special controversies. I can only
endeavour to present, in the briefest and clearest possible
form, such conclusions as may be confidently relied upon,
and such as appear most probable, and likely to be confirmed in the course of further study, as being supported
by the greatest amount of intrinsic and circumstantial
evidence.

The written traditions of the Freemasons are now very
numerous, but their texts exhibit so much disagreement
that it is a difficult matter to avoid confusion in an attempt
to arrive at their true value as historical muniments of the
Craft.

It will give more arrangement to our ideas, and at the
same time illustrate the variations that occur in these documents, if we consider them as divided into three clusters
or constellations, connected indeed very closely with one
another, yet each having its own centre of attraction and
its own boundaries.

The first of these we may suppose formed of the Regius
and Cooke *Codices*, which were compiled upwards of four
centuries and a half ago, when every book or record was a
written one. In the second class we may place all the known
versions of the Manuscript Constitutions (properly so-

called) with the exception of a particular group. A final cluster will comprehend the whole of the documents belonging to the Roberts Family, as arranged and classified by Dr. Begemann.

These three divisions will exhibit the written traditions of the Freemasons in what I shall venture to describe as their first, second and third manners respectively. The texts of the two earliest manuscripts evidently refer to a period when the forest law existed side by side with the ordinary law of the land. The documents in the second class (leaving out of sight for the moment the Spencer Family) point with equal clearness to an era coinciding with a later stage of English mediæval law. Lastly, in the "New Articles," which are only found in the Roberts Family, we meet with ordinances that belong to the class of *novellæ*. Their great importance is now unchallenged, but whether they were to be regarded as resting on any basis of actual fact, or as representing a past that never was in any sense a present, was, in less critical days, a moot point, on which the opinions of commentators were divided.

With regard to the cluster of documents, comprising the Regius and Cooke MSS., I shall first of all quote from a review of Dr. Begemann's *German* commentary on the older writing, by the late Mr. Speth. "The care," he observes, "with which Begemann has studied the Poem is shown by the fact that he is enabled to point out where the scribe has begun his day's work with a fresh pen, and where, towards the conclusion of each period, the pen becomes blunted by use, and the writer careless from fatigue. The most interesting part of his study is the determination of the particular district in which the document was compiled. A highly instructive essay on the dialects of England in the fourteenth century is the result, and a splendid description of the differences between the Northern, Midland, Eastern, Western, and Southern dialects of that period, and of the mixed dialects current in the portions bordering on each other with the influence one exercised over the other. Here, of course, he acknowledges his indebtedness to our English philologists, and though the subject is an intricate one, it is a pleasure to state that our Brother makes it fairly comprehensible to anyone who will take a little trouble to master it. But I am quite unable to give the impression made upon my mind of the magnitude of the task the doctor must have devoted years to. Neither do I feel myself competent to criticize his conclusions, as only a critic well versed in the study of our language could profitably do so" (*A.Q.C.*, vii, 34).

The diligence and acumen of Dr. Begemann are not, indeed, likely to be seriously impeached, and the highly important results attained by his critical and scientific methods have been welcomed and appreciated by all students in the same branch of research.

The Regius MS. has been described by an expert in manuscript literature, "as nothing more than a metrical version of the rules of an ordinary mediæval guild, or, perhaps, a very superior and exemplary sort of trades union, together with a number of pieces of advice for behaviour at church and at table, or in the presence of superiors, tacked on at the end."

The last hundred lines are taken from "Urbanitatis," a poem which Mr. F. J. Furnivall tells us he "was glad to find, because of the mention of the *booke of urbanitie* in Edward the Fourth's 'Liber Niger,' as we thus know what the Duke of Norfolk, of 'Flodden Field,' was taught in his youth as to his demeanings, how mannerly he should eat and drink, and as to his communication, and other forms of court. He was not to spit nor snite before his Lord the King, or wipe his nose on the table-cloth" (*Early Eng. Text. Soc.*, lxviii).

The passage referred to will be found in "Urbanitatis" (*ll.* 53, 54), and is thus given in the Regius MS. (*ll.* 743-46) :—

> Kepe thyn hondes, fayr and wel,
> From fowle smogynge of thy towel;
> Theron thou schalt not thy nese snyte,
> Ny at the mete thy tothe thou pyke.

The following lines also appear in both poems:—

> Yn chamber, amonge the ladyes bright,
> Hold thy tonge, and spend thy syght.

These rules of decorum read very curiously in the present age, but their inapplicability to the circumstances of the *purely operative* masons in the fourteenth or fifteenth century will be at once apparent. They were intended for *gentlemen* of those days, and the instructions for behaviour in the presence of a lord, at table, and in the society of ladies, would all have been equally out of place in a code of manners drawn up for use of a guild or craft of artisans.

A similar sense of the incongruity of the text of the Regius MS. with what we feel must have been the actual customs of the building trades, cannot but steal over us when perusing *Articulus Quartus* (*ll.* 143—46), where we meet with—

> By olde tyme wryten y fynde,
> That the prentes schulde be of gentyl kynde;
> And so sumtyme grete lordys blod
> Toke this gemetry, that ys ful good.

Upon the foregoing, Mr. Furnivall remarks, and the wish to which he gives expression will, I am sure, be echoed by most readers of the poem—"I should like to see the evidence of a lord's son having become a working mason, and dwelling seven years with his master.

> "'Hys crafte to lurne.'" (*E.E.T.S.*, xxii.).

The conclusion, therefore, as it seems to me, to which we are directed by the evidence, is that the persons to whom the Masonic poem was sung or recited, were a guild or fraternity from whom all but the memory or tradition of its ancient trade had departed. From some cause or other, then, upon which, in the absence of further evidence, we can only speculate without arriving at any definite conclusion, it would appear that at the date from which the Regius MS. speaks there was a guild or fraternity which commemorated the science, but without practising the art, of Masonry.

ARS QUATUOR CORONATORUM

A distinctive feature of the poem is an invocation of the "Holy Martyres Fowre," the tutelary saints of the building trades, an outline of whose story (though the legend concerning them has descended in many channels of transmission) may be given in a few words.

During the reign of the Emperor Diocletian, five Masons, or stone-squarers (*mirificos in arte quadratana*) refused to execute the statue of a pagan god, and in consequence were put to death. On the return of the Emperor to Rome, he commanded that all the soldiers in that city should march past and throw incense over the altar of Æsculapius. Four officers, however, who were *cornicularii*, having embraced the Christian faith, declined, and they also suffered death. The martyrdom of the Five is supposed to have taken place on the 8th of November, A.D. 298, and of the Four on the same day in A.D. 300.

The Nine were eventually interred in the same spot, a single festival, November 8th, being set apart for the five whose names had been preserved, and for the four who were only known (until their names were miraculously revealed in the ninth century) by their military rank. Upon the latter, Pope Melchiades—A.D. 310—bestowed the title of *Quatuor Coronati*, or Four Crowned ones, by which they are described in the more ancient missals and other formularies of public devotions, though in conjunction with the Five, who are referred to by name, and as Holy Martyrs.

In the seventh century Pope Honorius I erected a handsome church, in the form of a basilica, to the memory of the Four, out of the ruins of a temple of Diana, on the Coelian Hill. Into this, the church of the *Quatuor Coronati*, were removed, A.D. 848, the remains of the Nine Martyrs. Hence has arisen a certain amount of confusion, and the Four Officers, instead of the Five Masons, have become the patron saints of the building trades, while the occupation of the Five has survived under the name of the Four.

The church, which—after having been many times rebuilt —still exists, now bears the name of the *Quattro Incoronati*; according to some authorities, *Incoronati*, in modern Italian, being identical with the *Coronati* of mediæval Latin; while by others the word is supposed to be a corrupt form of the military term *Cornicularii*, which has been brought back into the Latin from the Italian as *Coronati*.

It has also been suggested that as there were two classes of decorated soldiers in the Roman Army, the higher being known as *Coronati*, and the lower as *Cornicularii*, so it may very probably have happened that the Four received a posthumous brevet at the hands of the faithful, a supposition which gains further strength if we bear in mind that crowns of martyrdom are also implied by the word *Coronati*.

From Italy, the vogue of the *Quatuor Coronati* as patron saints spread to Germany (*ante* 19) and France. According to the Martyrology of Du Saussay, the bodies of the Five were removed from Rome to Toulouse, and the relics of one of the number—St. Claudius—are mentioned in a Papal Bull of A.D. 1049 as reposing in the Church of Maynal, in the province of Franche Compté.

In many Flemish cities the name of *Vier Ghecroonde* (*Quatuor Coronati*) was given to a group of trades connected with the art of building, and associated for the purpose of forming an ambacht or corporation. According to Count Goblet d'Alviella, guilds of the *Vier Ghecroonde* (including Masons, Stone-cutters, Sculptors, and others) existed at Antwerp and Brussels in the fifteenth century. The members were known as "Companions of the Lodges" (*Gesellen van der logen*, or *logien*).

That the legend of the *Quatuor Coronati* must have penetrated into Britain at a very early date is quite clear. One of the chapters in Bede's *Historia Ecclesiastica* is headed, "Bishop Mellitus, by prayer, quenches a fire in his city"; and the record goes on to state that at Canterbury, where the miracle occurred—"The Church of the Four Crowned Martyrs was in the place where the fire raged most" (*erat autem eo loci, ubi flammarum impetus maxime incumbebat, martyrium beatorum Quatuor Coronatorum*).

In the opinion of Mr. Ireland, the Church of the Four Martyrs at Canterbury was erected about the time of St. Augustine, A.D. 597 (*History of Kent*, i, 157); and if this supposition is correct, we have the resulting inference that (in all probability) the first Christian edifice erected after the arrival of the "Apostle of the English" was dedicated to the patron saints of the building trades.

On the other hand, however, it is powerfully argued by my friend, Mr. C. Purdon Clarke, that the reason why the Church of the Four Martyrs at Canterbury withstood the fire better than the other churches and buildings was in consequence of its having been built in Roman times of either brick or stone, whereas the rest more probably belonged to the period of wholesale building of churches and monasteries which followed the conversion of the Saxons in A.D. 597, and were principally constructed of wood. He also says:—"It is beyond doubt that members of the *Collegia Fabrorum* in the British towns had, for a hundred years before the Saxon invasion, become Christians, and that, therefore, the Church of the *Quatuor Coronati*, the popular Saints of several trades, was more likely to have been built at a time when Canterbury possessed a large community of Christian craftsmen, than to have been founded by St. Augustine immediately after his arrival in A.D. 597." "The early Christian Church," he continues, "consisted principally of members of the industrial classes, all of whom were of necessity *magistri* or *operarii* of their respective trade *Collegia*" (*Vestigia Quat. Cor.*).

According, indeed, to Mr. H. C. Coote, Britain was abundantly furnished with churches when, in the fifth century, St. Germanus visited the martyrium of St. Alban at Verulamium (*Romans in Britain*, 414). This latter Saint received the crown of martyrdom A.D. 303, and the persecution of Diocletian doubtless extended throughout the whole of our island. The church (or cathedral) at

Winchester (the *Venta Belgarum* of the Romans), traditionally ascribed to the time of Lucius, the last of the British
Kings, with the clergy who belonged to it, must have greatly
suffered, but when the happier days of Constantine came it
was either rebuilt or restored, as we hear of it then as the
Church of St. Amphibalus, a Saint memorable as St. Alban's
teacher and fellow-sufferer (*Historic Winchester*, 4). In
parting with the legend of the Crowned Martyrs, I may
briefly state that, in my own judgment, the manner in
which it is referred to in the oldest document of the Craft
will fairly warrant the conclusion that the "Four" were
the Patron Saints of the most important section of the
building trades, during the splendour of Mediæval Operative Masonry, and until the period of its decay.

It was always contended by Dr. Begemann, even when
there were still missing links in the chain of proof, that the
Cooke MS. was the progenitor of the ordinary versions of
the Manuscript Constitutions. But whether the Edwin
of these later documents had previously figured as a patron
of the Masons under the designation of King Athelstan's
"youngest son," is a point which, in the absence of positive
evidence, no amount of exegetical skill can absolutely determine. I incline, however, strongly to the opinion that the
Edwin of early British history was a patron of the Craft
in early Masonic fable.

Athelstan, who is referred to by name in both the Regius
and the Cooke MSS., was the first King of all England, and
from this it is perhaps not unreasonable to suppose that the
legendary belief in his grant of a Royal Charter to the Masons
may have arisen (*ante*, 90). Further, let us recollect that
from the time of Athelstan down to the Norman Conquest,
and from the Conqueror to Edward I, and later, the oath
of allegiance was annually administered to every free man,
at what was called the View of Frankpledge—a distinguishing feature of the system of police, originating in Anglo-
Saxon times, upon which I have enlarged in an earlier
chapter (III).

The wording of this oath, as given in a publication of

1642, "You shall be true and faithful to our Soveraign Lord the King," is substantially the same as that of the corresponding "Charge" or inculcation which is met with in the Masonic Constitutions.

The two "obligations," to use a term with which some of my readers will be familiar, virtually stand on the same level as regards antiquity, and as survivals of still earlier forms their close resemblance is very suggestive of their common origin.

King Athelstan's youngest son, as we read in the Cooke MS., "Lovyd welle the sciens of Gemetry, and . . . he drewe hym to conselle and lernyd practyke of that sciens to his speculatyf, ffor of speculatyfe he was a master"— implying that he was amply skilled in the *knowledge*, as well as in the *practice*, of the science of geometry, and a proficient, so to speak, both in speculative and operative Masonry.

In the same manuscript, and also in the Masonic poem, it is stated that the craft of geometry was founded in Egypt by Euclid, and given the name of Masonry; and in reference thereto, the following are the observations of the late Albert Pike:—"Many of the symbols of the old religions of Pythagoras, and of the Hermetics of later days, were geometrical figures. . . . Some of these were symbolic because they represented certain numbers, even among the Assyrians and Babylonians. To the knowledge of these symbols, perhaps the name 'geometry' was given to avert suspicions and danger. The architects of churches revelled in symbolism of the most recondite kind. The Pyramids are wonders of geometrical science. Geometry was the handmaid of Symbolism. Symbolism, it may be said, is speculative Geometry."

In the preceding views all indeed may not concur, but the point should not escape us that in the oldest "cluster" of documents relating to our Society we meet with disquisitions and collections *which are very far removed from the mental range of the operative Masons to whom the Manuscript Constitutions were rehearsed at a later period.* This will accord with the supposition that Masonry, as a speculative science, declined or fell into decay, *pari passu*, with Masonry as an operative art.

Leaving the Regius and Cooke *codices*, which are of late fourteenth or early fifteenth century transcription, let me next pass to the second "cluster" of ancient Masonic writings, or, in other words, to the great bulk of the Manuscript Constitutions (properly so-called), of which the oldest dated form is the "Grand Lodge" MS. of A.D. 1583.

Between these periods there is a gap of more than a century and a half, during which the population dwindled, the builders almost died out, and the arts lost their vigour and beauty.

The Manuscript Constitutions of the Freemasons are ancient and more or less obsolete, when we first meet with them in the later history of the Society. Nor does an examination of more venerable texts, or of documents of a like stamp known to have been in existence at periods of time comparatively remote from our own, bring us any nearer to a comprehension of the circumstances under which they originated, the precise class of hearers for whom they were designed, or the particular purpose they were (in the first instance) intended to fulfil.

It is true, indeed, that from the two histories of or disquisitions upon Masonry of older date, we are justified in inferring that from the fourteenth century (and possibly earlier) there were associations of speculative or symbolical Masons (though I must be careful to state that on this point the judgment of some of the leading authorities is opposed to my own); also, in the "Constitutions" themselves it is plainly stated that at the admission of newcomers they were to be read over or rehearsed.

It is likewise true, that with regard to the group of documents which I have placed in the second class, many speculations, both curious and entertaining, have been advanced; but these, with a solitary exception, I must decline to pursue, as lying out of my way in the design I am now upon. In a *Tentative Enquiry* the late Mr. G. W.

Speth brought forward a singular hypothesis, his contention being that the cathedral (or church) builders of the Middle Ages were a separate class from the masons of the town guilds or companies; that the Manuscript Constitutions belonged to, and contained the codes of regulations *in use* among the church-building masons. The foregoing is the offspring of a lively fancy, and "Cathedral Builders," as an alternative title for the "Freemasons of the Middle Ages," having an attractive sound, has attained a certain vogue, but, unfortunately for the hypothesis (though advanced with great persuasive force by its gifted author), it is unaccompanied by even a shadow of proof, and is opposed to the known facts of history (*ante,* 103, 105).

Our accounts of the codes of regulations, or "Charges," are, indeed, only traditionary, and there is nothing to show that either in the sixteenth or fifteenth centuries, or earlier, they fulfilled any more useful purpose than the several versions of the Legend of the Craft, of which, in all copies of the Manuscript Constitutions, they form a part. We cannot trust those echoes of the past which are called the written traditions of the Freemasons. *Unless machinery is seen at work it is not possible to judge of its results.* Equally hard is it to form a judgment of the operation of the Masonic system of government in the Middle Ages from the dry statements which successive copyists of the old "Constitutions" have preserved or invented.

In a certain sense, therefore, the ancient muniments of the Craft may be described as "tombs without an epitaph." Some, however, of their general characteristics will be briefly enumerated, and an outline presented of a large subject still lying much in the dark, but upon which much recent light has been thrown by the monographs of Hughan and Begemann, and to these the interested reader is referred.

There is a remarkable circumstance connected with the Masons' trade to which, at this point, it will be convenient for me to advert.

By no other craft in Great Britain has documentary evidence been furnished of its having claimed at any time a legendary or traditional history.

That the Legend of the Craft was not written *uno tenore* will be patent to the most casual student, and the same remark will apply, though in a slightly modified degree, to the Charges or Codes of Regulations. In the former, especially, the usual indications of the union of different accounts, repetition, discrepancies, difference of language, force themselves repeatedly on our notice. These afford the clearest evidence not only of complexity of origin, but also of successive recensions. Dr. Begemann has made it quite plain that many of the recitals in the existing manuscripts have passed through numerous phases before reaching their present form, and I think therefore we may further assume that no small part of the original contents of the various "Books of Charges" (pre-dating the Regius and Cooke MSS.) must have been lost in the process.

In all probability, the earliest "History of Masonry," or "Legend of the Craft," was written either in Latin or in French.

The belief has many adherents that the mediæval Masons had a body of tradition derived from or through the Ancient Mysteries, a theory to which colour is lent by all versions of the Manuscript Constitutions, tracing the origin of Masonry in Egypt and the East.

In a book before me I find—"Egypt often *fossilized* rather than destroyed the earlier stages of her civilization and her art" (Conway, *Dawn of Art in the Anc. World*, 88); and again, "This is a small but significant example of the conservatism of Egypt, whereby she progressed, *not by supplanting one custom by another, but by enveloping the old in the new*" (*ibid.*, 61).

After the same manner, I believe that many of the old laws or disciplinary regulations of the earlier masons became fossilized or petrified, or, in other words, that they passed out of use, though retaining their hold on the written and unwritten traditions of the Society. Also,

I think we may safely assume, on even stronger grounds, that a parallel for the "conservatism of Egypt," referred to above, may be found in the customs of our own Craft, which in their descending course—as I shall venture to lay down with confidence—were not supplanted "one by another," but the entire body of them "progressed" to its ultimate goal, the purely speculative Masonry of our own times, "by enveloping the old in the new."

The Manuscript Constitutions are devoid of ambiguity with respect to the religion of Masonry before the era of Grand Lodges—"The first charge is this, that you be true to God and Holy Church, and use no error or heresy" (G. Lodge MS. No. 1); and in the next sentence of the same "Charge" there occurs—"You shall be true liegeman to the King of England," from which it has become an accepted doctrine, that all copies of the Craft Legend (or Charges) in either North or South Britain are of English origin.

On several of the documents there are endorsements, which not only point to a living Freemasonry at the date from which they speak, but also to the existence of a custom, requiring the Legendary history and the "Charges" to be read at the admission of new members of the Society.

The true text of the Manuscript Constitutions has been the subject of numerous theories, but the filiation of the Craft Legend, as traced with such infinite pains by Dr. Begemann, if we do no more, must at least be accorded the title of the dominant hypothesis. Yet there are two of the doctor's conclusions, from which, as lying outside the range of his strictly scientific methods, I shall, without derogating from the strength of his main position, venture to record my strong dissent. There is, in the first place, the recital in what has been termed the Plot text (of which we have examples in the W. Watson and other MSS.) that the "Charges" of the Freemasons had been seen and allowed by Henry VI and his Council, a statement with regard to which, though for reasons of a different (and mainly legal) character, I share the incredulity of Dr. Robert Plot (*ante*, 119). Secondly, there are the speculations of Dr. Begemann with regard to Hiram Abif, whose name admittedly appears in Bibles of older date than those of the Spencer Family of MSS., and therefore, whether it fell into absolute disuse, or the reverse, during the interval which occurred between the appearance of these publications respectively, must, in either view of the case, remain a pure matter of conjecture. There is also the *symbolic* (though *unwritten*) tradition which has gathered round Hiram's name, and this (though to anticipate somewhat), I am of opinion, has come down to us from very ancient times. I believe also that the class of persons who, in the fourteenth century, *or earlier*, constructed the original Craft Legend, were capable of understanding and did understand, to a larger extent than ourselves, the meaning of a great part of the Symbolism which has descended from Ancient to Modern Masonry. Symbolism, as Albert Pike so truly tells us, is the *Soul* of Masonry. I am unable to complete the metaphor by saying of what the *body* consists, but the garments in which it is clad—our Manuscript Constitutions—have come down to us from very remote times, and are the connecting links—in a corporeal sense—between Ancient and Modern Freemasonry.

I now pass to the third "cluster" of documents, or, in other words, to the "Roberts" Group or Family, containing the "New Articles," which have already been referred to at some length in previous passages of this book. From the evidence which these supply, it has been contended that the Society, re-modelled in 1717, was a Company of Freemasons, which at some previous time had relinquished the occupation that gave them a name. Moreover, if we follow Mr. Conder:—"The important fact that the Masons' Company dropped the prefix of 'free' from their title in 1665 shows clearly that at about that date a number of speculative masons formed themselves into a London Society, and were known as the *Society* of Freemasons, in contradistinction to the *Company* of Masons. From this London Society of Freemasons emanated, no doubt, several lodges of speculative masons, who, early in the next century (1717), met together and formed the nucleus of modern Freemasonry" (*Hole Crafte*, 208).

From one point of view, indeed, the foregoing may be regarded as at least a highly plausible conjecture, since it is quite possible that the disuse of the prefix "free" by the Masons' Company, in 1665, may have been one of the consequences resulting from the "New Articles" which (as *alleged* in the Roberts Print) were passed at a "General Assembly," held in 1663. But in the chain of proof that can alone substantiate the conclusion drawn by Mr. Conder there are missing many links, and until further evidence is forthcoming we can only look upon the written traditions, in what I have called their "third manner," as marking a period of expiring influences, when the old order of things was vanishing in the twilight that ushered in the new.

MASONS' MARKS

The short study of MASONS' MARKS with which the present chapter will be brought to a close, might have found a place in earlier sections of this work, but for reasons that hardly require pointing out it has seemed most desirable to proceed with it at the stage we have now reached, when the subject can be taken as a whole.

The marks are described by the Rev. C. W. King as "enigmatical symbols, which yet existing and in common use among ourselves, and among the Hindoos in their daily religious usages, can be traced backwards through Gnostic employment and Gothic retention, through old Greek and Etruscan art to their first source, and thus attest convincingly what country gave birth to the theosophy that made, in Imperial times, so large a use of the same *siglæ*" (*The Gnostics and their Remains*).

The same "enigmatical symbols" appear to have been freely used by the Hermeticists and Rosicrucians. Indeed, it has been asserted that not only the magical numerals, but also the curious alphabets which are given by Cornelius

Agrippa in his *Occult Philosophy,* may be found in their entirety among the marks of the Masons.

It is very remarkable that these marks are to be found in all countries—in the chambers of the Great Pyramid at Gizeh, on the underground walls of Jerusalem, in Herculaneum and Pompeii, on Roman walls and Grecian temples, in Hindustan, Mexico, Peru, Asia Minor—as well as on the great ruins of England, France, Germany, Scotland, Italy, Portugal and Spain.

Some of the foundation stones of the Harem Wall of Jerusalem are cut in the surface to a depth of three-quarters of an inch, but most of the characters are painted with a red colour like vermilion. In the opinion of the late Emmanuel Deutsch, who inspected them *in situ,* the signs were cut or painted when the stones were laid in their present position. He believed them to be Phœnician, and to be partly letters, partly numerals, and partly masons' or quarrymen's signs. Colonel Conder, however, points out that similar characters were used on coins and buildings up to Herod's time, and the marks cannot therefore be held to be decisive evidence as to date. Nevertheless, to use the words of the late Professor Hayter Lewis, they seem to give at least strong presumptive ground for the belief that in these splendid foundation stones we may see the actual work of the Phœnician Hiram for his great master, Solomon. More recently, such stones (as at Jerusalem), though worked with a different tool, have been found in the old Amorite City of Lachish, and, if we may assign this peculiar masonry to the ninth century B.C., we shall have found a near approximation to the date of the Wise King.

It is important, however, to bear in mind during the progress of our inquiry, that while marks were used by masons from very early times, they were also common, during the Middle Ages, to the generality of the other trades. Merchants' marks are well known to have existed during the Mediæval period, if indeed they have yet passed out of use, and it is but rarely that a black-letter book can be opened without one or two ciphers belonging to the author or printer being disclosed. In 1398 a system of marks was instituted at Aberdeen, for the different makers of bread in that town, while in England (and especially in London) by statutes of much earlier and much later dates, not only the bakers, but also the workers in the precious metals, the weavers, brewers, blacksmiths, and the members of numerous other trades—even including the tinkers—were required to use and put their own mark upon their own work.

Marks were also common to the guilds. In London we find them used by the Carpenters' Company down to 1597, by the Masons' Company until 1621, and so late as 1758 the Coopers' Company issued particular marks to the members of their trade.

By the Schaw Statutes, promulgated in 1598, for the regulation of the then existing Scottish Lodges, it was enjoined that the fellow craft or master shall have a mark, which, however, he may have adopted on his being made an entered apprentice, for the ancient records of Mary's Chapel, of the Lodge of Kilwinning, and of other Lodges of the seventeenth century, show that the possession of these devices was common alike to all apprentices and fellows, or masters, who chose to pay for them (Lyon, *Hist. L. of Edin.*, 73).

As well summed up by Mr. W. H. Rylands:—"Each Lodge in Scotland, in the seventeenth and eighteenth centuries, kept an independent book in which was registered the name, generally the mark, and the profession or trade of every member and each newly-entered apprentice" (*Tr. Hist. Soc. of Lanc. and Chesh.*, vii, 13).

According to the late Mr. E. W. Shaw, the marks were handed down from father to son, and those of the various members of one family could be distinguished by additional symbols. He also thought he could trace not only the mark of the master mason, the fellow, and the apprentice, but even what he termed "blind marks," or, in other words, the marks of those who were not actually members of the Lodge. He likewise held that by careful study the nationality of the workmen could be distinguished from the marks, and as a proof that such was the case used to point out some of the marks in Fountains Abbey as being of French extraction, and differing from those in this country.

With regard, indeed, to the marks, as a rule, being hereditary, the evidence is somewhat conflicting, but the late Professor Hayter Lewis thought that they often were, and that we might assume with great probability that the plan still existing of the same marks being continued in use (with certain modifications) by members of the same family was also a characteristic of the Mediæval masons. The Professor then asks:—"Was there any distinct mark which would serve to distinguish the members of any particular lodge, or company, or fraternity?" And in reply to his own question, observes:—"I may say shortly that I can see no sign which would thus define a separate group of workmen. Yet there are certain cases in which one would expect to find them, if, as we generally suppose, the companies were under clerical guidance." He goes on to say, that while in modern times and at the present day the marks are hidden away out of sight in the horizontal joints, so as to prevent the stones from being disfigured by them: this was very rarely the case in former times, and generally they were external and quite prominent enough to be easily seen (*Journ. Arch. Assoc.*, xlv).

On the modern custom of cutting the mark in such a manner as not to be seen when the stone is in its place, Mr. W. H. Rylands makes the following remark:—"I am inclined to refer the date when it became more usual to cut the mark on the bed of the stone at a little earlier than the year 1600, when the Craft had lost much of its former glory and power, and the marks themselves had lost, to a great extent, their value and symbolism" (*Op. Cit.*, 22).

In the opinion of the late Mr. Papworth—"Whilst such marks as were made by the ancient masons often took the place of a proper sign manual to a document, they then, as now, merely designated, or designate, the stone which each man worked."

"Occasionally," he adds, "a double mark is observable, one being supposed to be that of the foreman under whom the mason worked, the other that of the workman himself. Thus by these marks, in case of wrong or defective workmanship, the mason who had to make his work good could at once be known " (*Eng. Bdgs. in the Middle Ages*).

The books and authorities to be consulted on the general topic will be found in an excellent paper by the same gifted writer (*Dict. Arch. Publ. Soc.*, *s. v.* "Marks"). The whole subject, especially in connection with Freemasonry, was afterwards reviewed at some length in the ninth chapter of my *History of Freemasonry* (i. 455-66). It next engaged the attention of Professor Hayter Lewis, who may be said to have adopted a method of treating the subject which, for the first time, offered any prospect whatever of investing it with any real interest for advanced students of the Craft. (*Jrnl. Brit. Arch. Assoc.*, xlv, 145-54; *Tr. Quat. Cor. Lo.*, iii, 65-72; v, 195-201).

A further incentive to the study of Masons' Marks was supplied by Mr. W. H. Rylands, the results of whose researches were given to the world in a masterly paper— covering the whole ground—which was read in 1891 (*Tr. Histor. Soc., Lanc. and Chesh.*, vii, *n. s.* 123-208).

From the writings of the late Professor Hayter Lewis, which are referred to above, I extract the following:— "I am afraid that at present there is nothing before the fourteenth century to guide us but tradition. It is scarcely to be doubted that much will, however, eventually be found, as the Regius and Cooke MSS. date from the first half of the fifteenth, and clearly show that our Society was then well recognized. But we have, up to that time, so far as I can see, no direct link *except perhaps the Masonic Marks*, which, I have not the slightest doubt, came from the East. No doubt, owing to our traffic with these countries, such marks had been known in England before the Crusaders, but it was by the Crusaders that they were acclimatized here to the extent which we find have been the case.

"Go where you will, in England, France, Sicily, Palestine,

you will find all through the buildings of the twelfth century the same carefully worked masonry, the same masons' toolmarks, the same way of making them. Another century comes, and all is changed. Except in Scotland, where the old style continued to be used, the delicate tooling disappears, and in place of it we get marks made with a toothed chisel, which cover the whole surface with small regular indentions most carefully worked upright (not diagonally as before) and giving us another series of Masons' Marks which are sometimes of great use in regard to the origin and date of buildings.

"Putting together the information which we have, we find:—

"1st. That certain definite methods of marking the general surfaces of the stones characterized the Masonry of the styles which we call Norman and that this had apparently a Western origin.

"2nd. That in the thirteenth century there was introduced, with the Early Pointed Style, an entirely different method of finishing the surface and that the source of this method was apparently from the East.

"3rd. That Masons' Marks do not appear to have been commonly used in Europe until late in the twelfth century.

"4th. That some of the most prominent of these marks appear to have been used continuously, from very early times, in Eastern countries.

"What I believe as to crusading work in Palestine is, that the general design was sent from the great French Abbeys, and that the Master Masons, in directing the works (which must have required the aid of a great many of the skilled native workmen), learned from them and adopted the pointed arch and a general lightness of detail.

"I believe also that our Masons' Marks were adopted in Britain in a similar way, and that they were not used by the inferior workmen, but were the distinguishing marks of approval used by the Master Mason and the foremen under him. It is quite clear that some of these marks were used in England before the Crusaders, owing to the great traffic which existed with the East even as early as Charlemagne, but it was not until the eleventh century that their use became general."

It remains to be stated that, in the opinion of the same careful writer, all the evidence seems to point to there having been bands of skilled workmen attached to great monasteries, cathedrals, and in later times large cities, whose example and training influenced the districts round. When the works ceased they were lessened in number, the members dispersing here and there, and leaving their marks in various places, much as our masons do now at the finish of some great work. But he finds no distinct trace of the general employment of large migratory bands of masons going from place to place as a guild, or company, or brotherhood.

The Rev. A. F. A. Woodford (adopting the views of Mr. E. W. Shaw) thought that Masons' Marks, though originally alphabetical and numeralistic, ultimately became both symbolical and exoteric. That especially in the Middle Ages, if not at all times in the history of the building sodalities, the marks were outer tokens of an inner organization; that, taken from geometry, they constituted a sort of universal alphabet, which, with national variations, was a language the craftsman could understand (*Kenning's Cyclop.*, 459). Other writers of equal eminence have expressed themselves to a similar effect, but in the maze of conjecture to which we are conducted, a clue is presented by Mr. W. H. Rylands, which I think we shall do well to accept:—"If it be true," he tells us, "that ancient Masonry contained some amount of symbolism in which was embodied important secrets it would almost naturally follow that a certain amount of this symbolism would find an outcome in the marks."

The same diligent antiquary, in the exhaustive essay to which I have already referred, formulates a theory that a large number of marks—even some of those which have the appearance of being purely alphabetical—must be looked for in the geometrical bases of construction. Others, he considers, seem to be taken from the propositions of Euclid, and the many forms of the triangle are easily to be traced. In his interesting monograph, Mr. Rylands supplies much valuable information which is available in no other work. German marks are made the subject of a special study, and upwards of eleven hundred marks of all ages and countries are figured in the series of plates with which the essay is enriched.

The difficulty in explaining the prevalence of the same emblems in widely distant parts of the world is not confined to the student of Symbolism. It is shared by those who devote themselves to comparative mythology or folklore, and indeed by all who attempt to trace out the origin of ideas in the past. The conjecture is permissible, that were it possible to establish the existence of a mystic brotherhood, which in times far remote from our own had roamed over most of the old world, the Sphinx-like riddle might be read. But, alas for the supposition—though resting on a huge basis of learned credulity, it has no foundation whatever in ascertained fact.

In the very earliest epochs, three principal symbols of universal occurrence have been found—the CIRCLE, the PYRAMID, and the CROSS.

The CROSS is graven on the Temple-stones of Baalbec and stamped on the tiles from the Temple of Onias—occurring therefore at a period of at least a thousand years before the Christian era.

The TAU, or CRUX ANSATA (*the Cross with a handle*, Fig. 1) occupies a prominent place in the Egyptian Hieroglyphics, and is one of the most ancient and widely spread of the cruciform emblems. In his Fig. 1. famous work, Sir Gardner Wilkinson calls the TAU "the Sacred Sign, or the Sign of Life." It was regarded as a token of supreme power, and appears to have been either worshipped as the symbol of light and generation or feared as an image of death or decay.

The Croix Gammee, or Gammadion (Fig. 2), is also a cross, but the end of each arm of the cross is bent at a right angle. The name is given to it from each of the arms being like the *Gamma*, or third letter of the Greek alphabet. The name, however, by which it is most commonly known is a Sanscrit one, which in English orthography is written Swastika. In China it was called Wan, and in Northern Europe— where it was the emblem of Thor—the Fylfot. It is common both to the East and the West—is found on pottery of the respectable date of 200 B.C.—and has been used in Masonry down to the present day. According to the best authorities, the symbol was associated with the worship of the Sun, and the Swastika is in fact an abbreviated emblem of the Solar wheel with spokes in it, the tire and the movement being indicated by the crampons (Aynsley, *Symbolism of the East and West*, 52).

The Pentalpha, as ancient and common as the Swastika, is used by our Masons now (Fig. 3), but what it does (or did) mean remains a mystery. That it was Pythagorian has been already stated (*ante*, 53), but it was in vogue as a talisman or mark for some 2,000 years before that philosopher was born. In the opinion, however, of Mr. Rylands, it appears to have symbolized a very important basis of construction.

The Seal of Solomon, or Shield of David, likewise called the Hexapla or Hexalpha, is an hexagonal figure consisting of two interlaced triangles, thus forming the outlines of a six-pointed star (Fig. 4). Upon it was inscribed one of the sacred names of God, from which it was supposed to derive its talismanic powers. The spirit of the old talismanic faith is gone, but the form remains, and is everywhere to be found.

The Hour-Glass form, very slightly modified, has been used in every age down to the present, and in almost every country (Fig. 5). According to some good authorities, it was a custom (at the period immediately preceding the era of Grand Lodges) to inter an HOUR-GLASS with the dead, as an emblem of the sand of life having run out.

A figure resembling the Arabic numeral 4 is a very common and universal mark. It is probably in many instances an unfinished HOUR-GLASS, and occasionally has additional lines (Fig. 6).

Fig. 6.

The BROAD ARROW is also a mark which is everywhere to be found. Mr. Rylands says he has never examined a building without meeting with it, and it seems to have been in use from the very earliest times (Fig. 7).

Fig. 7.

The Indian TRISULA, or TRIDENT, is one of the oldest and most widely-spread symbols of the past. It has assumed many forms, and is alike common to the votaries of Brahminism (or Hinduism) in India, and the followers of Buddha in other parts of the East. It was the sceptre of Poseidon. The thunderbolt of Zeus was originally a TRISULA. The Hades of Mediæval drawings is always represented by a TRIDENT, and on our own coinage of the present day Britannia may be found with the same symbol in her hand (Fig. 8).

Fig. 8.

In the earliest era of operative Masonry, a geometrical figure, or canon, was adopted in all sacred buildings, which had an import hidden from the vulgar. This hieroglyphical device was styled VESICA PISCIS, being the rough outline of a fish, formed of two curves, meeting in a point at their extremities. It was held in high veneration, having been invariably adopted by Masons in all countries (Fig. 9).

Fig. 9.

Upon the whole we may now confidently assume that most of the characteristic signs now called Masons' Marks were originally developed at a very early period in the East, and have been used as distinguishing emblems of some kind throughout the Middle Ages in Persia, Syria, Egypt, and elsewhere. From thence they passed through mediæval Europe, and these Oriental types are still visible on the surface of the stones forming the walls of our old Abbeys and Cathedrals.

CHAPTER VI

*As in the transformation scene of some great Masque, so
here the waning and waxing shapes are mingled ; the new
forms, at first shadowy and filmy, gain upon the old ; and
now both blend ; and now the old scene fades into the background ; still, who shall say whether the new scene be finally
set up ?*—JOHN ADDINGTON SYMONDS

THOUGH Scotland seems to have borrowed some of her
early burghal laws from England, the general development
of her municipal history in the Middle Ages resembles
more closely that of the Continent than of England. This
was probably due to the weakness of the Royal authority
in Scotland, and in part, perhaps, to the intimate relations
between that country and the Continent. After the
thirteenth century Scottish burghs sought municipal prece-
dents in France and Flanders rather than in England.

Nothing, indeed, like the same wholesale appropriation
of funds and property devoted to the purposes of religion
by the guilds took place in Scotland at the time of the
Reformation, such as occurred in England. But the records
of the various trades in North Britain show that they suffered
to some extent in a similar way.

About 1430, however, Scotland became so much depopu-
lated by the wars with England that it was found necessary
to import craftsmen from France and Flanders; and, in
1431, King James I, "to augment the common weil, and
to cause his lieges increase in mair virteus, brocht mony
nobill craftsmen out of France and Flanders, and other
partes—for the Scottis were exercit in continuell wars frae

the time of King Alexander the Third to thay days. Thus were all craftsmen slane be the wars." James V. had also to plenish the country with craftsmen from France, Holland, and England. (Bain, *Aberdeen Guilds*, 73.)

About the year 1520 it became common in the leading burghs of Scotland for the magistrates to grant "Seals of Cause" (or local Charters) to the different bodies of craftsmen, specifying their rights and privileges. This brought into use the word "Incorporation"—*i.e.*, incorporated trades—in connection with the craft guilds, when the workmen in a particular town incorporated themselves together under a deacon convener, and established a convener court, or convenery, to look after matters that were common to all the different crafts.

It was impossible for a craftsman to carry on business on his own account within the burgh until he had become a free man, or free burgess, and to attain that position he had to furnish satisfactory evidence of his "habilitie" to exercise his trade. It was the practice at Aberdeen, for the applicant (with the assent of his fellow-craftsmen) to memorialize the Magistrates and Town Council to the effect—"That the petitioner, having learned the art and trade of a ——, is desirous of being admitted a Freeman of Craft of the Trade of Aberdeen." The application was then remitted to the Trade (or Craft) of the petitioner, who was next instructed to make an essay or maisterstick, after which, if found satisfactory, he was again presented to the Magistrates and Town Council, when, having taken the oath of allegiance, he was "admitted and received a Free Burgess of the Burgh of Aberdeen, of his own craft only." Journeymen and apprentices, although not members of the societies, were enrolled in the books of their own crafts, while the latter were entered in the books of the town, as well as in those of their craft, to enable them to claim the rights of an apprentice when they came to apply for their freedom. (Bain, 99, 106.)

A Seal of Cause was granted to the Masons, Wrights, and Coopers, in 1532, and shortly afterwards, in the opinion

of Mr. Bain, "Free" or "Speculative" Masonry was introduced into Aberdeen. "At the outset," he considers,
"Freemasonry was simply an adjunct of the original
association of craft masons; but gradually it became its
leading feature, and the Incorporation of Mason artificers
became what is now known as the Aberdeen Mason
Lodge."

A much earlier Incorporation was that of the Wrights
and Masons, created by a Seal of Cause of the Provost and
Magistrates of Edinburgh in 1475. This, like the Lodge,
assembled in St. Mary's Chapel, and in consequence we
meet with the Incorporation of Mary's Chapel, and the
Lodge of the same name.

The passing of fellow crafts at Edinburgh (Wrights and
Masons) was conducted, as at Aberdeen, by representatives
of the united trades, and in the latest edition of his famous
work, the historian of the Scottish Craft expresses a view
in which I think all will be found to coincide: "The
absence from the Kilwinning and Mary's Chaple archives,"
he remarks, "of any certification of a craftsman's ability to
serve the lieges in the station of a master mason, strengthens
the supposition that Lodges did not, in the seventeenth
century, possess the power of raising fellow-crafts to the
position of masters in Operative Masonry. The prescrip-
tion of a master mason's essay really lay with the 'House,'
i.e., the Incorporation," and whatever may have been
the practice in former times, the testing of a fellow-craft's
competency to undertake the duties of a master mason
had, in the period over which the Schaw Statutes extend,
been placed beyond the province of Lodges and invested
in the Incorporations. In certain districts where no Incorporations existed, Companies were formed to discharge
their functions. Thus we find that on October 26th, 1636,
a convocation of master tradesmen was held at Falkland,
under the presidency of Sir Anthony Alexander, Warden
General and Master of Work. The establishment of "Companies" of not less than twenty persons, in those parts
of Scotland where no similar trade Society existed, was

recommended as a means of putting an end to the grievances which were complained of, and rules were laid down for their guidance. These Statutes were "accepted" by the Lodge of Atcheson's Haven, at a meeting held in January, 1637, also presided over by Sir Anthony Alexander, whose signature is attached to the minutes; and further approved at a conference held with the same Lodge by Henrie Alexander, who succeeded his brother as Warden General and Master of Work—in 1638. (Lyon, *Hist. L. of Edin.*, 2nd edit., 18, 91, 95.)

The most complete picture we possess of the early Masonry of Scotland is afforded by the Schaw Statutes of 1598 and 1599. These are Codes of Laws signed and promulgated by William Schaw, Master of the King's Work and General Warden of the Masons, the one directed to the craft in general, the other to the Lodge of Kilwinning. From these two codes we learn very little with regard to the entry of Apprentices—simply that in each case it was booked—but on other points they are more communicative. Thus a Master (or Fellow Craft, which was a term importing the same meaning) was to be received or admitted in the presence of six Masters and two Entered Apprentices; his name and mark were also to be booked, together with the names of those by whom he was admitted, and of his Intenders (or instructors). No one was to be admitted, according to the earlier Code, without an Essay and sufficient trial of his skill and worthiness in his vocation and craft; or, according to the latter one, without a sufficient Essay and proof of memory and art of craft. A further regulation requires an annual trial of the art of memory and science thereof, of every Fellow Craft and Apprentice, according to their vocations, under a penalty if any of them shall have lost one point thereof.

Some of the Lodges held a controlling or directing power over other Lodges in their districts. The second of the Schaw Statutes—containing fifteen clauses, the first four of which I reproduce, either wholly or in part—defines these and their rank.

"xxviii., December, 1599.

"*First.*—It is ordanit that the warden witin the bounds of Kilwynning and vther placeis subject to thair ludge salbe chosin and electit zeirlie by monyest of the Mrs voitis of the said ludge vpoun the twentie day of December and that wn the Kirk of Kilwynning as the heid and secund ludge of Scotland and yrefter that the generall warden be advertysit zeirlie quha is chosin warden of the ludge, immediatlie efter his electioun.

"*Item.*—It is thocht neidfull and expedient be my lord warden generall . . . yt ye ludge of Kilwinning secund ludge in Scotland sall haif thair warden [present] at the election of ye wardenis wtin ye bounds of ye Nether Waird of Cliddsdaill, Glasgow, Air, & bounds of Carrik, [with power to the warden and deacon of Kilwinning to convene the remaining wardens and deacons within their jurisdiction either in Kilwinning or any other part of the west of Scotland].

"*Item.*—It is thocht neidful & expedient be my lord warden generall, that Edr salbe in all tyme cuming as of befoir the first and principall ludge in Scotland, and yt Kilwynning be the secund ludge as of befoir is notourlie manifest in our awld antient writts and that Stirueling salbe the third ludge, conforme to the auld priveleges thairof.

"*Item.*—It is thocht expedient yt ye wardenis of everie ilk ludge salbe answerabel to ye presbyteryes wtin thair schirefdomes for the maissonis subiect to ye ludgeis anent all offensis ony of thame sall committ."

It may be usefully noted that all the Operative terms or expressions, which were afterwards turned to Speculative uses by the Freemasons of the South—namely, Master Mason, Fellow Craft, Entered Apprentice, and Cowan—are mentioned in the Schaw Statutes, and appear to have been in common use in Scotland from the year 1598 down to our own times.

Patrick Coipland, the Laird of Udaucht, was granted, in 1590, by James VI, the office of Warden and Justice over the Art and Craft of Masonry within the counties of

Aberdeen, Banff, and Kincardine. This appointment, however, was clearly made for purposes of a purely local character, and, without a doubt, the powers granted to Coipland were entirely subordinate to the paramount authority of the Warden General.

A more prominent holder of a similar office to that held by the Laird of Udaucht, was Sir William St. Clair of Roslin, with regard to whose family and its alleged hereditary connection with the ancient Masonry of Scotland, much disputation and not a little confusion have arisen. There are two "St. Clair" Charters, neither of which are dated, but the earlier document has been assigned on the best authority to the year 1601, and the later one to 1628. The parties to the first Charter were William Schaw, the Warden General, and the Lodges then meeting at Edinburgh, St. Andrews, Haddington, Atcheson-Haven, and Dunfermline. The second Charter bears the names of the representative Lodges at Edinburgh, Glasgow, Dundee, Stirling, Dunfermline, St. Andrews, and of the masons and other crafts at Ayr. In the first Charter, the petitioners (with the sanction of William Schaw) consent that their nominee, Sir William St. Clair, shall purchase and obtain from the King, jurisdiction over them; and in the second (William Schaw being then deceased) a renewal is sought of the previous connection, because the former "letters of protection" had been consumed by fire. The connection, real or supposed, of any previous member of the St. Clair family, with Scottish Masonry, has been examined at considerable length by Mr. D. Murray Lyon in his famous "History." To bring the story, however, within the scope of the present work, it will suffice, at this point of the narrative, to relate, that in a letter dated February 27th, 1635, Charles I instructed the Commissioners of the Exchequer to call before them Sir William St. Clair of Roslin and examine him as to his pretending "ane heritable charge over the Maissons of our said Kingdome." They were also to order "that the Maissons be examined by the Magistrates of every toun, and the Sheriffs of every schyre"

(Rogers, *Memorials of the Earls of Stirling*, 229). It would appear from the evidence that the legality of the appointment of Sir Anthony Alexander (second son of the Earl of Stirling), conjointly with Sir James Murray, as "General Surveyors and Masters of Work" in 1634, was challenged by Sir William St. Clair. The dispute seems, however, to have been amicably arranged in 1636, with the result that Sir Anthony was sustained in his high office, and succeeded in it by his brother, Henrie Alexander, in 1637.

Two of the Lodges mentioned in the Schaw Statutes (1599), those of Edinburgh and Kilwinning, and with fair probability that of Stirling—the "third ludge of Scotland" —are in existence at this day. Several Lodges also, who figure in documents of only slightly later date—for example, the St. Clair Charters of 1601 and 1628—after undergoing vicissitudes of good and bad fortune, still live on, and are surrounded by a halo of antiquity, for which a parallel will be vainly sought in any other region of the globe.

With the exception of the Lodge of Edinburgh, however, the minutes of which body extend back to July, 1599, none of the existing records of the old Scottish Lodges are of earlier date than the seventeenth century. But the documentary evidence of that period is fairly abundant, and from the materials before me, I shall, in the first instance, present the best sketch in my power of the system of Masonry prevailing in Scotland during the era to which I have last referred—namely, from the close of the sixteenth down to the dawn of the eighteenth century. The records upon which I am mainly relying are those of the Lodges at Glasgow (1620), Kilwinning (1642), Scoon and Perth (1658), Aberdeen (1670), Melrose (1674), Dunblane (1675), and Dumfries (1687), the figures within parentheses denoting the years from which they commence; together with the minutes of the Lodge of Edinburgh—of unrivalled antiquity—and the other evidence of old Masonic customs so lavishly supplied by my friend, David Murray Lyon, in the latest edition of his monumental work.

It is most probable that, down to the close of the sixteenth century, there was only a single Lodge in each town or city which, as a matter of course, possessed all the rights and privileges belonging to the mason's trade. "Not the slightest vestige of authentic evidence, however," as we are well reminded by Mr. Lyon, "has ever been adduced in support of the legends in regard to the time and place of the institution of the first Scottish Masonic Lodge." To which may be added, that, while the entire group of really ancient Lodges in the Northern Kingdom are without any documents at all approximating to the dates of their foundation, several of them have occasion to deplore, not only the loss of their oldest records, but also the loss (in a historical sense) of any old records whatsoever. The true story, therefore, of the old Scottish Lodges could only be satisfactorily related in a series of "Lodge Histories," and this, on a limited scale, was attempted in my larger work (*Hist. of F.*, ch. viii).

The Lodge of Dundee asserts a traditional antiquity of more than a thousand years. It also claims as one of its former Masters David, Earl of Huntingdon—afterwards King of Scotland—to whom is ascribed the erection of a fine old cathedral, which was partially destroyed by fire in 1841. Apart however, from these genealogical *extravaganzas*, "our lady"—*i.e.*, St. Mary's—"ludge of Dundee," referred to in an indenture of 1583, is almost certainly represented by *one* of the *two* old Lodges, Nos. 47 or 49, which (claiming the same traditional antiquity) are working side by side in the mercantile capital of Forfarshire at this day.

To the Lodge of Glasgow St. John, for a long time, was conceded (in certain districts) a singular pre-eminence, by virtue of a Charter alleged to have been granted by Malcolm III, King of Scots, so far back as the year 1057. But the earliest authentic record of the Lodge occurs in a document bearing the date of 1620, which refers to its existence in 1613. "Ancient Stirling" claims a venerable antiquity, as representing the body of Masons who were engaged in the construction of Cambuskenneth Abbey, founded by David I, 1147. But, as previously remarked, it is probably identified with the "third ludge in Scotland," referred to in the Schaw Statutes of 1599, and also with "the Ludge of Stirlinge" one of the parties to the St. Clair Charter of 1628. "The masowns of the luge"—of whose successors in an unbroken line we possibly read in the existing "Lodge" minutes of 1670—are mentioned, under the year 1483, in the Burgh Records of Aberdeen.

According to its traditional history, the Lodge of Scone (now Scoon and Perth) was erected in very ancient times by those artificers who were employed to build the Abbey, the Palace, and the other buildings which were required in this early capital of Scotland. When, however, Perth became the capital of the Kingdom, the Lodge of Scone was removed to it, and remained there, when, at the close of the fifteenth century, the seat of government was transferred to Edinburgh. Nor can the position taken up by its historian (Mr. D. Crawford Smith) be seriously impugned, that if the antiquity of the old Lodges is to be determined by the ages of the churches or buildings with which they are specially connected, then it follows that the Lodge of Scone is the oldest of the Scottish Lodges.

There was a Masonic Convention at St. Andrews, in January, 1600, summoned by order of the Warden General. Of its proceedings no record has been preserved, but from a minute of the Lodge of Edinburgh dated November 27th, 1599, we learn that the Lodge of St. Andrews was charged to attend, "and that the Maisteris of Dindie and Perth be alsua warnit to convene."

The next reference to the Lodge of Scoon and Perth occurs in a parchment writing (in the archives of the Lodge), which is headed—"Mutual Agreement of 1658," and informs us that King James the Sixth of Scotland, by his own desire, had been entered "ffrieman, meassone, and fellow craft." This statement, Mr. Crawford Smith (with a somewhat robust faith) thinks is entitled to our confidence. The King, he tells us, made a state visit to Perth on the

15th of April, 1601, and was made a Burgess at the Market Cross. It would be on this occasion, he considers, that the King, being thirty-four years of age, "was entered by his own desire."

Of the same date (1658) and in the same document is a recital that—"ffrom the Temple of temples building on this earth (ane vniforme communitie, and vvnione throughout the whole world), ffrom which temple proceided one in Kilwinning, in this our nation of Scotland. And from that of Kilwinning many moe within this Kingdome, off which ther proceided the Abbacie and Lodge of Scone . . . as the second Lodge within this nation."

No other Lodge, as we are rightly told, has such traditions as the Lodge of Kilwinning, and not the least splendid of the series, according to the Rev. W. Lee Ker, is the tradition, "believed in so far back as 1658, in which the Lodge of Perth declares that the Kilwinning temple of Free Masons was the temple which was first instituted in Scotland, and that its foundation was laid about the year 1190" (*Mother Lodge Kilwinning*, 103). The same writer assures us—"that Kilwinning Lodge is the true Mother Lodge of Scotland is not a mere legend. On the contrary, a fair reading of Schaw's Statutes shows it to be a solemn truth." In support of this view, it is contended that in the Code of 1599, the Warden General "says explicitly in his first Item, that Kilwinning was *the heid* lodge, and in the third, that for reasons of expediency this was to be changed, that henceforth the Lodge of Edinburgh was to be the principal, and Kilwinning was to be the second lodge." In other words, from "a fair reading" of the famous document of 1599, may be inferred "that it ascribes the palm of priority and original supremacy in Scotland to the Lodge of Kilwinning."

The words, however, of William Schaw, in the third Item, "that Edinburgh shall be in all time coming, *as of before*, the first and principal Lodge of Scotland," are to my mind decisive as to the ruling of the Warden General with respect to the relative precedency of the two chief

Scottish Lodges, long prior to, as well as concurrently with, the date on which it was expressed.

It is quite possible, of course, that Kilwinning may have been the seat of the first Scottish Lodge, without that old court of Operative Masonry being the supreme Lodge in Scotland. To the curious reader, however, who is desirous of considering the rival pretensions of the two leading Lodges of the world at greater length, I commend the admirable "Histories" of Mr. D. Murray Lyon and the Rev. W. Lee Ker, in each of which (though with conflicting results) the whole evidence is carefully marshalled and summed up.

The customs of the old Scottish Lodges are of interest, as being in many instances, down to a comparatively recent period, survivals of usages pre-dating the era of Grand Lodges. But in the notes which next follow I am more desirous of depicting the Masonic practices of the seventeenth than of the eighteenth century. These, indeed, are in numerous cases indistinguishable, as a number of the customs which are first disclosed in connection with the earlier, continued to exist throughout the later period, and even overlapped the century which has just passed away. But the usages of the Scottish Craft, so far as they relate either to the system of Speculative (or Symbolical) Masonry, or to the admission of non-operative members, will only be dealt with in the present section, as known to be existing in the seventeenth century. Almost immediately afterwards, there are indications from which a ritual of more elastic proportions might be inferred, but the Masonic Symbolism of North Britain, as gradually assimilated with that of the South, will in due order of time form the subject of a separate study.

There was an ancient ceremony called "Fencing the Lodge," which consisted of prayer to God, and the purging by oath of the brethren from undue partiality in the consideration of matters coming before them as courts of Operative Masonry.

In the great majority of the Lodges, the Festival of St.

John the Evangelist was kept as a day of feasting and rejoicing. Wardens (except in the district of Kilwinning) were chosen on that date, and in numerous instances there was no other meeting in the year. At Melrose (1674) and other masonic centres, neither apprentices nor fellow crafts were to be received, "bot on Saint John's day."

Banquets, at the expense of newcomers, together with the practice of exacting from them gloves (or glove money), otherwise called "Clothing the Lodge," were in vogue at the close of the sixteenth, and the customs lingered until the second half of the eighteenth century.

The Schaw Statutes tell us that Oaths were administered to the masons. One, the "Great Oath," apparently at their entry; and the other, "the Oath of Fidelity," at intervals of a year; also, that no apprentice could be admitted a fellow craft, without an Essay (or masterpiece), "and sufficient trial of his skill and worthiness in his vocation and craft." It was the duty of his Intender to prepare and instruct the apprentice preparatory to passing. Examinations of the last "entered apprentices and others," to ascertain what progress they had made under their respective Intenders, continued to take place in the Lodge of Kelso on St. John's day, until 1741, and probably later.

The same Statutes ordain that a Warden shall rule each Lodge, and this regulation was carried out by the Lodge of Edinburgh in 1598, though in the following year the Deacon sat as President, with the Warden as Treasurer. The Deacon was the chief officer at Kilwinning in 1643, and at Haddington in 1697, while the Scone and Perth (1658), Aberdeen (1670), Melrose (1675), and Dunblane (1696) Lodges were in each instance ruled by the Master Mason.

Versions of the old Manuscript Constitutions, transcribed during the seventeenth century, are in the possession of the Lodges of Kilwinning, Stirling, Aberdeen, Melrose, and Dumfries. The Kilwinning MS. is in the handwriting of the Clerk of the Lodge of Edinburgh, and was written about the year 1665. In the early part of the eighteenth century it was a custom of the Lodge of Kilwinning to sell to Lodges receiving its charters copies of this document, which was termed "the old buik." Whether, indeed, the old Constitutions of the Freemasons fulfilled the same purpose in North and South Britain is indeterminable, but "there is no version known which can fairly be described as of purely Scottish origin, apart from exceptional, fanciful, and local additions, which do not materially affect the legitimate text" (Hughan, *O.C.*, 55).

"That Masonic Initiation was formerly a ceremony of great simplicity," observes Mr. Lyon, "may be inferred from the curtness of the Warden General's 'item' on the subject (1598), and also from the fact that a century after the promulgation of the Schaw Statutes, the MASON WORD was wont occasionally to be imparted by individual Brethren in a ceremony extemporized according to the ability of the initiator. The Word is the only secret that is ever alluded to in the minutes of Mary's Chapel, or in those of Kilwinning, Atcheson's-Haven, or Dunblane, or any other that we have examined of a date prior to the erection of the Grand Lodge. Further:—If the communication by Mason Lodges of secret words or signs constituted a *degree*—then there was, under the purely Operative régime, only one known to Scottish Lodges, viz., that in which, under an oath, apprentices obtained a knowledge of the Mason Word, and all that was implied in the expression" (*Hist. L. of Edinburgh*, 22).

According to a diarist of the seventeenth century, at the sitting of the Assembly (or Synod) in 1649, "Ther was something spoken anent the meason word, which was recommended to the severall presbytries for tryall thereof" (*Chronicle of Fife*, 9).

A little later we meet with the case of the Rev. James Ainslie, to whom, objection having been taken because he was a Freemason, the presbytery of Kelso—February 24th, 1652—expressed their belief "that there is neither sinne nor scandale in that word, because in the purest tymes of this Kirke, maisons haveing that word have been ministers" (*ante*, 111).

What the old Scottish Mason Word was, however, remains a mystery, and as the historians of the Craft are silent on this subject, the remarks of two writers, who were not of the Fraternity, may interest if they fail to convince.

Under the date of (about) 1678, the Rev. George Hickes, afterwards Dean of Worcester, writes:—"Hence I went to Halbertshire. This is a strong high tower built by the Laird of Roslin in King James the 5th time. The Lairds of Roslin have been great architects and patrons of building for these many generations. They are obliged to receive the Mason's word, which is a secret signall masons have thro'out the world to know one another by. They alledge 'tis as old as since Babel, when they could not understand one another, and they conversed by signs. Others would have it no older than Solomon. However it is, he that hath it will bring his brother mason to him without calling to him or you perceiving of the signe" (*Hist. MSS. Comm.*, xiii, 56).

I shall next quote from the "*Secret Commonwealth. . . .* By Mr. Robert Kirk, Minister at Aberfoil, 1691." After pointing our several mysteries, the Author observes (p. 64):—"Besides these I have found fyve Curiosities in Scotland, not much observ'd to be elsewhere. . . . 2. The Mason Word, which tho some make a Misterie of it, I will not conceal a little of what I know. It is lyke a Rabbinnical Tradition, in way of comment on Jachin and Boaz, the two Pillars erected in Solomon's Temple (1 Kings, vii, 21), with ane Addition of some secret signe delyvered from Hand to Hand, by which they know and become familiar one with another."

At Aberdeen it was ordained by the "Lawes and Statutes" of 1670, that certain privileged persons were to have the benefit of the Mason Word, free of all dues, save for the box, the mark, the banquet, and the pint of wine. Also—"We ordaine that no Lodge be holden within a dwelling house where there is people living in it, but in the open fields, except it be ill weather, and then let a house be chosen that no person shall heir or sie us.

"We ordaine lykewayes that all entering prentieses be

entered in our antient out-field Lodge, in the mearnes in the Parish of Negg, at the Stonnies at the poynt of the Ness."

Irregular "Makings" continued to disfigure the practice of Scottish Masonry, not only during the seventeenth, but until the second decade of the nineteenth century. The minutes of the Lodge of Edinburgh record "a great abuse" committed by John Fulltoun in 1679, who is charged with having taken upon himself "to passe and enter severall gentlemen without licence or commission from this place." Initiations, nevertheless, conducted without the precincts of the Lodge were subsequently freely ratified by "Mother Kilwinning," down to the middle of the eighteenth century, and by one of her daughter Lodges (conformably with rules enacted in 1765), members residing more than three miles from the place "where the box is kept," were permitted "to enter persons to the Lodge," a practice, "in the observance of which one Mason could, unaided, make another, indicating," to adopt the words of Mr. Lyon— "either the presence of a ritual of less elaborate proportions than that now in use, or a total indifference to uniformity in imparting to novitiates the secrets of the Craft."

The issuing by private Lodges of commissions, or, as they were afterwards termed, "dispensations," was also an evil of great magnitude, and led to frequent complaints with regard to the practice of brethren traversing the country and picking up what members they could for their own Lodges, to the detriment of those "locally situated."

The erection of branch Lodges by "dispensation" became so popular in Ayrshire, that in 1807 the villages of Monkton and Prestwick could boast, the former of two and the latter of one, each having its staff of officials apart from those of the Mother Lodge.

"William Schaw," observes Mr. Lyon, "in his ordinance for the reconstruction and government of the Scottish Lodges, made no provision for the admission of Theoretical Masons; yet in 1600, eighteen months subsequent to the issuing of his famous Statutes, we find him, with one such (the Laird of Auchinleck) at his elbow, engaged, like himself, in investigating and giving judgment in a breach of Masonic law on the part of the Warden of the Lodge of Edinburgh—a circumstance which establishes the fact that in the sixteenth century the membership of the Mason Lodges was not exclusively Operative" (*Hist. L. of Edin.* 85). John Boswell of Auchinleck, who was present at this meeting of the Lodge of Edinburgh (Mary's Chapel), on the 8th of June, 1600, appears to have taken part in its deliberations, and to have acquiesced in its decision. Like the Operative members present, he attested the minutes by his mark.

In the opinion of Mr. Lyon, "the grafting of the non-professional element on to the stem of the Operative system of Masonry had its commencement in Scotland probably about the period of the Reformation"—a view which is strikingly in accord with that of Mr. Bain, and gains additional strength from the declaration of the Kelso presbytery in 1652 (*ante*, 111, 182).

Besides the name of the Laird of Auchinleck, those of many other persons of distinction were inscribed on the roll of Mary's Chapel. Viscount Canada, eldest son of the Earl of Stirling, was admitted into the Lodge of Edinburgh, as a fellow of craft, conjointly with his brother, Sir Anthony Alexander, Master of Work to the King, and Sir Alexander Strachan, on the 3rd of July, 1634.

Henrie Alexander—third son of the first Earl of Stirling—who succeeded his brother Anthony as General Warden and Master of Work to the King, was admitted a fellow and brother in 1638. Two years later Alexander Hamilton, General of Artillery, was received as a fellow and "Mr." of the Mason Craft. The entries relating to the admissions of those candidates of gentle birth, though varying somewhat in form, were evidently intended to convey the same meaning, and the actual Masonic status, therefore, of General Hamilton, who was enrolled as a fellow and master, differed in no respect whatsoever from those of the other Speculative members, his seniors in the Lodge, who had been received as fellows or brothers of the craft.

Of forty-nine fellow crafts (or master masons) who belonged to the Lodge of Aberdeen in 1670—when the records commence—less than a quarter were of the Masons' trade. Among the members were clergymen, surgeons, merchants, and three noblemen, one of whom—Gilbert, tenth Earl of Errol—was then an old man, and presumably, therefore, must have joined the Society at a much earlier date.

John, seventh Earl of Cassillis, while only an apprentice, was elected Deacon or head of the Lodge of Kilwinning, in 1672. His immediate successors in that office were Sir Alexander Cunninghan, and Alexander, eighth Earl of Eglinton. In 1678 Lord William Cochrane (son of the Earl of Dundonald) was a warden.

At Dunblane the earliest records show that the Operative masons were in the minority. In 1696, when the minutes begin, William, second Viscount Strathallan, was the President (or "Master Mason"), Alexander Drummond of Balhaolie, the Warden, and John Cameron of Lochiel a member of the Lodge.

A common name in use to describe the non-operatives —generally persons of quality—who were admitted into the Scottish Lodges during the seventeenth century, was Geomatics; while the masons by trade were called Domatics. The former were also known as Gentlemen Masons, Theorical Masons, Architect Masons, and Honorary Members (Lyon, 87).

It should be recorded, that the membership of the Lodge of Glasgow, unlike that of other pre-eighteenth century Lodges, was exclusively Operative, and, though doubtless giving the Mason Word to Entered Apprentices, none were recognized as members until they had joined the Incorporation, which was composed of Mason Burgesses.

Before passing away from the seventeenth century, it will be convenient if I refer to a remark on an earlier page (124)

—"That in Irish academical circles Freemasonry was well known before the landing of William of Orange at Carrick Fergus in 1690."

Of the Freemasonry existing in Ireland before the era of Grand Lodges, merely a passing glance is afforded, and the glimpse we obtain of it is supplied by Dr. Chetwode Crawley in an introductory chapter to a recent Masonic work. He tells us that a custom prevailed during the seventeenth century in certain Universities of allowing a representative of the undergraduates to make a satirical speech, called a Tripos, at the annual meeting for conferring degrees. At Trinity College, Dublin, the "Tripos" (or speech) delivered, July 11th, 1688, amounts, in fact, to an attack on the authorities of the University, by the use of illustrations drawn from the Freemasonry of the day. For example:—

"It was lately ordered that for the honour and dignity of the University there should be introduced a Society of Freemasons, consisting of gentlemen, mechanics, porters, parsons, tinkers, freshmen [and others], who shall bind themselves by an oath never to discover their mighty no-secret; and to relieve . . . distressed brethren they meet with, after the example of the Fraternity of Freemasons in and about Trinity College, by whom a collection was lately made for a reduced Brother, who received [among other gifts]: 'From Sir Warren, for being Free-masonized the new way, five shillings.' "

The "Speech," which after this is continued in the Latin tongue, goes on to relate that the recipient of the "Collection" (to quote from the translation given by Dr. Crawley) then proceeded into the library of the University, where, anatomized and stuffed, stood the carcase of one Ridley, supposed to have been an informer against the Irish priests, upon whose remains he discovered the Freemasons' Mark (*privatum Fraternitatis notavit signum*).

Other passages in the "Speech" are not without significance to students of the Craft, but the foregoing will sufficiently "demonstrate," to use the words of Dr. Crawley,

"That the Fraternity of Freemasons was so well known in 1688, that a popular orator could count on his audience catching up allusions to the prominent characteristics of the Craft. The speaker was addressing a mixed assemblage of University men and well-to-do citizens, interspersed with ladies and men of fashion, who had come together to witness the chief University function of the year. His use of the theme proves that the Freemasonry known to him and his audience was conspicuous for its secrecy and for its benevolence. We can fairly deduce, too, that membership of the Craft was not confined to Operatives, or to any one class. Otherwise the catalogue of incongruous callings would be without point." (H. Sadler, *Mas. Repr. and Hist. Rev.*, Introd., xviii—xxv).

The exact period of the *eighteenth* century at which the evidence points with precision to the existence, in Scottish Masonry, of a plurality of degrees, cannot be affirmed. There is no room for doubt that the more ornate ritual of the English craft had penetrated into Scotland before the year 1730, and in the records of several Lodges there are entries from which it has been inferred that an alteration in the original simplicity of the old Scottish ceremonial may possibly have taken place at a much earlier date.

In 1701 an apprentice at Aberdeen was sworn "by the points," and, according to the Laws of 1670, which may possibly be based on English originals, at the "entering of everie entered prenteise," the "Measson Charter"—a form of the Manuscript Constitutions still in the possession of the Lodge of Aberdeen—was to be read to him. It is also worthy of our attention, that in these Statutes of 1670 there is the only allusion—ante-dating the era of Grand Lodges—to the practice of Lodges being held, and apprentices entered, in the open fields, of which an echo (or survival) is to found in the catechisms (or spurious rituals) which were extensively manufactured in the third decade of the eighteenth century.

In the Haughfoot minutes of 1702 we meet with the

following:—"Of entrie as the apprentice did, leaving out (the common judge). They then whisper the word as before, and the Master grips his hand in the ordinary way." From this may be inferred that the word was *then* accompanied by a grip, and the expressions used may even justify a belief that a *ceremony* of passing was practised by certain Scottish Lodges at that time. On St. John's day, 1708, two apprentices were admitted into the Lodge at Haughfoot, and received the word "in common form."

The Grand Lodge of England was established in 1717, and published its first printed *Book of Constitutions* in 1723. These notable events will form the subject of a separate study, but for the convenience of the reader it will be best if I first of all complete my sketch of the early Masonry of Scotland, which I shall bring down to the year 1751, combining therewith an account of the leading Masonic occurrences in the British Isles—these pertaining to the *original* jurisdiction of the Grand Lodge of England alone excepted—from the period immediately succeeding the creation of a governing body of Speculative (or Symbolical) Masons in 1717, down to that at which the system of "Grand Lodges," in the only countries wherein Freemasonry was of native growth, may be said to have become complete.

The minutes of the Lodge of Dunblane—under December 27th, 1720—record:—"Compeared John Gillespie, who was entered on the 24th instant, and after examination was duely passt from the Square to the Compass, and from an Entered Prentice to a Fellow of Craft." A copy of Dr. Anderson's *Book of Constitutions* was presented to the Lodge in September, 1723; and on December 27th, 1729, it was reported of two entered apprentices from the Lodge of Kilwinning, "that they had a competent knowledge of the *Secrets* of the MASON WORD" (Lyon, 444).

I shall next glean from the records of the Lodge of Edinburgh, where the following occurs:—

"Att Maries Chapell the 24 of August 1721 years— James Wattson, present deacon of the Masons of Edinr.,

Preses. The which day Doctor John Theophilus Desaguliers. . . late Generall Master of the Mason Lodges
in England, being in town and desirous to have a conference with the Deacon, Warden, and Master Masons of
Edinr., which was accordingly granted, and finding him
duly qualified in all points of Masonry, they received him
as a Brother into their Societie. Likeas, upon the 25th
day of the sd moneth, the Deacons . . . and other members
. . . together with the sd Doctor Desaguliers, haveing mett
att Maries Chapell. . . . John Campbell Esqr., Lord
Provost of Edbr. [and other] honourable persons were
admitted and received Entered Apprentices and Fellow-
Crafts accordingly" (*ibid.*, 611).

Relying on the above, Mr. Lyon has no hesitation in
ascribing Scotland's acquaintance with, and subsequent
adoption of, English Symbolical Masonry to the conference
which Dr. Desaguliers held with the Lodge of Edinburgh
in August, 1721.

According to Dr. Chetwode Crawley, with whom I am
wholly in accord, and whose words I reproduce:—"All
Freemasonry in existence to-day can be traced, through
one channel or another, to the Grand Lodge of England.
This general statement is particularly true of IRELAND.
The Freemasonry of Ireland in the days immediately
succeeding the erection of the Grand Lodge for London
and Westminster seems rather a part than a counterpart of
the new system. In less than eight years from the foundation of the Premier Grand Lodge, the Sister Grand Lodge
of Ireland stands forth as the compeer of the Grand Lodge
of England, to which alone it owes precedence."

To the research of the same talented writer we are
indebted for the fact that in 1725 the Grand Lodge of
Ireland was in existence in Dublin. On St. John's Day
(in Harvest) of that year, the Earl of Rosse was elected
Grand Master, and "the Masters and Wardens of the Six
Lodges of Gentlemen FREE MASONS" took part in the
proceedings. "The terms in which the ceremony is

Kingston G. M.

Netterville Dy. G. M.

No. (1)

By the Right Worshipful and Right Honourable Lord K I N G S T O N, Grand Master of all the Lodges of Free Masons in the Kingdom of *IRELAND*, the Right Honourable the Lord *Netterville*, Deputy Grand Master, the Honourable *William Ponsonby* and *Dillon Pollard Hamson*, Esquires, Grand Wardens.

WHEREAS Our Trusty and Well-beloved Brothers, *John Ireke and Thomas Cooke Esqrs James Condon, and Florence McCarthy* have besought Us, that We would be pleas'd to Erect a Lodge of Free Masons in the *Town of Michelito* and at of such Persons, who by their Knowledge and Skill in Masonry, may contribute to the well Being and Advancement thereof. We therefore duly weighing the Premisses, and having nothing more at Heart, than the Prosperity and true Advancement of Masonry, and reposing special Trust of Confidence in Our Trusty and Well-beloved Brothers, the said *John Ireke, Tho Ereol James Condon, Florence McArthy* — of whose Abilities and Knowledge in Masonry, We are satisfied, Do, by these PRESENTS, of Our certain Knowledge, and meer Motion, Create, Authorize, and Constitute the said *W. 1. 4th th. to be Mar: of the D Lsgn the D Ireke a Cooke*, to be Masters and Wardens of a Lodge of Free and Accepted Masons, to be held by them and their Successors lawfully admitted in the said *Town of York*; for ever. A N D We do hereby Give and Grant unto the said *Master a Junior Warden of the use of the Worshipfull bre in* and their Successors, full Power and lawful Authority from Time to Time to proceed to Election of new Master and Wardens, and to make such Laws, Rules, and Orders, as they from Time to Time shall think Proper and Convenient for the well Being and Ordering of the said Lodge, referring to Our Selves and Our Successors, Grand Masters and Grand Wardens of *IRELAND*, the sole Right of deciding all Differences which shall be brought by Appeal before Us and Our Successors, Grand Masters or Grand Wardens of *IRELAND* IN WITNESS whereof, We have hereunto set our Hands and Seal *of office this first* Day of *February* in the Year of our Lord God 1731 and in the Year of Masonry, 5731

Intratur per — — — — Tho Griffith Secretary

THE OLDEST EXTANT WARRANT IN THE WORLD 1731
No. 1 OF IRELAND. (Size of original, 11 inches by 8)

This Wart. So Long Missing thank god is Received & found the same On record, tho: — we Desire Under No 5 —

May the 2. 1754 —

Edie in

This is to certify that this Warrant No 1 granted to be held in the Town of Mitchelstown & many years dormant. has been revived by the Grand Lodge of Ireland & is hereby transferred to be held in future in the City of Cork by the present Master & wardens and their Successors for ever. Given under my hand in Provincial Grand Lodge in the City of Cork this 10th Day of August 1776 and of Masonry 5776 .. — — — Robert Davies P.G. M. M.

(ENDORSEMENTS ON THE BACK OF THE WARRANT)

described," remarks Dr. Crawley, "leave little room for doubt that the Grand Lodge was no sudden creation, but had been then in existence long enough to develop a complete organization of Grand Officers, with subordinate Lodges under its jurisdiction" (*Cæmentaria Hibernica*, ii). On December 2nd, 1725, a charter was granted by the Corporation of Cork to "the Master, Wardens, and Society of Free Masons, according to their petition." At the ensuing Festival of St. John—December 27th—a Grand Master and other officers were elected by the Freemasons of York; and Sir Thomas Prendergast, Senior Grand Warden of Ireland (under the Earl of Rosse), was appointed Junior Grand Warden of the Grand Lodge in London on the same date.

The records of the Grand Lodge of Munster begin on December 27th, 1726, a day which is also associated with the remarkable "Speech" of Dr. Francis Drake (author of *Eboracum*), the Junior Grand Warden of York. With the proceedings of a private Lodge, those of the Grand Lodge of Munster are intermixed, but it seems on the whole highly probable that the only distinction was in name, and that the membership was one and the same.

From the famous "Speech" delivered at York by Dr. Drake, on St. John's day (in Winter), 1726, I extract the following:—"*Edwin*, the first Christian King of the *Northumbers*, about the six hundredth year after *Christ*, and who laid the Foundation of our Cathedral, sat as Grand Master. This is sufficient to make us dispute the superiority with the Lodges at *London*. But as nought of that kind ought to be amongst so amicable a fraternity, we are content they enjoy the Title of Grand Master of *England*; but the *Totius Angliæ* we claim as an undoubted right." A further passage in the oration will bear quotation as being of great importance in the general history of Freemasonry. Drake speaks of "𝕰.𝕻.𝕱.𝕮. and 𝕸.𝕸.," meaning, no doubt, Entered Apprentices, Fellow Crafts, and Master Masons, and this is the earliest of all known references to the degrees of these names, from which may be inferred that they were wrought with the sanction, direct or implied, of a Grand Lodge. Upon this point, however, the York records down to the first period of somnolency of the Grand Lodge (1730) throw no light. As in earlier days, new comers continued to be "sworn and admitted" (*ante*, 122), but of the form (or forms) of their reception, we are left without a sufficiency of materials to construct even a plausible conjecture.

By the General Regulations of the Grand Lodge of Munster, "made at a Grand Lodge held in Corke, on St. John ye Evangelist's day, 1728," it was ordained that every Lodge should provide itself with a copy of Dr. Anderson's "Constitutions" of 1723.

There is no list of the Officers of the Grand Lodge of Ireland for the years 1726-29, but the Earl of Rosse, who was Grand Master in 1725, filled the same position in 1730. In the latter year John Pennell, Grand Secretary, published *The Constitutions of the* [Irish] *Free Masons*. This work is almost an exact counterpart of the English original, and the slight differences which exist are mainly due to the compilation of John Pennell being intermediate in point of date between Dr. Anderson's "Constitutions" of 1723 and 1738.

In 1731 the Grand Lodge of Munster passed under the sway of James, fourth Lord Kingston (who had been Grand Master of England in 1729), and during the same year (1731) this nobleman was elected to the chair of the Grand Lodge of Ireland, in connection with what appears to have been a re-organization of the latter body. The Grand Lodge of Munster is heard of no more, and from 1731 to the present date the succession of the Grand Officers of the Grand Lodge of Ireland is plain and distinct. The first Warrant of Constitution ever issued by a Grand Lodge was granted to the First Lodge of Ireland in 1731. In 1732 it was ordered by the Grand Lodge that "true and perfect Warrants should be taken out by all the Irish Lodges," and in the same year the first of a long series of ambulatory Warrants—to accompany Regiments on their tours of service—was granted to the second battalion of the 1st Foot.

In resuming the thread of SCOTTISH Masonic history, I shall do so by quoting in the first instance from an anonymous tract published at the Irish capital in December, 1731, which was included in the Dublin edition of Dean Swift's Complete Works (1760-69), but has been silently omitted from all those of subsequent date. It bears the name of *A Letter from the Grand Mistress of the Free-Masons*, and, as my friend Dr. Chetwode Crawley well observes, "it has no exact counterpart in the literature of the Craft." The pamphlet has many features of interest, but I am here concerned with the following passage only, which since the date of publication of the *Grand Mistress* was announced in *Cæmentaria Hibernica* (iii, pref. 2), it has become quite clear, could not have been inspired by, but must have been anticipatory of, expressions of a similar and almost identical kind, which are to be met with in the Chevalier Ramsay's "epoch-marking" Orations of 1737:—

"The famous old *Scottish Lodge* of *Kilwinnin*, of which all the Kings in *Scotland* have been, from Time to Time, Grand Masters without Interruption, down from the days of *Fergus*, who reigned there more than 1000 Years ago, long before the Knights of *St. John* of *Jerusalem*, or the Knights of *Malta*, to which two *Lodges* I must, nevertheless, allow the Honour of having adorned the antient *Jewish* and *Pagan Masonry* with many Religious and Christian Rules."

Mr. Lyon tells us that "the minutes of Canongate Kilwinning contain the earliest Scottish record extant of the admission of a Master Mason under the modern Masonic Constitution. This occurred on the 31st of March, 1735." The third degree is not referred to in the records of the Lodge of Kilwinning until 1736, nor in those of the Lodge of Edinburgh until 1738. The historian of Scottish Masonry is, however, of opinion, "That the degree in question was first practised north of the Tweed by the Edinburgh Kilwinning Scots Arms. This, the first purely Speculative (Scottish) Lodge, was constituted in 1729. Its original members were all Theoretical Masons, and the Earls of

Crawfurd, Kilmarnock, Cromarty, and Home; the Lords
Colville, Erskine, and Garlies, together with Sir Alexander
Hope of Kerse, were on the roll in 1736." (*Hist. L. of Edin.*,
190, 233.)

On the 15th of October, 1736, a form of circular was
agreed upon, by four (out of the six) Lodges "in and about
Edinburgh," to be sent to all the Scottish Lodges, inviting
their attendance either in person or by proxy, for the purpose
of electing a Grand Master. The election took place in
Mary's Chapel on Tuesday, November 30th, and thirty-
three of the hundred or more Lodges that had been invited
were found to be represented. No amendments having
been offered to the form of procedure, or to the draft of the
constitution of the Grand Lodge, a document was tendered
by the Laird of Roslin, and read to the meeting. In this
writing Mr. William St. Clair renounced any hereditary
claims he might possess "to be patron, protector, judge,
or master of the Masons in Scotland," and "so fascinated
do the brethren seem to have been with the apparent
magnanimity, disinterestedness, and zeal for the order
displayed in his 'Resignation,' that the success of the
scheme for his election was complete—the Deed was accepted,
and with a unanimity that must have been grateful to the
Lodge [Canongate Kilwinning], at whose instance it had
been drawn, the abdication of an obsolete office in Operative
Masonry was made the ground of St. Clair being chosen
to fill the post of first Grand Master in the Scottish Grand
Lodge of Speculative Masons." (Lyon, *ut supra*, 188.)

For a great many years, however, the Grand Lodge of
Scotland stood on a very anomalous footing with regard to
the ancient Lodges in that kingdom. There were several
Lodges which never joined the Grand Lodge at all, while
others did so and retired, though of the latter some renewed
their allegiance. For example, the Haughfoot Lodge (1702)
never resigned its independence; Glasgow St. John (1628)
only did so in 1850; and the Lodge of Melrose (1674) until
so late a date as 1891 refused to recognize any superior
authority to its own. The "Company of Atcheson Haven"

(1601-2) was struck off the roll in 1737, and only readmitted into the fold in 1814. "The Ancient Lodge, Dundee" (1628), appears not to have definitely joined the new organization until 1745, while other Lodges accepted Charters of Confirmation in the following order:—Dumfries Kilwinning (1687), 1750; St. John's, Kelso (1701), 1754; St. Ninian's, Brechin (1714), 1756; the Lodge of Dunblane (1696), 1760; St. John, Jedburgh (1730), in 1767. The Lodge of Scoon and Perth (1658), which received a charter of confirmation in 1742, was, in 1807, "upon a memorial to that effect, readmitted into the bosom of the Grand Lodge, from which for some years past she had been estranged."

There were other old Lodges which seceded (for longer or shorter periods) from the Grand Lodge, notably "Mother Kilwinning," and the Lodge of Edinburgh (Mary's Chapel), the cause of the schism being in either instance the same, namely, a jealousy of the one at the other being placed at the head of the roll.

In November, 1737, it was resolved that all the Lodges holding of the Grand Lodge should be enrolled according to their seniority, which should be determined from the authentic documents they produced, and in accordance with this principle (the existence of the further documentary evidence afterwards supplied by the earliest records of the Lodge of Scoon and Perth, and the Schaw Statutes of 1599, being at that time unsuspected), the first place on the roll was assigned to Mary's Chapel and the second to Kilwinning.

The brilliant oration of Andrew Michael (usually styled the "Chevalier" Ramsay), a native of Ayr, near Kilwinning, though probably unheard of in Scotland until several years after its delivery at Paris in 1737, has been commonly associated with the rise of a spurious tradition awarding the palm of priority over all the other Scottish Lodges to the Lodge of Kilwinning, by which all genuine Masonic tradition of a cognate character was swept away. From the "Oration" I extract the following:—"At the time of the Crusades in Palestine many princes, lords, and citizens associated themselves. . . . They agreed upon several ancient signs and symbolic words. . . . Some time afterwards our Order formed an intimate union with the Knights of St. John of Jerusalem. From that time our Lodges took the name of Lodges of St. John. This union was made after the example set by the Israelites when they erected the second Temple, who, while they handled the trowel and mortar with one hand, in the other held the sword and buckler.

"At the time of the last Crusades many Lodges were already erected in Germany, Italy, Spain, France, and from thence in Scotland, because of the close alliance between the French and the Scotch. James, Lord Steward of Scotland, was Grand Master of a Lodge established at Kilwinning, in the West of Scotland, MCCLXXXVI, shortly after the death of Alexander III, King of France, and one year before John Baliol mounted the throne. This lord received as Freemasons into his Lodge the Earls of Gloucester and Ulster, the one English, the other Irish."

With the foregoing should be compared the allusions to "The famous old *Scottish Lodge of Kilwinin*," and "the Knights of St. *John* at *Jerusalem*," which were printed at Dublin in 1731 (*ante*, 193).

The two passages I have given from Ramsay's celebrated Speech, and particularly the last one, have been turned to strange uses by the inventors of so-called "Scottish Rites" ——which were and are mere excrescences on the body of Pure and Ancient Masonry, as will be shown at a later stage. In connection, however, with the Lodge of Kilwinning, the reader (at this point) is requested to take note, that in the light of the evidence supplied by the Minute of 1658 (Scoon and Perth), and the pamphlet of 1731 ("*Letter from the Grand Mistress*"), there is no room for doubt that a traditional belief in the pre-eminence of "Mother Kilwinning" over the other Scottish Lodges must have extensively prevailed for some time before it received the *imprimatur* of Andrew Michael Ramsay, and passed into general acceptance as a cardinal feature of the remarkable "Oration" delivered by him in 1737.

A second edition of the English *Book of Constitutions* (to be presently noticed in more detail) was published in 1738. From its pages I extract the following:—"The *old Lodge* at YORK CITY, and the *Lodges* of SCOTLAND, IRELAND, FRANCE, and ITALY, affecting Independency, are under their own *Grand Masters*, though they have the same *Constitutions, Charges, Regulations*, etc., for substance, with their Brethren of *England*."

I shall next proceed with the histories of the Grand Lodges of Scotland and Ireland down to the close of the first and slightly overlapping the second half of the eighteenth century. During the whole of this period "The Old Lodge at York City" remained in a state of tranquil repose, and its temporary revival will be noticed in due chronological sequence when the annals of the Grand Lodge of England have been incorporated with the general narrative and brought down to the year 1761.

In the Grand Lodge of SCOTLAND, during the year 1740, the opening of a correspondence with the Grand Lodge of England was proposed and unanimously agreed to. In 1743, at the recommendation of the Earl of Kilmarnock, Grand Master, the first Military Lodge (under the Grand Lodge) was erected, the petitioners all belonging to "Colonel Lees' regiment," afterwards the 55th Foot.

During the same year (1743) the Lodge of Kilwinning, discontented with its secondary rank, resumed its independence, and for well-nigh seventy years continued to exist as an independent Grand Body, dividing with the Grand Lodge of Scotland the privilege of constituting Lodges in North Britain, as well as in places beyond the seas. About seventy "Kilwinning Charters" are supposed to have been issued down to the year 1803, but all traces of the greater number of them have disappeared. Many of the Lodges so established superadded the name of Kilwinning to that of the town or place where they carried on their work, but this compound title is by no means distinctive of the bodies so created, as the practice was also a common one among the Lodges erected by the Grand

Lodge, without their having any connection with the present No. O.

In 1745 the Associate Synod sought to disturb the peace of the fraternity, and eventually drew up a list of foolish questions which they required every Kirk-session to put to those under their charge. In other words, "A Synod of Scotch Dissenters attempted to compel the Free Masons of their congregations to give them an account of those mysteries and ceremonies which their avarice or fear hindered them from obtaining by a regular initiation" (A. Lawrie, *Hist. of F. in Scotl.*, 133). The Grand Lodge of Scotland did not take the slightest notice of these proceedings, and it is satisfactory to state that, notwithstanding persecution, and other obstacles, Freemasonry has ever steadily progressed in North Britain, and, as it has hitherto been, so is it justly held in the highest esteem.

Between 1745 and 1751 there is, in Scottish Masonry, very little, except the succession of Grand Masters, to record. The third Earl of Cromarty, who succeeded William St. Clair of Roslin, in 1737, was followed at yearly intervals in the chair of the Grand Lodge by eight other noblemen of the same rank, the last of whom—the sixth Earl of Buchan—was elected in 1745. Alexander, tenth Earl of Eglinton (a former Master of the Lodge of Kilwinning), was at the head of the Scottish Craft in 1750, and James, Lord Boyd (afterwards thirteenth Earl of Errol), eldest son of the last Earl of Kilmarnock, in 1751.

In 1740, under the Grand Lodge of IRELAND, as the Masons of that country still showed a want of alacrity in applying for what may be termed "Charters of Confirmation," the decree of 1732 was re-enacted, but in more peremptory terms:—"Such Lodges as have not already taken out Warrants are ordered to apply for them to John Baldwin, Esq., Secretary to Grand Lodge, or they will be proceeded against as Rebel Masons."

The next event of importance was the promulgation of the Irish Regulations of 1741, which are a virtual reproduction of Dr. Anderson's second *Book of Constitutions*, published in 1738. "The obvious explanation seems to be," remarks Dr. Crawley, "that the relations between the two organisations was such that, when the Grand Lodge of England adopted a new and expanded code, the Grand Lodge of Ireland held the code to be equally binding on that part of the Fraternity that happened to lie on this side of the Channel" (*Cæm. Hib.*, 11, 17).

To the research of the same diligent antiquary, we are indebted for the earliest known reference to the ROYAL ARCH. It occurs in a contemporary account of the proceedings of a Lodge at Youghall (No. 21) in 1743. The members walked in procession, and preceding the Master was—

"The Royal Arch carried by two Excellent Masons."

The next notice of the Degree in question will be found in Dr. Dassigny's SERIOUS *and* IMPARTIAL ENQUIRY *into the cause of the present Decay of* FREE-MASONRY *in the* KINGDOM *of* IRELAND, which, together with the General Regulations of the Grand Lodge, "Pursuant to the *English* Constitutions, approved of on the 24th of June, 1741," was printed at Dublin in 1744.

The *Enquiry* and the *Regulations* are not, however, two separate pamphlets bound up together, but form one homogeneous volume, the pagination running continuously throughout.

Dr. Dassigny tells us of the existence of an Assembly of Royal Arch Masons at York—from which city the degree was introduced into Dublin; that it was known and practised in London "some small space before"; and that the members thereof were "an organis'd body of men who have passed the chair."

The *Subscribers' Names* are printed in the volume, and among them are those of three women, one of which, the name of the Hon. Mrs. Aldworth, following that of Lord Allen, the Grand Master, occupies the second place on the list. The romantic story of this lady's initiation into Masonry when a girl of tender years has passed into general acceptance. Readers of history will, however, remember that the author of the famous *Decline and Fall of the Roman Empire* lays it down as a canon of criticism, that if a story is started long after the date of its alleged occurrence, and if it had not been heard of by any contemporary, it may be put down as a mere invention. In the case before us, the alleged initiation of the "Lady Freemason" derives no proof whatever from the evidence of contemporary witnesses, and the whole story hangs on the credibility which should be attached to a family tradition, *which was not recorded until a century after the event which is supposed to have given it birth.* [I differ from Mr. Gould over this matter. It was certainly believed by my friend Dr. Chetwode Crawley, who was the most careful and learned historian of Irish Freemasonry, and in my "Irish Master-Mason's Handbook" I have quoted, by his advice, Mr. E. Conder's version from *Ars Quatuor Coronatorum*, 1895, Pt. i.—F.J.W.C.]

Edward Spratt, Grand Secretary, author of the *General Regulations* of 1741 (printed in 1744), followed up that work by bringing out, in 1751, *The New Book of Constitutions, collected from the Book of Constitutions, Published in England, in the year* 1738. Both these compilations were adapted from the English original and were avowedly taken from Dr. Anderson's edition of 1738.

The Irish "Constitutions" of 1751 are dedicated to Lord Kingsborough, and in committing the "sheets" to the "Protection and Patronage" of that nobleman, Edward Spratt adds—"Not in Quality of an Author, a task I am in every way unequal to, but only as a faithful Editor, and Transcriber of the works of our learned and ingenious brother, *James Anderson*, D.D., dedicated to his Royal Highness, *Frederick*, Prince of Wales."

I must now pick up the thread of ENGLISH Masonic history, for which purpose a retrograde step in the story I am laying before my readers has become essential.

The only official account we possess of the foundation of

ANTHONY SAYER, GENTn.
The First Grand Master
By permission of the Board of General Purposes from the painting
in Grand Lodge

the Grand Lodge of England, and the first six years of its history, is contained in the second edition of Dr. Anderson's *Constitutions*, published in 1738:—

"After the Rebellion was over, A.D. 1716, the few *Lodges* at *London* . . . thought fit to cement under a *Grand Master* as the center of Union and Harmony, *viz.*, the *Lodges* that met,

"1. At the *Goose* and *Gridiron* Ale-house in St. *Paul's Church-yard*.

"2. At the *Crown* Ale-house in *Parker's-Lane*, near *Drury-Lane*.

"3. At the *Apple-Tree* Tavern in *Charles Street, Covent-Garden*.

"4. At the *Rummer* and *Grapes* Tavern in *Channel-Row*, Westminster.

"They and some old Brothers met at the said *Apple-Tree*, and having put into the Chair the *oldest Master* Mason (now the *Master* of a *Lodge*), they constituted themselves a *Grand Lodge* pro Tempore in *Due Form*, and forthwith revived the Quarterly *Communication* of the *Officers* of Lodges (called the 𝕲𝖗𝖆𝖓𝖉 𝕷𝖔𝖉𝖌𝖊), resolv'd to hold the *Annual* ASSEMBLY and Feast, and then to chuse a GRAND MASTER from among themselves, till they should have the Honour of a *Noble Brother* at their Head.

Accordingly

On St. *John Baptist's* Day, in the 3d Year of KING GEORGE I, A.D. 1717, the ASSEMBLY and *Feast* of the *Free and Accepted Masons* was held at the foresaid *Goose and Gridiron* Ale-house.

"Before Dinner, the *oldest Master* Mason (now the Master of a *Lodge*) in the Chair, proposed a List of proper Candidates; and the Brethren by a Majority of Hands elected MR. ANTHONY SAYER, Gentleman, *Grand Master of Masons*, who, being forthwith invested with the Badges

Mr. *Jacob Lamball*, Carpenter	*Grand*
Capt. *Joseph Elliot*	*Wardens*.

of Office and Power by the said *oldest Master*, and install'd, was duly congratulated by the Assembly who pay'd him the *Homage.*"

It should be carefully borne in mind, however, that this *revival* of the "Quarterly Communication" was *recorded* twenty-one years after the date of the occurrence to which it refers; also, that no such "revival" was mentioned by Dr. Anderson in the *Constitutions* of 1723.

Moreover, there were only annual meetings of the Grand Lodge during the three years next following, which took place on St. John's day (in Summer) in 1718, 1719, and 1720 respectively.

Anthony Sayer was succeeded by "George Payne, Esqr.," during whose year of office (1718) "several old Copies of the *Gothic* [*i.e.*, "*Manuscript*"] *Constitutions* were produced and collated."

The third Grand Master was the Rev. John Theophilus Desaguliers, LL.D., and F.R.S. (1719) by whom were "reviv'd the old regular and peculiar Toasts or Healths of the *Free Masons.*" In 1720 George Payne was elected for a second term, and the leading events of the year were—the burning of several Manuscripts—presumably copies of the old Masonic Constitutions—"by some scrupulous Brothers, that these Papers might not fall into strange Hands"; the holding of a "*Quarterly* Communication on *St. John Evangelist's* Day" (1720); and the enactment of a law, that the Grand Wardens should no longer be elected by the Grand Lodge, but be appointed, together with a Deputy Grand Master, by the Grand Master after his installation.

On the 24th of June, 1721 (twelve Lodges being represented at the Assembly and Feast), George Payne was succeeded by John, Duke of Montagu—the first of a long and unbroken series of noble Grand Masters—and the Society rose at a single bound into notice and esteem.

September 29th, 1721.—"His Grace's *Worship* and the *Lodge* finding Fault with all the Copies of the *old Gothic Constitutions*, order'd Brother *James Anderson*, A.M., to digest the same in a new and better Method" (16 Lodges).

THE "GOOSE AND GRIDIRON" TAVERN
Where the First Grand Lodge of England was originated
on June 24th, 1717.

December 27th, 1721.—"The Duke of Montagu appointed 14 learned Brothers to examine Brother *Anderson's* Manuscript, and to make Report" (20 Lodges).

March 25th, 1722.—"The *Committee* of 14 reported that they had perused Brother *Anderson's* Manuscript, viz., the *History, Charges, Regulations, and Master's Song*, and after some Amendments had approv'd of it; Upon which the *Lodge* desir'd the *Grand Master* to order it to be printed" (24 Lodges).

"*Grand Master* MONTAGU's good government inclin'd the better sort to continue him in the chair another Year; and therefore they delay'd to prepare the *Feast*.

"But *Philip*, Duke of *Wharton*, lately made a Brother, tho' not the *Master* of a *Lodge*, being ambitious of the Chair, got a Number of Others to meet him at *Stationers-Hall* 24 June, 1722, and having no *Grand* Officers, they put in the Chair the *oldest Master Mason* (who was not the *present* Master of a *Lodge*, also irregular), and without the usual decent Ceremonials, the said *old Mason* proclaim'd aloud.

"*Philip Wharton*, Duke of *Wharton*, Grand Master of *Masons* . . . but his Grace appointed no *Deputy*, nor was the *Lodge* opened and closed in due Form.

"Therefore the *noble* Brothers and all those that would not countenance Irregularities, disown'd *Wharton's* Authority, till worthy Brother MONTAGU heal'd the Breach of Harmony, by summoning the GRAND LODGE to meet 17 January 1723, at the *King's Arms*, when the *Duke* of *Wharton* promising to be True and Faithful," he was "proclaim'd" Grand Master in proper form (25 Lodges). At the same meeting, "G. Warden *Anderson* produced the *new* Book of *Constitutions* now in Print, which was again approv'd."

The Duke of Wharton's successor was the Earl of Dalkeith, who was elected on April 25th, and duly proclaimed (*in absentiâ*) on June 24th, 1723.

The meeting last referred to is the *first* of which any record has been preserved in the earliest Minute book of the

Grand Lodge, and the account of its proceedings on St. John's Day (in Summer), 1723, as recorded at the time, differs very materially from that furnished by Dr. Anderson in 1738.

There are also numerous discrepancies of subsequent date between the two narratives, owing, it may be assumed, in many instances, to the "Father of Masonic History" vainly endeavouring to reconcile the statements for which he was responsible in the *Constitutions* of 1723, with those that, in a measure, he was compelled to make, at the close of a long evolutionary process, or period of transition, commencing after 1717, and terminating at some time before 1738.

Upon the only contemporary record of events, I shall, therefore, mainly rely for the further story of the "Mother of Grand Lodges," the earliest Minute of which body informs us, that on June 24th, 1723, the Duke of Wharton presided as Grand Master, with Dr. Desaguliers as Deputy, and Joshua Timson, and "the Reverend Mr. James Anderson," as Grand Wardens. The election of the Earl of Dalkeith passed off harmoniously, but that of his Deputy, Dr. Desaguliers, was opposed, and only carried by a majority of one vote. The Duke of Wharton then proposed that "the Question should be put again in the General Lodge." Whereupon the action of the Duke became the subject of general protest, as being "unprecedented, unwarrantable, and Irregular, and the late Grand Master went away from the Hall without Ceremony."

At the next Quarterly Communication, held November 25th, it was, however, definitely settled that the Grand Master had power to appoint his Deputy, and the Grand Wardens. The "Master of the King's Head in Ivy Lane was expelled for laying several Aspersions against the Deputy Grand Master, which he could not make good," and it was

"Agreed, that no new Lodge, *in or near London*, without it be Regularly Constituted, be countenanced by the Grand Lodge, nor the Master or Wardens be admitted at the Grand Lodge."

The foregoing is given by Anderson in a mutilated form, and without the words in italics, among the New Regulations contained in his *Constitutions* of 1738, but by that date the authority of the Grand Lodge of England had vastly outgrown the expectations of its founders, by whom its jurisdiction was limited to the Cities of London and Westminster, or, in other words, the district or circle embraced by what were called the "Bills of Mortality," in the original "Constitutions" of 1723.

George Payne, John Theophilus Desaguliers and James Anderson are often mentioned in Masonic works as having planned and carried out what, by a strange misuse of terms, it has become the fashion to call the "Revival" of a governing body, in 1717. But there is not a scrap of evidence from which it may be inferred that any one of these early Grand Officers took part in the formation of the Grand Lodge. All three, indeed, had a share in the compilation of the first *Book of Constitutions*. Payne drafted the Regulations, Anderson "digested" the general subject matter, and Desaguliers wrote the Preface or Dedication. The work contains :—

III.—"The Constitution, History . . . of the Accepted Free Masons, collected from their General Records and faithful traditions." In this portion of the book, the highest Masonic *degree* that could have been present to the author's mind in 1723, is very plainly revealed in a passage relating to the secrets of the Ancient Lodges—"But neither what was convey'd, nor the Manner how, can be communicated by writing; as no Man indeed can understand it without the Key of a Fellow Craft."

IV.—"The Charges of a Free-Mason."

First Article.—"But though in ancient Times Masons were charg'd in every Country to be of the Religion of that Country or Nation, whatever it was, yet 'tis now thought more expedient only to oblige them to that Religion in which all Men agree, leaving their particular Opinions to themselves."

V.—"The General Regulations, compiled first by Mr. George Payne, Anno 1720."

Article 13 (called in the *Constitutions* of 1738, Old Regulation XIII).—"Apprentices must be admitted Masters and Fellow-Craft only here [*i.e.*, in the Grand Lodge], unless by a dispensation."

VI.—"The manner of constituting a New Lodge."

"The Candidates, or the New Master and Wardens," are described as "being yet among the Fellow-Craft."

The degrees of Speculative Masonry recognized by the Grand Lodge of England in 1723 were two in number, Entered Apprentice, and Fellow Craft *or* Master; the former combining the degrees of E.A. and F.C., and the latter being that of M.M., as we now have them. The first step in those days was called the "Apprentice Part," and the second or final step, the "Master's Part." By keeping this in mind, the wording of the Article I have extracted from the "General Regulations" of 1720, and which will be again referred to under the title of "O.R. XIII," is at once explained and reconciled with the context.

That only two degrees were recognized by the Grand Lodge in 1723 may, indeed, be considered to be placed beyond doubt by the subsequent legislation of 1725, to be cited under that year, and afterwards compared with the garbled and falsified version of the same which appears in the *Constitutions* of 1738.

The first *Book of Constitutions*, "for the use of the Lodges in London," and the "Brethren and Fellows in and about the Cities of London and Westminster," was approved by the Grand Officers, after whose names follow those of the Masters and Wardens of twenty Lodges—*i.e.*, the Four *old* (or original) Lodges, together with sixteen *new* Lodges, constituted between 1717 and 1723—all of which assembled in the Metropolis. In 1724, however, the very next year, there were already nine Lodges in the provinces, the earliest of which on the roll, if we may form an opinion from its position on the Engraved List, was the Lodge at the Queen's Head in the City of Bath.

The four Lodges—founders of the Grand Lodge—met in 1724:

1. At the GOOSE AND GRIDIRON, in St. Paul's Church-yard.

2. At the QUEEN'S HEAD, Turnstile, *formerly* the CROWN, in Parker's Lane.

3. At the QUEEN'S HEAD, in Knave's Acre, *formerly* the APPLE TREE, in Covent Garden.

4. At the HORNE in Westminster, *formerly* the RUMMER AND GRAPES, in Channel Row.

With the exception of Anthony Sayer, the Premier Grand Master, who is cited on the roll of No. 3, all the eminent persons who took any leading part in the early history of Freemasonry, immediately after the formation of a Grand Lodge, were members of No. 4. In 1724 No. 1 had twenty-two members, No. 2 twenty-one, No. 3 fourteen, and No. 4 seventy-one. The three senior Lodges possessed among them no member of sufficient rank to be described as "Esquire"; while in No. 4 there were ten noblemen, three honourables, four baronets or knights, two general officers, ten colonels, four officers below field rank, and twenty-four esquires. Payne and Desaguliers, together with the Rev. James Anderson, were members of this Lodge.

Returning to the *Constitutions* of 1723, the book introduces three striking Innovations. It discards Christianity as the (*only*) religion of Masonry, forbids the working of the "Master's Part" in private Lodges, and arbitrarily imposes on the English Craft the use of two compound words—Entered Apprentice and Fellow Craft—which had no previous existence in its terminology. Against these deviations from established usage the brethren rebelled, and the more earnestly because it gradually became apparent that the Grand Lodge, designed at first as a governing body for London and Westminster, was slowly but surely extending its authority over the whole country.

The first of these Innovations, the drawing a sponge over the ancient "Charge" "to be true to God and the

Holy Church," was doubtless looked upon by many Masons
of those days in very much the same manner as *we*
now regard the absence of any religious formulary whatever in the so-called Masonry of the Grand Orient of
France.

The second, as we shall presently see, was triumphantly
swept away on November 27th, 1725; and the effect of the
third will be perceptible in the course of events, which it
becomes my next duty to relate.

In 1724 the political state of Persia was one of great
confusion. The "Sophy," or head of the "Sufawi" dynasty,
had been deposed by an Afghan chief, son of Meer Vais,
who, inheriting his father's power, seems also to have
been called by his name in the English newspapers. Prince
Tahmasp (or Thaumas), the rightful heir, or young
"Sophy," exercised a precarious sovereignty over a small
number only of the aggregate of provinces which, down to
1722, had constituted the Kingdom of the captive Shah,
his father. The situation, therefore, of the Persian Crown
Prince, with a usurper in possession of his capital (Ispahan),
seems to have afforded the Jacobite faction in England, or
at all events certain of their number, who, for one reason
or another, were desirous of turning into ridicule the proceedings of the Freemasons, with some of the texture for
an allegory, of which the earliest notice occurs in the *Daily
Post*.

September 3, 1724.—"Whereas the truly ANTIENT NOBLE
ORDER of the Gormogons, instituted by the . . . First
Emperor of China, many thousand years before Adam
. . . and of which . . . Confucius was Œcumenical Volgee,
has lately been brought into England by a Mandarin,
and having admitted several gentlemen into the Mystery
. . . they have determined to hold a Chapter at the Castle
Tavern in Fleet Street. . . . There will be no drawn
Sword at the Door, nor Ladder in a dark Room, nor will
any Mason be receiv'd as a Member till he has renounced
his Novel Order and been properly degraded. N.B.—The
Grand Mogul, the Czar of Muscovy, and Prince Tochmas

are enter'd with this Hon. Society; but it has been refused to the Rebel Merriweys, to his great Mortification. The Mandarin will shortly set out for Rome."

The story was next taken up in the *Plain Dealer*:—

September 14, 1724.—"I will not be so partial to our Worshipful Society of FREE *and* ACCEPTED MASONS to forbear reproving them. . . . 'Tis my opinion that the late Prostitution of our *Order* is in some Measure the betraying it. The weak heads of *Vintners, Drawers, Wigmakers, Weavers,* etc., admitted into our *Fraternity,* have not only brought contempt upon the Institution, but do very much endanger it."

The editor of the *Plain Dealer* concludes by presenting his readers with two letters, the first addressed by Hang Chi (the "Mandarin") to himself, and the last written from Rome, by Shin Shaw, "to the Author of the first."

But the fullest account of the Order is given in the second edition of the *Grand Mystery of the Freemasons Discover'd,* published October 28th, in the same year. This contains "Two Letters to a Friend—the first, concerning the Society of FREE MASONS; the second, giving an Account of the most Ancient Order of GORMOGONS." In the latter, Verus Commodus—whose signature is attached to both—observes, "I cannot guess why so excellent and laudable a Society as this of the GORMOGONS, should think it worth their while to make it an Article to exclude the *Free-Masons.* . . . Except there be any Truth in what I have heard reported. . . . The Report is this, That the Mandarin [Hang Chi] has declared, that many years since, Two unhappy busy persons who were *Masons* [*Anderson* and *Desaguliers*], having obtruded their idle Notions [*Book of Constitutions*] among the Vulgar Chineze, of *Adam,* and *Solomon,* and *Hiram* . . . being Crafts-men of their Order; and having besides, deflower'd a venerable OLD Gentlewoman [taken unwarrantable liberties with the Operative Charges and Regulations], under the Notion of making her an *European* HIRAMITE (as they call'd it) . . . they were hang'd Back to Back, on a gibbet. . . .

And ever since, it has been an Article among the Gormogons, to exclude the Members of that Society, without
they first undergo a solemn *Degradation.* . . . If ever you
hear from me again on this subject, it will be in a few
REMARKS on that empty Book called *The Constitutions,*
etc., of the *Free-Masons,* written, as I am told, by a *Presby-
terian Teacher,* and pompously recommended by a certain
Orthodox, Tho' Mathematical Divine."

The *British Journal* of December 12, 1724, has the
following:—"We hear that a Peer of the first Rank, a
noted Member of the Society of *Free-Masons,* hath suffered
himself to be degraded as a member of that Society,
and his Leather Apron and Gloves to be burn't, and
thereupon enter'd himself as a Member of the Society of
Gormogons."

The founders of the Gormogon Order—if there was more
than one—may have been, and I think were, malcontent
Freemasons. That there were dissensions in the Craft
during 1723, 1724, and later, admits of no doubt, and I
apprehend that both in religion and politics the brethren
were arrayed in opposing camps. Of the Whigs and
Tories, or supporters respectively of the King and the
Pretender, very little need be said ; but the religious differences, we may confidently assume, were such as could
not fail to arise when the old creed of the Freemasons, a
profession of the Christian faith, was blotted out, and a new
one, "leaving their particular opinions to themselves," was
substituted in its place. Other Innovations (to which I
have previously referred) were introduced into English
Masonry in 1723, and to all combined, but perhaps chiefly
and especially to the *New* Charge, "Concerning God and
Religion," which embodied a latitudinarian doctrine equally
obnoxious to the Church of Rome and the Catholic adherents
of the Pretender, we must look, I think, for the real origin
of the delusive Club, or Fraternity, commonly (though
erroneously) supposed to have been the only serious rivals
of the Freemasons.

It was in thorough harmony with the character of Philip,

Duke of Wharton, to have first of all cast in his lot with the Masons, and afterwards—if he did not directly originate—to have become an active supporter of the Gormogons. That he was a prominent member of the so-called "Order" there can be no doubt whatever, and it is quite within the limits of possibility that it sprang into existence as the creation of his lively fancy. But without crossing the boundary of reasonable presumption, we may fairly conclude that he became the ruling spirit of the mysterious association, whose periods of activity, from 1724 when HANG CHI, the Mandarin (*i.e.*, Duke of Wharton), first appears on the scene, corresponded so closely with his own.

I shall next refer to Hogarth's well-known plate, *The Mystery of Masonry, brought to Light by the Gormogons*, which it may be supposed made its original appearance shortly after the publication of Shelton's English edition of the *History of Don Quixote*, reproducing the "cuts" or illustrations of Charles Antoine Coypel (from which Hogarth borrowed freely), in 1725. The plate is a coarse and very indecent attack upon the Freemasons, the "*Ladders, Halters, Drawn Swords,* and *Dark Rooms,*" mentioned in the *Plain Dealer*, and again in the *Grand Mystery of the Freemasons Discover'd*, at once suggest both the title of the plate, and at whose instigation it was undertaken by Hogarth.

A book held out by a figure at the entrance to a tavern almost certainly refers to the pamphlet last cited (*Grand Mystery*). Closed casements and a lighted candle are meant, of course, to indicate the "Dark Rooms" within. A man in the garb of an apprentice, with his head between the spokes of a ladder, is evidently intended to represent the Rev. James Anderson, whose position there is doubtless emblematic of a custom imputed to the Masons in a scurrilous pamphlet published in 1723. "The Venerable Old Gentlewoman" described by Verus Commodus in his fable is represented by a woman on an ass, and this feature of the engraving, therefore, can have had no other object than a desire to make the author of the *Book of Constitutions* figure in as ridiculous and contemptible a light as possible.

Lastly, under the disguise of the "Crazy Knight of La Mancha," it seems possible that we may identify Philip, the first and last Duke of Wharton? If not, indeed, our research will be vain among the other notabilities of that day, for any one man whose exploits as a Freemason, Gormogon, and modern Knight Errant, could have been sufficiently notorious to win for him the distinction of being made to combine all three of these rôles, by Hogarth in his travesty of Coypel.

The allegory begun in the *Daily Post, Plain Dealer,* and other publications of 1724, was continued by the Duke of Wharton, through the medium of *Mist's Journal,* August 24th, 1728. In a curious apologue, the noble writer has encased his satirical remarks in the same historical framework with which we have already become familiar from the Gormogon literature of 1724. George I and the Pretender are again referred to as *Meryweis* and the *Young Sophi* respectively, as in the *Daily Post* and *Plain Dealer* of that year, and while the Hanoverian dynasty is grossly lampooned, the head of the Stuart (royal) family is described as the "greatest Character" of the age.

There are faint traces of the Gormogons down to the year 1730, but the Order is no longer heard of as an existing society after the death of the Duke of Wharton in 1731.

In addition, however, to the fulminations of the Gormogons, many publications appeared after 1723, in which the *Book of Constitutions* and its author were openly derided. As a consequence, though it is possible that by some persons it may be merely deemed a coincidence, we find that Dr. Anderson was not present at any meeting of the Grand Lodge between St. John's Day (in Summer), 1724, and the recurrence of that Festival in 1731.

From the numerous attacks upon him during this interval, I extract the following, which appeared in *An Ode to the Grand Khaibar,* a publication of 1726:—

" So pleased with Dreams the 𝔐𝔞𝔰𝔬𝔫𝔰 seem,
 To tell their Tales once more they venture ;
And find an Author worthy them ;
 From Sense and Genius a 𝔇𝔦𝔰𝔰𝔢𝔫𝔱𝔢𝔯.
In doggerel Lyrics worse than Prose,
 Their Story he again rehearses ;
But nothing of a Poet shows,
 Excepting Fiction in his Verses."

In 1724—November 21—the Duke of Richmond being Grand Master, the Earl of Dalkeith proposed a scheme for raising a fund of General Charity for distressed Masons, which was adopted. A committee, called the "Committee of Charity," was appointed to manage the Fund and distribute relief; it is now the "Board of Benevolence." The powers of the committee were greatly extended in 1730, and still more so in 1733, when it was determined:— "That all such business which cannot be conveniently despatched by the Quarterly Communication, shall be referred to the Committee of Charity"; and "that all Masters of Regular Lodges, together with all present, former, and future Grand Officers, shall be members of that committee." This established what is now known as the Board of Masters—composed of the same members —which still meets four times a year to settle the *agenda* for Grand Lodge, prior to entering upon its duties as the Board of Benevolence. In 1725—November 27—at a Grand Lodge, "with former G. *Officers* and Those of 49 *Lodges*":—

"A Motion being made that such part of the 13th Article of the Gen^{ll.} Regulations relating to the making of Ma^{sts.} only at a Quarterly Court may be repealed, and that the Ma^{st.} of Each Lodge, with the consent of his Wardens and the Majority of the Brethren, being Ma^{str.}, may make Ma^{sts.} at their discretion. Agreed, *Nem. Con.*"

The Duke of Richmond was succeeded as Grand Master by Lord Paisley, after whom came the Earl of Inchiquin. Under this nobleman Provincial Grand Masters were appointed to office, and the Square, Level, and Plumb Rule, ordered to be worn by the Master, Senior and Junior Wardens respectively, of every private Lodge.

The next event of importance was the regulation of the precedency of the Lodges, a task which was confided to the Grand Officers—namely, Lord Colerane, Grand Master; Alexander Choke, the Deputy; and Nathaniel Blackerly and Joseph Highmore, the Senior and Junior Grand Wardens respectively.

They performed their task in 1728, at the close of which year James, Lord Kingston, whose name is resplendent in the annals of Irish Freemasonry, was proclaimed as Grand Master.

The Engraved List of 1729 enumerates 54 Lodges, 42 of which are in London, 11 in the country, and 1 (founded by the Duke of Wharton) at Madrid. It is described as "A List of Regular Lodges according to their Seniority and Constitution"—words which are here met with for the first time.

It is both curious and noteworthy that the number of Lodges shown in the Engraved List of 1725—namely, sixty-four—should have fallen to fifty-four in 1729, and, without doubt, reflects the general feeling of discontent which must have pervaded the Masonic body, or at least that section of it most closely affected by the growing despotism of the newly-established Grand Lodge. An incident arising out of the arrangement of "the Regular Lodges according to their Seniority and Constitution" is worth recording:—

July 11, 1729.—"The officers of the Lodge at the Queen's Head in Knave's Acre, represented that their Lodge was misplaced in the printed Book, whereby they lost their Rank, and humbly prayed that the said mistake might be regulated. Bro. Choke, late D.G.M., acquainted the Grand Lodge that the several Lodges stood in the List according to the date of their Constitutions. . . . The said complaint was dismissed" (*G.L. Minutes*).

The Lodge in question—the one from which the first Grand Master, Anthony Sayer, was selected—met in 1716 at the Apple-Tree Tavern in Charles Street, Covent Garden, and still survives, as the Lodge of Fortitude and Old

Cumberland, No. 12. The three senior Lodges of the original four were not represented on the Committee of Precedence, otherwise the unmerited supersession of original No. 3 (which will again claim our attention) could not possibly have occurred.

On December 29th, 1729, it was enacted by the Grand Lodge that "Every *New Lodge*, for the Future, shall pay two *guineas* for their *Constitution* to the General *Charity*." This had reference to the Act of Constituting the Lodge, and must not be confused with a Lodge Warrant, which was an instrument unknown at the time. The Ceremony of Constituting the Lodge was to be the personal Act of the Grand Master, or his representative. When the Act was performed by the Grand Master, or his Grand Officers, a certificate was given of the due Constitution of the Lodge, which served the purpose of the later Warrant.

The other early Documents, also erroneously termed Warrants, were simple Deputations, authorizing some competent Brother, named therein, to constitute a regular Lodge in due form. The Deputations, like the Certificates, fulfilled the same duty as the present Charters or Warrants of the Grand Lodge.

The Duke of Norfolk was proclaimed and installed on January 29th, 1730. All the former Grand Masters (with the exception of the Duke of Wharton) were present, and "walk'd one by one according to Juniority—viz.: *Lord* Colerane, *Earl* of Inchiquin, *Lord* Paisley, *Duke* of Richmond, *Earl* of Dalkeith, *Duke* of Montagu, Dr. Desaguliers, George Payne, Esq., and Mr. Anthony Sayer."

In the course of the same year, however, as we learn from the minutes of Grand Lodge, the first Grand Master of Masons had not only fallen into poverty and decay, but he had also seriously transgressed the Regulations of the Society.

April 21, 1730.—"Then the Petition of Brother Anthony Sayer, formerly Grand Master, was read, setting forth his misfortunes and great poverty, and praying Relief. The Grand Lodge took the same into their consideration, and it was proposed that he should have £20 out of the money received on acc$^{t.}$ of the General Charity; others proposed £10, and others £15. The Question being put, it was agreed that he should have £15, on acc$^{t.}$ of his having been Grand Master."

August 28, 1720.—"A paper signed by the Master and Wardens of the Lodge at the Queen's Head in Knave's Acre, was presented and read, complaining of great Irregularities having been committed by B$^{ro.}$ Anthony Sayer, notwithstanding the great ffavours he hath lately received by order of the Grand Lodge."

December 15*th*, 1730.—"B$^{ro.}$ Sayer attended to answer the complaint made against him, and after hearing both parties, and some of the Brethren being of Opinion that what he had done was clandestine, others that it was irregular, the Question was put whether what was done was clandestine, or irregular only, and the Lodge was of opinion that it was irregular only—Whereupon the Deputy Grand Master told B$^{ro.}$ Sayer that he was acquitted of the charge against him, and recommended it to him to do nothing so irregular for the future."

The precise offence committed by the earliest of "Grand Masters" cannot, indeed, be determined with exactitude, but the evidence clearly points to his having been among the conspirators who sought to undermine the authority of the Grand Lodge.

In the same year two spurious rituals, or catechisms, made their appearance, one of which, *The Mystery of Free-Masonry*, an anonymous publication, was printed in the *Daily Journal* of August 15th; and the other, "*Masonry Dissected*, by Samuel Prichard, late Member of a Constituted Lodge," was announced as being on sale, in the issue of that paper for October 20th, 1730.

The two catechisms invite a comparison. In the older one, two degrees are referred to, and in the later form three. Both texts were frequently reprinted. *Masonry Dissected* ran into four editions in less than as many weeks; while the *Mystery of Free-Masonry* was reprinted from the *Daily*

Journal by a host of newspapers, both at home and abroad. It was also published by Benjamin Franklin in the *Pennsylvania Gazette* of December 8th, 1730, and we again meet with it as late as 1742 in the *Westminster Journal*, of May 8th, in that year.

The Mystery of Free-Masonry and *Masonry Dissected*, it will be seen, appeared within a few months of each other, and I have already called attention to the fact that, while the catechism of slightly later date speaks of three degrees, in the earlier one only two are referred to. Other discrepancies occur, as invariably happens with this class of publications; but, leaving these spurious rituals for what they are really worth—and it may be remarked that the value set upon them has never been a high one—we may occasionally, from amid a mass of otherwise unintelligible matter, pick out an item or suggestion calculated to throw light on the past of Freemasonry. Of this, the limitation of the number of degrees to two by all the catechisms which preceded *Masonry Dissected* affords an illustration. Many persons outside the actual pale of Freemasonry would know the precise number of degrees worked in the Lodges, though their knowledge of what transpired when the said degrees were conferred on candidates would be, at best, pure conjecture. Hence, while brushing aside as worthless all pretended revelations of Masonic secrets, we may nevertheless accept statements—to be found in these catechisms—relating to matters which were not secrets at all, but were known facts, at the time they were published to the world.

Masonry Dissected, as already observed, made its first appearance in October, 1730, and, being in pamphlet form, was so cordially welcomed by the enemies and rivals of Freemasonry, that a fourth edition was published during the second week of the ensuing November. On the 15th of December in the same year (1730), in the *Daily Post*, and on the 16th of December, in the *Daily Journal*, there was the following advertisement:—

"*This Day is Published,*
A DEFENCE OF MASONRY; occasioned
by a Pamphlet, call'd MASONRY DISSECTED.
Rarus Sermo illis, & magna Libido Tacendi.
Juv. Sat. II.
Printed for J. Roberts, near the Oxford Arms in Warwick
Lane. Price 1s."

Of the treatise thus announced no known copy is in
existence, but it was reproduced in the *Free Masons' Pocket
Companion* for 1738, and the *New Book of Constitutions*,
published in the same year. That the writer was a man
of learning, a master of style, and an able polemic, there
was ample proof on every page of the publication. But
the authorship of the piece was for a long time enveloped
in mystery, and all the guesses hazarded with regard to
it down to a comparatively recent date (1891), my own
not excepted, fell very wide of the mark. The writer,
however, is now known to have been "Martin Clare,
A.M. and F.R.S." The motive for secrecy seems to
have been, that the real aim of Clare, or those by whom
his pen was set in motion, was to convey to the world that
the reply to *Masonry Dissected* was the production of some
impartial critic, and in no wise merely a pamphlet written
to order for the Freemasons. This view is sustained by
the letter from "Euclid" (almost certainly Dr. Anderson
himself), which is given in the *Constitutions* of 1738, immediately after the *Defence of Masonry*. In this the writer
observes:—"The *Free Masons* are much obliged to the
generous Intention of the unbiass'd *Author* of the above
Defence: Tho' had he been a Free Mason, he had in time
perceived many valuable Things suitable to his extended
Views of Antiquity, which could not come to the *Dissectors'*
Knowledge; for they were not intrusted with any Brothers
till after due Probation."

From a variety of evidence, however, which will be found
collected in my *Memoir of Martin Clare* (*A.Q.C.*, iv, 33-
41), we may clearly infer that the name of the real author
was a very open secret, at least among the class of persons

who may be described as the "Masonic Authorities," both at the time of publication and for a good many years afterwards.

The tract is in all respects a most remarkable production, and as it has been twice reprinted in the publications of the *Quatuor Coronati* Lodge (*Q.C.A.*, i and vii), it will be unnecessary to do more than refer the reader to the first chapter for the ostensible grounds on which it was published to the world, and to the later ones for a very successful attempt on the part of the writer to resist the attack made on Freemasonry, by boldly and resolutely carrying the war—to use a familiar figure of speech—into the enemies' country.

There is only one passage in the Defence to which I shall particularly allude:—"There appears to be something like *Masonry* (as the *Dissector* describes it) in all regular societies of whatever denomination: ·They are *All* held together by a sort of *Cement*, by Bonds and Laws that are peculiar to each of them, from the Highest to the little Clubs and Nightly Meetings of a private Neighbourhood. . . . There is the Degree of *Enter'd Prentice*, Master of his Trade, or *Fellow Craft*, and Master, or the *Master* of the Company" (chap. ii).

In the last sentence of the preceding extract, the Fellow Craft is described as "Master of his Trade"—meaning the highest grade, rank, title, or degree (existing separately from the *offices* of the Society), as then known to, or at least recognized as such by, the writer of the essay.

Francis, Duke of Lorraine, the first Royal Freemason, was admitted into the Craft, by virtue of a Deputation from Lord Lovell, Grand Master, at the Hague, in 1731.

Other Deputations, we are told by Dr. Anderson, were granted by the two next rulers of English Craft—namely, by Viscount Montagu, for constituting Lodges at VALENCIENNES and PARIS, in 1732; and by the Earl of Strathmore, "to eleven *German* gentlemen, good Brothers, for constituting a *Lodge* at HAMBURG," in 1733.

In the last named year (1733) there occurs the first

reference to "a Master's" or "a Master Masons' Lodge,"
a subject to which I shall again refer in connection with
the Degrees of Pure and Ancient Masonry, but mention
in this place, as the institution of distinct Lodges for the
working of the "Master's Part," like the earlier evidence
adduced under the year 1730, is of particular value in our
researches, as pointing to a date from which we may infer
a gradual progression in what, shortly afterwards, became
an accepted system of three degrees.

The *Free Mason's Pocket Companion* was brought out
by William Smith, in London and Dublin, in 1734-5. Full
particulars of both editions are given by Dr. Crawley in
his *Cæmentaria Hibernica* (ii), where also will be found
a reproduction of the Dublin issue. In the present connection, the manuals are chiefly of interest as explaining
the action taken by Dr. Anderson—February 24th, 1735—
in requesting permission from the Grand Lodge of England,
to publish a second edition of "the General Constitutions
of Masonry, compiled by himself." "He further represented that one William Smith, said to be a Mason, had,
without his privity or consent, pyrated a considerable part
of the Constitutions of Masonry aforesaid to the prejudice
of the said Br. Anderson, it being his sole property."

The Minutes of Grand Lodge next inform us, under
March 31st, 1735—"Then a Motion was made that Dr.
James Anderson should be desired to print the Names (in
his New Book of Constitutions) of all the Grand Masters
that could be collected from the beginning of time," also of
the other Grand Officers, and of the Grand Stewards,
"Because it is Resolved, that for the future, all Grand
Officers (except the Grand Master) shall be elected out of
that Body."

Viscount Weymouth was proclaimed as Grand Master
(in succession to the Earl of Crawford) in April, 1735, and
appointed as his Junior Grand Warden, "*Martin Clare*,
A.M. and F.R.S."

In the following December, at a meeting of the Grand
Lodge, "GEORGE PAYNE, Esq., formerly *Grand Master*

in the Chair; *Martin Clare*, the G.W., acted as *Dep. Gr. Master*, and *James Anderson*, D.D., and *Jacob Lamball* [the first Senior Grand Warden of Masons], *Grand Wardens*, pro Tempore."

The Master of the recently constituted Stewards' Lodge reported that the Junior Grand Warden, Martin Clare, had entertained it with an excellent Discourse, which it had seemed to the members and visitors was "Worthy of being read before the Grand Lodge itself—which was accordingly done, it being received with great attention and applause."

The Oration or "Discourse" of Martin Clare—Deputy Grand Master in 1741—was translated into several foreign languages, and reprints of it will be found in the *Pocket Companion* for 1754, the *Masonic Institutes* of Dr. Oliver, and other publications.

The sequence of "Noble Grand Masters" was duly preserved in 1736 and 1737, beyond which there is nothing to record, except that in the latter year—November 5, 1737 —at an "Occasional Lodge" held in Kew Palace, under the Mastership of Dr. Desaguliers (who had similarly presided at the Initiation of the Duke of Lorraine), Frederick, Prince of Wales, was admitted a member of the Society.

On the 25th of January, 1738, George Payne and Dr. Desaguliers, former Grand Masters, together with many actual and other former Grand Officers, and the Officers of the Stewards' and Sixty-six other Lodges, being present, "the Grand Lodge approved of the *New* BOOK of *Constitutions*, and order'd the Author, Brother *Anderson*, to print the same."

A DIGRESSION ON DEGREES

Scholars and antiquarians take but a languid interest— there is no use in disguising it—in the history of Modern Masonry. They do not believe that the system of Masonry as understood by the founders of the first Grand Lodge, is capable of indefinite expansion. Degrees, in their judgment, cannot be multiplied *ad infinitum*. But the history and origin of Ancient Masonry are regarded by them in quite a different manner. These, they are not only willing, but eager, to study and investigate, yet an unwelcome doubt obtrudes itself which checks, if it does not wholly dissipate, the ardour of their research.

Conjointly with the old MS. Constitutions (or written traditions of the Society), which are of undoubted antiquity, the symbolical teaching in our Lodges—though possessing a remoteness of origin less assured—has a peculiar fascination for all genuine votaries of archæology.

Here, however, the doubt referred to creeps in, and the scholar or antiquary who has a longing to trace the antiquity of our symbolism is checked by similar reflections to those which occurred to Gibbon, who kept back an hypothesis he had framed with regard to the real secret of the Ancient Mysteries, "from an apprehension of discovering what never existed"; and to the elder Disraeli, who, much in the same way, excused his imperfect speculations with respect to the shadowy and half-mythical Rosicrucians. But if the Symbolism of Masonry, or a material part of it, can be proved with reasonable certainty to ante-date the year 1717, the doubt upon which I have enlarged will disappear, and with it, we may venture to hope, the present disinclination on the part of really competent investigators to extend their researches into the only field of inquiry— the domain of Ancient Masonry—which offers any prospect whatever of rewarding the patient student of our antiquities, by a partial revelation of the origin, and by the recovery of some portion, at least, of the lost learning of the fraternity.

Under the Grand Lodge of England, within the first decade of its existence, there was a ceremonial, or, to vary the expression, certain ritual and emblematical observances were wrought in the Lodges, and whether these were then new or old is, shortly stated, the main issue for our determination. If the Symbolism of Masonry was in existence before the era of Grand Lodges, there is practically no limit whatever of age that can be assigned to it (*ante* 54); or, to put it in another way, if we once get beyond or behind the year 1717—*i.e.*, into the domain of Ancient Masonry, and again look back, the vista is perfectly illimitable, without a speck or shadow to break the continuity of view which is presented to us.

To accept, indeed, for one moment (as it has been finely observed) the suggestion that so complex and curious a system, embracing so many archaic remains, and such skilfully adjusted ceremonies, so much connected matter, accompanied by so many striking symbols, could have been the creation of a pious fraud or ingenious conviviality, presses heavily on our powers of belief, and oversteps even the normal credulity of our species.

Dr. Stukeley tells us in his *Diary* that on January 6th, 1721, he was made a *Freemason*, and in his *Common Place Book*—"I was the first person made a freemason for many years. We had great difficulty to find members enough to perform the ceremony. Immediately after that it took a run, & run itself out of breath thro' the folly of the members."

The doctor also records in the *Diary* that at a meeting of the Grand Lodge, held on June 24th, 1721—"The G^{d.} M^{r.,} Mr. Pain . . . read over a new sett of articles to be observ'd." These were the famous "General Regulations," afterwards printed in the *Constitutions* of 1723, consequently the admission of Stukeley (in January, 1721) must have taken place before the working of the "Master's Part" was forbidden, except in the Grand Lodge, and therefore while the old and original laws (or customs) of the Society remained in force.

Of the Masonic Symbolism *inherited* in 1717, and presumably still existing in 1721, I shall begin with the remark, that the Rev. C. J. Ball (one of the first Oriental scholars of our day), in a lecture delivered before the *Quatuor Coronati* Lodge, on June 24th, 1892—*The Proper Names of Masonic Tradition*, a `Philological Study*—of which some fragments only, and these the least important of the whole, could be printed (*A.Q.C.*, v, 136-41), seems to me to settle beyond dispute, not only that what we now call the Third

Degree existed before the era of Grand Lodges, but that, having passed through a long decline, its symbols had become corrupted, and their meaning (to a great extent) forgotten, when the step itself—then known as the "Master's Part," is first heard of (*i.e.*, unequivocally referred to) in any print or manuscript to which a date can be assigned (1723).

To what extent the "Master's Part" was *worked* in Stukeley's time there are no means of determining, though it is worthy of consideration whether the difficulty, at his initiation, in finding "members enough to perform the ceremony," may not have consisted in getting together a sufficient number of brethren to work *both* steps of Masonry? The first, or "Apprentice Part," was communicated in a very simple manner in Scotland, and the practice lingered until a comparatively late period. One Mason, unaided, could, and often did, make another. Without, indeed, contending that there was an equal simplicity of ritual in the South, the usage in the North goes a long way towards proving that there could not have been any very elaborate *ceremony*, in London, at the reception of an Apprentice, in 1721. The difficulty, however, in finding a sufficiency of brethren to constitute the *dramatis personæ* in working the Master's Part may well have been, and probably was, a real one. Upon the doctor's avowed reason for becoming a Freemason, I have already enlarged, and to the remark on a previous page that Ashmole may have been "influenced by similar feelings, which he satisfied in the same way" (*ante*, 54), I shall add that the statement of the latter in his *Diary* (*ante*, 116) that he was the "Senior Fellow" at a Lodge held in the Masons' Hall, London, in 1682, *may*, and, I think, *does*, mean that he had acquired the higher *step* as well as *grade*.

The Freemasons, as we are told by Aubrey, on the authority of Sir William Dugdale, the close and intimate friend of Elias Ashmole, "are known to one another by certayn signes and watch-words. . . . The manner of their adoption is *very formall*." That there was a plurality of "signs and words" we also find stated in *Harleian*

MS., 2054, dating from about 1665; while a plurality of the former ("certain *secret signes*") is mentioned by Dr. Plot in 1686 (*ante*, 99, 115, 119).

The existence of an Arabic MS. of the fourteenth century, in which "a sign or pass-word known to the Masonic brotherhood" is referred to, has also been affirmed by a very high and very trustworthy authority.

Still, "all feet tread not in one shoe," and I do not for a moment contend that what seem to myself to be perfectly legitimate inferences from the evidence before us will be regarded in a precisely similar light by other students in the same branch of research.

My next proceeding will be to consider the question of Masonic degrees, within a smaller compass, and to establish, if I can, according to strictly legal methods, that the Symbolism recognized by the Grand Lodge of England in 1723 differed in no shape or form from that which must have previously been in vogue among the London Lodges, prior to the formation of a governing Masonic body, in 1717.

Antiquity of time fortifieth all titles, and supposeth the best beginning the law can give them.

So, at least, runs an old legal maxim, and from that time of Payne, Anderson, and Desaguliers, down to that of William Preston and Laurence Dermott, and from the time of Preston and Dermott down to the generation of which we ourselves form a part, the belief that a system of degrees existed, and not merely a solitary degree, has not been assailed. It was left for a German writer to do this—J. G. Findel, the author of a *History of Freemasonry*, the first edition of which appeared in 1862, or, at least, I am so informed; but the point is not material, and it will answer all purposes if I say, that I am acquainted with no earlier enunciation of the theory that, to use the somewhat cumbrous phraseology of the translated work—"There was but one degree of Initiation in the year 1717."

Truly, no sandier foundation was ever discovered for a fallacy more futile than this! The Grand Lodge of England was established on St. John's Day (in Summer), 1717, Anthony Sayer being the first Grand Master. The second meeting of the Grand Lodge took place on the recurrence of the same Festival in 1718, and George Payne was elected Grand Master. There was a third meeting in June, 1719, when Dr. Desaguliers succeeded Payne; and a fourth on St. John's Day, 1720, when the latter was elected Grand Master for a second time. During the year thus begun the General Regulations of the Society were compiled by George Payne, the Grand Master, who, as we learn from Dr. Stukeley, "read over a new sett of articles to be observ'd," and these were afterwards printed in the first *Book of Constitutions*, which appeared in 1723.

In the 13th "Article" of these "General Regulations" there is the well-known proviso that Apprentices were only to be admitted Masters and Fellow Craft in the Grand Lodge, unless by a dispensation.

Until a few years ago this clause was very erroneously interpreted, and the fundamental principle of literary criticism—the principle that an author's meaning is to be read *out* of his words, and not *into* them—was totally disregarded. All commentators seem to have determined what the author of the *Book of Constitutions* (transcribing the "General Regulations" of George Payne) ought to have said, and then they set themselves to prove that he practically said it.

"Commentators doubtless have their use, but they are liable to err in a sense in which documents are not. If the commentators contradict the documents, there is an end of them, and we may pass on" (E. A. Freeman, *Histor. Essays*, 342).

I leave, therefore, the "General Regulations" of 1721 and 1723, that is to say, so far as they point (as they do with the utmost clearness) to a system of *two*, and not of *three* degrees, the latter being the number which Dr. Anderson was supposed to have had in his mind when publishing his work of 1723. The simple fact being, that the titles of Fellow Craft and Master Mason, which really meant the same thing in the phraseology of Scottish Operative Masons, were also used as words of indifferent application by the doctor in his *Book of Constitutions*.

Let us next consider the weighty authority which the "General Regulations" possess. We have seen that they were first compiled by George Payne, as Grand Master, in 1721, and that Payne had previously been elected Grand Master in 1718, exactly one year after the original formation of the Grand Lodge. To that early date, therefore, his knowledge of the existing secrets of the Society must certainly be carried back, and for how much longer his acquaintance with them may fall within the limits of reasonable inference or conjecture, I shall ask my readers to estimate for themselves. In my own judgment, however, it is not credible for an instant that the Symbolism of Masonry was tampered with, and expanded *at the only meeting of the Grand Lodge*—June 24th, 1717—which took place *before* we find Grand Master Payne in the chair of that august body, precisely a twelvemonth afterwards.

Unless, therefore, we disbelieve George Payne, also his successor as Grand Master, Dr. Desaguliers, and Dr. James Anderson, and their testimony on the subject is wholly uncontradicted on any point, we are bound to acquiesce in the decision that a Masonic system of two degrees was certainly inherited by the Grand Lodge of Speculative Masonry at its formation in 1717.

The earliest evidence which bears on the subject of the degrees of Masonry having been communicated in three distinct steps, is contained in the *Transactions* of the *Philo-Musicæ et Architecturæ Societas*, London, which begin on the 18th of February, 1725, and end on the 23rd of March, 1727. The records of this Society are included among the *Quatuor Coronati* publications (*Q.C.A.* IX.), and from the *Prolegomena* of the Founders I extract the following:—

"On the Eighteenth Day of February (1725) this Society was Founded and Begun at The Queen's Head near Temple Barr. By us the Eight Underwritten, Seven of which did Belong to the Lodge at the Queen's Head in Hollis Street.

And were made Masons There. In a Just and Perfect
Lodge Vizt M^r· Willm· Gulston and M^r· Edmund Squire . .
were made Masons the 15th of December, 1724 [and others]
were made Masons the 22d of December, 1724, By . . The
Duke of Richmond, Grand Master, Who then Constituted
the Lodge. Immediately after which Charles Cotton, Esqr·,
was made a Mason by the said Grand Master M^r· Papillon
Ball . . and Seign^r· Francisco Xaverio Geminiani were made
Masons the 1st of February [1725]. M^r· Thomas Marshall
. . was made a Mason at the George in Long Acre Sometime
before the said M^r· William Gulston . . and M^r· Edmund
Squire were Regularly Pass'd Masters in the before mentioned Lodge of Hollis Street. And before We Founded
this Society A Lodge was held Consisting of Masters Sufficient for that Purpose In Order to Pass Charles Cotton . .
Papillon Ball and . . Thomas Marshall Fellow Crafts. In
the Performance of which M^r· William Gulston Acted as
Senior Warden."

The *Minutes* of the Society inform us:—

"The 15th Day of April, 1725 . . M^r· James Murray did
attend and was made and admitted according to the Fundamental Constitution and Orders."

"The 12th day of May, 1725—
. . Brother Charles Cotton Esq^e·
Broth^r· Papillon Ball
Were regularly passed Masters
Brother F X° Geminiani
Was regularly passed fellow Craft & Master
Brother James Murray
Was regularly passed Fellow Craft."

There are *no other entries in the Minutes* which relate
to a plurality of degrees, or extend beyond the statement
that a candidate was "made a Mason in order to qualify
him to be admitted a Member of the Society." The proceedings, therefore, as recorded under May 12th, 1725,
invite a careful scrutiny. *Standing alone*, the entires of
that date are not inconsistent with the supposition that

the ceremony of "passing" in the case of all the four "Brothers" was one and the same.

Master and Fellow Craft—at that time—were convertible terms, according to the phraseology of the Grand Lodge (*ante*, 205). Moreover, *if* a second and third degree *are* referred to, how can it be explained why *both* were conferred on F. X. Geminiani, and only *one* on James Murray? *Taken, however, with the allusions of earlier date* to Charles Cotton and Papillon Ball, the entries of May 12th, 1725, relating to these "Brothers," are generally held to indicate that after having been "made Masons," and before being "passed Masters," they received the intermediate degree of Fellow Craft. This step of Masonry, indeed, which (if the above view is a correct one) *we meet with for the first time* under the year 1725, is plainly shown to have been an *addition* to the ceremonies worked by the Lodge in Hollis Street—which were two in number—and the new degree was apparently communicated by members of the *Society* who formed themselves into a *Lodge* for that purpose.

Thomas Marshall, it may be observed, who became a Fellow Craft, together with Cotton and Ball, is not referred to as having received any further degree, though also a Founder, and until March, 1726, a Member of the Society.

It seems to myself, however, not entirely free from doubt, whether the step communicated to Cotton, Ball, and Marshall, at the same meeting, was the present second or the present third degree. At that date, there could have been few persons who were capable of rehearsing the "Master's Part," and the step of February, 1725, may have been again communicated—in a more correct manner—to Cotton and Ball in the following May. But without labouring this point, and even conceding, for the moment, that *three* degrees are plainly referred to in the "records" under examination—on the other hand, the entire body of evidence from 1723 to 1730, that has come down to us, is conclusive with respect to two degrees, and no more, having been worked in the Regular Lodges.

The members of the *Philo-Musicae* Society were called "to an account for making Masons irregularly" in December, 1725, by the Duke of Richmond, who was then in the chair of the Grand Lodge. But it was ordered that the letter of the Grand Master "do lye on the Table," and during the remainder of its short span of life, the association of musical Brethren continued to qualify candidates for membership by initiating them (when requisite) into the mysteries of the Craft.

The *new* method of communicating the *old* secrets of Masonry—which originated at some period after 1723—crept very slowly into favour, and it was not until the *fourth* decade of the eighteenth century that the existence of a *third* degree met with any general recognition. This is worthy of very careful consideration, because the period during which evolutionary changes were in progress has been somewhat arbitrarily restricted within narrower limits than there is evidence to support. The "Epoch of Transition," as I have elsewhere ventured to term the space of time that intervened between the formation of the first Grand Lodge and its cumulation of degrees, extended not only down to, but beyond, the year 1730, a date connected with certain events of weight and importance to which I have previously referred.

The two catechisms of 1730 reflect very clearly the absence of uniformity, at that time, in the manner of conferring the degrees. *The Grand Mystery* alludes to two steps of Masonry only, and informs us that "There is not one Mason in a Hundred that will be at the Expence to pass the Master's Part, except it be for Interest."

In *Masonry Dissected*, which particularizes three steps, there is also, under a thin veil of affected candour, what is really a violent attack upon, and impeachment of, the Grand Lodge, and for this reason, we may suppose, it was selected by Martin Clare (the champion of that body), as affording a very natural pretext for the publication of his learned *Defence*, in which the denunciations levelled at the Freemasons were triumphantly refuted. From a passage already quoted it is quite clear that only two degrees were in the contemplation of Clare when his essay was composed. The description of "Master" *or* "Felloe Craft" is in strict harmony with the *Constitutions* of 1723, and all the ritualistic evidence of that or any earlier period that has been handed down to us. After 1723 there were three degrees or *steps*, but the old system died hard, and (even in the absence of confirmatory evidence) it would be safe to conclude that the practice of communicating the Masonic secrets according to the new method could not have been officially recognized until after the *Defence of Masonry* saw the light. Clare evidently wrote as one of the older school, and the carefully chosen words in which he describes the gradations of Masonic rank as existing in 1730, are indicative not only of his own adherence to the usage of ancient times, but they also point—as I think may plainly be deduced—in the direction of the author of the *Defence* being the mouthpiece of the Grand Officers.

That he was so regarded, not only in London, but likewise (to some extent) in the provinces, we have direct proof in the minutes of a Lodge formerly meeting at the Saracen's Head, Lincoln, from which I extract the following:-

October 2nd, 1733.—Present, Sir Cecil Wray, Baronet, Master, with other members, and six visitors (Esquires), "When Brother Clare's Discourse concerning Prichard, as also . . . our By Laws were read."

August 6th, 1734.—"Brother Clare's Discourse relating to P———d was read."

Through Sir Cecil Wray—Deputy Grand Master in 1734 —who was Master of a London Lodge, with Martin Clare as his Senior Warden, in 1730, the *Defence of Masonry*, by the latter, no doubt found its way to Lincoln. The entry of August 6th, 1734, is a singular one, and tends to show that the full mention of Prichard's name was a slip on the part of the scribe who recorded it, the motive for secrecy being, as the other evidence (*i.e.*, the letter from "Euclid," printed with the *Constitutions* of 1738), seems to point out, the desire of Martin Clare, and those with whom he was acting in concert, to conceal the fact that the counterblast to *Masonry Dissected*, was, in reality, a manifesto of the Grand Lodge. It may be usefully noted in connection with the above, that the minutes of the Lodge wherein the "Discourse" (or *Defence of Masonry*) is referred to (the chair of which was filled by the Deputy Grand Master in 1734), only mention two degrees—those of apprentice and master—as being worked by the Lincoln Masons of 1732-42. They also show that the higher step was conferred in a "Lodge of Masters," but not too often or too easily, as we may judge from the circumstance that persons of high social standing (including Sir Christopher Hales, Baronet, son-in-law of Sir Cecil Wray), were members of the Lodge for several years, before being adjudged "well qualifyed and worthy," and thereupon admitted to the Master's degree.

At this point it may be conveniently mentioned that two degrees only are referred to in the "General Regulations" given in the Irish *Constitutions* of 1730, and the *Pocket Companion* of 1735; also, that when the French Lodge in London "*à l'enseigne du Duc de Lorraine*" was constituted—August 17th, 1732—by the Earl of Strathmore, the only members particularized by the Grand Master, were "*le Maitre, les Surveillants, les Compagnons, et les Apprentifs de la Loge Française.*"

In the same year, however—1732—besides the first degree, those of "F.C. and M." were worked by a London Lodge, No. 83 (*Eng. Rite,* 23); but it should be carefully borne in mind that this occurred *after* the publication of Prichard's pamphlet, and is the earliest known example of a system of *three* degrees having been adopted in the Regular Lodges.

From 1730 until 1738 new comers were admitted into Masonry, according to the old system and the new. After the latter year, indeed, the differences of procedure continued to linger, but the point on which I am now dwelling is the important fact that from 1725 to 1730, and from 1730 until the publication of the *Constitutions* of 1738, there is not a scrap of evidence from which we may infer that three degrees of Masonry were practised with the sanction (or recognition) of the earliest of Grand Lodges, either express or implied.

What was anciently called the "Master's Part," and is now the Third Degree, must have fallen into comparative disuse, when Masonry put on its modern attire, which may be described as the period beginning about the year 1723, and approaching a conclusion in 1738. After 1725, all Lodges—new or old—were empowered "to make Masters at their discretion," but many (and apparently the great majority) of them could not or did not, and the few that were able to work the "Superior" degree were known and described as Masters' Lodges. This term, in the opinion of Mr. Hughan, was applied to two classes of meetings. The first, where Lodges worked the degree on certain days in each month; and the second, where Lodges assembled as Master Masons only. According to this view of the case, some of the Lodges worked the Master's cere-mony at stated times only, while others, not caring to meet except as Master Masons, left to the ordinary Lodges the task of communicating to candidates the earlier secrets of the craft. In process of time, however, the Lodges in the first class appear to have set as little value on the Master's degree as those in the second class did on the previous ceremonial. Thence arose the custom of looking to certain Lodges for the working of the Master Mason's ritual, which bodies were specially known and described as "Master's Lodges," though all Lodges existing at the time were equally entitled to work the ceremony.

Four members of a London Lodge, who had been "made Masons," were admitted "Masters" (without receiving any intermediate degree), on April 29th, 1727; and six others were similarly "admitted" in a "Master's Lodge" on March 31st, 1729 (Hughan). This is the earliest known reference to a Master's Lodge.

The subject has also been dealt with in an exhaustive essay by the late Mr. John Lane, to which the reader is

referred. (*A.Q.C.* i. 167—175.) Masters' Lodges continued
to exist, and are described in the official lists down to the
beginning of the nineteenth century.

They appear to have been established with the object
of instructing generally in the Master's degree, which, therefore, was conferred in some instances as a second, and in
others as a third, step in Masonry.

When the Grand Lodge set its official seal on the order
in which the two moieties of the old "Apprentice Part"
should be conferred, there is no evidence to determine. All
we know with certainty is, that *two* degrees are officially
recognized by the *Constitutions* of 1723, and *three* by the
Constitutions of 1738. In the earlier work the words
Master and Fellow Craft are used as convertible terms; in
the later one they import different meanings. Entered
Apprentice, and Fellow Craft *or* Master, were the degrees
or *steps* of 1723; and Entered Apprentice, Fellow Craft, *and*
Master, were those of 1738.

For example, in the latter publication (1738), Old Regulation XIII is transformed into—"*Apprentices* must be
admitted *Fellow Crafts* and *Masters* only here"; while
the "New Regulation" at the same number, which is
supposed to reproduce the Law passed in the Grand Lodge
on November 27th, 1725, is headed "On 22. *Nov.*" (of that
year), and reads—"The *Master* of a Lodge, with his
Wardens and a competent *Number* of the Lodge assembled
in due Form, can make *Masters* and *Fellows* at Discretion"
(*ante*, 213).

But, notwithstanding the order of precedence finally
accorded by the Grand Lodge to the several moieties of
the "Apprentice's Part" as degrees, the evidence shows
that for many years after 1738 they were conferred for the
most part in continuing steps. In November, 1753, it was
enacted by the Grand Lodge, that no Lodge "be permitted to *make* and *raise* the same Brother at one and the
same Meeting, without a dispensation from the Grand
Master." Only two ceremonies are specially referred to in
the minutes of my own Lodge—the Moira, No. 92—from

the date of its formation in 1755 down to the year 1767, the "making" of Masons, and the "raising" of Masters. These "steps," however, were not conferred on "the same Brother at one Meeting," except in a solitary instance:—

April 2nd, 1766.—"Bʳ. Samuel Garnatt was made a Mason in due form, and likewise Rais'd Master by desire."

From the examples given (which could be greatly multiplied) it is reasonable to conclude that no approach to uniformity in the "making of a Mason" (*i.e.,* in the method of imparting the secrets of the first *two*, or continuing steps of the *three* degrees), could have been established in the Lodges, until many years after 1738.

It is probable that the Grand Lodge entered very reluctantly upon the task of determining which section of the old "Apprentice Part" should take the position of the first degree. The choice ultimately made (1738) soon, however, became publicly known (1742), and, as will hereafter be more particularly referred to, it differed *in toto* from the sequence of the degrees as published by Prichard in his spurious ritual of 1730.

The Royal Arch was the first of the "additional degrees," extraneous to the system of Pure and Ancient Freemasonry, and that the seed was sown, from which it ultimately germinated, by the alteration of the Mason's Creed in 1723 there cannot be a doubt. The degree was certainly worked from about the year 1740, and presumably from an earlier date. The members of the Royal Arch are described by Dr. Dassigny, in 1744, as "a body of men who have passed the chair" (*ante*, 199). At that date, however, the *degree* of Installed (or Past) Master was unknown, nor is there any evidence of its being in existence until some years after the formation of the Schismatic Grand Lodge of England in 1751. It would therefore appear that the communication of the secrets of the Royal Arch was the earliest form in which any esoteric teaching was specially linked with the incident of Lodge Mastership, or, in other words, that the *degree* of the Royal Arch was the complement of the Master's *grade*. Out of this was

ultimately evolved the degree of Installed Master, a ceremony not sanctioned by the Regular (or Constitutional)
Grand Lodge of England until 1810, and of which I can
trace no sign among the "Ancients" until the growing
practice of conferring the "Arch" upon Masons not properly
qualified to receive it brought about a *constructive* passing
through the chair, which, by qualifying candidates not
otherwise eligible, naturally entailed the introduction of a
ceremony, *additional* (like the "Arch" itself) to the simple
forms known to Payne, Anderson, and Desaguliers. In
passing from this branch of the subject, it may be observed
that, while unrecognized by the legitimate Grand Lodge
of England (in the eighteenth century), the "Arch" and
"Chair" degrees were frequently communicated in the
Regular Lodges, and it is probable, from quite as early
dates as they were practised by the "Ancients" or
"Schismatics."

As there are no early records of the Grand Lodge of
IRELAND, and the custom of publishing the histories of
private Lodges, which is otherwise universal, does not
prevail in the sister kingdom, many details of Masonic life
and activity are withheld from us, which would probably
throw considerable light upon the interesting question of
"degrees." We know, however, that the *English Constitutions* and Spurious Rituals were always reproduced in
IRELAND, where the latter especially flourished with a
luxuriant growth. From the evidence supplied by the
Irish *Constitutions* of 1730, and the *Pocket Companion* of
1735, it is apparent that (as in England) only *two* degrees
were then recognized by the Grand Lodge.

Their expansion, therefore, must have occurred after the
latter year, and, judging by such light as we possess, it is
reasonable to assume that in adopting a system of three
Masonic Steps, the *Irish* simply followed the example set
by the *English* Grand Lodge in 1738.

At that date, it should be recollected, there were in
existence Grand Lodges of England, Ireland, and Scotland,
and consequently—if we suppose the necessity for a choice

to have arisen—it was equally open to them all to determine the order of priority of the first two degrees. The Grand Lodge of England, as I have endeavoured to show, struck out a path of its own, the action of the Grand Lodge of Scotland is veiled in some obscurity, but the Grand Lodge of Ireland, for reasons we cannot fathom, instead of adopting the *authorized* English system of 1738, must eventually have accorded its official sanction to the progression of the degrees, as given by Samuel Prichard in his *unauthorized* publication of 1730.

As we have already seen, the *only* degree (of a speculative or symbolical character) known in the early Masonry of SCOTLAND was that in which the Legend of the Craft was read, and the benefit of the MASON WORD conferred. From the operation of causes, however, which, though largely debated, have not yet passed out of the region of conjecture, the greater number of the additional ceremonies, adopted in many quarters as Masonic, and labelled the "HIGH DEGREES," have been described as of Scottish origin. Indeed, not content with this—as St. Andrew was the Patron Saint of Scotland, and of the Lodges there, the new degrees manufactured in France were called not alone Scottish, but St. Andrew's degrees. These *Scots* degrees, as I have elsewhere ventured to term them, in contradistinction to the ceremonies actually practised by *Scottish* Masons, appear to have sprung up about the year 1740, in all parts of France. Afterwards, in Continental Europe, besides the legion of Scots degrees, we meet with the STRICT OBSERVANCE, and the (so-called) ROYAL ORDER OF SCOTLAND, each placing its origin in North Britain. A still later example of the common practice of affecting a connection with Scotland is afforded by a well-known and highly influential body—the ANCIENT AND ACCEPTED SCOTTISH RITE.

From the circumstance that Scots Masonry was unknown before the delivery by Andrew Michael Ramsay of his famous speech in 1737, and appeared shortly afterwards, the two have been represented as cause and effect—which, indeed, was almost certainly the case, but the oration of the "Chevalier" and the Continental perversions of Freemasonry that followed in its train are supposed by some good authorities to be themselves merely links in a far-reaching chain of events, extending over a long series of years.

The Scots Degrees smoothed the way for the Templar movement in Masonry, called the STRICT OBSERVANCE, and the key to the problem which confronts us in either instance, it is contended, may be found in the extent to which the Jesuits moulded the Stuart agitation, ending with the rising of 1745-6.

Early in the eighteenth century, when English Masonry put on its modern attire, its secret organization was continued under a Grand Lodge, and this body was established during the same period which, after the death of Louis XIV, became the signal for the Jacobite risings that were suppressed in 1716. Among those who took up arms for the Pretender were many prominent Freemasons. Some were executed, and others found refuge on the Continent. Among the latter was the Earl of Winton, afterwards Master of the famous "Roman Lodge" (founded by Scottish Masons in Rome) at the time of its suppression in 1737; and if we may believe the French historians, it was by another of these exiles, Charles Ratcliffe, who, after his elder brother was beheaded, assumed the title of the Earl of Derwentwater, that the first Lodge in France was founded at Paris in 1725.

In a recent pamphlet Mr. R. Greeven lays great stress on "the struggles of the Duke of Wharton [1724] and the Society of Gormogons at first to control and afterwards to counteract Freemasonry in England for Jacobite purposes in connection with the Pretender at Rome." At a much earlier date, however, the several printed notices of the Gormogons formed the subject of an interesting study by Dr. Kloss (1847), by whom three conjectures were advanced:—I. That the Oecumenical Volgi (or Head of the Order) was no less than the Chevalier Ramsay, then at

ANCIENT SUMMONS OF A LODGE AT NUREMBERG IN 1778

Rome in attendance upon Charles Edward Stuart ("the young Sophi of Persia"). II. That the movement was a deeply-laid scheme on the part of the Jesuits to attain certain ends; and III. (though without attaching to it any importance), that in the Gormogons we meet with the precursors of the Schismatic Masons, or "Ancients" (*Gesch. der Fr. England, Irland, Schottland*, 90).

It is next suggested that, in his famous speech of 1737, "Ramsay—connected by his hearers with the Young Pretender both by religion and tutorship—was appealing in the name of crusading tradition, to a society of which the back-bone consisted of Scotchmen waiting only for a favourable opportunity, eventually presented in 1745, for invading England with French assistance to enthrone a Romanist aspirant already seriously preparing himself for the contest." Shortly after the speech was delivered, there followed the deluge of Scots degrees, and throughout the whole of them the influence of Ramsay's rhetoric is apparent, in the underlying fiction that Scottish crusaders—sword in one hand and trowel in the other—discovered a lost and sacred word in the vault of the Temple at Jerusalem.

The numerous Scots Lodges soon assumed the powers of Grand Lodges, and at an early stage began to manufacture new degrees connecting the Scots Masons with the Knights Templars.

If the statements of the Baron von Hund are to be credited, there is the clearest possible evidence that in 1743 substantially the entire Rite or System, afterwards so well-known under the title of the STRICT OBSERVANCE, was in full working order under the guidance of leading Jacobites and with the direct approval of the Young Pretender. This Rite was based upon the fiction that at the time of the suppression of the Templars, and the execution of their last (historical) Grand Master, his alleged successor, Pierre d'Aumont, with seven other knights, took refuge in Scotland, and there preserved the occult wisdom and the due succession of the Order. For certain reasons also, these knights were said to have joined the Guild of Masons in that Kingdom, and thus to have given rise to the Society of Freemasons.

The Baron von Hund declared that he was received into the Order of the Temple at Paris, by the Knight with the Red Feather (or Chief Superior), in the presence of the Earl of Kilmarnock, and with Lord Clifford acting as Prior. A solemn pledge, he averred, prevented his revealing the identity of the Knight with the Red Feather, though in effect he allowed it to be inferred that the presiding officer on the occasion of his being knighted as a Templar, was no other than the Young Pretender himself. He stated, moreover, that he had been specially presented, as a distinguished member of the Order, to Prince Charles Edward, shortly after the ceremony of 1743. The history of "Templarism in Masonry" is next to be traced in the proceedings of the Chapter of Clermont (1754), the Knights of the East (1756), and the Emperors of the East and West (1758), after which—in 1767—the curtain falls on the first act of the Templar drama, and the scene shifts to Germany, where the princes and nobles for nearly two decades, received the new Order of Chivalry with enthusiasm. Throughout the Continent of Europe, Pure and Ancient Masonry almost vanished, and no less than twelve reigning princes—bound by vows of unquestioning obedience to Unknown Superiors—were active members of the STRICT OBSERVANCE, in 1774.

The oath of implicit obedience to Unknown Superiors was the leading characteristic of the Order, and on taking it new comers received a promise—the breach of which ultimately broke up the organization—that those Superiors would impart to them an occult Wisdom, which (as a matter of fact) we know that the historical Knights Templars could never have possessed.

At the death of von Hund, in 1776, there was a period of confusion, and his papers were searched with the object of ascertaining who was the real head of the Order, but nothing was discovered beyond the circumstance that von Hund evidently believed Prince Charles Edward Stuart to be the man. The Young Pretender was then duly communicated with, and with the result, according to one set of writers, that he not only disclaimed being Grand Master of the STRICT OBSERVANCE, but also that he was a Freemason at all; while by others, it is affirmed (and with perhaps the greater show of reason) that the Prince was compelled, by the altered circumstances of his cause, to repudiate any relations with Freemasonry. A few years later, at the Congress of Wilhelmsbad, in 1782, it was resolved and declared that the Freemasons were not the successors of the Knights Templars. From that moment the STRICT OBSERVANCE, as a system, practically ceased to exist.

If we adopt the conclusions of Mr. Greeven and the late Dr. Kloss, the influence of "Scots abroad," and of Scottish legend (real or supposed), on the Masonry of the Continent, ceases to be a wholly obscure enigma. If we do not, however—and in the absence of further evidence there will always be a conflict of opinion with regard to the direction in which our judgment ought to incline—then the wholesale manufacture of degrees, supposed to hail from Scotland, but having no real connection with that country, which spread like a pestilence throughout Europe, will remain among the phenomena that baffle the research of all students of Freemasonry.

End of the Digression

The merits of the *Constitutions* of 1738, as containing the only record of certain eighteenth-century facts, are unquestionable; but it is much to be regretted that, in his desire to exhibit the Craft to the best advantage, Dr. Anderson should have claimed as its rulers at some period or other nearly every celebrity of ancient or modern times. Thus we have Noah and his sons figuring as the "Four Grand Officers," and among the Ancient Grand Masters are gravely enumerated the names of Nimrod, Moses (with Joshua as his Deputy), Solomon, Nebuchadnezzar, and Augustus Cæsar. The list of Modern Grand Masters is drawn up on an equally comprehensive scale, and includes the names of Alfred the Great, Edward the Confessor, Cardinal Wolsey, and Sir Christopher Wren—to whose "neglect of the office," shortly after 1708, is attributed the decay which immediately preceded the so-called "Revival" of 1717.

Professor John Robison, the eminent Scottish mathematician, in his now forgotten *Proofs of a Conspiracy* (1797), comments very justly "upon the heap of rubbish with which Anderson has disgraced his Constitutions of Freemasonry, *the basis of Masonic History.*" The evil is to be deplored, but may be minimized by our totally disregarding any statements of the doctor, excepting only such as relate to the early proceedings of the Grand Lodge —published with the sanction and approval of the Grand Officers, and others who were personal actors in the events to which they refer.

In *The New Book of Constitutions*, "The CHARGE concerning God and Religion" is made to read—"In ancient Times the Christian Masons were charged to comply with the Christian Usages of each Country where they travell'd or work'd," which takes the place of—"In ancient Times Masons were charg'd in every country to be of the Religion of that Country or Nation, whatever it was," which appeared in the *Constitutions* of 1723.

"Whether the Grand Lodge disagreed with Dr. Anderson in reference to this particular matter," observed the late Mr. H. J. Whymper, "we do not know, but we do know there was some disagreement, and we see by the 1738 'Constitutions' that Dr. Anderson virtually disavowed the 1723 statement." (*Religion of F.*, 38.) As we shall presently find, at some time after 1738, two parties were formed, the Grand Lodge of England (established in 1717) taking the Deistic, and the Masons who claimed to be the representatives of Ancient Masonry taking the Christian side—the latter adopting Dr. Anderson's statement of 1738, that Masons were anciently enjoined to comply with Christian customs in foreign lands; while the former went back to his older declaration of 1723, that in bygone times

Masons were enjoined to be of the religion of any country in which they might happen to reside.

A list is given of the Lodges in and about London and Westminster, and among them we find three "whose *Constitution* is immemorial," being the survivors of the Four by whom the Grand Lodge was founded in 1717, namely, the Lodges at the KING'S ARMS, removed from the GOOSE AND GRIDIRON, *now* the LODGE OF ANTIQUITY; at the HORN, removed from the RUMMER AND GRAPES, *now* ROYAL SOMERSET HOUSE AND INVERNESS; and at the QUEEN'S HEAD, removed from the APPLE TREE, *now* FORTITUDE AND OLD CUMBERLAND. Of the last named we learn that "the members came under a *new constitution*, tho' they wanted it not," which ought to have resulted, though it *has not*, in the restoration of the Lodge to its rightful position on the Grand Lodge roll. The Lodges enumerated form a total of 106, and after the names of thirteen there follow the words "Where there is also a *Master's Lodge*."

The first organized rebellion against the authority of the Grand Lodge took place shortly after the promulgation of the *Constitutions* of 1723, and the second, or a revival of the old one, must have closely followed the publication of the *Constitutions* of 1738. The discontent which ultimately assumed the proportions of a Schism in English Masonry is commonly supposed to have originated in 1739, and the theory has much to recommend it, though for reasons entirely differing from those which are ordinarily brought forward in its support.

The true story of the Great Division I shall, in the next chapter, endeavour to relate, and as preparatory thereto it will be best if I next proceed to bring up the general narrative to the point from which the memorable division in the English Craft can be examined as a whole. For this purpose it will be essential to take a brief glance at the progress of Masonry on the Continent. Persecutions of the Freemasons occurred in Holland, 1735; in France and Italy, 1737; at Vienna, 1743; and in Switzerland, 1745. Moreover, in the year 1738, a formidable Bull was issued by the Pope, not only against the Freemasons themselves, but against all those who promoted or favoured their cause.

There is evidence that the English Craft was also falling into disfavour, from the series of mock processions that appear to have been begun by the "Scald Miserables" in 1741, and continued in 1742, 1744 and 1745. A print of the procession, designed and engraved by Benoist, was published in 1742. The proceedings of the "Scald Miserables," which were intended to exhibit a mockery of the public procession of the Freemasons to the Grand Feast, resulted in the latter abandoning all outdoor display, and confining their operations within the limits of their own assembly. Money, however, must have been plentiful with the organizers of the buffoonery, for the mock processions could not have been otherwise than very costly affairs, from which may be inferred that there were influential people in the background, who shared in the design of holding up the Freemasons to ridicule and contempt.

In 1743—May 4th—Horace Walpole, in a letter to Sir Horace Mann, says:—"The Freemasons are in so low repute now in England, that one has scarce heard the proceedings at Vienna against them mentioned. I believe nothing but a persecution could bring them into vogue here again. You know, as great as our follies are, we even grow tired of them, and are always changing."

A notable figure passed off the stage in 1744, in the person of Dr. Desaguliers, one of the triumvirate to whom the foundation of the earliest of Grand Lodges has loosely been ascribed. The other members were Dr. James Anderson and George Payne. The Author of the original *Book of Constitutions* died in 1739, and the second of our Grand Masters in 1757.

In 1747 Lord Byron was elected Grand Master, and during his nominal presidency, which lasted for a period of five years, the affairs of the Society were much neglected. The same Grand Officers and Grand Stewards continued in office, which is the more remarkable, because the honours of the Craft were much coveted.

The first English Military Lodge was established in 1750, and attached to the 31st Foot. In the following year (as will presently be more fully referred to) the Rival Body in the English Craft had assumed form and cohesion, and if technicalities are disregarded, the members may be said to have been governed at that date by a Grand Lodge, though sometimes disguised under the title of a Grand Committee.

Lord Byron was succeeded by Lord Carysfort in 1752, and Dr. Thomas Manningham was appointed Deputy Grand Master.

In 1755, it was "Ordered that every certificate granted to a Brother of his being a Mason shall for the future be sealed with the seal of Masonry, & signed by the G.S." (*Grand Secretary*). A new edition of the *Book of Constitutions*, in which the original version of the "CHARGE concerning God and Religion" (1723) is reproduced, was published in 1756.

There next await our consideration letters written by Dr. Manningham in 1756 and 1757 respectively, which were published a few years ago in the columns of the *Jaarboekje voor Nederlandsche Vrijmetselaren*, or Dutch *Freemason's Annual*.

The first letter was dated December 3rd, 1756, and forwarded, by order of the Grand Master, the Marquis of Carnarvon, to the Provincial Grand Lodge of Holland. It runs:—

"Gentlemen & Brethren,—

"The Marquis of CARNARVAN, Grand Master of Masons, being absent in the Country, has occasion'd my Neglect in not answering your Letters address'd to our late worthy Grand Master, Lord CARYSFORT, & communicated the Contents to his Lordship, as well as to the present Grand Master.

"As I presume the English Tongue is understood by several of our Brethren in *Holland*, I thought it more advisable to send my Answer in English, than French.

"The Grand Master is at all times willing to oblige the Craft, & is very sorry it is not in his Power to grant the Request contained in your Letters: as I am not perfect

Master of the French Language, perhaps I may have mistook & interpreted their Purport wrong; therefore I now write them as I understood them, & annex the Grand Master's Answer to the separate Articles.

"1st. You desire the Grand Master's Permission to hold Scotch Lodges, & institute the Brethren according to their Method.

"This cannot be allow'd, as we know no Distinction of Lodges, Free Masonry being the same in all Parts of the World; I am sure it ought to be so, or it could never be general: Unless you are cautious, you may be misled. By your kind Letter, I find the craft flourishes in *Holland*, & I sincerely wish it may without Cavils and Dissentions.

"The Methods of Lodges will sometimes differ a little, but I trust not materially, & that the ancient Land Marks will always continue. Of late some fertile Genius's here have attempted considerable Innovations, & their manner of working in Lodge, they term sometimes Irish, another Scotch Masonry, why or wherefore they themselves best know; this I am certain of, all Innovations in our Society must tend to Confusion. Harmony & Union in Masonry all the world over, is to be wish'd for & cultivated. I dare believe the Brethren in *Holland* will subscribe to such Unanimity, & choose to be known as Free Masons, without other appellative Distinctions, & will excuse the Grand Master from saying, He cannot grant your first request, wch seems to design Innovations, or new Methods, if not Variation in the Signs, Tokens, & Words, & thereby ruin, instead of support, the Society. . . .

"The Grand Master desires his Respects to all the Brethren with you, particularly the Members of your Lodge, & I beg leave to add my Compliments likewise, who am

"Gentlemen & Brethren,

"Y$^{r.}$ most obed$^{t.}$ & affect$^{te.}$ humble serv$^{t.}$

"T. MANNINGHAM, D.G.M.

"London,

"3 Dec$^{r.}$ 1756."

The second letter—July 12th, 1757—may be appropriately introduced in the words of Mr. L. H. Hertzveld to Mr. J. G. Findel, as appearing in the *Freemasons' Magazine* of August 15th, 1858:—

"A witness whose honour and competence no one can dispute, has risen from the tomb after more than one hundred years' slumber, to testify to some historical facts.

"By means of a happy event, there has come into my hands a communication from the famous Deputy Grand Master of England, Bro. Manningham, to the then Grand Lodge of the Netherlands, dated London, 12th July, 1757, which proves (1) That no higher degrees, with the only exception of the three craft degrees, belong to pure ancient Freemasonry; (2) That before 1717 the now existing rituals have been worked; (3) That the introduction of the so-called high degrees took place after 1740.

" '*Dr. Manningham to Bro. Sauer at the Hague, July 12th,*
1757.

" 'Sr ∴ & Br ∴

" 'I am quite asham'd that your obliging Letter should lay by me so long unanswer'd, but I hope you will excuse me when I assure you it was not owing to Neglect or Disrespect, but want of Opportunity to satisfye myself on some Points, relating to the Variety of Masonry wch. you mention under the Name of Scotch Masonry.

" 'I was determin'd to consult our Brethren in *Scotland*, particularly our Brother, Lord ABERDOUR, who is Son & Heir to the Earl of MORTON, & an exceedingly good Mason; as such He has fill'd the chair in *Scotland*, & his Lordship is now elected Grand Master in *England*, on the Marquis of CARNARVAN's Resignation.

" 'Lord ABERDOUR & all the Scotch Masons (or rather Scotch Gentlemen that are Masons) that I have convers'd with, & I have made it my Business to consult many, are entirely unacquainted with the Forms & Titles you mention, & wch. you justly call the charlatanery of Masonry. Amongst some of our lowest Brethren, I have met with,

& frequently heard of such Irregularities; Irregularities I justly call them, because they deviate so much from our usual Ceremonies, & are so full of Innovations, that in process of Time, the antient Landmarks will be destroy'd. by the fertile genius of Brethren who will improve or alter, if only to give Specimen of their Abilities, & imaginary consequence; so that, in few Years it will be as difficult to understand Masonry, as to distinguish the Points or Accents of the Hebrew or Greek Language, now almost obscur'd by the Industry of Criticks & Comentators.

" 'Three foreign Gentlemen and Masons lately visited the Lodge I belong to, & were introduc'd by me to the Grand Lodge & the Grand Feast; by discoursing with these Gentlemen I find *Germany, Holland,* & *Switzerland* in some Places have Orders of Masons unknown to us, viz., Knights of the Sword, of the Eagle, of the Holy Land, with a long train of et caetera's; surely these Points of Masonry must be wonderfull; I am certain they are very new; beside, these dignified & distinguish'd Orders I find have Signs, Tokens, &c., peculiar to their respective Dignities, & adorn themselves with different colour'd Ribbons.

" 'I shall be glad with your Assistance & the Assistance of the Brethren in *Holland,* to settle these intricate & confus'd Points, & wish to know (especially from the Brethren who distinguish themselves by the Denomination of Scotch Masons) from whence they receiv'd their constitution, the Grand Master of *Scotland,* who I presume they acknowledge Head of their Society, being entirely unacquainted with their Order: To Lord ABERDOUR & several other Scotch Noblemen, & Gentlemen that are good Masons, I have communicated your Letter, likewise the Information I receiv'd from those foreign Brethren, one of wch. was an Officer in the Dutch Service; but from the strictest Enquiries I can make, can only say they have rack'd their genius with Endeavours to make Masonry unintelligable and useless.

" 'These Innovations are of very late Years, & I beleive the Brethren will find a Difficulty to produce a Mason, acquainted with any such Forms twenty, nay, ten, Years. My own Father has been a Mason these fivety Years & has been at Lodges in *Holland, France,* and *England.* He knows none of these ceremonies: Grand Master PAYN, who succeeded Sr. CHRISTOPHER WREN, is a stranger to them, as is likewise one old Brother of Ninety, who I convers'd with lately; this Brother assures me He was made a Mason in his youth, and has constantly frequented Lodges, 'till rend'red incapable by his advanc'd Age, & never heard, or knew, any other Ceremonies or Words, than those us'd in general amongst us; such Forms were deliver'd to him, & those he has retain'd: As to Knights of the Sword, Eagle, &c., the knowledge of them never reach'd his ears, till I inform'd him of them. The only Orders that we know are Three, Masters, Fellow-Crafts & Apprentices, & none of them ever arrive at the Honour of Knighthood by Masonry; & I beleive you can scarcely imagine, that in antient time the Dignity of Knighthood flourish'd amongst Free Masons; whose Lodges here to fore consisted of Operative, not Speculative Masons. Knights of the Eagle, Knights of the Sword, I have read in Romance, the great Don QUIXOTE himself was Knight of the Brazen Helmet, when He had vanquish'd the Barber. Knights of the Holy Land, St. John of Jerusalem, Templars, &c., have existed, & I beleive now exist in the Knights of Malta, but what is that to Masonry? I never heard that those Orders or Honours were obtain'd by skill in Masonry, or that they belong'd to the Fraternity of Free Masons, tho' I do not doubt they have now, & have had, many Free Masons worthy Members of their Order & Honour, but imagine they did not think such Titles obtain'd by Masonry alone.

" 'Universal Benevolence, Brotherly Love, Friendship & Truth, acting by the Square & living within Compass, are or ought to be, the Tenets of Masonry, the Rule & Guide of our Actions. Let us be good Masons, we may look with Scorn, on other Honours or Titles, it is at all Times in our Power to be good Masons, & I think we ought to be contented, & not search the aerial Fields of Romance for additional Titles. Use our utmost Endeavour Dear Brother to prevent a realy valuable Society, from degenerating, and being lost in Obscurity, by aiming at Titles, to which the very nature of our Society cannot give us a Claim.

" 'The only distinction of Ribons or Jewels, that we make in our Lodges, you will find in our Book of Constitutions; viz., Grand Officers wear their Jewels gilt, pendant on blue Ribons, & their Aprons lin'd with blue; Those Brethren that have Serv'd the Office of Steward at our Grand Feast (from wch. number all Grand Officers, except Grand Master, must be elected) wear their Jewels of Silver on red Ribons, & line their Aprons with red; all other Brethren wear white Aprons and their Jewels pendant on white Ribons, neither are they suffer'd to wear other Jewels than the Square, Level and Plumb, the Compass belonging only to the Grand Master. . . .

" 'If the Master of the Lodge is absent, the past Master, or the Senior warden of the Lodge supply his Place, just as the private Regulations of such Lodge direct.

" 'Our Healths in Lodge are first, the King & the Craft, wth. 3, 3. 2d The Grand Master, wth. 3, 3, the D.G.M. & G.W's. wth. 3, then we drink past G.M., foreign Brethren of Distinction by Name as the Emperor, King of *Prussia*, &c., after that the general Toast of the Craft.

" 'The Marquis of CARNARVON has resign'd the Chair to Lord ABERDOUR, who is now G.M., & our worthy Br. REVIS, D.G.M., but I have permission to sign this Letter as D.G.M., & if you favour us with a Line, take the same Method as before by Mr. HOPP's secretary, who will convey your Commands to me, & I will take care they are properly honour'd.

" 'The late & present G.M. desire their Respects to our Brethren, please to accept likewise of the Respects of

" 'Dr. Sr. & Br.

" 'Yr. most affect. Br. & obedt. humble servt.,

" 'T. MANNINGHAM, D.G.M.

" 'JERMYN STREET,

" '12 July, 1757."

OLD CERTIFICATE OF THE "ANCIENTS" GRAND LODGE
Date, 1805

There are only two expressions in the Manningham letters which call for remark. In the first place, the doctor tells us that Grand Master Payne, "who succeeded Sir Christopher Wren, *is* a stranger" to the ceremonies of the Continent. But Payne, who was in his grave when the letters were written, certainly did not "succeed" Wren, even if we were to transmute the fable of the latter's Grand Mastership into a fact. The explanation probably is, that the mention of Payne in the present tense was purely a slip on the part of the writer, while in the allusion to the great architect having presided over the Society, an unfortunate reliance on the imaginative history related by Dr. Anderson is plainly to be detected. Lastly, "The only Orders we know," observes Dr. Manningham, "are three—Masters, Fellow Crafts, and Apprentices." There were no more and no less. But this, as I have endeavoured to show in the recent DIGRESSION, was not always the case; although it is evident that the falsification of Old Regulation XIII by Dr. Anderson in the *Constitutions* of 1738 was entirely unknown to the Deputy Grand Master of 1757. A similar ignorance with respect to the actual number of degrees recognized by the Grand Lodge from 1717 until 1738, as we shall presently see, was displayed by the author of the *Illustrations of Masonry*, in the last quarter of the eighteenth century, and by the representatives of the older of the two rival Grand Lodges of England, when arranging the preliminaries which were followed by the memorable UNION of these Societies, in 1813.

CHAPTER VII*

FOR many years a violent controversy raged around the history of the rival Grand Lodges in England, and some writers preferred to call it "The Great Schism."

The researches of the late Mr. Henry Sadler in the archives of the Grand Lodge clearly proved that the second Grand Lodge was founded by Irish Masons who had settled in London. In 1751 these Irish Masons established a body which they termed "The Grand Lodge of England according to the old Institutions," and they gave themselves the name of "Ancients," and the members of the Senior Grand Lodge they termed "Moderns."

They claimed that the members of the Senior Grand Lodge had made changes in the ceremonial about the year 1730, but that they themselves had remained faithful to the ancient rules, landmarks, and customs of the Order.

Laurence Dermott himself stated that "The Ancients under the name of Free and Accepted Masons according to the old Institutions, and the Moderns under the name of Free Masons of England, though similar in name, yet differ exceedingly in makings, ceremonials, knowledge, Masonic language, and installation, so much that they always have been, and still continue to be, two distinctive societies totally independent of each other."

In 1756 "A Book of Constitutions" appeared for the use of the Ancient Masons under the name of *Ahiman Rezon*, and this was adopted by all Masons in England and America who followed the Ancients' workings, whilst the members of the Moderns or Regular Grand Lodge adhered

---

* *Vide* Preface to Revised Edition.

to *Anderson's Constitutions*, which was first published in 1723. Mr. E. L. Hawkins says, "What were the precise differences in the rituals of the Ancients and Moderns it is now perhaps impossible to discover, as from their esoteric nature they were only orally communicated; but some shrewd and near approximation to their real nature may be drawn by inference from the casual expressions which have fallen from the advocates of each in the course of their long and generally bitter controversies."

It had already been said that the Regular Grand Lodge is stated to have made certain changes in the modes of recognition in consequence of the publication of Samuel Prichard's book, *Masonry Dissected*. These changes, as we traditionally learn, have simple transposition of certain words by which that which had originally been the first became the second, and that which had been the second became the first. Hence Dr. Dalcho, compiler of the original *Ahiman Rezon* of South Carolina, who was himself made in an Ancient Lodge, and was acquainted with both systems, says:—"The real difference in point of importance was no greater than it would be to dispute whether the glove should be placed on the right or on the left."

A similar testimony as to the character of the changes is furnished by an address to the Duke of Atholl, a Grand Master of the Grand Lodge of Ancients, in which it is said:—"I would beg leave to ask whether two persons standing in the Guildhall of London, the one facing the statues of Gog and Magog, and the other with his back on them, could with any degree of propriety quarrel about their stations, as Gog must be on the right of one and Magog on the right of the other. Such then, and far more insignificant, is the disputatious temper of the seceding that on no better grounds than the above they choose to usurp a power, and to aid in open and direct violation of the regulations they have solemnly engaged to maintain, and by every artifice possible to be devised endeavour to increase their numbers."

It was undoubtedly to the relative situation of the pillars and the appropriation of their names that these innuendoes referred; as we have them now, they were made by the change effected by the Grand Lodge of Moderns, which transposed the original order in which they existed before the change, and in which order they are still preserved in the Continental Lodges.

In his *Masonic Facts and Fictions*, Mr Henry Sadler shows clearly that a very strong Hibernian element was found in the membership of the new Masonic body; and Laurence Dermott, who was appointed their Grand Secretary, and afterwards became their Deputy Grand Master, was himself an Irishman. He was born in 1720 in Ireland, initiated in 1740, installed as Master of No. 26 at Dublin in 1746, and in the same year became a Royal Arch Mason; soon afterwards he came to London and worked as a Journeyman Painter. He joined a "Modern Lodge" in 1748, but soon afterwards became an "Ancient." He became Grand Secretary in 1752, and was Deputy Grand Master from 1771 to 1777, and again from 1783 to 1787, four years after which he died.

Hawkins says "That, though he began his career in London as a Painter, working twelve hours a day for his master, he was able to make some valuable presents to Grand Lodge, and in its later records he was described as a Wine Merchant."

Even as regards Bye-laws an Irish model seems to be adopted, as the following occurs in the minutes of the Grand Committee, April 1st, 1752.

"A copy of the Bye-laws for private Lodges as written by the late Grand Secretary was read and compared with Bro. Dermott's copy of the Bye-laws of his former Lodge, No. 26, in the City of Dublin, and the latter being deemed the most correct it was Unanimously Resolved that the most correct copy should be received and acknowledged as the only Bye-laws for private Lodges in future, and public thanks be given to Bros. Philip M'Loughlin and J. Morgan for their good intentions and trouble in drawing up the former Bye-laws."

The first Constitutions of the Ancients were also derived

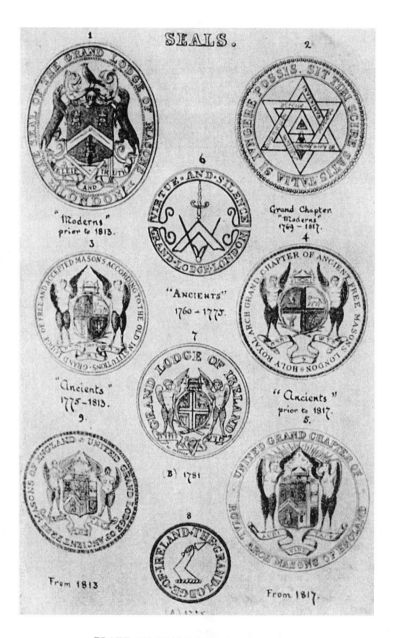

PLATE OF SEALS FOR COMPARISON

from Ireland; the seals of the Ancients and of the Grand Lodge of Ireland were almost identical, and a small Irish seal showing an arm with a hand grasping a trowel was very commonly used by the Lodge of the Ancients.

In their Warrants also they copied Ireland. The first one known was dated November 16th, 1772, and the seal is affixed by being impressed on two pieces of narrow ribbon of blue and gold colour as in the old Irish seals, whilst the Moderns never used ribbons for the seals of their Warrants. The Irish system of registering members was used by the Ancients, whilst the Moderns did not adopt it for over thirty years.

Sadler states "That the first register of the Ancients and the earliest existing register of the Grand Lodge of Ireland are almost identical, whilst the Moderns used different systems." The Ancient Grand Lodge minutes of March 1st, 1758, contained the following:—"Heard a letter from Mr. John Calder (G.S.) in Dublin, wherein he assured the Grand Lodge of Ancient Masons in London that the Grand Lodge of Ireland did usually concurr in a strict Union with the Antient Grand Lodge in London, and promised to keep a Constant Correspondence with them. Order'd that the Grand Secretary shall draw up an answer in the most respectful and Brotherly Terms wherein the General thanks of this Grand Lodge shall be convey'd and to show them that we will to the utmost of our powers promote the welfare of the Craft in General."

We are also told by Sadler of a footnote added to the Grand Lodge minute of December 27th, 1755, in which Dermott remarks:—"This year, 1755, the Modern Masons began to make use of Certificates, though the Ancient Masons had granted Certificates from time immemorial."

Here, again, the Irish and the Ancient Grand Lodges issued Certificates in Latin and English, whilst the Moderns never did so. These and many other coincidences seem clearly to prove that the Ancients had an Irish origin, and were not seceders from the original Grand Lodge of England.

As a final and, to our mind, conclusive argument, Mr.

Sadler gives a copy of a letter from James Heseltine, then Grand Secretary of the Moderns, dated "D'rs Commons, 8th Aug., 1769," and written to Mr. Geo. Stable of White-haven, who had made inquiries of him as to the Ancients. Heseltine naturally strongly disapproves of them and their doings, and has no opinion of their social position or their ways. He makes every charge he reasonably can against them. "Yet it will be observed," says Sadler, "that the words *seceders* or *schismatics* are not to be found in this long and carefully worded document; nor does the writer even insinuate that these terms might with propriety be applied to them."

The Ancients maintained that they alone preserved the ancient tenets and practices of Masonry, and that the regular Lodges had altered the Landmarks and made innovations. They certainly had peculiar marks of their own, as Dermott himself states. He says that "A Modern Mason may safely communicate all his secrets to an Ancient Mason, but that an Ancient cannot with like safety communicate all his secrets to a Modern Mason without further ceremony. For as a Science comprehends an Art (though an Art cannot comprehend a Science), even so Ancient Masonry contains everything valuable among the Moderns, as well as many other things that cannot be revealed without additional ceremonies."

There is little doubt that these differences consist of changes in the third degree and the introduction of the Royal Arch.

The Ancients were very largely instrumental in introducing Masonry into foreign countries and into America, where they organized several Provincial Grand Lodges, including those of Massachusetts, Pennsylvania, New York, Virginia, and South Carolina, where their Lodges were called "Ancient York Lodges."

We must admit that the Moderns did make innovations in the rituals, but there is a strong probability that these were made because of the flood of spurious publications which appeared at about that time, and that they were intended to distinguish impostors from true brethren.

The Earl of Blesington was prevailed upon to accept the office of Grand Master in 1756.

As already stated, "a Strict union with the Antient Grand Lodge in London" was established by the Grand Lodge of Ireland in 1758. The third Duke of Atholl was Grand Master of the "Ancients" from 1771 to 1774; and the fourth Duke from 1775 to 1781, and again from 1791 to 1813. The former was Grand Master of Scotland in 1773—when an *entente cordiale* was established between the *two* Grand Lodges under his jurisdiction—and the latter in 1778.

Towards the close of the century, wherever there were British garrisons, the authority of the "Ancient" or (as it was often called) the "Atholl" Grand Lodge was slowly but surely extending, while that of the older Grand Lodge of England was as steadily diminishing. At the close of 1789, forty-nine Army warrants had been granted by the seceders, and upon the influence which the "Atholl" and the Irish "Travelling Lodges" exercised both in the Old World and the New, Mr. Gould has enlarged in a previous work (*Military Lodges, passim*).

A motion in favour of a Union with the "Moderns" was made, but defeated, at the December meeting of the Grand Lodge, in 1797. [*Here the revision of this portion of the work terminates.*—F.J.W.C.]

Returning to the older Grand Lodge of England, or let me say, in the present connection, passing from the ANCIENTS to the MODERNS, we find that in 1761, during the Grand Mastership of Lord Aberdour, the "Grand Lodge of ALL England at York" awoke from a slumber of uncertain duration, and held meetings for a long period. It seems to have warranted about ten subordinate Lodges, created the Lodge of Antiquity a Grand Lodge, and recognized five degrees of Masonry—the three of the Craft, the Royal Arch and Knight Templar. The records come to an end in 1792, but there is evidence from which we may infer that the "Grand Lodge of ALL England" lingered until the early years of the nineteenth century.

What Mr. Hughan has well described as "the pernicious fiction of the 'Ancients' being 'York Masons' " may be incidentally referred to. In the *Ahiman Rezon* of 1756 the Regulations for Charity are described—

"As practised in *Ireland*, and by York Masons in England." So there is really no doubt that the "Ancients" wished to be regarded as "York Masons," though without an atom of justification to the claim.

Lord Blayney became Grand Master of the older Grand Lodge of England in 1764, and during his administration the Dukes of York, Cumberland, and Gloucester—sons of Frederick, Prince of Wales—were admitted to the membership of the Society. All the sons of George III, except the Duke of Cambridge, it may be observed, were numbered among the Royal Freemasons of later date.

It was carried by a vote of the Grand Lodge, in 1769, that the Society should be incorporated, but the design was abandoned in 1771. A New Hall was opened in Great Queen Street, and the building dedicated to MASONRY, in 1776. In the following year a dispute arose among the members of the Lodge of the Antiquity—the Senior Lodge on the roll—and the contest having been carried into the Grand Lodge, the result was a minor schism, which lasted for the space of ten years. William Preston and ten others were expelled from the Society in 1779, but they claimed to have carried the real Lodge of Antiquity with them in their retirement from the Grand Lodge. Matters were adjusted, and things returned into the *status quo ante*, in 1789, the Lodge of Antiquity, in the interim, masquerading as a Grand Lodge.

The last *Book of Constitutions* containing the "History of Masonry from the Creation" was published in 1784. In 1790 Lord Rawdon, better known as the chivalrous Earl of Moira, was appointed Acting Grand Master, at first under the Duke of Cumberland, and subsequently under the Prince of Wales. In 1799 it was enacted by Parliament that all societies, the members of which were required to take any oath not authorized by law, should be deemed unlawful combinations, and their members should be liable to a penalty. The Bill, however, owing to the united efforts of the Duke of Atholl and Lord Moira, was much modified in its passage through Committee, and the Act was ultimately framed so as to embrace as participants in its immunities all Lodges of Freemasons complying with its requirements. The first definite proposal for a Union, made in either of the rival Grand Lodges, as we have already seen, took place in 1797. The next attempt to effect a fusion of the two Societies came from the other side, and similarly fell to the ground, but it soon became evident that the divided bodies of English Freemasons were bent on a complete reconciliation, which the misguided efforts of the ruling authorities on either side might retard, though only for a time.

During the pendency of the two Grand Lodges, the usage prevailed of requiring brethren who had been admitted to the degrees under one system to go through the ceremonies a second time under the other. This custom, however, was by no means a universal one. Frequently, in an "Ancient" Lodge, the "Business" was "Modern," and quite as often, in a "Regular" Lodge, the work was carried out in the "Ancient" way. Indeed, of a divided allegiance, where the members of a Lodge held warrants from *both* Grand Lodges—meeting under one or the other as caprice might dictate—there are some examples.

The Royal Arch was worked under both systems—with the sanction of their rulers, and as a step of lawful Masonry by the "Ancients." The attitude of their rivals, as represented by the older *Grand Lodge*, was one of non-recognition, but the leading Grand Officers were warm supporters of the degree.

In the sacred cause of charity, however, all differences between the two sections of the English Craft seem to have vanished from the scene. Of this we possess enduring monuments in the Royal Masonic Institutions for Girls, founded by the titular "Moderns" in 1788; and in the Royal Masonic Institution for Boys, founded in truly fraternal rivalry, ten years afterwards, by the brethren in the opposite camp.

After a pause in the negotiations for a Union—during which there were mutual recriminations, though happily for the last time—it was Resolved, at a meeting of the Regular Grand Lodge:—

"That this Grand Lodge do agree in Opinion with the Committee of Charity that it is not necessary any longer to continue in Force those Measures which were resorted to, in or about the year 1739, respecting irregular Masons, and do therefore enjoin the several Lodges to revert to the Ancient Land Marks of the Society."

The way was accordingly paved for a Union by the creation of a special board, called the "Lodge of Promulgation," which, according to its warrant, was "constituted for the purpose of promulgating the Ancient Land Marks of the Society, and instructing the Craft in all such matters as might be necessary to be known by them, in consequence of, and in obedience to, the Resolution passed by Grand Lodge, April 12th, 1809." In the result, it was settled (1810) that the ceremony of Installation was a Landmark, and the Masters of London Lodges were duly "summoned for the purpose of being regularly Installed as Rulers of the Craft."

In the *actual* or original degrees of Masonry, that is the first three, with the exception of the opportunities selected under the two systems for the communication of secrets, there appears to have been no real difference between the procedure (or ceremonial) of the rival fraternities. The minutes of the Lodge of Promulgation inform us of "the restoration of the proper words of each degree," and the virtual adoption of the method of working among the "Ancients," which has been relied upon as affording decisive proof of the "Moderns" having finally *returned* to the old ways—I regard myself from an entirely different aspect, and consider that it points with certainty to "an alteration" *for the first and only time*, "in its established forms," by the earliest of Grand Lodges.

In 1813—May 12th—the Prince of Wales declining a re-election, the Duke of Sussex was installed as his successor.

In November of the same year, the Duke of Atholl resigned in favour of the Duke of Kent. The latter was placed in the chair of the "Ancient" Grand Lodge, December 1st, and on the St. John's Day following, the Freemasons of England were re-united in a single Society. *One* Grand Lodge was then constituted, and at the close of the proceedings, on the motion of the Duke of Kent, the Duke of Sussex was unanimously elected "Grand Master of the United Grand Lodge of Ancient Freemasons of England," and his Royal Highness received the homage of the Fraternity.

According to the Articles of Union:—

II.—"It is declared and pronounced that pure Ancient Masonry consists of three degrees, and no more; viz., those of the Entered Apprentice, the Fellow Craft, and the Master Mason (including the Supreme Order of the Holy Royal Arch)."

V.—For the purpose of establishing uniformity of working, nine expert brethren of each Fraternity were to be formed into a *Lodge of Reconciliation*, "for the purpose of obligating, instructing, and perfecting the Masters, Past Masters, Wardens, and Members" of the Lodges "in both the forms."

VII.—The existing Past Masters were rendered members of the Grand Lodge, but of those subsequently qualified, one only was to attend from each Lodge. The privilege, however, was extended to all Past Masters in 1818.

VIII.—"The two first Lodges under each Grand Lodge to draw a lot in the first place for priority, and to which of the two the lot No. I. shall fall, the other to rank as No. 2; and all the other Lodges shall fall in alternately." In the result, to the "Grand Masters," the Senior Lodge of the "Ancients" was allotted the highest position on the united roll, and the "Lodge of Antiquity"—one of the founders of the Grand Lodge of 1717—had to content itself with the second place. The other Lodges, of which there were nominally 359 and 641 on the winning and losing sides respectively, "fell in alternately" in like manner. But as many Lodges, under both systems, had ceased to exist, only 647 were actually carried forward at the Union, exclusive of the Grand Stewards' Lodge, which was continued at the head of the list without a number.

A new *Book of Constitutions* was published in 1815, and the "Charge concerning God and Religion" is as follows:— "Let a man's religion or mode of worship be what it may, he is not excluded from the Order, provided he believes in the glorious Architect of heaven and earth, and practise the sacred duties of morality."

Very excellent service was performed by the Lodge of Reconciliation, of which the last notice in the official records occurs in the proceedings of September, 1816, when the "Masters, Officers, and Brethren were thanked by the Grand Lodge for their unremitting Zeal and Exertion in the cause of Free-Masonry."

In 1817 the two Grand Chapters of the Royal Arch were amalgamated.

An attempt was made in 1834 to establish a Charity for Aged Freemasons. This resulted in what was called the "Asylum Scheme." An Annuity Fund for Males was subsequently formed in 1842, and extended to the widows of Freemasons in 1849, which was separately administered until 1850, when it effected a union with the Asylum.

The Duke of Sussex, who continued to preside over the Society until his death, was succeeded by the first Earl of Zetland in 1843. Four years later, the words "Free Man" were substituted for "Free Born" in the Declaration to be signed by candidates at their Initiation.

In 1856—March 5th—at a meeting of the Grand Lodge, it was Resolved Unanimously:—

"That the Degree of Mark Mason or Mark Master is not at variance with the ancient landmarks of the Order, and that the Degree be an addition to and form part of Craft Masonry; and consequently may be conferred by all regular Warranted Lodges, under such regulations as shall be . . . sanctioned by the Grand Master." The resolution, however, was negatived when the minutes were brought up for confirmation in the following quarter. A Grand Lodge of Mark Master Masons was formed in London during the same year, but it has not been recognized by the "United Grand Lodge" of the Craft. We find then, among the conflict of laws under the various Grand Lodges, that in England the Royal Arch is recognized, and the Mark degree is not; in Scotland, the Royal Arch is not, but the Mark is; and in Ireland both are recognized. The earliest known reference to the Mark degree, it may be observed, occurs in the Minute book of a Royal Arch Chapter at Portsmouth, under the date of September 1st, 1769.

In 1870, Lord Zetland retired from the Grand East, and was succeeded by Earl de Grey and Ripon, who, however, subsequently becoming a Roman Catholic, retired from Masonry in 1874. The office of Grand Master was then accepted by the Prince of Wales, who had been initiated by the King of Sweden in 1869, and the Heir Presumptive to the throne was installed amid the plaudits of a vast assemblage of British Masons in 1875. Two years later the Dukes of Connaught and Albany were invested as Senior and Junior Grand Wardens respectively, and in 1885 Prince Albert Victor, eldest son of the Prince of Wales, was initiated by the Grand Master in person. King Edward VII, on his accession to the throne, laid down the Grand Mastership, in which he was succeeded by the Duke of Connaught, but graciously consented to act as the Protector of the Craft. On his death in 1910, King George V became Patron of the Boys and Girls Institution; whilst Queen Mary became Grand Patroness, and Queen Alexandra Chief Patroness of the Girls Institution. Prince Arthur of Connaught was initiated in 1911.

In 1913 Grand Lodge acquired the Crowe Collection of historical documents, warrants, diplomas, etc., the unique result of nearly thirty years' world-wide search and study.

The Freemasons' War Hospital was opened in Fulham Road in August, 1916, and after doing invaluable work during that terrible period, is now a permanent Masonic Nursing Home.

Especial Grand Lodges were held in the Albert Hall on June 24th, 1917, to commemorate the bicentenary of the forming of the First Grand Lodge of the World in 1717; and in 1919 for the celebration of peace; each being attended by some 8,000 brethren, and many deputations from other English-speaking Grand Lodges in the Colonies and America.

The connection of our Royal Family with the Craft was further strengthened by the initiation of H.R.H. the Prince of Wales in 1919, followed after a short interval by his brother Prince Albert.

The number of Lodges on the roll to June, 1920, is 3,566. Of these, 810 are held in the London District, 2,028 in the Provinces, and 728 (which includes two in Military Corps) in places beyond the seas.

In SCOTLAND—November 30th, 1756—Lord Aberdour was again elected to the office of Grand Master, which is the first instance of a re-election since the institution of that Grand Lodge. During this nobleman's first term of office, it was resolved, "that the Grand Master for the time being be affiliated and recorded as a member of every Daughter Lodge of Scotland." The use, by Lodges, of "Painted Floor Cloths," was forbidden in 1759, and the practice of issuing diplomas (or certificates) was adopted by the Grand Lodge in 1768.

The three Steps of Masonry crept very slowly into general use. In the Lodge of St. Machar, at Aberdeen, down to the year 1775, while 260 members had taken the first degree, only 137 had been admitted to the second and third. The custom of numbering the Scottish Lodges began at first unofficially, about 1790, and a renumbering, atter the healing of the Kilwinning Schism, took place in 1816.

In 1799—May 26th—It was resolved by the Grand Lodge, "that they sanction the *Three Great Orders of Masonry*, and these alone, of APPRENTICE, FELLOW CRAFT, and MASTER MASON, being the ancient order of SAINT JOHN."

The Earl of Moira, Acting Grand Master of England, and Commander-in-Chief of the Forces in Scotland, was present at the Grand Election of 1803. "In the course of the evening, the Earl, in an eloquent and impressive address, related at considerable length the conduct of the Grand Lodge of England to the Ancient Masons, and stated that the hearts and arms of the Grand Lodge to which he was attached, had ever been open for the reception of their seceding Brethren, who had obstinately refused to acknowledge their fault; and though the Grand Lodge of England differed in a few trifling observances from that of Scotland, they had ever entertained for Scottish Masons that affection and regard which it is the object of Free Masonry to cherish, and the duty of Free Masons to feel." (Laurie, *Hist of F.*, 168.)

The Prince of Wales was elected Grand Master and Patron in 1805, and Lord Moira filled the position of Acting (or virtual) Grand Master in 1806 and 1807. In the latter year a reconciliation was effected with the Lodge of Kilwinning. The "Mutual Agreement" of the Lodge of Scoon and Perth (1658) was produced, but the Schaw Statutes of 1599 (*ante*, 173) were not—probably for the reason that their existence was at that time unknown. Ultimately, it was agreed that the Lodge of Kilwinning should be placed at the head of the Scottish roll without a number, and that her daughter Lodges should rank according to the dates of their charters. This gave umbrage to the Lodge of Edinburgh, whose supersession by its ancient rival was not without influence in fomenting a spirit of discontent, which resulted in a new Schism, and threatened at one time to lead to a multiplicity of Grand Lodges. The breach, however, was not healed until 1813.

Four years later the Grand Lodge of Scotland renewed its former edict of 1799, respecting the degrees of Masonry being restricted to three.

The laws or "Constitutions" were revised in 1829, and the Fund of Scottish Masonic Benevolence was established in 1846. The New Freemasons' Hall, 98, George Street, Edinburgh, was consecrated and inaugurated in 1859. In 1872 the Past Master ceremonial of Installation was recognized by the Grand Lodge, *not* for the purpose of introducing a new degree into Freemasonry, but to authorize the ritual of Installed Master as used in England, and thereby remove the disqualification which prevented Scottish Past Masters from being present at the Installation of Masters in English Lodges. The number of Lodges on the roll at the present time is 900, of which 22 are in Edinburgh, and 420 abroad.

New Regulations for the better government of the Freemasons of IRELAND were published in 1768. These ordain that "Every Master and Warden at his first Entrance [into the Grand Lodge] shall stand such Examination as the Grand Master . . . shall appoint" (IX); That, "Any Person who has been made a Mason in a Clandestine Manner, contrary to the Rules of the Grand Lodge, shall not . . . sit in any Regular Lodge, until such Lodge . . . shall have him first entered and passed over the usual Courses over again, as if the same had never been performed before" (XXV); That, "No Army Lodge on the Registry of this Kingdom, shall be charged with . . . annual Contributions, except for the Time they remain on *Dublin* Duty" (XXVI); And, that "No Army Lodge shall for the future make any Townsman a Mason, where there is a registered Lodge held in any Town where such Lodge do meet; and No Town's Lodge shall make any Man in the Army a Mason, where there is a warranted Lodge held in the Regiment, Troop, or Company, or in the Quarters to which such Man belongs" (XXVII). These Regulations eventually gave place to *The Constitution of* FREE-MASONRY, *or* AHIMAN REZON, published in 1807. Both Codes are printed by Dr. Crawley in his Cœmentaria *Hibernica* (iii). The Laws passed in the interval between the two publications are given in the later one, from which I extract the following:

Oct. 1, 1789.—"That no Masonic transaction be inserted in a newspaper by a brother, without permission from the Grand Lodge."

In 1805, a schism blazed forth in the Grand Lodge of Ireland. It had smouldered since 1800, when Alexander Seton, an unscrupulous barrister, had been appointed Deputy Grand Secretary, but without the additional emoluments of Deputy Grand Treasurer, which he had expected. Seton fomented local jealousies, seized the Grand Lodge archives, and retained adverse possession of the Grand Lodge premises. Many of the Lodges in the North of Ireland followed his standard, and were joined by others misled by his specious circulars. Driven from Dublin in 1807, after a struggle, conducted with unseemly virulence on his part, he organized at Dungannon a schismatic body, which he called the GRAND LODGE OF ULSTER. Worsted in a law suit, in which he sought to recover damages from the Grand Lodge of Ireland for his expulsion, his influence rapidly waned, and the Grand Officers whom he had attracted by misrepresentations, repudiated the short-lived Masonic power. The final blow was dealt in 1814, when it was agreed between the Grand Lodges of England and Ireland that no countenance should be shown to Seton's adherents. The disaffected Lodges speedily returned to their obedience, and the Grand Lodge of Ireland received their submission with wisdom and toleration.

The roll of Irish Lodges probably reached its highest figure about the year 1797, when scarcely a village in the Kingdom was without its "Masonic Assembly." Afterwards, however, a period of dormancy set in, and out of a total of 1,020 members in the calendar of 1816, more than one-half are available (in accordance with the Irish practice) for re-issue to New Lodges. At the present time of writing there are 530 Irish Lodges, of which 59 are in Dublin, 43 abroad, and six in Military Corps. There are about

28,000 members under the Irish Constitution. Of a grand total of at least 409 Ambulatory Lodges, which are *known* to have been constituted by the Grand Lodges of the British Isles, it may be remarked in conclusion, a much larger number were warranted by the Irish than by any other Grand Lodge. The influence exercised by these travelling bodies was immense, and the general subject, though lying outside the scope of the present, has been considered by me at some fulness in a previous work (*Military Lodges*).

CHAPTER VIIa

[As the "Higher" or "Additional" degrees have been so slightly touched on in the previous chapter, I think it would be convenient to the reader to have a concise account of those in use in England and the United Kingdom.— F.J.W.C.]

THE ROYAL ARCH

This is the earliest known of the additional degrees having been introduced from 1737 to 1740, when it was certainly conferred in London.

Laurence Dermott took the degree of Royal Arch Masonry in 1746, and therefore clearly could not have invented it. As a degree it is mentioned in the minutes of the Ancient Grand Lodge of March 4th, 1752, when a complaint was made against certain brethren who had pretended to give the degree without knowing anything about it. The earliest known record of the degree being actually conferred is a minute of the Fredericksburg Lodge, Virginia, U.S.A., stating that on December 22nd, 1753, three brethren were raised to the degree of Royal Arch Masons.

The earliest record in England is 1758, when several brethren were "Raised to the degree of Royal Arch" in a Lodge Meeting at the Crown at Bristol, this being a Modern Lodge. It is the only degree officially recognized by, and attached to, Craft Masonry, and is only practised in English-speaking countries. At one time in England only Past Masters were eligible for the degree, and the ceremony called "Passing the Chair" was arranged to meet the technical difficulties. In Scotland Royal Arch Masonry is separate from the Grand Lodge, and not officially recognized. In Ireland it is recognized as in England.

269

THE MARK MASTER'S DEGREE

This is certainly ancient, and is frequently referred to in the latter half of the eighteenth century as being well known. Many Scottish Lodges have Mark Books dating back to the seventeenth century, including one of the sixteenth century. It is not officially recognized by Grand Lodge, but has its own governing body, H.R.H. the Duke of Connaught being the Grand Master, as he is of the Craft and Arch Degrees.

The oldest Mark Lodges in England had generally Scottish charters. The degree was also worked under the assumed authority of a Craft Warrant, according to ancient usage— *e.g.*, in the minute books of the old Royal Arch Chapter at Portsmouth in 1769; again in the Marquis of Granby Lodge No. 124, Durham, in 1773; and in St. Thomas's Lodge No. 124, London, in 1777. Originally there were two degrees, the Mark-Man and the Mark-Master, conferred respectively on Fellow Crafts and Master Masons, but now they are combined, and conferred on Master Masons only.

ROYAL ARK MARINER

This is a side degree worked under the authority of Mark Lodges, but having no real connection of any kind.

CRYPTIC DEGREES

These are conferred in Councils, and consist of the four degrees of "Most Excellent Master," "Royal Master," "Select Master," and "Super-Excellent Master." These are conferred under a Constitution originating from the Grand Council of New York, U.S.A., in 1871; the English Grand Council being actually established in 1873. In Scotland the degrees were introduced in 1878 from Illinois, U.S.A., and the Grand Council formed in 1880. These degrees are not worked in Ireland.

THE ANCIENT AND ACCEPTED RITE

This is a system of thirty-three degrees, including the three Craft Degrees, which, though claimed, are not worked but left to Grand Lodges. From the fourth degree to the fourteenth compose a *Lodge of Perfection*, and are named as follows:—*Secret Master*, *Perfect Master*, *Intimate Secretary*, *Provost and Judge*, *Superintendent of the Buildings*, *Elect of Nine*, *Elect of Fifteen*, *Sublime Elect*, *Grand Master Architect*, *Royal Arch of Enoch*, and *Scottish Knight of Perfection*. The next two degrees, *Knight of the Sword and of the East* and *Prince of Jerusalem*, comprised a *Council of Princes of Jerusalem*. The next degree, *Knight of the East and West* is given in a *Lodge of Knights of the East and West*; and *Knight of the Eagle and Pelican, Sovereign Prince Rose Croix of H.R.D.M.* is worked in a *Chapter of Rose Croix*. Then from the nineteenth to the thirtieth are controlled under a *Council of Kadosh* and are named *Grand Pontiff*, *Venerable Grand Master*, *Patriarch Noachite*, *Prince of Libanus*, *Chief of the Tabernacle*, *Prince of the Tabernacle*, *Knight of the Brazen Serpent*, *Prince of Mercy*, *Commander of the Temple*, *Knight of the Sun*, *Knight of St. Andrew*, *Grand Elected Knight K.H.* or *Knight Kadosh*. The thirty first and thirty-second degrees are conferred in *Consistories*, and are *Inspector Inquisitor Commander* and *Sublime Prince of the Royal Secret*.

The last degree, *Sovereign Grand Inspector General*, is conferred in the *Supreme Council of the Thirty-third Degree*.

The degrees are very interesting and elaborate, and the Rite is highly esteemed all over the world.

The Supreme Councils generally recognized as "Regular" are—Southern Jurisdiction of the United States of America at Washington; the "Mother Supreme Council of the World," founded 1801.

(Many of the degrees are, of course, much older than this date, but the Rite was then finally arranged in thirty-three degrees)—

France and dependencies	... ...	founded	1804
Spain		,,	1811
Northern Jurisdiction, U.S.A., at New York		,,	1813
Belgium		,,	1817

Ireland ...	...	...	...	...	founded	1824
Brazil ...	...	...	...	...	,,	1829
Peru ...	...	...	...	...	,,	1830
Columbia	...	...	...	...	,,	1833
Portugal	...	...	...	...	,,	1842
England	...	...	...	...	,,	1845
Scotland	...	...	...	...	,,	1846
Uruguay	...	...	...	...	,,	1856
Argentine	...	...	...	...	,,	1857
Colon (Cuba) ...	...	...	...	...	,,	1859
Mexico ...	...	...	...	...	,,	1860
St. Domingo	...	...	...	...	,,	1861
Venezuela	...	...	...	...	,,	1865
Paraguay	...	...	...	...	,,	1870
Guatemala	...	...	...	...	,,	1871
Greece	...	...	...	...	,,	1872
Switzerland	...	...	...	...	,,	1873
Dominion of Canada ...	...	...	...	,,		1874
Italy ...	...	...	...	...	,,	1876
Chili ...	...	...	...	...	,,	1899
Egypt ...	...	...	...	...	,,	1907
Serbia ...	...	...	...	...	,,	1912
Holland	...	...	...	...	,,	1913

ROYAL ORDER OF SCOTLAND

This is almost, if not quite, as old as the Royal Arch Degree, and its history is very curious. The Grand Lodge is now at Edinburgh, and all other Lodges out of Scotland are ruled by Provincial Grand Lodges. Its legend claims that the first of the two degrees of which it consists— namely, "Heredom of Kilwinning"—was originated in the reign of David I, King of Scotland, and the second part ("Rosy Cross") was instituted by Robert the Bruce after the Battle of Bannockburn on St. John's Day (in summer), 1313. He revived the degree of Heredom, and incorporated with it a civil order of Knighthood named the "Rosy Cross," which he conferred upon a party of Templars who had repaired to Scotland to help him. A Grand Lodge of this Royal Order of Scotland was established by Bruce at Kilwinning, "with reservation of Office of Grand Master to himself and his successors on the Scottish throne." Originally the membership of the order was limited to sixty-three, none being entitled to it but Scotsmen, and possibly their allies, the Irish. Mr. C. Fox-Thomas gives many interesting details in his sketch of the history of the Order. Mr. Murray Lyon says:—"As regards to the claim of antiquity and of royal origin that are set up in favour of this Rite, it is proper to say that modern enquiries have shown them to be purely fabulous. The Fraternity of Kilwinning never at any period practised or acknowledged other than the Craft Degrees, neither does there exist any tradition worthy of the name Local or National that can in the remotest degree be held to identify Robert Bruce with a holding of Masonic Courts or the Institution of a Secret Society of Kilwinning."

Every degree, however, has its traditional history, and this is sufficiently interesting to be well worth preserving. The King of Scotland is still considered the perpetual Grand Master, and a chair is always kept vacant for him.

Curiously enough, the Royal Order was known and practised in England long before it was known in Scotland, there having been a Grand Master in London at least as early as 1741; whilst in July, 1750, there were five Chapters in London and one at Deptford. In 1752 a Chapter was warranted in Virginia, North America, but its history is unknown. In 1750 a Grand Chapter was warranted at the request of William Mitchell, a Scottish teacher of languages at The Hague, and of Jonas Kluck, who resided there, stating that there were a number of members of the Royal Order residing at The Hague, and asking for a warrant for a Provincial Grand Lodge to be held there.

A request was granted, and Mr. Mitchell was installed in London as Provincial Grand Master for The Hague, his Patent being dated July 22nd, 1750, at the sign of the Golden Horse Shoe, in Cannon Street, Southwark.

Apparently, however, Mr. Mitchell changed his mind, and did not return to The Hague, but settled in Scotland and assumed the position of Grand Master of the Order. The Provincial Grand Lodge which was warranted for The Hague therefore seems to have become the Grand Lodge of the Order in Scotland, which now governs all the world. There was a Provincial Grand Lodge at Paris which had twenty-six Chapters under its obedience in 1811, some of which were in Belgium and others in Italy.

At the present time there are Provincial Grand Lodges in New Brunswick and Nova Scotia; Hong-Kong and the open ports of China; Western India; Ontario and Quebec; United States of America; Natal; Cape Colony; the Canton of Geneva; and the Straits Settlements, as well as others in England and Scotland.

This Order also is not worked in Ireland.

THE UNITED RELIGIOUS AND MILITARY ORDER OF THE TEMPLE AND OF ST. JOHN OF JERUSALEM, PALESTINE, RHODES AND MALTA

This Order is very exclusive, and practically uses the ritual of the original Knights Templars, although it cannot claim a direct descent from the Ancient Military Order. The earliest known reference in the world to the Masonic degree of this name occurs in the records of St. Andrew's Chapter, Boston, dated August 28th, 1769, when William Davis was accepted and "made by receiving the four steps, that of Excellent, Super-Excellent, Royal Arch, and Knights Templars." The oldest dated reference to the degree in England is on a draft of a certificate of 1779 from the York Grand Lodge, signed by the Grand Secretary. This was the only Grand Lodge that ever officially recognized the Templar degree as Masonic in Great Britain and Ireland during the eighteenth century. The first governing body of the Order was formed in London in 1791 as a Grand Conclave by the celebrated Thomas Dunckerley. In Ireland "The High Knights Templars of Ireland, Kilwinning

Lodge," was warranted to meet in Dublin by the Earl of Eglinton on October 8th, 1769. He was "Most Worshipable Grand Master of Mother Kilwinning Lodge in Scotland," which was then (quite mistakenly) considered the custodian of the High Degrees. The warrant was really only a Craft Warrant, but it was used for years from 1702 as an authority to confer the Royal Arch, Knight Templar, and Rose Croix Degrees, and with other Irish Lodges formed the "Early Grand Christian Encampment of Ireland," which was the first governing body in that country. From Ireland "a Grand Assembly of Knights Templars" was constituted in Edinburgh in 1806, but shortly afterwards a second governing body was formed in Scotland by Alexander Deuchar, called the "Chapter General," dating from 1811. These bodies existed side by side until 1909, when they united and formed one Great Priory for Scotland. The present Great Priory of England dates from 1872 (replacing the previous "Grand Conclave"), and that of Ireland from 1836. There are also Great Priories in the United States and Canada, whilst bodies of the order exist in all English-speaking countries.

An interesting Templar body exists in Switzerland, under the title of The Great Priory of Helvetia, which is recognized by the Great Priories of England and Scotland, and is a descendant of the Templar system of Von Hund and the "Strict Observance." Its degrees are "Brothers of St. Andrew, Novice Esquire, and Knights Beneficent of the Holy Cross."

THE MASONIC AND MILITARY ORDER OF THE KNIGHTS OF
ROME, OF THE RED CROSS OF CONSTANTINE, KNIGHTS
OF THE HOLY SEPULCHRE, AND KNIGHTS OF ST. JOHN

These degrees are said to have been conferred from 1780, but are not as widely known or practised as the Templar degrees.

THE ROSICRUCIAN SOCIETY

The study of Mysticism, Hermetic Science, and Alchemy was widely pursued in the Middle Ages, and an attempt was made in 1614 by John Valentine Andrea, of Wurtemburg, a well-known theologian and philosopher, with others, to draw the students of these studies together to further research. He published a book containing an account of an imaginary alchemist, whom he called Christian Rozenkreus, and a society of Rosicrucians, who devoted themselves to the healing art, and possessed semi-miraculous powers. Intense interest was aroused, the legend being accepted as truth, and from that time onward societies pursuing these studies more or less seriously have existed in Europe and America. The Society of Rosicrucians in Anglia was founded in 1866 by two well-known mystics, Robert Wentworth Little and Kenneth R. H. Mackenzie.

Little was a prominent mason, and secretary of the Institution for Girls. He found some old Hermetic rituals in the cellars of Freemasons' Hall, and, in conjunction with Mackenzie, who had received certain grades whilst residing in Germany, formed a Society for research in all subjects connected with Mermeticism and Freemasonry, and the cult is flourishing in England, Scotland, and America, with subordinates elsewhere. There are nine degrees, in three groups, governed by a Supreme Magus.

There are other small bodies, such as the "Allied Degrees," which control the degrees "Knights of Constantinople," "Red Cross of Babylon," "St. Lawrence the Martyr," "Grand High Priest," "Secret Monitor," and "Grand Tyler of King Solomon," but these are of minor interest.

Anyone desiring information as to any of these various Rites and Orders, can obtain it at Freemasons' Hall, or Mark Masons' Hall, in Great Queen Street, W.C., or at the Office of the Supreme Council of the Thirty-third Degree, 10, Duke Street, St. James's, S.W.

ANCIENT FRENCH COMMEMORATIVE ENGRAVING
Dated 1789
(The middle plaque is in Sepia. The remainder in black)

CHAPTER VIII

The homely Freemasonry imported from England has been totally changed in every country in Europe, either by the imposing ascendancy of French brethren, who are to be found everywhere ready to instruct the World, or by the importation of the doctrines, and ceremonies, and ornaments of the Parisian Lodges.—PROFESSOR JOHN ROBISON (1798).

FRANCE

ACCORDING to the stream of French writers, all following more or less blindly in the footsteps of Lalande, the celebrated astronomer, whose *Franche-Maçonnerie* appeared in 1773, the first Lodge in France was founded by the Earl of Derwentwater and other British Jacobites, at Paris, in 1725. The last Earl of Derwentwater, it may be observed, was James Ratcliffe, executed for high treason in 1716, but the title was assumed by his brother Charles, who succeeded in escaping to France. The latter is said to have been followed in the chair of "Grand Master" in 1736 by Lord d'Harnouester, which is apparently a corruption of "Darwentwater," and, if so, will render the story a little clearer by removing some of the obscurities which have gathered round its text. For example, with respect to the succession of Grand Masters, and if the titular Earl of Darwentwater (according to the French orthography) really figures in the list, he was probably elected for the first time in, and is identical with the Lord *d'Harnouester* of, 1736. As strengthening this supposition, though at the same time introducing a new element of confusion, I shall quote from a German publication of 1744, which affirms that in 1736 the Earl of Darwentwater was chosen by the French Lodges

277

to succeed *James Hector Maclean*, a previous Grand Master.

Masonry encountered no opposition until 1737, when it experienced some arbitrary treatment in Paris at the hands of Hérault, the Lieutenant of Police. The famous Speech of the Chevalier Ramsay was delivered in the same year.

The Bull of Pope Clement XII had no effect in France, but many attempts were made to ridicule Freemasonry in the public journals and on the stage.

A great Masonic Festival was held at Luneville on June 24th, 1738, at which Lord d'Harnouester (or Derwentwater) resigned his office of Grand Master, and the Duc d'Antin was chosen in his stead. The administration of this nobleman is chiefly to be remembered in connection with the profusion of so-called "Scots degrees" to which I have referred in a previous chapter (VI).

The Duc d'Antin died on December 9th, 1743, and on December 11th Prince Louis de Bourbon, Count de Clermont, was elected Grand Master. The first French Code of Masonic Laws was published on the same day. The Grand Lodge now assumed the title of *Grande Loge Anglaise de France*.

Prince Louis remained at the head of the Craft until his death in 1771. This period is associated with the increase and development of the so-called Higher Degrees, for example: Scottish Master, Clermont Chapter (1754),Knights of the East (1756), and Emperors of the East and West (1758). The last two degrees especially were productive of infinite discord in the Grand Lodge, which from 1755 had adopted the name of the *Grande Loge de France*. The "Emperors" constituted a second independent Grand Lodge, and also among the "Knights of the East" (who were mainly tradesmen) a schism arose, resulting in the formation of a Sovereign Council, in 1762. By order of the Grand Master the Knights of the East were suspended, and the suspension lasted until 1771. The number of Lodges in Paris at this time was about eighty. There were others in the Departments—for instance, three at Rouen, and several at Bordeaux.

The next period commences with the nominal rule of the Duc de Chartres, afterwards the Duc d'Orleans—'Citizen Egalité"—and ends with the complete outward extinction of Freemasonry in the stormy days of the Revolution. The Duc de Luxembourg was elected Substitute-General. Attempts were next made to amalgamate the so-called "Higher Degrees" with the Grand Lodge, and in March, 1773, the *Grande Loge Nationale de France* was established. After this was accomplished, the Duc de Chartres was installed as Grand Master, and on December 27th, 1773, the *Grande Loge Nationale* became the *Grand Orient de France*. At the same date, a commission (which never entered upon its duties) was appointed to report on the Higher Degrees, and in the interim all Lodges were directed to work in the three symbolical degrees only. Nevertheless, the so-called "Higher Degrees" continued to flourish: for example, the *Scots Philosophic Rite*—a school of Hermeticism—at Avignon; the *Elus Coens*; the *Contrat Social*; the *Academie des Vrais Macons*; the *Philalethes* and the *Philadelphians*; the *Rose-Croix Chapter*, at Arras; and finally Cagliostro's *Rit Egyptien*. For the purpose of controlling these and some other systems (or rites) the Grand Orient decided to create a *Chambre des Grades* (1782).

At the instance of A. L. Roettiers de Montaleau, the leading Mason of his time, a *Grande Chapitre Général de France* was formed in 1784, which, after amalgamating with a rival Grand Chapter, was definitely established, in 1787, as the *Chapitre Metropolitain*, with the right to grant the Higher Degrees. The Grand Orient had reduced these Degrees to four, thereby investing with its official sanction the *Rit Moderne*, in accordance with which most of the French Lodges work at the present day. The *Chapitre Metropolitain*, it may be remarked, considered an aggregate of eighty-one degrees as desirable. About the end of the period under examination, the Rose-Croix entered upon a new lease of life at Rouen, and maintained a separate existence by the side of the Grand Orient.

The troublous times of the Revolution put an end to

Masonic activity. The greater number of the Lodges closed their doors. The Grand Master, now "Citizen Egalité," publicly renounced Freemasonry in February, and was guillotined in November, 1793. In the following year there was hardly a sign of Freemasonry anywhere in France.

When quieter times came, Roettiers de Montaleau (to whom the reader has already been introduced), from the remnants of the old Lodges, constructed, not as Grand Master, but as *Grand Vénérable*, a new Grand Orient, in 1795. This institution was sanctioned by the Police authorities in 1798, and in the following year the *Grand Lodge—i.e.*, the governing body of the French Craft prior to the formation of the Grand Orient of 1773—after a spasmodic revival in 1796, was virtually absorbed by its latest rival, and the one and only Grand Orient (or Grand Lodge) was solemnly proclaimed and installed.

By the side of the Grand Orient, however, two other Masonic powers were speedily established. In 1804— September 22nd—Comte De Grasse Tilly established at Paris a Supreme Council 33° of a new body calling itself the *Ancient and Accepted Scottish Rite*. This, indeed, was descended in a direct line from the "Emperors" of 1758, and it is possible from the Chapter of Clermont of 1754. But the highest portion of the new and imposing Masonic superstructure was undoubtedly constructed at Charleston, South Carolina, in 1801.

A Grand Scots Lodge was formed—October 22nd—by the Supreme Council 33°, which elected Prince Louis Buonaparte as its Grand Master. But when Prince Joseph Buonaparte—subsequently King of Naples—was nominated as the head of the Grand Orient, the *three* powers were resolved into *one*, by treaty of December 3rd in the same year. Marshals Massena and Kellermann were chiefly instrumental in bringing about this result. In 1805, however, the pact was dissolved, and while the Grand Scots Lodge had drawn its last breath, the Grand Orient and the Supreme Council of France have since existed side by side. All subsequent attempts at union have failed. At the request of the Emperor Napoleon (whose membership of the Craft is a disputed point) the Arch-Chancellor, Prince Cambacères was appointed *Grand Maître Adjoint* of the Grand Orient in 1805, and elected Sovereign Grand Commander of the Supreme Council 33° in 1806. Thus all strife was avoided without a formal union of the two associations. Masonry flourished exceedingly, and the calendar of 1814, in which year Cambacères resigned both positions, shows that 886 Lodges and 337 Chapters were then actually at work.

After 1814, the office of Grand Master of the Grand Orient was not again filled up, but simply *Grand Maîtres Adjoints* were appointed, until 1852. During this period the distinction between the Grand Orient as a democratic, and the Supreme Council as an aristocratic institution, became more and more marked. A new temple for the Grand Orient was inaugurated at Paris in 1843.

The political events of 1848 led to many attacks upon Freemasonry, in which, too, the clerical party joined, consequently the Lodges were looked upon with suspicion by the Government. For this reason the Grand Orient—January 9th, 1852—elected as Grand Master Prince Lucien Murat, who was a very active ruler for a time, but resigned in 1861. He was succeeded by Marshal Magnan, who was *appointed* by the Emperor Louis Napoleon, though he was not even a Mason at the time, and had to be initiated before entering upon the duties of his office.

Magnan died in 1865, and another soldier, General Mellinet, followed him in the chair. The position of Grand Master was abolished in 1871, and at the head of the Grand Orient there has since been a *President de l'Ordre*. It only remains to be added that in consequence of the removal by the Grand Orient from its "Book of Constitutions" of the paragraphs affirming the existence of a "Great Architect of the Universe," the Grand Lodge of England appointed, in December, 1877, a Special Committee of eleven (of which Lord Leigh and the present writer are the only surviving members) to consider the proper course to be pursued. Two months later, the Committee, in their report, declared the "alteration" to be, in their judgment, "opposed to the traditions, practice, and feelings of all true and genuine Masons from the earliest to the present time."

Similar action was taken in other jurisdictions, and in most States where the English language is spoken the Grand Orient of France has long been regarded as having parted with all claim to be looked upon as a Masonic body. There are altogether 462 Lodges, 77 Chapters, and 21 Councils at work under the Grand Orient. Of the Lodges, 89 are in Paris and its outskirts. The membership is about 40,000.

Under the auspices of the SUPREME COUNCIL, there has of late been established a *Grande Loge de France*, which works in the three Craft degrees, while the Supreme Council itself takes sole charge of the 4°—33°. The new Grand Lodge is desirous of putting a stop to the discussion in Lodges of political and religious questions, a practice which distinguishes the Masonry of France from that of the generality of other countries, where the consideration of such questions is forbidden. The atheistical doctrine of the Grand Orient is said not to be shared by the Supreme Council of France. On the roll of the *Grande Loge de France* are 128 Lodges, of which 55 are in Paris and its outskirts. It has 7,600 members.

In 1914 a Regular and Independent Grand Lodge of France and the Colonies was established in Paris, and recognized by the Grand Lodge of England and other Grand Lodges. It works on the lines of English Masonry, and the Rectified Rite of Switzerland. It has at present 9 Lodges and others are in the process of formation.

THE GERMAN EMPIRE

The first mention of Freemasonry in connection with Germany is the appointment of *Fredericus du Thom* as Provincial G.M. for the circle of Lower Saxony, by the Duke of Norfolk in 1729-30, but this appears to have been a sort oi honorary appointment, as Du Thom is a person entirely unknown in German Masonic history.

FREDERICK THE GREAT
Prominent in all Degrees known at the time.

Next, the Earl of Strathmore, 1733, is stated to have granted to "eleven German Masons, good brothers," a deputation to open a Lodge at Hamburg; but the deputation was evidently not acted upon, as no trace of a Lodge between 1733-1737 can be found.

The first German Lodge was established at Hamburg on December 6th, 1737, under Charles Sarry. It consisted of 7 members then, and no mention is made of any English Warrant. In point of fact, the W.M., Luttmann, only had it registered in England in October, 1740, and he was a few days later appointed Prov. G. Master. On his return to Hamburg, the Lodge—in July, 1741—took the name of ABSALOM.

The first German Lodge had the honour of initiating at Brunswick, on the 14th of August, 1738, the Crown Prince of Prussia (later Frederick the Great), who thereupon opened a private Lodge of his own at his castle of Rheinsberg. This is the starting point of Freemasonry in Prussia. The King's Lodge ceased when Frederick left for the first Silesian War, but with the King's permission another was then—September 13th, 1740—formed at Berlin. Out of this Lodge originated the oldest of the Prussian Grand Lodges: The Grand National Mother Lodge of the THREE GLOBES, in Berlin.

I.—THE GRAND NATIONAL MOTHER LODGE OF THE THREE GLOBES IN BERLIN*

This was originally formed at Berlin, as a private Lodge, on September 13th, 1740, under the name of "AUX TROIS GLOBES." It soon erected Lodges itself at Meiningen, Frankfort-on-the-Maine, Breslau, and Halle, after the fashion of those times, and thereupon styled itself, from June 24th, 1744, the GRAND ROYAL MOTHER LODGE. It also founded two Lodges at Berlin: EINTRACHT, which is the oldest of the *Berlin* daughter Lodges (1754), and AUX TROIS

---

* Owing to the Great War, and the attitude adopted by the German Lodges, no intercourse between them and the Allies is allowed at present (1920), nor is this likely to be quickly altered.

COLOMBES (1760). The latter is now the Grand Lodge ROYAL YORK (No. III). After this time there was a great confusion of Masonic systems at Berlin, and in August, 1766, the Rite of the STRICT OBSERVANCE was adopted. In 1772 the title was altered to GRAND NATIONAL MOTHER LODGE, when Prince Frederick August, of Brunswick, was appointed Grand Master, who remained in that position till 1799. In 1772 the Prince's uncle, Duke Ferdinand of Brunswick, was appointed Grand Master of the STRICT OBSERVANCE, and there can be no doubt that when the Convent of Wilhelmsbad was held, in 1782, the THREE GLOBES expected the centre of gravity to be shifted to Berlin. But the Convent decided otherwise, Ferdinand remained as nominal Grand Master of the STRICT OBSERVANCE, and the THREE GLOBES formally declared themselves independent of that Order in 1783.

In 1797 a new system of 7 degrees was adopted, which, with a few alterations, is still in force, and forms the basis of the present Masonic edifice; it was revised in 1883.

In 1798 a Royal Edict was issued granting certain privileges to the three Prussian Grand Lodges. In 1799 the present Masonic Hall was bought. In 1839 the Grand Lodge joined the "Prussian Grand Master's Union," and in 1873, together with the two other Prussian Grand Lodges, the "Grand Lodge League of Germany." Under this Grand Lodge are 156 St. John's (*i.e.*, Craft) Lodges, 69 Scottish Lodges, 354 Benevolent Institutions, and 16,346 active members; 116 of the St. John's Lodges are domiciled in Prussia proper, 16 in other German States, 1 in the Brazils, and 1 in China.

II.—THE GRAND NATIONAL LODGE OF GERMAN FREEMASONS
IN BERLIN

This Grand Lodge was founded by J. W. von Zinnendorf, one of the most remarkable Masons that ever existed, on December 27th, 1770. Zinnendorf was instrumental in bringing about the connection between the THREE GLOBES and the STRICT OBSERVANCE. He was Grand Master of the former, and a warm supporter of the latter, but in 1766 he renounced the STRICT OBSERVANCE, and in the following year retired altogether from the THREE GLOBES. Zinnendorf had obtained from C. F. von Eckleff (1765) the Swedish Ritual, and also a warrant of constitution, on the strength of which he founded—commencing in 1768—about twelve Lodges. These, in 1770, formed a new Grand Lodge.

A compact with the Grand Lodge of England, by which (Frankfort alone dissenting) all Germany was virtually handed over to the Zinnendorf body, was concluded in 1773, and the new Grand Lodge obtained the protection of Frederick the Great in 1774. It also benefited by the Royal Edict of 1798, already mentioned. Disputes with the Grand Lodge of Sweden arose, but were eventually settled, and a formal treaty between the two Masonic powers was concluded in 1819. A Revision of the Ritual took place about 1840, but only so far as words and expressions were concerned—nothing else was altered. Since then the assertion that the Society of Freemasons is directly descended from the Order of the Knights Templar has been dropped, and a spiritual succession is now only maintained. In 1840 Prince William of Prussia (later Emperor Wilhelm I) was initiated, and in 1853 his son (later Emperor Frederic II) joined the Society. The latter, as "Master of the Order," presided over the Grand Lodge from 1860 until 1874. In 1889 Prince Frederick Leopold of Prussia was initiated, in 1894 he was appointed Protector of the three Prussian Grand Lodges, and in 1895 "Master of the Order" (or Grand Master). In this jurisdiction there are 7 chapters, 28 St. Andrew's Lodges, 151 St. John's Lodges, 148 Benevolent Institutions, and 15,300 active members; 84 of the Craft Lodges are in Prussia proper, and the others in the different German States.

III.—THE GRAND LODGE OF PRUSSIA, CALLED ROYAL YORK
OF FRIENDSHIP, IN BERLIN

The THREE GLOBES founded a Lodge in Berlin, "AUX
TROIS COLOMBES," in 1760, which, from July 27th, 1765,
when Edward, Duke of York (brother of King George III),
was initiated in it, took the name of ROYALE YORK DE
L'AMITIE. The Lodge then obtained a Warrant of Constitution from England, and in 1768 severed its connection with
the THREE GLOBES. It next founded several daughter
Lodges, and on June 11th, 1798, divided into four Lodges,
who then constituted themselves a Grand Lodge of Prussia,
but the present name was only assumed in 1845. All
matters concerning ritual are controlled by a committee,
called the "Innermost Orient," but their recommendations
must be approved by the Grand Lodge. When the Grand
Lodge of Hanover was closed in 1867 most of the Lodges in
that jurisdiction joined the ROYAL YORK, and six of these
still work according to their old Ritual. There are in this
system 12 Inner Orients, 81 St. John's Lodges, 124 Benevolent Institutions, and 6,300 active members; 59 Lodges are
in Prussia proper, and 8 in other German States.

IV.—THE GRAND LODGE OF HAMBURG

The oldest German Lodge was founded at Hamburg on
December 6th, 1737, and its Master was, on October 30th,
1740, appointed Prov. Grand Master of Hamburg and Lower
Saxony. As such, Lüttman legitimated Lodge St. George,
and constituted other Lodges at Brunswick, Hanover, Got-
tingen, Celle, Copenhagen, Oldenburg, and Schwerin, within
about ten years. When the STRICT OBSERVANCE spread
over Germany, the then Prov. Grand Master, Janisch (in
1765), joined the Order without, however, entirely severing
his connection with the Grand Lodge in London. In 1774
the Lodge EMANUEL, and in 1776 FERDINANDE CAROLINE
were constituted at Hamburg. FERDINAND OF THE ROCK,
in the same city, also joined the Prov. Grand Lodge. In
1783, when the STRICT OBSERVANCE practically ceased to

exist, it was thought expedient to return to the old system of Freemasonry of 1737, and in July, 1786, Dr. von Exter was officially installed as Prov. Grand Master. F. L. Schroeder, one of the most prominent German Masons, was then elected Master of Lodge EMANUEL, and he began his great work of reformation. He built up the present system, which consists of the three Craft Degrees only, a Ritual, the centenary of which was celebrated on June 29th, 1901, and the constitution of the Grand Lodge, which is nothing but a representative body of all the subordinate Lodges, no other votes being allowed except the Grand Master's. In 1811, when the power of Napoleon was at its height, and all the States on the Continent were subservient to his will, the Grand Lodge of Hamburg declared its independence, and it has since worked as a Sovereign Masonic body. It became a member of the Grand Lodge League of Germany in 1873. Hamburg has particularly cultivated the establishment of German Lodges "beyond the seas," and from 1893, when the celebrated Edict of 1798 was adjudged to be obsolete and out of force, Prussian territory has also been opened to the missionary efforts of this Grand Lodge. It rules over 62 Lodges, 1 Prov. Grand Lodge (at Berlin), 60 Benevolent Institutions, and 4,000 active members; 6 of the Lodges are at Hamburg, 9 in Prussia proper, 20 in different German States, 1 at Copenhagen, 1 at Constantinople, and 6 in South America.

V.—THE GRAND NATIONAL LODGE OF SAXONY IN DRESDEN

The first Lodge in Saxon territory was founded in 1738 by Count Rutowsky, "AUX TROIS AIGLES," at Dresden; others soon followed, and formed a Grand Lodge, which, after an existence of some years, joined the STRICT OBSERVANCE in 1762. Benevolence has always been a special feature of Freemasonry in Saxony, and conspicuously so in times of famine (1772). Another characteristic is the support it has extended to the "Freemasons' Institute," a large School founded in 1773, and still flourishing. Towards the

close of the 18th century the Government was opposed to
the Craft, but the worst was averted, although some of the
Lodges stopped work for a while. In 1805 negotiations
began for the formation of a Saxon Grand Lodge, which
was successfully concluded in 1811. Some of the Lodges
were afterwards compelled to forsake it when parts of the
country were, in 1815, at the Vienna Congress, handed over
to Prussia. Two Lodges are still independent: MINERVA
and BALDWIN—both at Leipsic. There are 28 Lodges, 112
Benevolent Institutions, and 4,414 active members. Some
of the Saxon Lodges are the largest in Germany (as regards
membership), for example, at Dresden, THE THREE SWORDS,
696; and the GOLDEN APPLE, 631; and at Leipsic, the
Apollo, 374 members.

VI.—THE GRAND LODGE OF THE SUN IN BAYREUTH

In 1741 the Margrave Frederick of Brandenburg-
Culmbach established a Lodge of his own at Bayreuth,
which, in 1744, took the title of Grand Lodge, and founded
Lodges at Erlangen and Anspach. It afterwards joined
the STRICT OBSERVANCE, and when the principality was
united with that of Anspach (1769) the "Directorium"
was shifted to the latter place. When both fell to the
Prussian Crown (1799) Masonry languished, but again
revived under a Provincial Grand Lodge, established by
the ROYAL YORK OF FRIENDSHIP.

This connection, however, was of short duration, because
in 1810 Bayreuth was given to the Crown of Bavaria, and
the Lodges thereupon formed first of all an independent
Provincial Grand Lodge, and, in 1811, assumed the *title*
of an independent *Grand* Lodge. Down to 1857 little progress was made, but since that date a number of highly
intellectual Grand Masters, such as Feustel, Bluntschli,
and Lowe, have done excellent work. The Ritual is that
of Fessler, with slight alterations and improvements. Some
Lodges, indeed, work in a different manner, but this is
sanctioned by the Grand Lodge on the condition that once

a year the official Ritual is used. In the FREIBURG Lodge, at Baden, a Book with blank leaves lies on the altar instead of the Bible. It is maintained that while a Mason is obliged to believe in the G.A.O.T.U., he has the right to do so according to his own fashion, and the blank leaves are intended to represent that he is at liberty to inscribe his own particular belief thereupon. In 1882 a Provincial Grand Lodge (which now has five Lodges) was established in Norway, which at the time caused some opposition, but these Lodges are now fully recognized, and the Grand Lodge of Norway works harmoniously with them. There are 40 Lodges, 52 Benevolent Institutions, and 2,842 active members.

VII.—THE GRAND MOTHER LODGE OF THE ECLECTIC FREE-
MASONS' UNION, IN FRANKFORT-ON-THE-MAINE

The first regularly constituted Lodge at Frankfort appears to have been the UNION (still existing), which was formally established in 1742. It formed a Lodge at Marburg in 1745, and another at Mayence, in 1758. Greater activity prevailed from 1761, and particularly in 1764, when the Emperor Joseph II was crowned. In 1765 the Lodge was requested to join the STRICT OBSERVANCE, and some of the daughter Lodges did so, but Frankfort held aloof, and J. P. Gogel obtained a patent as Prov. Grand Master from London. When in 1773 the Grand Lodge of England concluded a Treaty with von Zinnendorf, whereby all the Lodges in Germany holding English warrants were handed over to his Grand Lodge, Frankfort demurred, and this was the cause of a complete rupture with London in 1782, when Gogel's successor (Passavant) was not confirmed by the Grand Master of England, who, in lieu thereof, referred the matter to Berlin. In the same year the Convent at Wilhelmsbad had taken place. The STRICT OBSERVANCE was *in extremis*, and a number of Lodges which were dissatisfied with the position of affairs issued a circular letter in March, 1783, which was signed by the Provincial Grand Lodges of

Frankfort and Wetzlar, recommending the formation of what was at once called the ECLECTIC UNION. This arrangement continued until 1823, when the Provincial Grand assumed the title of a Grand Lodge, owing, it is said, to some dispute that had arisen concerning the admission of non-Christians, and partly because the Grand Duke of Hesse-Darmstadt wanted all Lodges in his Grand Duchy to be under Darmstadt. "High Degrees" are absolutely forbidden by the Constitutions. Since 1814 the Oath has been recited, but not taken. There are 25 Lodges, of which 6 are at Frankfort, 6 in Prussia, 9 in different German States, 55 Benevolent Institutions, and 3,000 active members.

VIII.—THE GRAND FREEMASONS' LODGE OF CONCORD IN DARMSTADT

This Grand Lodge was formed in 1846 by the Lodges KARL OF THE DAWNING LIGHT, Frankfort, ST. JOHN THE EVANGELIST, Darmstadt, and FRIENDS OF CONCORD, Mayence, former members of the ECLECTIC UNION, who were opposed to the "Humanitarian" principle, which was then, as it is now, a leading dogma of the Frankfort Craft. KARL afterwards (1878) rejoined the ECLECTIC UNION. In 1859 the Grand Duke gave instructions that the Lodges at Alzey, Giessen, Offenbach, and Worms, should join the Grand Lodge of Darmstadt. The two Lodges at Freidberg (1862) and Bingen (1867) were also formed under the same obedience, so that all the 8 Lodges, with 17 Benevolent Institutions and 742 active members, on Hessian Territory, belong to one Grand Lodge.

IX.—THE FIVE INDEPENDENT LODGES OF GERMANY

Besides the eight Grand Lodges already alluded to, there are five Lodges in Germany which owe allegiance to no Grand Lodge, and are acknowledged as regular Masonic bodies by the whole fraternity. They are doing good Masonic work, and are not likely to give up their independence, unless the Masonry of Germany should ever become sufficiently consolidated to admit of the formation of a United (or General) Grand Lodge. They possess an aggregate of 69 Benevolent Institutions, and a total membership of 1,328 in 1920.

I. MINERVA OF THE THREE PALMS, LEIPSIC

The Lodge was founded in 1741, under the name of the THREE COMPASSES, and after sundry vicissitudes of fortune assumed its present title and joined the STRICT OBSERVANCE in 1766. But, tiring of the folly, about 1782, it declared itself independent, and has remained so. Nevertheless, a good deal of the strict discipline of the old Templar *régime* is still to be found in its organization, which consists of the three degrees, directory, inner circle, and three "overmasters," one of whom is the Master of the Lodge. The Ritual was originally that of the Templar System, but it has been repeatedly altered and modified, particularly in 1829. There are 461 members.

2. BALDWIN OF THE LINDEN, LEIPSIC

Eleven Freemasons—among them some nine members of MINERVA—were the founders of this Lodge, which was constituted in 1776 by the GRAND NATIONAL LODGE at Berlin. In 1807 it declared its independence, but in 1809 accepted a new constitution from Hamburg. In 1815 it joined the Grand Lodge of Saxony, but left it in 1824, and since then has maintained its independence. It has a membership of 396. The three degrees only are worked.

3. ARCHIMEDES OF THE THREE TRACING BOARDS, IN ALTENBURG

This Lodge was founded in 1742, and declared itself independent in 1786. From 1788 to 1793 it joined—temporarily—the ECLECTIC UNION. With the beginning of the nineteenth century a period of great activity set in;

the old oath was done away with, and new constitutions
were drawn up. The Lodge has worked in the German
language from the day of its constitution, and is probably
the oldest Lodge in existence that has done so. The
membership is 280. The Benevolent Institutions are
very richly endowed; one of them was granted £5,000 by
the town on the day of the 150th Jubilee of the Lodge.
Three degrees only are worked. The brilliant Altenburg
School of Masonic historians and writers is inseparably
connected with this Lodge.

4. ARCHIMEDES OF ETERNAL UNION AT GERA

This was a kind of branch of the Altenburg Lodge, by
which body it was formally constituted in 1804. Several
Grand Lodges, however, refused to acknowledge its "regu-
larity," so an English warrant was obtained in 1806 through
the good offices of the Prov. Grand Lodge at Hamburg.
But when the latter, from a *Provincial*, developed into a
Grand Lodge (1811), the Grand Lodge of England struck off
her roll all German Lodges under the former *Provincial*
jurisdiction. The Lodge at Gera thereupon became independent, and has remained so ever since. The Princes of
Reuss have always been members and patrons of this Lodge.
The present Master is Mr. Robert Fischer, the well-known
President of the UNION OF GERMAN FREEMASONS. The
membership is 195.

5. KARL OF THE WREATH OF RUE, AT HILDBURGHAUSEN

Karl, Duke of Mecklenburg-Strelitz, was a prominent
Freemason and Prov. Grand Master of Hanover (under
England). At his instance this Lodge was established in
1786, and it received a Warrant of Constitution from London
in 1787. Duke Frederic of Saxe-Hildburghausen (son-in-
law of Duke Karl) was the first Senior Warden of the Lodge,
and he afterwards assumed the Protectorate, granting many
privileges, and himself initiating several members of the
Ducal family. The connection with England was severed

MARSHAL BLUCHER AS MASTER OF THE LODGE OF MÜNSTER
From a rare engraving

during the time of the Napoleonic wars, and the Lodge became independent. Members, 60.

THE UNION OF GERMAN FREEMASONS

This is not a Lodge, but rather a club or circle of Free-masons associating for literary and benevolent purposes. The original idea was the consideration and formation of reformatory proposals to be taken up by the Lodges whose members are members of the club; also to foster the idea of a general union of all Lodges. All Masons in good standing can become members by paying an annual sub-scription of 3s. The Board of Management calls an annual meeting at one of the towns where a Lodge is established; these meetings take place without Ritual or Masonic forms. The members, who number about 3,000, are drawn from all the German Systems.

THE GERMAN HIGH-DEGREES

Out of the *eight* German Grand Lodges, *five*, viz., Ham-burg, Saxony, Bayreuth, Frankfort, and Darmstadt (this is the order of seniority), practise none but the three Craft degrees. The *three* Prussian Grand Lodges work as follows: The GRAND NATIONAL LODGE (No. II), 10 degrees; the THREE GLOBES (No. I), 7 degrees; and the ROYAL YORK (No. III), 3 degrees, together with a virtual fourth, *Schot-tischer Meister* (Innermost Orient). Grand Lodge No. II uses the expression "Higher Degrees"; the THREE GLOBES call them "Steps of Knowledge," which is a distinction without a difference, as separate initiations for each of the steps take place; and the ROYAL YORK practises the 4th degree as a sort of "Royal Arch." It is from the members of the 4th degree that the "Innermost Orient" of Grand Lodge No. III is formed, a committee by which all matters concerning dogma and ritual are controlled.

A peculiarity of the German High Degrees is that they form part and parcel of the organization of the Grand Lodge. In England the Grand Lodge exercises a close supervision over the three Craft degrees and the Royal Arch, but everything additional to these is under the exclusive control of a totally distinct organization. Thus the three degrees are thoroughly independent of the "higher degrees." None of the officers of the Grand Lodge are bound by law to have higher degrees, and the higher degrees have no veto (through their representatives) in matters decided by the Grand Lodge. In the German Grand Lodges, Nos. I and II, above mentioned, the position is exactly reversed.

The system of the GRAND NATIONAL LODGE (No. II) consists of 10 degrees. Of these, 1 to 3 form the St. John's Lodge, 4 and 5 the St. Andrew's Lodge, 6 to 9 the Chapter. The 10th degree is only given at Berlin, as a sort of Honorary Degree; it is called Apprentice of Perfection; its distinctive outward mark is a red cross worn round the neck, and the members are styled "KNIGHTS OF THE RED CROSS."

The Grand Lodge transacts all business of the 5 degrees. At the head of the Grand Lodge is the Grand Master, assisted by his grand officers. The Chapter transacts all business of the degrees from No. 6 to No. 10, *and all matters of System and Ritual* are exclusively within its control. There are four kinds of Chapters—those who work 6 and 7; 6, 7, 8; 6, 7, 8, 9; and the Grand Chapter INDISSOLUBILIS at Berlin. At the head of the whole System is the *"Ordensmeister"* (Master of the Order), who at the present time is Prince Frederick Leopold of Prussia.

The System of the THREE GLOBES consists of 7 degrees: 1 to 3, St. John's Lodge; 4, General Scottish Lodge; 5 to 7, Chapter or Inner Orient. Beyond that point the Grand Lodge consists of no more than 63 and no less than 25 members, who are appointed out of the members residing at Berlin or its immediate neighbourhood. Once a year all Masters of Lodges are summoned to Berlin for the Session of Grand Lodge (in May). The Grand Lodge is governed by the "Union Directory," consisting of 7 members elected out of members of the 7th degree. At the head of the "Union Directory" is the "National Grand Master" and his Deputy. The "Union Directory" is the Representative and Executive Power of the Grand Lodge. To it are also specially confided *all* matters of System and Ritual; it is officially styled "Keeper, Improver, and Dispenser of Masonic Knowledge." All decisions on the above points are subject to its veto. There is also a "Legislative Assembly," which meets once a year; its decisions are, however, subject to the confirmation of the "Union Directory."

The three Prussian Grand Lodges have come to an understanding that their brethren of the higher degrees can attend the respective meetings in all of the three systems. As a consequence of the high degrees, none but Christians are admitted to the membership of the GRAND NATIONAL LODGE and the THREE GLOBES; and as a consequence of the understanding above alluded to, the ROYAL YORK has lately issued a circular to its Lodges, to the effect that candidates for initiation are to be reminded that none but Christians can attain the 4th degree in that jurisdiction.

These so-called high degrees, in the way they are at present worked at Berlin, are a most serious obstacle in the way of the unification of German Masonry. Of course, they are not the only one; there is also a certain jealousy among the different Grand Lodges. It is often asserted that this feeling only exists in the smaller Grand Lodges, which, however, seems to be a mistake. The smaller Grand Lodges would more easily give their consent to form a single "National Grand Lodge" than the three larger ones, who are more tenacious of their position and influence.

Thus there is no rallying point at present. But besides this, the five Grand Lodges that work no high degrees cannot see that they would improve their position, their Masonic knowledge, and general co-operation, *even if* a National Grand Lodge of all *Craft Lodges* was formed. This would only be an *outward* unification. The difficulty would still remain, that the greater part of the Lodges thus united would *not* be independent in their action and decision, but amenable, as at present under the Prussian Grand Lodges, to outside control. On the other hand, the larger Grand Lodges have stated, through their most prominent brethren, that they cannot do without the higher degrees which they now have. The GRAND NATIONAL LODGE (No. II) has said:—"As in the human body the blood circulates through the whole body, so with us the fund of knowledge circulates from the higher to the lower degrees, and you cannot sever the connections between all our degrees. You cannot cut off a man's head nor even his legs without mortally injuring his vitality, and just as little can you cut off one of our degrees." The THREE GLOBES have made a similar declaration, to the effect that they cannot do without the higher degrees, that practically Masonry is an unlimited field, although they admit at the same time that the whole of Masonic knowledge is contained in the degrees of Entered Apprentice, Fellow-Craft, and Master Mason. In conferring these— the St. John's or Craft—degrees, the German Lodges concur in essentials, while differing to a considerable extent in forms and methods. Hence a variety of rituals are in use. It is also worthy of remark, that the German Masons, with a scrupulous fidelity, have adhered to the manner of imparting the secrets of the first two degrees, as practised under the *Regular* Grand Lodge of England, prior to its Union with the "Ancients" in 1813.

AUSTRIA AND HUNGARY

A Lodge—THE THREE STARS—is said to have been established at Prague by Count F. A. Sporck, afterwards Governor of Bohemia, on returning from his travels in 1726, or at all events prior to 1729. Other Lodges were subsequently constituted from Prague, in Galicia, Hungary, Luxembourg, Styria, and Moravia.

The first Vienna Lodge—THE THREE FIRING GLASSES —was established in 1742, but closed, by order of Maria Theresa, in the following year. The members, however, among whom was her husband, Francis of Lorraine (afterwards Emperor) continued to meet in secret. A second Lodge—THE THREE HEARTS—was formed at the Austrian capital, in 1754; and a third, ROYAL MILITAIRE, in 1761. Maria Theresa regarded Freemasonry with disfavour, but the influence of her Consort was sufficiently potent to procure for it a certain measure of toleration, though powerless to protect it from occasional outbursts of persecution.

Other Lodges were founded at Vienna, in the Tyrol, Lombardy, and Illyria, but Freemasonry in Austria had passed under the yoke of the STRICT OBSERVANCE when the Empress Maria Theresa died, in 1780.

The territory of St. Stephen in the eighteenth century comprised the Kingdom of Hungary, or "Mother Country," the Principality of Transylvania, and the Kingdoms of Croatia and Sclavonia. The first Lodge in the "Mother Country"—TACITURNITAS—at Pressburg, is known to have existed in 1766, and eight other Hungarian Lodges were established between 1769 and 1771. Four Lodges were also formed in Transylvania, the first in 1750 and the last (of which the name has been preserved) in 1769. One of these, bearing the curious title of ST. ANDREW OF THE THREE SEA-LEAVES, gave birth to some daughter Lodges. THE THREE DRAGONS was established at Varasd (Croatia) in 1774. In Southern Hungary, under the influence of the two Counts, John Draskovich and Stephen Niczky, Lodges were founded at Glina (1764-69) and Agram (1771), and (also in Croatia) a "FREE CARPENTERS' LODGE" was established at Varasd (1772), which was soon afterwards transformed into a Masonic one, under the name of PERFECT UNION.

Lodges were likewise formed at Eszek, the capital of Sclavonia, and at Kreutz (a country centre).

These Lodges, in 1775, created a National Masonic Rite, under the name of MASONRY OF FREEDOM, or PROVINCE (*i.e.*, *Grand Lodge*) OF LIBERTY, but it was commonly known as "The Draskovich Observance, or Rite." The new power was short lived, but did much good during its brief span of life.

Under the Emperor Joseph II—1780-83—four Lodges were instituted at Vienna, and nine in other Austrian

States. During the same period two Lodges each were constituted in Bohemia and Moravia, three in Galicia, eleven in Hungary, and one in Transylvania.

A Grand Lodge—ruling over forty-five Lodges—for Austria and its dependencies was established in 1784. An Imperial Edict in the following year ordered that not more than three Lodges should exist in any single town, while those that were at work in any place which was not a "Seat of Government" were summarily suppressed.

The consequences may be supposed. The newly-formed Austrian Grand Lodge, together with its Provincial Grand Lodges, passed off the scene, and the general discontent of the Craft betokened the beginning of the end.

Then came the French Revolution. The Freemasons were regarded with suspicion. The Austrian Lodges voluntarily closed in 1792, and those in Bohemia during the following year.

Masonry in Hungary had a slightly longer life, but by an Edict of 1795 all Secret Societies in the Austrian dominions were ordered to dissolve.

There was a short Masonic revival at Vienna during the French occupation of 1805, and again in 1809-12. In 1867, after the Civil War, Masonry revived in Hungary, though in Austria it continued to be forbidden. In 1918, after the Great War, a Grand Lodge of Vienna was formed with 14 Lodges and 1,010 members, and it is to be hoped it will be successful. A Lodge, UNITY IN THE MOTHER LAND, was founded at Buda-Pesth in 1868, and this, with six daughter Lodges, formed, on January 30th, 1870, the ST. JOHN'S GRAND LODGE OF HUNGARY. The three Craft degrees only were recognized or tolerated by this governing body.

In 1869, however, a Lodge, MATTHIAS CORVINUS, established under the auspices of the so-called "Ancient and Accepted *Scottish* Rite" (after a vain application to the Grand Lodge of *Scotland*) obtained a warrant from the GRAND ORIENT OF FRANCE. This likewise warranted daughter Lodges, and the united body, in November, 1871,

founded the GRAND ORIENT OF HUNGARY. Ultimately
the Grand Lodge and the Grand Orient amalgamated
under the title of the SYMBOLIC GRAND LODGE OF
HUNGARY, on March 23rd, 1886. "Freedom of Con-
science" is acclaimed by this Grand Lodge, and the preamble
of its Statutes follows rather closely that of the GRAND
ORIENT OF FRANCE. There are 82 Lodges, with a total
membership of 6,134.

[Since the foregoing was written the present (1920) Government has suddenly closed all the Lodges, and forbidden
Freemasonry in Hungary. The furniture and properties
have been seized, and the funds distributed in other directions, whilst all officials found to be members have been
dismissed and imprisoned.—F.J.W.C.]

SWEDEN—DENMARK—NORWAY

Four Grand Lodge Systems follow the SWEDISH RITE.
These are the Grand Lodges of Sweden, Denmark, and
Norway, and the so-called GRAND NATIONAL LODGE OF
GERMAN FREEMASONS, at Berlin. The Rite is based upon
an alleged Templar origin of Freemasonry; and in imitation of that Knightly Order, all Europe is divided by it
into provinces. Germany occupies the seventh province,
Denmark the eighth, Sweden the ninth, and Norway the
tenth. The others are allotted, but unoccupied, because,
by Freemasons elsewhere, the theory of a Templar origin
was long ago buried in the grave of the STRICT
OBSERVANCE.

1.—SWEDEN

Considerable light has recently been thrown on the early
history of Freemasonry in Sweden, by the publication of
official documents, taken from the archives of the Grand
Lodge. These cover the periods from 1735 to 1774, and
from the latter date to 1800, and were printed respectively in 1892 and 1898. We learn that Count Axel
Ericson Wrede-Sparre (who was initiated at Paris in 1731)

founded a Lodge at Stockholm in 1735, which lasted until 1746.

The Baron (afterwards Count) C. F. Scheffer, next appears on the scene. This worthy, it would appear, was made a Mason in "Prince Clermont's Lodge" at Paris, in 1737, and also obtained there "the other two St. John's," as well as "two Scottish degrees," all of which incidents in his career, if they ever occurred, it seems to myself, must at least have been slightly antedated in the narrative I am recording. At Paris Scheffer formed the acquaintance of the "Count of Darwentwater, Charles Radclyffe"—Grand Master of the Freemasons of France from 1736 to 1738—who granted— November 25th, 1737—a Deputation authorizing the Baron to constitute Lodges in the Kingdom of Sweden, to accept candidates for the first three degrees, and to nominate Masters of Lodges. These Lodges were to be under the jurisdiction of the French Grand Master, until they elected a ruler of their own. The original of this important document is stated to be still extant at Stockholm, signed and sealed by the "Count of Darwentwater, and countersigned by T. Moore, Grand Secretary and Keeper of Seals." In the same archives is a copy of "Rules" "for the Lodge constituted at Stockholm by our dear and worthy Baronet of Scheffer." These "Rules," we learn, were confirmed by "Macleane, Grand Master of France," October 22nd, 1735; and again, by the "Count of Darwentwater," October 27th, 1736. This evidence is also confusing, as, apart from that portion of it which bears on the *vexata quæstio* of the early Grand Masters of France, it is difficult to believe that the Continental were so much in advance of the British Masons as to have possessed a well-known and recognized system of *three* Craft Degrees in 1737.

In 1743-4 a Lodge was constituted at Stockholm by General (later Field-Marshal) James Keith, English Provincial Grand Master for Russia. This was called "General Keith's Lodge."

A so-called "Guards' Lodge," also at the capital, had a brief tenure of existence in 1751. In the same year one

Sorbon founded a Lodge, which was called by his name, but he left it in 1752, in order to become a founder and Deputy Master of ST. JEAN AUXILIARE.

This famous Lodge was constituted—January 13th, 1752 —by Count Knut Carlsson Posse, who had received a Deputation from Prince Louis de Bourbon, Comte de Clermont, Grand Master of France. Posse was elected "Grand Master" of ST. JEAN AUXILIARE, a title bestowed on Masters of Lodges at the time in France, and, following that custom, also in Sweden. At this period, seven Masonic degrees were worked in Stockholm, as shown in as many columns on the roll of members of the Lodge: 1 to 3, St. John's; 4 and 5, St. Andrew's; 6, St. John's Trusty Brethren's; 7, Elected Brethren's. Subsequently the Lodge was described by the following titles:—"SWEDEN'S MOTHER LODGE; THE FIRST REGULAR SWEDISH LODGE; THE COUNTRY'S GRAND FREEMASONS' SOCIETY"; and "THE COUNTRY'S GRAND LODGE," or "SWEDISH COUNTRY'S LODGE."

Count Wrede-Sparre and Baron Scheffer both joined ST. JEAN AUXILIARE in 1753. Immediately afterwards the latter was elected Grand Master of Sweden by the "Mother Lodge," and he remained in that position until 1774, though, as no Grand Lodge was formed until 1760, Sweden had only a Grand Master from 1753 to that year.

King Adolf Fredrik took upon himself—July 7th, 1753— the "Chiefmastership over all Societies of Freemasons in the Kingdom," and became the first Protector of the Swedish Craft. He is also said to have been the Master of a Lodge bearing his own name. But there is no certainty that the King was ever regularly initiated, and the so-called "King's Lodge"—ADOLF FREDRIK—was not officially recognized (as a regular Lodge) until 1762. In the same year—September 7th—the King declared himself Protector of the newly-constituted "LODGE OF THE SWEDISH ARMY" (*Svenska Arméens*), and was enrolled as No I on its list of members. The glorious career of this famous "Military Lodge" was brought to a close in 1788.

The Freemasons' Orphanage in Stockholm was founded by the "Mother Lodge" in 1753, and a French Lodge, L'UNION, constituted by the same authority in 1759. At the close of the latter year there were six regular St. John's Lodges in Sweden and Finland:—St. JEAN AUXILIARE, ST. ERIK, ST. EDWARD, and L'UNION, in Stockholm; SALOMON Á TROIS SERRURES, in Gothenburg; and ST. AUGUSTIN, in Helsingfors.

Among the members of Lodge ST. EDWARD was Charles Frederick Eckleff, who, to slightly anticipate, seems to have constructed a ritual, founded principally on the French "High Degrees," which became the basis of the present Swedish System. By virtue of a Deputation received from some unknown authority, Eckleff first of all established, in 1756, a new St. Andrew's Lodge, under the name of L'INNO-CENTE; and afterwards—December 25th, 1759—a Grand *Chapter*, bearing the same title. In connection with the latter, he was elected "Master of the Order," which empowered him to constitute new Lodges, and accordingly—May 1st, 1760—he duly founded one, called the SEVENTH ST. JOHN'S LODGE, of which he became the leading Master.

In 1760 a Swedish GRAND LODGE was established, comprising the seven St. John's Lodges—ST. JEAN AUXILIARE now losing its power of constituting other Lodges, and being ranged on a level with the other six.

The St. Andrew's Lodge, L'INNOCENTE, and the Grand Chapter of the same name, were also placed on the roll, but without numbers. Baron Scheffer continued to hold the office of Grand Master, and Eckleff was elected his Deputy, so that the latter was at one and the same time Master of the Order, Deputy Grand Master, Master of the St. Andrew's Lodge, L'INNOCENTE, and Master of the SEVENTH ST. JOHN'S LODGE.

Charles Tullmann, Secretary to the British Embassy at Stockholm, received an *English* patent as Provincial Grand Master of Sweden, in 1765, and constituted several Lodges. But in 1770 the Grand Lodge of England recognized the Grand Lodge of Sweden as a Sovereign Masonic power, on the representation of Count Scheffer, its Grand Master. In consequence, the "English," or "Tullmann," Lodges soon ceased to exist.

In 1771, King Gustavus III and his brothers, Charles and Frederick Adolf, were initiated, and the King became Patron of the Craft. The three Royal brothers became members of the Grand Chapter in 1773.

In 1774, Duke Charles was elected "Master of the Order," and National Grand Master, in succession to Eckleff and Scheffer respectively. In this year the Grand Chapter was invested with the highest authority, and the general title was assumed of the SWEDISH GRAND COUNTRY'S LODGE.

In 1779, when Duke Charles was placed at the head of the VIIth Province of the STRICT OBSERVANCE, in Germany, he resigned the office of National Grand Master in favour of his brother, Frederick Adolf.

In 1780 Gustavus III erected a IXth Province of the Order of the Temple, in Sweden, and Duke Charles was installed VICARIUS SALOMONIS of the same. Since then the supreme chief of Swedish Freemasonry has been accorded that title, and the Grand Lodge of Sweden has been styled the IXth Province.

In 1781 Duke Charles resigned his position as head of the STRICT OBSERVANCE in Germany, and between 1796 and 1800 devoted his energies to the compilation of new Constitutions and new rituals for all the degrees.

The STRICT OBSERVANCE and the SWEDISH RITE formed the two branches of what has been called the Templar descent theory. Both systems were introduced into Germany, and on the formation of the GRAND NATIONAL LODGE in Berlin, the Swedish branch of Templarism (under Zinnendorf) was for some considerable period the only powerful competitor of the STRICT OBSERVANCE.

The SWEDISH RITE has been described as a mixture of English Freemasonry, of the "Scots" degrees of the French, of Templarism, and of certain ideas peculiar to the Hermetic or Rosicrucian Fraternities. It is also affirmed that the mystical teachings of Emmanuel Swedenborg are discernible in the doctrines of the RITE.

There are three clusters of degrees, St. John's, St. Andrew's, and Chapter degrees respectively. Above or beyond these is a sort of 10th degree, consisting of three steps of honour, and at the head of the whole system is the so-called VICAR OF SOLOMON.

On succeeding to the throne in 1809, Charles XIII resumed the office of Grand Master, but two years later resigned it in favour of his adopted heir, Bernadotte (Charles XIV), retaining, however, the position of VICARIUS SALOMONIS. The late "Master of the Order," or "Vicar of Solomon," was King Oscar II, by whom our own King—Edward VII—was initiated in 1868. The King of Sweden, Gustav V, is the National Grand Master, and the Crown Prince his Deputy; and there are in the jurisdiction 13 St. Andrew's and 28 St. John's Lodges, with a total membership of about 8,000.

II.—DENMARK

ST. MARTIN, the first Danish Lodge, was established at Copenhagen, in 1743, by a member of the THREE GLOBES at Berlin; and the second, ZERUBBABEL, by seceders from the first Lodge, in 1744. Afterwards, both Lodges received English Charters, and ultimately amalgamated, under the name of ZERUBBABEL OF THE NORTH STAR.

English and Scottish Provincial Grand Lodges for Denmark and Norway were severally erected in 1749 and 1753. In 1765 the English Provincial Grand Lodge—which was the only survivor—went over to the STRICT OBSERVANCE, and became the Prefecture BENIN.

A Lodge, which still exists—MARIA OF THE THREE HEARTS—was instituted at Odense in 1791. It was named after the Danish Crown Princess, Maria Sophie Fredericke, whose father, Prince Charles of Hesse-Cassel, Grand Master, gave the Lodge its warrant. In 1817 Prince Christian—

afterwards Christian VIII—and in 1841 his son, Frederick VII, were initiated in this Lodge.

In 1792, on the death of Ferdinand of Brunswick—the conqueror at Minden—Prince Charles became the sole head of the Danish Lodges. Prince Charles died in 1836, and the Crown Prince, afterwards Christian VIII, assumed the Protectorate of the Lodges, which he held during the remainder of his life. His son and successor, Frederick VII, became Grand Master of the Grand Lodge of Denmark on ascending the throne in 1848. This King remodelled Danish Masonry on the Swedish system, the first three degrees of which do not, however, differ materially from our own. At the present time King Christian X is Vicar of Solomon, and Master of the Order. There are 3 St. Andrew's, 11 St. John's, and 18 "Instruction" Lodges, with a total membership of 5,338.

III.—NORWAY

This country, until 1814, formed part of the Kingdom of Denmark, which had not then adopted the Swedish Rite. But in that year the Norwegian Lodges came under the rule of the Grand Lodge of Sweden. The first Lodge in Norway, St. Olaus, is said to have been constituted in 1745. Another, Christian of the Dark Helmet, was established at Trondhjem, in 1780; and a third, Charles of the Norwegian Lion, at Bergen, in 1786. That there were others in the eighteenth century may be safely inferred, but no record of them has come down to us. A Field Lodge is stated to have been in existence at Kongsberg—the Norwegian silver mines—during the war of 1807-09.

The Grand Lodge, however, became independent again when the kingdoms separated in 1905. The King is no longer Grand Master, but the rule is democratic. There are 3 St. Andrew's Lodges and 13 of St. John, with a membership of 5,812.

HOLLAND

The authentic history of Dutch Masonry dates from the initiation of the Duke of Lorraine, afterwards the Emperor Francis I at the Hague, "by virtue of a *Deputation* for a *Lodge* there," which was presided over by the Rev. Dr. Desaguliers, in 1731 (*ante*, 219). After this, according to general report, there were permanent Lodges meeting at the Hague, Du GRAND MAITRE DES PROVINCES REUNIS, in 1734, and LE VERITABLE ZELE (under an English warrant) in 1735. During the latter year there were also Lodges in Amsterdam and Rotterdam. The Craft then fell into disfavour with the States General, but the Lodges resumed work in 1744.

In 1756—December 27th—fourteen Lodges, several of which were of English and one of Scottish origin, founded the NATIONAL GRAND LODGE OF THE NETHERLANDS.

But the Grand Lodge of England was either only dimly aware of the existence of the new Masonic power, or did not recognize its exclusive territorial jurisdiction, as it continued to constitute Dutch Lodges. This state of affairs, however, was put an end to in 1770, when the Grand Lodge of England agreed not to issue further charters in Holland, though stipulating that the Lodges under English warrants should have full and perfect liberty either to remain under the jurisdiction of the English Provincial Grand Master for foreign Lodges, or to join the national organization.

Prince Frederick William, second son of King William I, was elected Grand Master of Holland in 1816, of Belgium in 1817, and of a Grand Orient, with jurisdiction over the Lodges in both these countries, in 1818. A little later (1830) Belgium obtained its political, and shortly afterwards its Masonic, independence. Prince Frederick remained at the head of the Dutch Craft until his death in 1881.

According to Dr. H. W. Dieperink, "the *Order* of Freemasons in the Netherlands is composed of three different systems, which have each their separate administration, laws, and finances. These are the Symbolic Degrees, the Higher Degrees, and the Division of the Master's Degree. The first system is governed by the Grand Orient, the second by the Grand Chapter, and the third by the Chamber of Administration (for that portion of the Rite)." Of the degrees of the Craft, we are told by another authority, "that the words and pass-words of the first two are exactly the reverse of the English usage, and the battery in all three degrees is entirely different." From which may be inferred that the Dutch, like the German Masons, continue to impart the secrets of the first two steps of Masonry in the manner originally prescribed by the earliest of Grand Lodges.

The High Degrees of the Netherlands, also called Red Masonry, acquired their name in 1803. They consisted until recently of—1st, *Elu* or Select Master; 2nd, the three Scots Grades; 3rd, Knight of the Sword, or of the East; and 4th, Sovereign Prince Rose-Croix, but there is now a Supreme Council 33° working the usual degrees of that Rite.

The Division of the Master's Degree comprises Elected Master and Sublime Elected Master, which are now combined in a single degree. It is merely an elaboration of, or perhaps it would be better to say an addition to, the third degree.

The jurisdiction of the Grand Orient extends over 108 Lodges, of which 31 are in South Africa, and 22 in the Dutch Colonies. The membership is estimated at 4,800.

Belgium

English Lodges were established at Alost in 1765, at Ghent in 1768, and at Mons in 1770. The latest of the three, La Parfaite Union, claims (though on wholly insufficient evidence) to have been originally constituted by the Duke of Montagu, Grand Master of England, in 1721. Under Joseph II, Masonry, in what was then the Austrian Netherlands, greatly flourished, but all the Lodges, with the exception of three, were closed by that Emperor in 1786.

Others, indeed, continued to exist, but *all* Lodges, including the privileged *three*, were formally prohibited from assembling by an edict of 1787.

During the closing year of the eighteenth century, and until 1814, the Masonry of Belgium was conducted under the ægis of the Grand Orient of France. Then followed the union of the Belgian and Dutch Lodges, which has already been narrated. The GRAND ORIENT OF BELGIUM was constituted in 1833. There are 24 Lodges under its jurisdiction, with a total membership of about 4,100. There is also a Supreme Council 33° which controls a few Craft Lodges in addition.

LUXEMBURG

The central authority of the Craft in this Grand Duchy is a SUPREME COUNCIL (not, however, of the so-called "Ancient and Accepted Scottish Rite"), which was established in 1849. The jurisdiction is the smallest one known, and consists of a single Lodge, LES ENFANS DE LA CONCORDE —founded in 1803—with a membership of 100.

RUSSIA

Freemasonry in the dominions of the Czar may be said to date from 1732, in which year General James Keith (brother of the last Earl Marischal) was Master of a Lodge either at Moscow or St. Petersburg. This famous soldier of fortune, who had entered the Russian Service in 1728, received an English patent as Provincial Grand Master in 1740. Masonry in Russia assumed at different times and concurrently all the varying forms under which it was known in Europe, and it will be sufficient to state that from 1762 to 1782 an indigenous Rite named after its chief supporter, Count Melisino, flourished; that in 1765 the STRICT OBSERVANCE, and in 1771 the SWEDISH RITE, found a footing in the Empire. In 1772, Lieutenant-General Yelaguin was appointed Provincial Grand Master under England, and a large increase of Lodges was the result. In 1774, however, Yelaguin, at the head of seven Russian

Lodges, shifted his allegiance, and became Prov. G.M. under the SWEDISH RITE. A Provincial Grand Chapter—PHŒNIX —was next constituted at St. Petersburg in 1778, by the same authority, with Prince Gagarin as its chief. In the following year Gagarin succeeded Yelaguin as Prov. G. Master, and established what was nominally a NATIONAL GRAND LODGE, though, until 1782, when it threw off the foreign yoke, it remained in reality a Swedish Provincial Grand Lodge.

In 1794, at the wish of the Empress Catherine, the Lodges closed their doors, but ten years later, under the liberal-minded Alexander, a revival took place.

A GRAND DIRECTORAL LODGE, under Sweden, was formed in 1811, of which, at the instance of the Czar, Beber was elected Grand Master. In 1815, the "High Degrees" caused dissension, and the system split into two parts, the Grand Lodge ASTRÆA—a purely Craft body—and a revived Provincial Grand Lodge under the SWEDISH RITE. In 1819, the former had twenty-four Lodges on its roll, and the latter only six. Three years later (1822), by a decree of the Emperor, which is still in force, Freemasonry in Russia was finally suppressed. Whether it will experience a resurrection in the future of a regenerated Russia remains to be seen.

POLAND

Prior to 1739 there were in existence some Lodges at Warsaw, but these were all closed in that year in consequence of the Bull of Pope Clement XII.

A little later the Craft revived, and many Lodges sprang into existence. The THREE BROTHERS, constituted at Warsaw in 1744, developed into a Grand Lodge, with Count Augustus Moszynski as Grand Master, in 1769. This nobleman, however, accepted the secondary position of Prov. Grand Master, under England, in the following year. A general dormancy of the Lodges occurred after the first partition of Poland, in 1772. On their resuming labour, in 1773, there was a struggle for supremacy between the STRICT

OBSERVANCE, the GRAND ORIENT OF FRANCE, and the ROYAL YORK LODGE, at Berlin, which lasted until 1781. In that year, CATHERINE OF THE POLE STAR—which had been reconstituted by the ROYAL YORK in 1780—received an English patent as a Provincial Grand Lodge, and the rivalry of the STRICT OBSERVANCE and the GRAND ORIENT OF FRANCE ceasing, was converted into an independent GRAND ORIENT OF POLAND, in 1784.

But again political events disturbed the tranquillity of the Craft. In 1792 the second partition of Poland took place, and in 1794 its final dismemberment. After a long period of inactivity, the former Provincial Grand Lodge, CATHERINE OF THE POLE STAR, and also the NATIONAL GRAND ORIENT, resumed work in 1810. Further political changes occurred in 1815, but Masonry continued to prosper, and in 1818 there were thirty Lodges under the jurisdiction of the Grand Orient. Clouds, however, soon afterwards appeared on the horizon, and by an Imperial rescript, the practice of assembling as Freemasons in what from 1794 had been generally described as the "Grand Duchy of Warsaw," was prohibited, in 1821. A year later, a similar Ukase was issued in Russia, and in either instance there appears to have been ample justification for the action of the Czar. The resuscitated Kingdom of Poland may again achieve a Grand Lodge, but at present things are in abeyance.

SWITZERLAND

Of the twenty-two Cantons now forming the Swiss Confederacy, the first in which Masonry effected an entrance was GENEVA, where a Lodge was established in 1736. The next year witnessed the formation of an English Provincial Grand Lodge. In 1745 there were six Lodges.

From nearly as early a date as at GENEVA the Society had obtained a footing in VAUD, BERNE, ZURICH, and BASLE. But in 1745, in consequence of a decree of the Great Council of BERNE, the Lodges closed their doors, which, after an interval of about fifteen years, they reopened, but in every instance, *in the then confederated States*, under the banner of the STRICT OBSERVANCE.

In GENEVA the UNION OF HEARTS (at a later period the "Mother Lodge" of the Duke of Kent) was established in 1768, and in the following year ten Lodges met, and erected the INDEPENDENT GRAND LODGE OF GENEVA. The pure and ancient Masonry of Britain was alone practised by the subordinates of this Grand Lodge.

During the "Reign of Terror" all Masonic work ceased.

The second period of Swiss Masonry lasted from 1795 to 1814-16, and the allegiance of the Lodges was chiefly divided between the GRAND ORIENT OF FRANCE and the SCOTS DIRECTORY OF THE VTH PROVINCE—a modified form of the STRICT OBSERVANCE. A notable event was the formation, in 1810, at Lusanne (VAUD) of the NATIONAL GRAND ORIENT OF FRENCH HELVETIA, or, as it was more commonly called, GLAIRE'S HELVETIC RITE. The third period begins in 1816, after the fall of Napoleon. The systems existing were the GRAND ORIENT OF FRANCE, the HELVETIC RITE, the SCOTS DIRECTORY, and the LODGE OF HOPE at BERNE, constituted by the GRAND ORIENT OF FRANCE, in 1803.

The French Lodges gradually dissolved, and HOPE became, in 1818, an English Provincial Grand Lodge. Four years later the BERNE and VAUD Lodges (the HELVETIC RITE having passed off the scene) joined in forming a NATIONAL GRAND LODGE OF SWITZERLAND, recognizing three degrees only.

This left only two governing bodies, the NATIONAL GRAND LODGE, at BERNE, and the SCOTS DIRECTORY at BASLE, in the field; and these, uniting, formed the present GRAND LODGE ALPINA on July 24th, 1844. It has 35 Lodges under its jurisdiction, with a membership of 4,200.

ITALY

In the uncertain period of Italian Freemasonry, a Lodge is said to have been founded at Florence by Lord George

Sackville, in 1733, and others are also traditionally reported
to have existed at Milan, Verona, Padua, Vicenza, Venice,
and Naples, in 1735. But the minutes are still preserved
of the ROMAN LODGE, in the STATES OF THE CHURCH,
from the year 1735 down to the time of its final closure—
when the Earl of Winton was "Great Master"—in 1737.
Shortly afterwards (1738) the thunders of the Vatican were
launched against the Freemasons, and the series of Bulls
issued against the Society by successive Pontiffs have been
carefully enumerated by the present Pope, from whose
Encyclical Letter of April 20th, 1884, I transcribe the
following:—"The first warning of danger was given by
Clement XII in 1738, and his Edict was confirmed and
renewed by Benedict XIV (1751). Pius VII followed in
their steps (1821); and Leo XXII, in his Apostolic Edict,
'*Quo Graviora*' (1825), embraced the acts and decrees of
the earlier Popes on this subject, and ordered them to be
ratified for ever. To the same effect, Gregory XVI (1832),
and very often Pius IX (1846, 1865, etc.), have spoken."
(*De Secta Massonum.*)

In the opening years of the second half of the eighteenth
century, Lodges under England were established in the
TWO SICILIES, TUSCANY, VENETIA, GENOA, and SARDINIA.

The STRICT OBSERVANCE swept over Italy in 1777, and
a little later there was a general cessation of Masonic work.
Then came the French domination, and with it a system of
Grand Orients. After the fall of Napoleon, edicts of
suppression were issued by the various States, and from
1821 to 1856 not a Lodge existed in any part of what is
now the Kingdom of Italy.

In 1859 some Masons congregated in a Lodge at Turin,
and the example was followed at Genoa, Milan, Pisa,
Florence, Leghorn, and Rome. On the 1st of January,
1862, twenty-two Lodges being represented, the GRAND
ORIENT OF ITALY was proclaimed at Turin. This body
has been several times reconstructed, and absorbed the
SUPREME COUNCIL, 330, at Palermo, in 1873. There are
204 Lodges in the jurisdiction, of which 38 are in foreign

countries (Roumania, Servia, Egypt, Barbary, North Africa, South America, and China).

A *new* GRAND ORIENT OF ITALY—at Milan—with a following of 42 Lodges, is mentioned in a circular of the Swiss GRAND LODGE ALPINA (1901). At present the Grand Orient is at Rome, and has 482 Lodges with 20,000 members.

SPAIN

The first Lodge in Spain was founded in 1728 by the Duke of Wharton at Madrid, and the second was constituted later in the same year by the Grand Lodge of England at Gibraltar. In 1740 Philip V issued an edict against the Craft, and a further decree of Ferdinand VII, in 1751, condemned the Freemasons to death without the formality of a trial. Brighter times came, and in 1767 a Grand Lodge was formed, which in 1780 became a Grand Orient. In 1811 there were four governing Masonic bodies, two Grand Orients, and two Supreme Councils 33°. Another persecution took place in 1814, then came the popular movement under the patriot Riego (1820), the Jesuits were expelled, the Inquisition abolished, and the old liberal constitution regranted. For four years the Craft flourished, but a new insurrection broke out, and Ferdinand VII was charged by the populace with being a Freemason himself, because he had not re-established the Inquisition. By the aid of French troops the old prerogatives of the King were restored, and the Fraternity suppressed. Riego was shot, and in 1825, a Lodge at Granada having been forcibly entered, the seven Master Masons present were hanged, and an apprentice (who had just been initiated) was sent for five years to the galleys.

The next period of Spanish Masonry extends to the year 1868, when Queen Isabella was deposed, and throughout the whole of it there is darkness and uncertainty. In 1869 the Craft once more emerged into the light of day, and in 1887 the names are mentioned of the GRAND ORIENT OF SPAIN, the GRAND NATIONAL ORIENT, and the

SYMBOLICAL GRAND LODGE, with a following of 247,220 and 28 Lodges respectively. These numbers, if, indeed, even approximately correct, have since declined, and at the present time there exists in Madrid a GRAND ORIENT (or GRAND LODGE), with 109 subordinate Lodges and 5,920 members. Grand Lodges were also mentioned as having their seats at Seville and Barcelona, the former with twenty-six, and the latter with fifteen daughter Lodges. These are not now known ; but there is a Symbolic Regional Grand Lodge of Catalana-Balcar at Barcelona with 8 Lodges and 200 members, and a Supreme Council at Madrid.

PORTUGAL

An English Lodge was established at Lisbon in 1735, and the progress of the Craft was uninterrupted, until suddenly arrested by a royal edict in 1743. On the banishment of the Jesuits in 1761 Masonry revived, but again declined on the death of Joseph II in 1777. Lodges, however, continued to exist at Lisbon, Coimbra, and Oporto, also in the shipping. The Lodge REGENERATION was constituted on board the frigate PHŒNIX in 1797, and shortly afterwards created five other Lodges. The superior authority was then confided to a committee (*commissao do expediente*), consisting of six delegates, under whose benign rule Masonry penetrated into every part of the Kingdom. A GRAND LODGE OF PORTUGAL was established in 1800 (or 1805). During the French invasions the Craft languished, and there were successive revivals, followed by intermittent and savage persecutions, in 1810, 1821, and 1834. In 1848 there were three Grand Lodges, a Grand Orient, and an Irish Provincial Grand Lodge.

All the National organizations coalesced in 1869 and formed the UNITED GRAND ORIENT OF LUSITANIA. This was joined by the four Irish Lodges in 1872, who thereupon laid down their *Provincial* title, and resolved themselves into a Single Lodge, REGENERACAO IRLANDEZA (*Irish Regeneration*). Eleven years later (1883) there was a schism, and a new Grand Lodge was established. Still more recently (1892) the Lodges REGENERACAO IRLANDEZA and OBREIROS DO TROBALHO seceded from the United Grand Orient (on the ground of its having departed from the fundamental principles of Freemasonry), and formed the GRANDE LOJA DE PORTUGAL. The calendars, however, of current date, only mention the UNITED GRAND ORIENT OF LUSITANIA, which has an apparent following of 79 Lodges, 34 Triangles, and 2,748 members.

GREECE

Lodges were founded by the Grand Orient of France at Corfu, in 1809 and 1810, and by the Grand Lodge of England —PYTHAGORAS, still existing—in 1837. A GRAND LODGE OF GREECE—of which all traces have vanished—is supposed to have been formed at the same island about 1840. On the mainland there were, in 1867, eight (Italian) Lodges, which met and constituted themselves into an independent Grand Lodge. Irregular Masonic centres were subsequently established, but in 1898 the Grand Lodge of 1867, by a combination with its only surviving rival, became the sole governing body of the jurisdiction, with the title of the GRAND ORIENT AND SUPREME COUNCIL 33° FOR GREECE. It rules over eighteen Lodges, with a membership of about 1,000.

BULGARIA

A Grand Lodge was founded in 1917, and has eleven Lodges, with about 1,000 members.

TURKEY

There were Lodges at Smyrna and Aleppo in 1738, and from about ten years later till the present time others have been constituted at irregular intervals by many of the European Grand Lodges or Grand Orients.

ROUMANIA

Twenty Lodges (of foreign origin) united in forming the NATIONAL GRAND LODGE OF ROUMANIA in 1880. The next year two SUPREME COUNCILS were established, one of the RITE OF MEMPHIS 95°, the other of the ANCIENT AND ACCEPTED SCOTTISH RITE 33°. In 1882, a GRAND CHAPTER OF THE ROYAL ARCH was added; and in 1883, a GRAND LODGE AND TEMPLE OF THE SWEDENBORGIAN RITE. The Grand Master of all these bodies is (or was) one and the same person. Statistics fail me with respect to the majority of these associations, but the "National Grand Lodge of Freemasons" had a following of twenty-seven Lodges before the war; no recent statistics are at present available.

SERVIA

Private Lodges, under foreign warrants, were established at Belgrade and elsewhere, and in 1919 the GRAND LODGE OF SERBIA, CROATIA, AND JUGO-SLAVIA was formed, with seven Lodges and 270 members.

MALTA

After early persecutions, caused by the Papal Bull of 1738, the LODGE OF SECRECY AND HARMONY was formed on the island, and in 1789 reconstituted from England, as No. 539. All the officers were KNIGHTS OF MALTA. If we may credit Besuchet, Napoleon Buonaparte was initiated at Valetta in 1798. (*Précis Hist. de la F.M.*) Since 1815 the island has been the seat of an English Provincial (or, as now termed, a District) Grand Lodge. Tunis was incorporated with the Malta district in 1869.

CHAPTER IX

*To the popular world the necessity for secrecy seems a weak
point in our structure, but when examined by the light of practical working in the past, and in Oriental Communities where
ancient systems still survive, the concealment of their methods
of working is shown to be a necessity of the greatest importance.
It was the discovery of the uses and construction of the square,
level, and plumb rule, and a few powers in geometry, which,
gained by ages of experimental working, were regarded as
precious jewels of knowledge. The builders often became the
masters of the situation, and did not fail to bargain for and
obtain privileges, which together with their mysteries they safe-
guarded with jealous care.*—SIR C. PURDON CLARKE.

PERSIA—INDIA

ASKERI KHAN, a Prince of PERSIA, ambassador of the Shah
at Paris, was admitted a member of the Craft in that city
in 1808. A similar experience befell the Mirza Abul Hassan
Khan—also a Persian Ambassador—who was made a Mason
by the Earl of Moira, in London, in 1810. During the same
year Sir Gore Ousely, English Ambassador *at* the Court of
the Shah, was appointed Provincial Grand Master for
PERSIA, but there is no evidence to show that any Lodges
were ever established in that country by any external
authority.

The earliest stationary Lodges in INDIA, which must all
have partaken more or less of a military character, were
established at Calcutta in 1730, at Madras in 1752, and at
Bombay in 1758.

The rivalry between the two Grand Lodges of England was reflected in the Indian Lodges, but the "Brethren" of Madras anticipated in a very happy manner the complete "Union" of 1813, by the "Atholl" or "Ancient" Masons, and the Regular Masons or titular "Moderns," who amalgamated under General Horne, in 1786.

In the senior Presidency, however, the animosities between the Regular Masons and the Schismatics lingered until 1813, when, under the benignant sway of the Earl of Moira, ACTING GRAND MASTER OF INDIA, Masonry in Bengal took firm root in the land, and flourished as it had never done before.

In Bombay, the most brilliant era of the Craft is inseparably connected with the memory of Dr. James Burnes, by whom, in order to throw open the portals of Freemasonry to native gentlemen, a Lodge—RISING STAR OF WESTERN INDIA—was established in December, 1843. At the first regular meeting there were two initiations, one of the candidates being a Parsee and the other a Mahommedan, both ranking among the most highly cultured of their own people; and, in the following July, there were present in Lodge nine native brethren, three of whom were followers of Zoroaster, two of Confucius, and four of Mahomet, but all assembled with the followers of Christ to worship the Masons' God. In the three Presidencies—with Aden and Burma—there are at the present time 139 Lodges under the English, and 44 under the Scottish jurisdiction.

In both PERSIA and INDIA, however, there are certain customs peculiar to the building trades, which possess an interest for Freemasons. These are graphically described by my friend, Sir C. Purdon Clarke, in an interesting essay, *The Tracing Board in Modern Oriental and Medieval Operative Masonry*, from which I extract the following:—"So well concealed are the methods used by Oriental craftsmen to produce the work which often puzzles us by its complexity, that travellers have been deceived with believing that by some intuitive faculty the Eastern master builder is able to dispense with plans, elevations and sections, and start the foundations of the various parts of his structure without a precise predetermination of the bulk and requirements of the several parts. To all appearances the PERSIAN master builder is independent of the aid of plans. Actually he has first of all worked out the general scheme, not as our architects do, on plain paper, but on a sectional lined tracing board, every square of which represents either one or four square bricks. *These tracing boards are the key to the mystery of their craft,* and masons will understand the significance of the discovery that they represent in miniature scale the floor of the master builder's work room." (*A.Q.C.* vi., 100.) The great antiquity of the PERSIAN tracing board and system of enlargement by squaring is illustrated (among other proofs), and especially with respect to the use of drawn plans, by a reference to the Chaldean Statue in the Louvre of a princely builder or architect, who is represented as sitting with a tracing board on his knee.

During his sojourn in INDIA, the same close observer, though unsuccessful in finding among the native methods of working a connection with the squaring system of Modern PERSIA and Ancient EGYPT, was so fortunate as to discover a new system of proportion, which may prove a key to certain racial problems now a mystery. At Madura he was able to study Craft work in progress, carried on by men who were conforming strictly to rules which, at the least, possessed an antiquity of a thousand years. The ARCHITECT CASTE, conjointly with Surveyors, Carpenters, and Joiners, claim descent from VISWACARMA, the Heavenly Architect, and to them belong some 32 or, as some reckon, 64 books of the Shastras, of which they, not the priests, are the custodians. The consequence has been, that while the practical part of the science continued to be followed up amongst themselves as a kind of inheritance from generation to generation, the theory gradually became lost to the whole nation, if not to the whole world. At the celebrated Pagoda of Cochin, in Travancore, a further discovery was made—a room specially set apart for the temple achitect, the walls of which were covered with full-sized tracings of figures and temple furniture of all sorts. "This concession of a special room within the precincts of the temple," in the opinion of Sir C. Purdon Clarke, "should be noted, as in European medieval records the setting apart of a portion of a building in course of erection for the use of masons is frequently mentioned, and the practical necessities of their craft and its mysteries led," he believes, "in course of time to the peculiar arrangement and ornaments of the modern Lodges of Speculative Masonry."

The East India Islands

Lodges holding charters from European jurisdictions exist at Ceylon, Sumatra, Java, Celebes, and Borneo. In the Philippines there were, until the recent political changes, four Spanish Lodges at Manila, the capital, but the activity of the Craft is gradually being resumed under charters from the American Grand Lodges. A system of corrupted Freemasonry is practised in these islands by the members of the Katapunan Society. This was originally a revolutionary association formed by the leaders of the people during their revolt against Spanish rule.

The Far East

Lodges constituted from Great Britain or Ireland exist in the Straits Settlements, Siam, China, and Japan, and at the most important treaty-port in the Chinese Empire—namely, Shanghai—there are two Lodges under other foreign jurisdictions, which hold German and American warrants respectively. In China, moreover, there exists what by many persons is regarded as a kind of indigenous Masonry, which has likewise penetrated into some of the Colonies and dependencies of certain European powers, for example, Sumatra, Java, the Straits Settlements, and Burma.

The first of the Secret Societies of China, in age, dignity, and importance, is called the Triad from its native name of *San-ho-hwi*, or "three united," the three being Heaven,

Earth, and Man. Another term by which it is known is *Thian-ti-hwi*, or "Heaven and Earth Alliance" (*Hung-league*), the explanation of both names being the same—viz., that when Heaven, Earth, and Man unite in restoring the Ming dynasty, the perfect triangle will be formed, and universal peace will be the result.

Although a good deal was whispered about them, the ways of the Society were enveloped in mystery, so long as the members were confined to the "Middle Kingdom." But when they began to spread into SUMATRA, JAVA, and the STRAITS SETTLEMENTS, their doings were made public.

Until the overthrow of the Ming dynasty (1644), the TRIAD sodality seems to have been a benevolent association of the most exalted character—mystical, philosophic, and religious—but the Manchu Conquest transformed it, from about the year 1674, into a band of rebels and conspirators.

The grand symbol of the Society is a triangle, which appears in every ceremony; while the foot-rule, the scales, and weights are laid in the sacred "bushel" upon the altar before the opening of a Lodge. The altar and the seat of the presiding officer are in the East. The members call each other brother, worship one God, and possess a system of grips and signs. On his admission, a candidate becomes dead to everyone except to members of the League, and considers himself (after entering the Society) to have been newly-born. The last ceremony is drinking blood—a few drops of his own in a cupful of arrack, emphasizing the vow of secrecy. The blood sacrifice is a very ancient custom, and covenants sworn to in the same manner as is now done by the TRIAD sodality—viz., by the shedding of blood—are recorded as having taken place so early as the period of the Chan dynasty—*i.e.*, 1122 B.C.

Very much later, but still at a time comparatively remote from our own (1520), Fernando de Magalhaens, or, as we are wont to call him, Magellan, discovered the PHILIPPINE Islands, and the King of Cebu proposed a treaty, to be ratified by the ceremony of blood-brotherhood, after the native custom. Magellan assented, and the ceremony was performed.

As in Masonry, there are Lodges of Instruction for the benefit of zealous members of the TRIAD Society.

On examining the ritual, a difficulty is encountered in the numerous allusions to the Buddhist and Taoist symbolism. Concerning the former we are fairly well informed, but about the latter very little is known.

Enough has been said, perhaps, to show that the analogy between this Chinese Society and Freemasonry is possibly something more than a coincidence. In the view of the leading authority on the history and procedure of the TRIAD fraternity—"For those who believe in the unity of the human race, it will seem less strange that there should exist a marked resemblance between both societies, and they will more readily comprehend the similarity of the symbols and institutions of these societies. If the theory of the unity of the human race be the more correct one, it would be very likely that the nations, when they spread themselves from the supposed cradle of mankind—the plains of Middle Asia—over all the world, retained the notion that they were once all brethren and formed one family. . . . Perhaps Masonry divided itself into two branches: one passing to the West, and the other directing itself to the East, and finding a fertile soil for its development in CHINA" (Gustave Schlegel, *Thian-ti-hwi, or Heaven-Earth League*, viii).

On the other hand, Mr. Herbert A. Giles, while admitting that—

"From time immemorial we find the square and compasses used by Chinese writers, either together or separately, to symbolize precisely the same phases of moral conduct as in our own system of Freemasonry"—

goes on to say—

"It has ever been accepted as a physical axiom in CHINA that 'Heaven is round, Earth is square'; and among the relics of the nature-worship of old, we find the altar of Heaven at Peking *round*, while the altar of Earth is *square*.

By the marriage of Heaven and Earth, the conjunction of the circle and the square, the Chinese believe that all things were produced and subsequently distributed, each according to its own proper function. And such is, in my opinion, the undoubted origin of the terms 'square and compasses' as figuratively applied to human conduct by the earliest ancestors of the Chinese people."

Mr. Giles then notices the coincidences to which Sir Chaloner Alabaster had recently called attention, as existing between the old religion of CHINA and the ritual and observances of our Craft (*ante*, 3); and after pointing out that a Chinese character, relied upon by the latter, had only been introduced some four hundred years after Christ, when the period of the old religion of CHINA had long since passed away, expresses himself in the following terms,—"The Chinese language contains many characters apparently Masonic in form, but almost all these coincidences vanish for the most part into thin air when we recollect that the written symbols of CHINA are no longer what they were." (*Freemasonry in China*, 14, 19).

ASIA MINOR

The LAW OF DAKHIEL, as prevailing among the ARABS of ASIA MINOR, forms the subject of an interesting essay by Mr. S. T. Klein, who carefully considers the possible explanation it may afford of the curious incident narrated in 1 *Kings*, xx. 31-33, as pointing to certain signs and words being in use in those times for the purpose of recognition, and to there having been a sacred bond of union between Ahab, Benhadad, and the messengers. (*A.Q.C.*, ix., 89.)

Besides the nomads of the Syrian Desert, observances more or less akin to those of the Freemasons are ascribed to the YESIDIS—otherwise *Nasrani*, *i.e.*, "Nazareans"— who accept neither the Bible nor the Koran, and are scattered to the number of about 300,000 over ASSYRIA, MESOPOTAMIA, the North of SYRIA, KOORDISTAN, ARMENIA, and ASIA MINOR; the BEGTASCHI, who belong to a society founded by BEKTÂSH of BOKHARA, who lived in the fifteenth century, and is buried in ASIA MINOR; the DRUSES; and the ANSARIYEH. To all of these sects I have referred in the opening chapter of this *History*, but to the curious reader I commend a remarkable essay by the Rev. Haskett Smith, who contends that the DRUSES are none other than the original subjects of HIRAM, King of Tyre, and that their ancestors were the builders of SOLOMON's Temple. Their signs and tokens, though not their passwords, are stated by the same writer to bear a close resemblance to those of the Freemasons. (*A.Q.C.*, iv., 8.) Personally, however, I adhere to the opinion already expressed, that if such coincidences actually do exist, then the sectaries of MOUNT LEBANON must have *adopted* some of the practices of our Society. But the inclination of my own judgment, based on the writings of persons long resident in the LEVANT, is in the direction of the real bond uniting the DRUSES and the ANSARIYEH respectively, being, in the case of either sect, a mystery which time has not yet revealed.

AFRICA

In the North of the "Dark Continent" we find at Alexandria a GRAND ORIENT OF EGYPT, with a membership of about 100; and at Cairo a GRAND NATIONAL LODGE, with a following of 68 Lodges. Several European Masonic powers, including ENGLAND, SCOTLAND, ITALY, and FRANCE, are also represented in the valley of the Nile, England having a Provincial Grand Lodge for Egypt and the Soudan, with 14 Lodges. In ALGERIA and MOROCCO, Masonry may be said to fall exclusively within the French sphere of influence, and in TUNIS mainly so, though in this Regency an independent GRAND LODGE was established in 1881.

On the WEST COAST OF AFRICA there are several Lodges under ENGLAND and one under IRELAND. Others exist in SENEGAL, the AZORES, and ST. HELENA, holding French, Portuguese, and English warrants respectively.

In the Negro Republic of LIBERIA there is a GRAND

LODGE—constituted in 1867—with 8 daughter Lodges, and a membership of 250.

A remarkable essay on *Secret Tribal Societies of West Africa*, by Mr. H. P. F. Marriot, can only be cursorily referred to. These associations are religious, mystical, political, and judicial. "The Science of Life and Death," or, to use another expression, "The Worship of Death," is taught in the highest, and even hinted at in the inferior societies. In most (or all) of the associations, there exists a system of degrees or steps. A clue to the influences brought to bear upon the development of the secret tribal associations has been suggested. It is to this effect— "There exists in EGYPT a Society called SIRI, which is from an Arabic word, meaning secret or magic. Forms of it are in many parts of the SOUDAN and SENEGAMBIA. It is a Society for the study of Occult Science, and was introduced into AFRICA by the Arabs. It still retains some of the ancient Cabalistic mysteries of the Hebrews in the Arabic language, as well as the science of Astrology. It is a key to the understanding of the rites, ceremonies, etc., of African religion, and the practices of African Secret Societies." (*A.Q.C.*, xii., 66-93.)

SOUTH AFRICA

The first of a long series of Dutch Lodges was established at Cape Town in 1772, and since the final cession of the Cape Settlement to Great Britain in 1814, the Freemasons owning fealty to the Grand Orient of the NETHERLANDS have always acted in perfect harmony with those working under warrants from the Grand Lodges of the BRITISH ISLES. At the present time, in Cape Colony, Natal, the Transvaal, the Orange River Colony, Rhodesia, Nigeria, Mashonaland, etc., there are 185 English, 35 Scottish, 23 Dutch, and 4 Irish Lodges, making a grand total of 247, exclusive of some others—more or less clandestine—which are not recognized by the dominant Masonic Powers.

In the SOUTH AFRICAN ISLANDS, there are French Lodges at RÉUNION (or BOURBON) and MADAGASCAR. A Portu-

guese Lodge exists at MOZAMBIQUE. At the MAURITIUS
there are (or were) three Lodges holding French charters,
and until quite lately an equal number under the Grand
Lodges of the BRITISH ISLES, but one of these, INDEPEN-
DENT, No. 236 on the roll of the Grand Lodge of IRELAND,
has, at the present time of writing, disappeared from the
list.

THE WEST INDIES

In the large group of islands lying east of Central and
north of South America, there are 45 British Lodges,
and a solitary Irish one. The districts where Masonry
flourishes with the greatest luxuriance are JAMAICA,
BARBADOES, BERMUDA, and TRINIDAD. Lodges holding
French charters are (or were) existing at MARTINIQUE and
GUADELOUPE.

A GRAND LODGE OF CUBA was established in the early
part of the last century, and after a most chequered career
was once more revived and reorganized in 1899. During
its latest dormancy, however, a GRAN ORIENTE NACIONAL
sprang into temporary existence. The GRAND LODGE
had, in 1901, a following of 102 subordinates, with a total
membership of 6,000.

In PORTO RICO, the other island in what was formerly
the *Spanish* WEST INDIES, a Grand Lodge was formed at
Mayaguez in 1885. After a slumber of three years, this
body met in 1899, and transferred its seat to San Juan.
The GRAN LOGIA SOBERANA DE PUERTO RICO has 15 Lodges
within its jurisdiction, and a membership of 396. This is
now under the U.S.A.

HISPANIOLA, HAYTI, or SAN DOMINGO, formerly included
in the *French* WEST INDIES, is now divided into two Negro
Republics, one of which—in the west—has taken the name
of HAYTI, and the other—in the east—that of SAN DOMINGO.
In the former there are two GRAND ORIENTS, the older of
which (1836), at Port-au-Prince, has 75 Lodges on its roll;
of the junior body (1886) no particulars are forthcoming.
In the district now called SAN DOMINGO there is a GRAND

ORIENT (1866) with 13, and a GRAND LODGE (1891) with 13 Lodges.

If we go back, however, to the second half of the eighteenth century, it will be found that what is now one of the most popular and widely diffused of the vast array of Rites which claim to be Masonic, was cradled in what was then indifferently known as the island of HISPANIOLA, HAYTI or SAN DOMINGO. Among the French colonists were four men, Stephen Morin, Germain Hacquet, the Comte Alexander F. A. de Grasse Tilly, and Jean Baptiste Marie de la Hogue, whose names will duly figure in the story I am about to relate.

In 1761 Stephen Morin received a patent from the Grand Council of the EMPERORS OF THE EAST AND WEST, and the GRAND LODGE OF FRANCE, then temporarily united, power being given him to establish a symbolic Lodge, also to confer the higher degrees and the rank of Inspector. The "EMPERORS OF THE EAST AND WEST" controlled a Rite consisting of twenty-five degrees, which has ordinarily been known as the RITE OF PERFECTION, or of HEREDOM.

In 1763 Morin went from Paris to SAN DOMINGO, which he made his headquarters, or Grand Orient, for the "High Degrees" in the New World. He also created a Council of PRINCES OF THE ROYAL SECRET (25°) at Kingston, JAMAICA, in 1770, and appointed numerous Deputy Inspectors General for the purpose of propagating the Rite, granting them roving commissions with powers very similar to his own. Of the filiation of these powers there is no complete record, but the first Deputy Inspector appointed by Morin was Henry A. Francken, of Kingston, JAMAICA, who afterwards went to New York, and established a LODGE OF PERFECTION at Albany, in that State. At the outbreak of the revolution at SAN DOMINGO in 1791 (after which nothing further is heard of Stephen Morin), the French settlers were obliged to flee, and many of them sought refuge in America. The Comte de Grasse Tilly and his father-in-law, J. B. M. de la Hogue, were created Deputy

Inspectors General at Charleston, in 1796, and a similar rank was conferred upon Germain Hacquet at Philadelphia in 1798.

Down to the year 1801, the highest degree known either in the WEST INDIES or AMERICA was that of PRINCE OF THE ROYAL SECRET, the twenty-fifth and last of the RITE OF PERFECTION. But on the 31st of May, 1801, there was organized a new governing body of a new Rite, into which the RITE OF PERFECTION had been transformed. It was named the SUPREME COUNCIL OF SOVEREIGN GRAND INSPECTORS GENERAL OF THE THIRTY-THIRD DEGREE FOR THE UNITED STATES OF AMERICA. It recognized the "Constitutions" of 1762, the "Secret Constitutions," and the "Constitutions of 1786." The last named are the supreme law of the Rite, and purport to have been sanctioned by Frederick the Great, as its Governor and head. Whether, indeed, the "Grand Constitutions of 1786" more properly belong to the authentic, or to the legendary, history of this Rite is a question that has been fiercely debated, but by the generality of readers, perhaps, the words of the French proverb will be deemed much in point— *"Pour qui ne les croit pas, il n'est pas de prodiges."* ("There are no miracles to the man who has no faith.")

De Grasse Tilly, as his patent informs us, was a member of the SUPREME COUNCIL at Charleston, and Grand Commander for life of the *French* WEST INDIES, in 1802, at the close of which year he returned with de la Hogue to SAN DOMINGO, and founded a SUPREME COUNCIL at Port-au-Prince. Both men were then *Sovereign Grand Inspectors General* (S.G.I.G.)—*i.e.*, members of the 33rd degree.

In 1803 the Negroes again attained the upper hand, and the Whites were once more driven out of SAN DOMINGO. Hacquet arrived in Paris early in 1804, and was adroit enough to induce the GRAND ORIENT OF FRANCE to accept the twenty-five degrees of the RITE OF PERFECTION. "The hand of time," said the GRAND ORIENT, in a circular of 1819, "had now [1804] effaced in France the remembrance of these degrees, which had gone out from its own bosom;

even of some that were exclusively French; so that they were brought back there as strangers, and were not reclaimed." In September, 1804, De Grasse Tilly, aided by de la Hogue and three other S.G.I.G., who had also come from SAN DOMINGO, organized and established a SUPREME COUNCIL FOR FRANCE at Paris; and in the following month a GRAND SCOTS LODGE.

The GRAND ORIENT OF FRANCE thought it advisable to make a Union with these bodies, and by a concordat the GRAND SCOTS LODGE was merged in the GRAND ORIENT, and the SUPREME COUNCIL became a co-ordinate branch of it. But this arrangement came to an end in 1805. All the SUPREME COUNCILS of the so-called ANCIENT AND ACCEPTED SCOTTISH RITE in the world trace their descent from Charleston, De Grasse, the SUPREME COUNCIL, or the GRAND ORIENT OF FRANCE.

CENTRAL AND SOUTH AMERICA

It has been shown that in 1804 the Comte de Grasse introduced a new system or Rite of thirty-three degrees into FRANCE, under the title of the ANCIENT AND ACCEPTED SCOTTISH RITE. Its success in FRANCE was instantaneous and phenomenal, and it speedily became a favourite with the LATIN races. The Rite penetrated and made its ground secure in SPAIN, PORTUGAL, MEXICO, and SOUTH AMERICA, while, to come to our own day (with the exceptions that will be presently noticed), what Lodges there are in the Republics of CENTRAL and SOUTH AMERICA are governed either by SUPREME COUNCILS or by GRAND ORIENTS, of which SUPREME COUNCILS form part.

SUPREME COUNCILS and SOVEREIGN GRAND INSPECTORS GENERAL, 33°, were each supposed by members of the Rite to possess, on the whole, powers greatly in excess of those appertaining to GRAND LODGES and GRAND MASTERS. SUPREME COUNCILS could confer at pleasure the 33rd degree, and the persons so honoured could not only create SUPREME COUNCILS where none existed, and add to the number of their own degree (S.G.I.G.), but it was extensively believed that, like the Scots Masters—whose assumed powers were afterwards, in some shape or form, successively exercised by the Chapter of Clermont, the Knights of the East, the Emperors of the East and West, and the Strict Observance—they could, at any time or place, personally impart, either with or without a ceremony, the secrets of the three Craft degrees.

The Grand Orient system was a French invention, and has since been adopted by other Latin nations. *In theory*, a Grand Orient is an organization consisting of several sections, usually a Supreme Council, Grand Chapter, and Grand Lodge, each with exclusive power over its own degrees. *In practice*, the Supreme Council is always the predominant partner, and its Grand Commander is the Grand Master of the united body.

In Mexico, besides a Supreme Council, there are several distinct Grand Lodges. A circular, issued—June 14th, 1901—by one of the latter, declares:—"That the Bible, the Great Light of Masonry, is to be found on its altars; and that no women are admitted into the Lodges,"—from which an opinion may be formed of the so-called "Masonry" of the Republic, as practised under the ægis of the Gran Dieta Simbolica, now happily defunct. The most important, founded 1865, has 15 Lodges, with over 1,000 members.

A Grand Orient for Central America—comprising the Republics of Costa Rica, Guatemala, Honduras, and San Salvador, was established in Guatemala, in 1887. Under it are 18 Lodges, exclusive of 7 which are ruled by the Grand Lodge of Costa Rica—formed in 1899—and 3, holding British charters, in Nicaragua. A Grand Lodge of Guatemala has 12 Lodges; that of Salvador has 5; that of Panama 6 Lodges; and that of Yucatan has 9.

In South America, there is in Brazil the Grand Orients of Brazil at the capital, and of the Rio Grande do Sul, at Porto Allegre, with a following of 390 and 39 Lodges respectively. Single Grand Orients exist in Argentina (115), Chili (49), Colombia (5), Paraguay (9),

PARANA (13), URUGUAY (18), and VENEZUELA (9). The figures within parentheses denote the number of Lodges in the several jurisdictions, so far as I have been able to discover them.

There is a GRAND LODGE OF PERU—reorganized in 1852 —with a following of 6 Lodges.

Besides the national organizations, Lodges under various European jurisdictions exist in many of the Republics, and in all of the larger capitals. ENGLAND is represented by 22 Lodges in SOUTH AMERICA, and AMERICA by 3—under charters granted from MASSACHUSETTS—in the "District of CHILI."

In GUIANA, Lodges have been from time to time constituted by HOLLAND and FRANCE within their respective spheres of influence, and BRITISH GUIANA, at the present moment, besides having a SCOTTISH Lodge at Demerara, is itself the seat of an ENGLISH Province, with a roll of 6 Lodges, one of which, however, is at work in CHILI (*Valparaiso*) and another in URUGUAY (*Monte Video*).

CHAPTER X

*In a subject so comprehensive, it is necessary to light our
match,—as Bacon was proud to say he did,—at every man's
candle.*—CHARLES BUCKE.

So, on your patience ever more attending,
New joy wait on you! Here our play hath ending.
PERICLES: *Prince of Tyre*

THE UNITED STATES OF AMERICA

THE three oldest Lodges on the Continent of North America
are ST. JOHN's, at Boston, Massachusetts; SOLOMON's at
Savannah, Georgia, and (again) SOLOMON's at Charleston,
South Carolina. The first of these bodies, all of which are
of English origin, was established in 1733, and the last two
in 1735. But there was formerly in existence a still older
Lodge at Philadelphia, with records dating from 1731, and
which is presumably referred to—December 8th, 1730—as
"one of the *several* Lodges erected in this Province," by
Benjamin Franklin, in the *Pennsylvania Gazette*. All the
evidence points in the direction of this having been an
independent or non-tributary Lodge, assembling by inherent
right, and acknowledging no higher authority than its own.
It has, indeed, been contended that the Lodge was constituted by Daniel Coxe, to whom a Deputation was granted—
June 5th, 1730—by the Duke of Norfolk, as Provincial
Grand Master for the Provinces of New York, New Jersey,
and Pennsylvania. But all the known facts are inconsistent
with the supposition that the powers conferred by this
Deputation were ever exercised by Coxe, and even if we

PORTRAIT OF GENERAL WASHINGTON
By permission of the Board of General Purposes from the painting in
Grand Lodge

concede the possibility of certain official acts having been performed by him, though unrecorded, the conclusion is irresistible that these could not have occurred until *after* the formation of the Lodge at Philadelphia, with an Immemorial Constitution, and existing "records dating from 1731." Of this Lodge, which met sometimes as a private, and sometimes as a Grand Lodge, Benjamin Franklin was the Master and Grand Master in 1734.

The first Lodge held under written authority was established by Henry Price, Provincial Grand Master of New England, at "The Bunch of Grapes" Tavern, in Boston, on August 31st, 1733.

In 1734, Franklin published an edition of the English *Book of Constitutions*, and entered into a correspondence with Henry Price, "whose deputation and power," he understood, "had been extended over all America," asking the latter to confirm the Brethren of Philadelphia in the privilege of holding a Grand Lodge annually in their customary manner. As Price's reply has not been preserved, and the collateral evidence is in the highest degree confusing, what he actually did in response to the application from Franklin must remain, to a large extent, the subject of conjecture. But there seems no room for doubt that the Lodge (and Grand Lodge) never, until 1749, worked under any sanction which was deemed superior to its own. The authority actually held, as well as the powers exercised by Price, have been much canvassed, but it will be sufficient to state that all the action of the first Provincial Grand Master of New England was recognized in the Mother Country by the Grand Lodge.

A Master's Lodge, with Henry Price as Master, was founded at Boston in 1738. On the death of Robert Tomlinson, who succeeded Price—as Prov. G.M. of New England—in 1737, Thomas Oxnard—an Initiate of the first Lodge at Boston—received a patent as Provincial Grand Master of North America, in 1743.

Benjamin Franklin was appointed Provincial Grand Master of Pennsylvania, by Oxnard, in 1749, but in the following year William Allen, Recorder of Philadelphia, presented a deputation from the Grand Master of England (Lord Byron), appointing him to the same office, and on his authority being duly recognized, nominated Franklin as his Deputy.

At the death of Oxnard, in 1754, a petition was drawn up recommending Jeremy Gridley as his successor. The document states that "Mr. Henry Price, formerly Grand Master, had resumed the chair *pro tempore*," and closes with the remark that since the establishment of Masonry at Boston, in 1733, Lodges in Philadelphia, New Hampshire, South Carolina, Antigua, Nova Scotia, Newfoundland, Rhode Island, Maryland, and Connecticut, "have received Constitutions from us."

By the terms of Gridley's patent, which was received in 1755, his authority was restricted to those parts of North America for which no Provincial Grand Master had been appointed.

A self-constituted Lodge at Boston—ST. ANDREW'S—which afterwards numbered among its members some of the most influential men of the city, received a Scottish warrant —*granted* four years previously—in 1760.

In 1766, there were, in addition to those in Boston, thirty (English) Lodges on the roll of the Province. Of these, three were military Lodges, four were in Massachusetts, three in Rhode Island, six in Connecticut, and one each in New Hampshire, South Carolina, Maryland, Virginia, New Jersey, and North Carolina.

In 1767 Gridley died, and in the following year John Rowe was installed as his successor. Immediately afterwards, steps were taken to form a Provincial Grand Lodge under Scotland, and a petition to that effect was drawn up and signed by the Masters and Wardens of ST. ANDREW'S Lodge, and of three Lodges attached to Regiments in the British Army—all four Lodges having a common bond in working according to what was commonly known as the "Ancient System."

The petition was granted in 1769, and a commission was

issued appointing Joseph Warren, Grand Master of Masons, in Boston, New England, and within one hundred miles of the same. Two of the Regimental Lodges, which had taken part in the movement, were present at the inauguration of the new governing body, but they were never any more than a nominal part of it; St. Andrew's was really the Provincial Grand Lodge.

In the same year—August 28th—a section of St. Andrew's, calling itself a Royal Arch Lodge, held its first recorded meeting, and the minutes contain the earliest account of the conferring of the degree of a Knight Templar that has yet been discovered either in manuscript or print.

By a further Scottish patent—dated March 3rd, 1772—Warren was appointed Grand Master for the Continent of America. The body over which he presided began to issue charters in 1770, and at a later period (1782) adopted the title of the "Massachusetts Grand Lodge," its rival, under John Rowe, retaining the appellation of "St. John's."

Returning to Pennsylvania, in 1758 the so-called Ancients gained a foothold in Philadelphia, and from that date the Lodges under the older sanction began to decline. A Provincial warrant was received from the Ancient or Schismatic Grand Lodge of England in 1764. By the Grand Body so established many warrants were granted for Lodges in other States as well as in Pennsylvania. All the other Lodges formed in the Province before the invasion of the Ancients soon after ceased to exist.

In what is now the State of New York, no trace of any Lodge, created before the administration of George Harrison, has been preserved. This worthy was appointed Provincial Grand Master in 1753, and during the eighteen years he held office granted warrants to a large number of Lodges, five of which still exist, and head the roll of the existing Grand Lodge of New York. One of these, Mount Vernon, No. 3, was originally constituted by the members of Lodge No. 74 in the Second Battalion of the 1st Foot, who, on leaving Albany, in 1759, gave an exact copy of their Irish Warrant to some influential citizens, which was exchanged for a Provincial Charter in 1765.

Masonry came into Virginia from several distinct sources, and, except perhaps in a single instance, without the intervention of Provincial Grand Masters. The earliest Lodge is said to have been founded at Norfolk by Cornelius Harnett in 1741, and, with good show of reason, it has been suggested that the Provincial commission was superseded by a deputation, or "constitution," from the Grand Lodge of England in 1753. To PORT ROYÁL KILWINNING CROSS LODGE—whose name indicates its source of origin—has been assigned the date of 1755. Other charters were issued from Scotland—by the Grand Lodge—in 1756 and 1758, to Lodges at Blandford and Fredericksburg. The latter had previously existed as an independent Lodge, but for what period is uncertain. Washington was initiated in this Lodge on November 4th, 1752, and in the following year—December 22nd, 1753—we find among its records the earliest known *minute* referring to the actual working of the Royal Arch degree.

In what were then the other colonies of British North America, Lodges gradually sprang into existence, either under direct or delegated authority from the Mother Country. The introduction, however, of Masonry into Florida has some distinctive features, with which I shall bring this portion of the narrative to a close.

A charter for holding a Lodge "by the stile and title of Grant's East Florida Lodge," was issued by the Grand Lodge of Scotland in 1768. But this, after the fashion of the "Ancients" (whose influence was shortly to become paramount in the New World), appears to have been regarded as an instrument authorizing the meetings of a Provincial Grand Lodge. Accordingly, on May 3rd, 1771, this "Grant's Lodge," acting as a Grand Lodge, issued a charter to ten persons at Pensacola, who, "for some time past had been members of Lodge No. 108 of the Register of Scotland, held in his Majesty's Thirty-First Regiment of Foot, as the said Regiment was about to leave the

Province." The new Lodge—St. ANDREW's, No 1 West Florida—continued to work at Pensacola until the cession of Florida to the Spaniards, when it was removed to Charleston, South Carolina. It will be seen that the founders of the first *Stationary* (though in the light of subsequent events it may be more appropriate to say *Civil*) Lodge in Florida were all members of an Army or "Travelling" Lodge attached to a British Regiment. It is also not a little remarkable that one and the same Military Lodge should have been in the first instance "Modern" (1750), next Scottish (1761), then "Ancient" (1802), and finally "Scottish" once more (1805), without any break of continuity in its existence. I shall be excused for adding that this feature of its Masonic history had entirely faded out of recollection in the 31st Foot, when a new English Lodge was established in that corps at Gibraltar, with myself as the first Master, in 1858.

During the Revolution, communication with the Mother Grand Lodges in North and South Britain was largely interrupted, and in most cases wholly ceased. When hostilities commenced, there were Provincial Grand Lodges, in real or nominal existence, in Massachusetts (for New England), New York, Virginia, South Carolina, North Carolina and Georgia, under the Regular Grand Lodge of England; in Pennsylvania under the "Ancients" (*ante*, chap. vii); and in Massachusetts (for the Continent of North America), under the Grand Lodge of Scotland.

It is a curious circumstance and deserves to be recorded, that in most of the Provinces the members of the "Ancient" Lodges evinced a greater disposition to espouse the cause of the Colonies, while the "Moderns" were more generally inclined to side with the Crown.

The first man of distinction to lay down his life in the cause of American Independence was Joseph Warren, the Scottish Provincial Grand Master, and leader of the "Ancients" in Massachusetts, who was killed at the battle of Bunker Hill, where, though commissioned as a Major-

General, he fought as a Volunteer. Among the Provincial
Grand Masters of the "Moderns," whose sympathies were
enlisted in the opposite direction, were John Rowe, whose
action paralysed the ST. JOHN's Grand Lodge at Boston;
William Allen, of Pennsylvania, who attempted to raise a
regiment for the British Army; Sir Egerton Leigh, of
South Carolina, who, foreseeing the approaching storm,
left for England in 1774; and Sir John (son of the more
famous Sir William) Johnson of New York, who cast in his
lot with the Royalists at the commencement of the war.

The death of Joseph Warren raised a constitutional
question of much complexity. What was the *status* of the
Grand Lodge after the death of the Grand Master? It
was disposed of by the *election* of Joseph Webb to the
position of "Grand Master of Antient Masonry" in the
State of Massachusetts. This, if we leave out of consideration the Lodge (and Grand Lodge) at Pennsylvania in 1731,
was the first sovereign and independent Grand Lodge in
America, and the second was the Grand Lodge of Virginia,
which was established in the following year.

Many Military Lodges were in active existence during
the war, the most renowned being AMERICAN UNION,
which received a charter from John Rowe (of Boston), and
was attached to the "Connecticut line." On December
27th, 1779, at Morristown, New Jersey, the Lodge celebrated the Festival of St. John. There were present a
large number of members and visitors—among the latter
being General Washington. A form of petition to the
several Provincial Grand Masters, to be signed on behalf
of the Army Lodges and the Masons in each military line,
for the appointment of a Grand Master for the United
States of America, was approved. Accordingly, at "a
convention Lodge from the different lines of the Army and
the departments, held in due form under the authority
of AMERICAN UNION LODGE, at Morristown, the sixth
day of March, in the year of Salvation, 1780," a duly
appointed committee presented their support. Washington
was naturally designated for the office of Grand Master,

and it would seem that the representatives of the Army Lodges hoped that the movement, if successfully carried out, would obliterate all distinction between "Ancient" and "Modern" Masons. Their idea also appears to have been to have a National Grand Master and Grand Lodge, with Deputy Grand Lodges, similar to the previously existing Provincial Grand Lodges in the several States. The project, however, of a national governing organization was finally abandoned, and, though revived on many subsequent occasions, has never been regarded with more than a languid interest by the vast majority of Grand Lodges in the United States.

In New York, prior to the war, Masonry was a monopoly of the "Moderns," but when the British Army occupied New York City, with it came "Ancient" Masonry. A Provincial Grand Lodge was organized in 1782 by three stationary and six Army Lodges. Of the latter, one was Scottish and one Irish, but the remaining seven were "Ancient" Lodges.

Within seven years after the close of the War of the Revolution, the system of Grand Lodges with Territorial jurisdiction was firmly established. It became an accepted doctrine that the Lodges in an independent State had a right to organize a Grand Lodge; that a Grand Lodge so created possessed exclusive jurisdiction within the State; and that it might constitute Lodges in another State in which no Grand Lodge existed, and maintain them until a Grand Lodge should be established in such State.

The following independent Grand Lodges, created in accordance with these principles, existed in 1790:—In Massachusetts (two, ST. JOHN's and MASSACHUSETTS), New Hampshire, Connecticut, New York (*Ancient*), Pennsylvania (*Ancient*), New Jersey, Maryland, Virginia, North Carolina, South Carolina (two, *Ancient* and *Modern*), and Georgia.

For some time after the Revolutionary period, there were two methods of working, as there had been before, but as the "Ancients" and "Moderns" assimilated in each jurisdiction, one mode was adopted, which embraced more or less the peculiarities of both systems. Gradually, in States where there were two Grand Lodges, they amalgamated. A union of the rival bodies at Boston was effected in 1792. In the two other leading jurisdictions, all opposition to the "Ancients" had simply melted away. The Grand Lodges established by the Schismatic Grand Lodge of England in Pennsylvania and New York simply declared their independence, the former in 1786 and the latter in the following year. In Pennsylvania there were no "Moderns" left to either conciliate or coerce, but in New York the Lodges under the older English sanction (which survived the period of the Revolution) one by one fell into line and became component parts of the Grand Lodge, which at the present time, as regards the number of its Lodges, its total membership, and the extent of its jurisdiction, takes the lead of all the other Grand Lodges in the United States.

The battle-ground of the fiercest contest between the "Ancients" and the "Moderns" was in South Carolina. For nearly twenty years each party had a Grand Lodge in active operation, and the contest was maintained for many years after it had ceased elsewhere in America, and after the Union had taken place in England.

In 1800 there were in the United States 11 Grand Lodges, having 347 subordinate Lodges, and a membership of 16,000.

During the first quarter of the nineteenth century the history of the American Craft was quiet and uneventful, but a storm then arose that well-nigh swept the great Fraternity from the land. William Morgan, a mechanic of Batavia, New York, who was reported to be about to publish a volume disclosing the secrets of the Freemasons, was kidnapped and carried off. What his fate was has never been ascertained. Whether his abductors murdered him, whether he died from exhaustion and fright, and they were compelled to conceal his body, or whether he was supplied with the means for removing to another country, a most searching investigation, extending over a period of six years, utterly failed to disclose.

An Anti-Masonic party was thereupon formed in New

York, and the excitement gradually spread into other States. With the full belief that it would sweep the old political division out of existence, a candidate for the Presidency was nominated in 1832. The other candidates (of the two recognized parties), Andrew Jackson and Henry Clay, were Masons and Past Grand Masters. In the result, the former was elected by an overwhelming majority, the Anti-Masons only carrying the State of Vermont. This was a death-blow to political Anti-Masonry, but it continued to struggle feebly for a few years longer before realizing that it was actually dead.

In the United States there have been many fierce and embittered contests, but no other has approached in intensity that which was carried on for several years by the Anti-Masons.

No society, civil, military, or religious, escaped its influence. No relation of family or friends was a barrier to it. The hatred of Masonry was carried everywhere, and there was no retreat so sacred that it did not enter. This, of course, was disastrous to the growth and progress of the Institution. Masonic work almost entirely ceased, most of the Lodges suspended their meetings, and many of them surrendered their charters.

Eventually, however, the tide of popular feeling began to turn. Dormant Lodges were revived. Surrendered charters were restored. The alarm at the outer door was again heard, as the best men in the community sought admission into the Society.

The most important of the National Conventions which have been summoned from time to time in order to consider matters common to, or affecting the whole of the jurisdictions, appears to have been that held at Baltimore, on May 8th, 1843. Fifteen Grand Lodges were represented. It was in session for ten days. With great unanimity a system of work and lectures was adopted. It was settled at this meeting, and the usage has since prevailed, that the business of the Lodges should be conducted in the third degree. The issuing of Grand Lodge certificates and a plan for a National Masonic Convention to meet once in three years were recommended to the Grand Lodges.

The scheme, however, of a National Convention, meeting triennially, has never been carried into effect.

Brigham Young, with about 1,500 other Mormons, was expelled from Masonry by the Grand Lodge of Illinois, in 1844. Six years later—at the close of the first half of the century just expired—there were, in the United States, 28 Grand Lodges, having 1,835 subordinate Lodges, with a membership of 66,142; but the extraordinary growth of Masonry which has since taken place altogether precludes my doing more than record in a tabular statement the statistics relating to the dates of formation of the fifty existing Grand Lodges of the Republic, together with the respective totals of their Lodges and members, as given by Past Grand Master Jesse B. Anthony, of New York.

During the Civil War more than a hundred Military Lodges were chartered by the Grand Lodges of the North and South, but the experience gained during that great conflict was decidedly opposed to their utility.

What is commonly known and described as the AMERICAN RITE consists of nine degrees, viz. : 1—3, Entered Apprentice, Fellow Craft, and Master Mason, which are given in Lodges, and under the control of Grand Lodges; 4—7, Mark Master, Past Master, Most Excellent Master, and Royal Arch, which are given in Chapters, and under the control of Grand Chapters; 8, 9, Royal Master and Select Master, which are given in Councils and under the control of Grand Councils. To these, perhaps, should be added three more degrees, namely, Knight of the Red Cross, Knight Templar, and Knight of Malta, which are given in Commanderies, and are under the control of Grand Commanderies.

There are also the degrees of the so-called Ancient and Accepted Scottish Rite, which attract the most influential section of the Craft, and the degree of Sovereign Grand Inspector General (33°) may be described as the innermost sanctuary of the Masons of the United States.

The three degrees of the Craft are commonly but erroneously referred to in America as the York Rite, an expression for which the origin must be sought in the assumption of the term, "York Masons" by the "Ancients" in the year 1756 (*ante*, 258).

There is, or may be, a Grand Lodge, Grand Chapter, Grand Council, and Grand Commandery in each State, whose jurisdiction is distinct and sovereign within its own territory. There is no General Grand Lodge, or Grand Lodge of the United States; but there is a General Grand Chapter, Grand Council, and Grand Encampment, to which the Grand Chapters, Grand Councils, and Grand Commanderies of some, but not all, of the States are subject.

There is no uniform usage as to the membership of Grand Lodge, or the mode of appointment of Grand Officers.

The utmost freedom is accorded to visiting brethren. While any member of a Lodge possesses the right to object to, and thereby exclude, any visitor, this right is very rarely exercised. The result is that often there are as many visitors present in an American Lodge as there are members.

The fifty independent jurisdictions of the United States are in every respect a happy family, conforming in their boundaries to plainly marked political lines; and while they may differ in minor methods of administration, all follow the broad lines plainly marked out by the usages, customs, and landmarks of the universal Craft. Almost every Grand Lodge possesses a Charity Fund. Another most efficient means of aiding the distressed is the agency of Masonic Homes for Freemasons, their widows and orphans. A number of these organizations are now in successful operation in many of the States.

Each of the Grand Lodges, Chapters, Councils, and Commanderies publishes an annual volume of its *Proceedings*, and with the greater number there appears a Report on Correspondence. The writers of these Reports, in a general survey of the progress of the Society in all parts of the globe, have gradually added to the bare narrations of facts their comments on Masonic law, and their criticisms on the decisions made in other jurisdictions. The Reports, of course, vary in interest according to the experience and literary ability of the writers by whom they are compiled, but owing to a well-established law of natural selection, the best men eventually come to the front, and those who have made their mark in the minor role of Reporter to a Grand Chapter, Council, or Commandery, are transferred to a higher sphere of usefulness, and become the critics and reviewers of the practice and procedure of the Family of Grand Lodges.

STATISTICS AT DATE OF WRITING

Grand Lodges	Date of Formation	Number of Lodges	Number of Members
Alabama	1821	550	32,538
Arizona	1882	28	3,149
Arkansas	1832	561	22,133
California	1850	383	64,095
Colorado	1861	135	20,239
Connecticut	1789	112	29,416
Delaware	1806	22	2,698
District of Columbia	1810	30	11,857
Florida	1830	237	14,749
Georgia	1786	667	50,620
Idaho	1867	65	5,681
Illinois	1840	869	167,286
Indiana	1818	567	90,000
Iowa	1844	532	62,461
Kansas	1850	418	51,202
Kentucky	1800	592	51,000
Louisiana	1812	235	20,588
Maine	1820	206	23,386
Maryland	1787	116	19,420
Massachusetts	1777	269	78,203
Michigan	1844	439	96,403
Minnesota...	1853	272	36,986
Mississippi	1818	372	21,745
Missouri	1821	643	74,201
Montana	1866	104	9,902
Nebraska	1857	275	28,136
Nevada	1865	23	2,032
New Hampshire	1789	80	11,248
New Jersey	1786	208	49,788
New Mexico	1877	51	4,338
New York	1787	872	230,770
North Carolina	1771	445	27,257
North Dakota	1889	117	11,233
Ohio	1808	554	122,373
Oklahoma...	1892	438	32,335
Oregon	1851	148	16,496
Pennsylvania	1786	507	131,954
Rhode Island	1791	37	9,832
South Carolina	1787	272	19,636
South Dakota	1875	148	12,908
Tennessee	1813	455	31,434
Texas	1837	864	56,071
Utah	1872	21	2,841
Vermont	1794	109	15,174
Virginia	1777	328	28,467
Washington	1858	209	23,900
West Virginia	1875	151	20,711
Wisconsin	1843	282	34,877
Wyoming	1874	34	4,087
Philippine Islands	1912	43	2,894
Porto Rico	1885	42	2,000

Totals:—51 Grand Lodges, 15,415 Lodges, and 1,942,747 Members.

In twenty-three (or more) of the States there are Negro Grand Lodges, but the Coloured are not recognized by the other (fifty-one) Grand Lodges.

CANADA AND NEWFOUNDLAND

Tradition marks the year 1738 as the date of the constitution of the first Masonic Lodge, in what is now the Dominion of Canada. This Lodge was warranted at Annapolis Royal, in Nova Scotia, by Erasmus J. Phillips, Fort Major of the pioneer fortress, under the authority of Henry Price, the Prov. G.M. of St. John's Grand Lodge at Boston, Massachusetts. Phillips was initiated in "the first Lodge in Boston" in 1737, while on a visit to that town. On his return to Annapolis, he opened the Lodge, thus sowing the first seeds of Craft fellowship in the Maritime Provinces. The position given him by Price was that of Deputy Grand Master—but within a short period he became Provincial G.M.—and by his authority the first Lodge at Halifax was warranted in 1749-50, with Brigadier-General Edward Cornwallis as Master.

A Grand Lodge was formed by a minority of the Lodges, in 1866, but it was shortly afterwards merged in the existing Grand Lodge of Nova Scotia, which was regularly organized in 1869.

The first Province west of the Maritime Provinces to constitute Lodges was Quebec, in 1759-60. These Lodges were military and civil—military for a short time after the conquest, and civil from 1761-2. They were governed by a Provincial Grand Lodge *("Moderns")*. This body had an active existence until 1791, when the "Ancients" warranted a Provincial Grand Lodge under Prince Edward, afterwards Duke of Kent, who was in command of the forces at Quebec. Both these organizations did good work, but that of the Moderns was not an active factor after 1800. In 1813, when the rival Grand Lodges of England joined hands, a Provincial Grand Lodge, under the present United Grand Lodge of England, took charge of the jurisdiction of Quebec. In 1791 the Province of Canada (Quebec) had been divided into Upper and Lower Canada, under William Jarvis and Prince Edward, as Provincial Grand Masters respectively. Both these appointments were made by the Ancients. In 1822-3 the Provincial Grand Lodge of Lower Canada was divided for Masonic purposes into two districts, one—Quebec and Three Rivers, the other—Montreal and William Henry. The two Provinces had separate Legislatures until 1841, when for civil purposes they were united, Lower Canada being afterwards known as Canada East, and Upper Canada as Canada West. The dividing line between these Provinces from 1791 was the Ottawa River, and no change was made when they were united in 1841.

In 1855 a secession took place from the Provincial Grand Lodge of Upper Canada, and an independent Grand Lodge was established. Two years later, the Provincial Grand Lodge (dating from 1792), formed "THE ANCIENT GRAND LODGE OF CANADA." In 1858 these two bodies united under the title of the GRAND LODGE OF CANADA, by which organization Lodges were formed, not only in Canada West, but also in Canada East.

The Grand Lodge of QUEBEC was formed in 1869, and exercises Masonic jurisdiction over the Province of Quebec, formerly Canada East. But three of the Lodges in Montreal still retain their English warrants, and have hitherto declined to affiliate with the Colonial Grand Lodge.

At a later period, in recognition of the position attained by the Grand Lodge of Quebec (Canada East), the words "In the Province of Ontario" (Canada West) were added by the Grand Lodge of Canada to its title.

The Grand Lodge of Alberta was formed in 1905, and that of Saskatchewan in 1906.

There are nine Provinces in the Dominion of Canada, and nine Grand Lodges:—

Grand Lodges	Date of Formation	Number of Lodges	Number of Members
Alberta	1905	103	7,984
British Columbia	1871	80	7,951
Canada (Ontario)	1858	457	66,457
Manitoba	1875	78	7,600
New Brunswick	1867	42	3,898
Nova Scotia	1869	75	7,124
Prince Edward Island	1875	15	881
Quebec	1869	66	8,286
Saskatchewan	1906	135	8,861

Totals:—9 Grand Lodges, 1,051 Lodges, and 119,042 Members.

NEWFOUNDLAND

There are ten English and two Scottish Lodges in this island, which has not yet thrown in its lot with the Dominion.

OCEANIA

The leading group of islands which fall within the limits of the present section are called by geographers AUSTRALASIA, and all of the colonies into which they are now divided were originally dependencies of NEW SOUTH WALES. In VICTORIA, WESTERN AUSTRALIA, SOUTH AUSTRALIA, QUEENSLAND, TASMANIA, and NEW ZEALAND, there are now independent Governments, but the "Mother City" of Australian Masonry, as might naturally be expected, is Sydney, the capital of the parent colony. Regimental, in the first instance, paved the way for Stationary Lodges, and the earliest of the latter—AUSTRALIAN SOCIAL—was established by warrant of the Grand Lodge of Ireland, in 1820. Many Lodges were afterwards formed in all parts of AUSTRALASIA by the three jurisdictions of the British Isles, and after some hasty declarations of independence by unruly minorities, Grand Lodges have now been established, in strict accordance with Masonic usage, in all of the Colonies:

Grand Lodges	Date of Formation	Number of Lodges	Number of Members
South Australia	1884	83	6,540
New South Wales	1888	289	27,000
Victoria	1889	232	19,200
New Zealand	1890	267	15,000
Tasmania	1890	33	1,500
Western Australia	1900	94	4,000
Queensland	1903	62	2,000

Totals:—7 Grand Lodges, 1,060 Lodges, and 75,240 Members.

In QUEENSLAND there is a Grand Lodge, but there are English, Scottish, and Irish District (or Provincial) Grand Lodges, with a following of 54, 58, and 23 Lodges respectively, forming a total of 135. Probably all will soon unite.

WESTERN AUSTRALIA is also the seat of a Scottish Masonic Province, with 34 Lodges, and there is a solitary representative (in each case) of the English and Irish jurisdictions, making an aggregate of 36 in addition to those on the roll of the Grand Lodge.

Apart from the above, ENGLAND still retains control over two Lodges—one in NEW SOUTH WALES and the other in VICTORIA—and IRELAND over one, in SOUTH AUSTRALIA.

TASMANIA has no Lodges under the authority of other Masonic powers, working side by side with those on the roll of its own Grand Lodge. In NEW ZEALAND the English, Scottish and Irish Lodges have united, and formed a Grand Lodge, which flourishes with 267 Lodges and 15,000 members.

There are four Lodges holding British warrants in the FIJI Archipelago; two, one English and the other French, in NEW CALEDONIA; and one Scottish and two (or more) American Lodges in the SANDWICH or HAWAIIAN Islands.

APPENDIX

THE following is the wording of the "Grant of Arms," and is published for the first time by kind permission of the Board of General Purposes:—

"To all and Singular to whom these Presents shall come, Sir Henry Farnham Burke, Knight Commander of the Royal Victorian Order, Companion of the Most Honourable Order of the Bath, Garter Principal King of Arms, Sir William Henry Weldon, Knight Commander of the Royal Victorian Order, Clarenceux King of Arms, and Charles Harold Athill Esquire, Member of the Royal Victorian Order, Norroy King of Arms, Send Greeting; WHEREAS, His Majesty by Warrant under His Royal Signet and Sign Manual bearing date the thirteenth day of June last, signified unto the Right Honourable Edmund Bernard Talbot (commonly called Lord Edmund Bernard Talbot) Knight Grand Cross of the Royal Victorian Order, Companion of the Distinguished Service Order, one of His Majesty's Most Honourable Privy Council, and Deputy to the Most Noble Bernard Marmaduke, Duke of Norfolk, Earl Marshal and Hereditary Marshal of England, that He had been graciously pleased to give and grant His Royal Licence and Authority that the United Grand Lodge of Antient Free and Accepted Masons of England may bear on its Common Seal, Shields Banners or otherwise, certain Armorial Bearings and Supporters therein, more particularly set forth, provided the same be first duly exemplified according to the Laws of Arms, and recorded in the College of Arms, otherwise the said Royal Licence and Permission to be void and of none effect, AND FORASMUCH as His Lordship did by Warrant under his hand and the Seal of the Earl Marshal bearing

351

date the twenty eighth day of the same month authorize and direct Us to exemplify such Armorial Ensigns and Supporters accordingly, KNOW YE THEREFORE that We the said Garter, Clarenceux and Norroy in obedience to the Royal Command in pursuance of His Lordship's Warrant and by virtue of the Letters Patent of Our several Offices, to each of Us respectively granted do by these Presents exemplify the Arms following, for the said United Grand Lodge of Antient Free and Accepted Masons of England, that is to say;

"Per pale Gules and Quarterly Azure and Or; dexter on a Chevron between three Castles, Argent a pair of Compasses extended of the third; sinister a Cross quarterly of the fourth and Vert; between, in the first quarter a Lion rampant of the third; in the second an Ox passant Sable; in the third a man with hands elevated proper, vested of the fifth the Robe Crimson lined with Ermine; and in the fourth an Eagle displayed also of the third; the whole within a Bordure of the first charged with eight Lions passant guardant of the third, And for the Crest, On a .Wreath of the colours, A representation of an Ark supported on either side by a Cherub proper with the Motto over in Hebrew characters 'Holiness to the Lord.'

"And by the authority aforesaid, I the said Garter Principal King of Arms do further exemplify the Supporters following that is to say; On either side A Cherub proper, the whole as in the margin hereof are more plainly depicted to be borne and used by the said 'United Grand Lodge of Antient Free and Accepted Masons of England,' on its Common Seal, Shields Banners or otherwise pursuant to the tenor of the said Royal Warrant and according to the Laws of Arms; IN WITNESS whereof We the said Garter, Clarenceux and Norroy Kings of Arms have to these Presents subscribed Our names and affixed the Seals of Our several Offices this ninth day of July in the Tenth year of the Reign of our Sovereign Lord George the Fifth by the Grace of God of the United Kingdom of Great Britain and Ireland and of the British Dominions beyond the Seas, King

Defender of the Faith, etc., and in the year of Our Lord
one thousand nine hundred and nineteen.

> (signed)   "H. FARNHAM BURKE.   *Garter.*
> (signed)   WILLIAM H. WELDON.   *Clarenceux.*
> (signed)   C. H. ATHILL.   *Norroy.*"

[The above signatures appear in one line.]

INDEX

INDEX

A

Aberdour, Lord, 248, 250, 257, 264.

Accepted Masons, the, 99, 111, 114, 115, 119-21, 145.

Acception (or Lodge), the, 111, 115.

Act of Constituting a Lodge, the, 215.

Additional Degrees, the Royal Arch and Installed Master's, 235, 237, 259-61, 269. Mark Master, 270. Royal Ark Mariner, 270. Cryptic, 270. Ancient and Accepted Rite, 270. Royal Order of Scotland, 272. Order of the Temple, 274. Red Cross of Constantine, 275. Rosicrucian Society, 276. Allied Degrees, 276. Foreign novelties, 237-41, 278, 290, 293, 307, 309, 328, 342. See Degrees, Knights Templar, Mark, and Rites.

Adopted Masons, the, 99, 120-1.

Africa, North and West Coast of, Lodges and Secret Tribal Societies, 324-5. South of, British, Dutch, and Irish Lodges, South African Islands, 325.

Agrippa, Henry Cornelius, one of the greatest of the Occult Philosophers, 56, 161.

Ahiman Rezon, the Book of Constitutions of the Ancient Grand Lodge of England, 252, 253, 258, 266.

Ainslie, Rev. James, objection taken to, in 1652 on account of his being a Freemason, 182.

Alabaster, Sir C., on the Early Symbolism of China, 3, 323.

Albert, H.R.H. Prince, 264.

Albertus Magnus, 56.

Aldworth, Mrs., the alleged Lady Freemason, 199.

Alexander, Sir Anthony, Warden General, 173, 176, 185.

Alexander, Henrie, Warden General, 173, 176, 185.

Alexandra, H.M. Queen, 263.

Algeria, 324.

Allen, William, Prov. G.M., Pennsylvania, 334, 338.

Alnwick Records, the, 121.

America, Central and South, invaded by the Ancient and Accepted Scottish Rite, Supreme Councils, and S.G.I.G., 33°, 329. Grand Orients, Mexico, Women in Lodges, Masonry in Central and South America, 330. Lodges chartered by foreign jurisdictions, 331.

America, United States of, Ancient York Lodges, organized by the Ancients, 256. Freemasonry in, the oldest Lodges, 332. Daniel Coxe, Benjamin Franklin, Henry Price, 332-3. Provincial Grand Lodge for North America, 334. The "Ancients," 335. Washington's Mother Lodge, 336. The War of Independence, 337. The Ancients sided with the Colonists, the Moderns with the Crown, 337. Convention of the Army Lodges, 338. Fusion of Moderns with Ancients, 340. Abduction of William Morgan, political Anti-Masonry, 340. National Conventions, 341-2. The American Rite, 342. Masonic Customs, 343. Statistics, 345.

Ancient and Accepted Rite, 270.

Ancient and Accepted Scottish Rite, the, 237, 280, 298, 316, 329, 342.

Ancients, English Masons, the, 236, 252-61, 265, 318, 335, 336-40, 343.

Anderson, Dr. James, ordered to digest the old Gothic Constitutions, 202. His Book approved, 203. A member of the Horne Lodge, 207. Attacks on, 209, 211, 212. Author of a Letter from Euclid, 218. Second edition of his Book of Constitutions sanctioned, 220-1. His death, 244. Cited or quoted, 82, 101, 114, 117, 121, 126, 142, 200,

209, 219, 225-7, 236. His First
Book of Constitutions, 189, 192,
202, 204-7, 212, 223, 226, 231, 234,
242, 253. His Second Book of
Constitutions, 192, 197, 199-201,
205, 206, 218, 220, 221, 231, 232,
234, 241, 242, 251.
Andrea, Johann Valentine, the re-
puted founder of the Rosicrucian
Fraternity, 48, 50, 51, 276.
Ansariyeh of Syria, the, 2, 324.
Anthony, Jesse B., 342.
Anti-Masonry in America, 340-1.
Antiquity, Lodge of, 243, 262. See
Lodges, English, the Four Old.
Apprentice, the French passed, called
Compagnon, Aide, Valet, Varlet,
or Garçon, 27-8.
Apprentice Part, the, 206, 224, 234, 235.
Apprentice Pillar, Legend of the, 64.
Aprons, worn by the Mediæval
Masons, 66, 74.
Arabic MS. of 14th Century referring
to Masonic Symbolism, 225.
Architects, a term of modern English
use, 71. Indian Caste of, 319.
Architecture, Monasteries the Cradle
of, in Germany, 16. Passes under
the control of the Lay Guilds, 17.
Gothic and Saracenic, 57. Early
and Middle Pointed, and Perpen-
dicular Styles, 62-3, 92. Scottish,
64, Gothic, a Stranger in Italy,
101. In 14th Century, the great
art of the age, 104. Tracing Board
in, 318.
Argentina, 330.
Arms of, the Masons and Freemasons,
117. Grant to Grand Lodge of
England, 351.
Ashmole, Elias, philosopher, chemist,
and antiquary, made a Free Mason
at Warrington in 1646, 112.
Attended a Lodge at Mason's Hall,
London, in 1682, 116. Cited, 49,
51, 52, 54, 99, 100, 113, 120, 224.
Asia, Freemasonry in, 317.
Asia Minor, the Law of Dakhiel, the
Yesidis, Begtaschi, Druses and
Ansariyeh, 323-4.
Assembly, 81, 84, 85, 109, 130.
Annual, 14, 81, 86, 87, 89, 93, 131,
136. Common, 83, 97. General,
82, 83, 88, 94, 97. Lawful, 82, 89,
91, 99. Triennial, 86, 87, 89, 130,
136. Unlawful, 91, 92, 94, 98.

Athelard, Scholar and Philosopher of
Bath, Geometry introduced into
England by, 62.
Athelstan, the first King of All
England, invokes the prayers of the
Culdees at York, A.D. 936, 14.
Grants a Charter to the Masons, 14.
His name preserved in the Legend
of the Craft, 14. Cited, 85-7, 90,
96, 126, 130, 131, 135-7, 153.
Atholl, the Dukes of, Grand Masters
of the Ancients, 253, 257, 259, 261.
Aubrey, John, Author of the
"Natural History of Wiltshire,"
his account of churches erected
all over Europe, by travelling
Freemasons armed with Papal
Bulls, 99, 100, 114, 224.
Australasia, Freemasonry in, Aus-
tralia, New Zealand, Tasmania,
348-9.
Austrian Empire, Freemasonry in,
the Craft persecuted, 297. Early
Lodges, Francis of Lorraine, Maria
Theresa, 296. Free Carpenters'
Lodge, a Grand Lodge, cessation
of Masonic Work, A.D. 1792-3;
revival A.D. 1918, 297-8. Revival
in Hungary, Symbolic Grand Lodge,
Frontier Lodges, 298; all Lodges
closed A.D. 1920, 299.
Azores, the, 324.

B

Babyngton, Thomas, cited in the
"Paston Letters," 1464, as Master
and Sovereign of the Order of the
Temple of Syon, 107.
Bacon, Francis, Lord Verulam, 50.
Bacon, Roger, 56.
Ball, Papillon, 228-9.
Ball, Rev. C. J., learned Orientalist,
"The Proper Names of Masonic
Tradition," a Philological Study
by, 223.
Baltimore, National Convention at,
341.
Banquets, 181.
Begemann, Dr. W., on the Manu-
script Constitutions, 129-46. Cited
48, 114, 128, 146-8, 153, 156-9.
Begtaschi, the, 3, 323.
Belgium, Grand Orient of, 307-8.
Benhadad, King of Syria, 323.
Bernadotte, Marshal, 304.

Black Death, the, 30, 91.
Blayney, Lord, English Grand Master, 258.
Blesington, Earl of, English Grand Master, 257.
Blood Brotherhood, 321.
Boileau, Etienne, Provost of Paris, compiler of the *"Livre des Métiers,"* 26, 27.
Book M., the, 46.
Borneo, 320.
Boswell, John, Laird of Auchinleck, present at the Lodge of Edinburgh, in 1600, 110, 185.
Boyd, Lord, Scottish Grand Master, 198.
Branch Lodges, 184.
Brazil, 330.
British Columbia, 348.
Broad Arrow, the, a Mason's Mark, 169.
Brother Book of 1563, 19, 22, 23.
Bruce, Sir W., of Balcaskie, Master of the King's Works, 73.
Brunswick, Duke Ferdinand, and Prince Frederick of, 284.
Buhle, J. G., his theory that the Rosicrucians developed into the Freemasons, 51.
Bulgaria, 315.
Bulls, Papal, 58, 98, 114, 243, 278, 309. Modern series of, 312.
Buonaparte, Joseph, 280. Louis, 280. Napoleon III, 281. Napoleon I, 316.
Burma, 320.
Burnes, Dr. James, 318.
Byron, Lord, English Grand Master, 244, 245.

C

Cambacères, Prince J. J. R., Grand Maître Adjoint of the Grand Orient of France, 281.
Cameron, John, of Lochiel, 186.
Canada, early Lodges in, 346. Provincial Grand Lodges, 347. Grand Lodges and Statistics, 347-8.
Canada, Viscount, admitted a fellow of Craft in the Lodge of Edinburgh, 1634, 185.
Carnarvon, Marquis of, English Grand Master, 245, 250.
Carysfort, Lord, English Grand Master, 245.

Cassilis, John, seventh Earl of, Deacon of the Lodge of Kilwinning, 1672, 186.
Cathedral builders, 156.
Celebes, 320.
Cementarius, 74, 78.
Certificates, 245, 264.
Ceylon, 320.
Chance Coincidences, the doctrine of, may explain the assumed exchange of Masonic signs by travellers with aboriginal natives, 2.
Charge, the Apprentice, to be given, 121.
Charges, the Book of, 130, 131, 134, 136.
Charity, Committee of, 213.
Chaucer, Geoffrey, Clerk of the Works 1389, 73.
Chichester inscription relied upon as proving the existence in Britain of a *collegium fabrorum*, 11.
Chili, 330.
China, in early days a mystic faith took a Masonic form, 3. Lodges in, 320. Triad Society, its past and present aims, 321. Blood Brotherhood, Buddhist and Taoist Symbolism, possible antiquity of Masonry in the East, 322. Square and compasses figuratively applied to human conduct, 323.
Church, supposed influence of the, A.D. 1000, 58.
Circle, the, 167.
Clare, Martin, author of "A Defence of Masonry," 218. Oration of, as Junior Grand Warden, 221. His description of the two degrees recognized in 1730, 231.
Clarke, Sir C. Purdon, 152, 318, 319.
Clay, Henry, American statesman and Grand Master, 341.
Clermont, Louis Comte de, French Grand Master, 278.
Clifford, Lord, 240.
Clothing the Lodge, 181.
Clugny, the Abbey of, 78.
Cochin, the Pagoda of, 319.
Coipland, Patrick, Warden of Masonry, 174.
Colerane, Lord, English Grand Master, 214, 215.
Colleges, the Roman, accompanied the Legions to Britain, 11. Compared with Guilds, 12. General

features of, 12. Speculations with regard to, 13. Alleged connection with the Culdees, 14. The Craft Guilds of France, 26. The Companionage, 44. The Magistri Comacini, 65. In Britain, 152.

Columbia, 330.

Comacenus, the late Latin term for a native or inhabitant of Como, 79.

Commissions or Dispensations, 184.

Como, Masters of. See Magistri Comacini.

Compagnons de Liberté, 33, 42.

Compagnons du Devoir, 33, 42.

Companies, the London, 105. The Scottish, 172.

Companionage, the, 25, 28. Composed of three divisions, 31. The Sons (Enfants) of Solomon, Maître Jacques and Maître (or Père) Soubise, 31. Tour of France, Customs, 32. Titles and Emblems, Houses of Call, 33. Nicknames, Howling, the Topage, 34. Annual Assemblies, 35. The Accolade or Guilbrette, 35. Contests and Battles, 36-7. Legendary History, 37. Schisms, Masonic Influence, 38-9. Secret Ceremonial, A.D. 1651. Story of the First Three Companions, 39. Antiquity of the Three Families. 41. Hiramic Legend, 42. Other Legends, 44. Filiation of the Society, 44.

Companions (in France), Foreign, Passing, 34. Story of the First Three 40-2.

Concord, Grand Lodge of, at Darmstadt, 290.

Conder, Edward, Historian of the Masons' Company of London, 105, 110, 112, 116, 117, 159.

Confessio Fraternitatis, the, 47, 50, 51.

Confréries, the French, 29, 30.

Congregations, in England, 91-3, 98, 130.

Connaught, H.R.H. Duke of, 263.

Connaught, H.R.H. Prince Arthur of, 263.

Constitutions, Ancient and Accepted Scottish Rite, 329. *English*, 252, 258. See also Anderson, Dermott, and Manuscript. *French*, 278, 281. *German*, 18, 21, 23, 79. See Brother Book, Strasburg, and

Torgau. *Irish*, 192, 198, 200, 232, 236, 266. *Scottish*, 266.

Conventicles, 91-2.

Cooke, Matthew, 133.

Coote, H. C., author of *The Romans of Britain*, 11, 12, 152.

Cornwallis, Brig.-Gen. Edward, 346.

Costa Rica, 330.

Coterie, or Cotterie, a term used by the French Stonemasons, 30, 34.

Cotton, Charles, 228-9.

Cowan, a Scottish operative term, 174.

Coxe, Daniel, 332-3.

Crawley, Dr. W. J. Chetwode, 124, 187, 190, 193, 199, 200, 220, 266.

Cromarty, Earl of, the Second Scottish Grand Master, 198.

Cross, the, 167.

Crowe Collection of documents, 263.

Crusaders, Influence of the, on Western Art, 57, 59, 84, 164, 195.

Crux Ansata, the, 167.

Cryptic Degrees, 270.

Culdees, the, in Britain before St. Augustine, 13. Officiating Clergy at York, and their prayers invoked by King Athelstan, A.D. 936, 14. Supposed connection with the Roman Colleges, 14.

D

Dakhiel, the Law of, as prevailing among the Arabs of Asia Minor, 323.

Dalcho, Dr., compiler of the original *Ahiman Rezon*, 253.

Dalkeith, Earl of, English Grand Master, 203, 213, 215.

Dallaway, Rev. J., 103.

d'Alviella, Comte G., 7.

Dassigny, Dr. F., reference by, in 1744, to the Royal Arch, 199, 235.

d'Antin, Duc, French Grand Master, 278.

d'Aumont, Pierre, Templar Grand Master, 239.

David I of Scotland, 177, 272.

David, Shield of, 168.

Defence of Masonry, A, by Martin Clare, 218, 230.

De Grasse Tilly, Comte A. F. A., 280, 327-9.

De Gray and Ripon, Earl of, English Grand Master, 263.

De la Hogue, J. B. M., 327-9.
De Molay, Jacques, Grand Master of the Templars, 39.
Degrees, General Progression of the, one only in early Scottish Masonry, 182. The Mason Word, 182. Introduced into Scotland from England, 188. The first purely speculative Scottish Lodge, 193. Two Steps recognized by the Grand Lodge of England in 1723, the Apprentice Part and the Master's Part, 206. Three mentioned in 1726 by the Junior Grand Warden of York, but not practised in that City, 191-2. Privilege of making Masters restored to the Lodges, 213. Spurious Rituals, 216-7. Two Steps referred to by Martin Clare in 1730, 219. Master's Lodges, 220. A Digression on Degrees, 221-41. Dr. Stukeley on, 223. Their meaning obscured, 224. Method of Communication very formal, 224. A plurality of, 228. Two only in 1723, 226. Earliest mention of three, 227. New System discouraged by the Premier Grand Lodge, 230. Not practised until after 1730 in the Regular Lodges, 232. Official recognition, 234. Royal Arch and Past Master, 235. Irish System, 236. So-called Scots Degrees on the Continent, 237-40, 246, 248. Three Orders only in Britain, 249, 265. Alterations in the established forms, 260-1. The Mark, 262, 270. Scottish Ceremonial, 264, 266. *Foreign Systems*, African, 325. American, 342. Austrian, 298. Dutch, 307. French, 278-80, 300-1, 328. German, 284, 287, 290, 291, 293. Russian, 309. Swedish, 300-1, 304. Swiss, 311. See Additional Degrees, Knights Templar, Mark, and Rites.
Denmark, Freemasonry in, 304. Of German Origin, but re-modelled on the Swedish system, 305.
Deputations, 215, 219.
Derham, Elias de, Ingeniator, 71, 73.
Dermott, Laurence, 225. Grand Secretary of the Ancients, 254. Cited, 255-6, 269.

Derwentwater, Earl of, Grand Master of France, 238, 277, 300.
Desaguliers, Dr. J. T., the learned natural philosopher, his visit to the Lodge of Edinburgh, 190. The third of the historic Grand Masters, 202. The first Royal Freemasons initiated by, 219, 221. His death, 244. Cited, 204, 205, 207, 209, 215, 225-7, 236, 306.
Devizor, 73.
Devoir, in the Companionage, a Rule or Code, Villes du, 32.
d'Harnouester, Lord. See Derwentwater.
Dieperink, Dr. H. W., 306.
Digression on Degrees, 221-41.
Director or Master, 73.
Dispensations or Commissions, 184.
Disraeli, Isaac, 222.
Divisions (Masonic), the Great English, 243, 252-61.
d'Orleans, Duc, afterwards Citizen Egalité, French Grand Master, 279.
Dotzinger, Jost, Chief Judge of the Steinmetzen Fraternity, 18.
Drake, Dr. F., his Speech as Junior Grand Warden of York, 191.
Druses, the, 2, 324.
Dugdale, Sir W., his Story of Churches erected by travelling Freemasons armed with Papal Bulls, 99, 113, 120, 224.
Dundee, "Our Lady luge of," 68, 177.

E

East India Islands, 320.
Eckleff, C. F. von, 285, 302.
Eclectic Union, Grand Lodge of the, at Frankfort, 290.
Edward VII, King, Past Grand Master of Freemasons, 263. Cited, 304.
Edwin of Northumbria, held an assembly, and began the erection of the Minster Church at York; his name and fame preserved in the Legend of the Craft, 14. Cited, 137, 153, 191.
Eglinton, the eighth Earl of, Deacon of the Lodge of Kilwinning, 186, 275.

Egypt, the supposed home of the earliest Mysteries, 4. Squaring System of, 319. Magical Society in, 325.

Egyptian, or Hermetic Art, the, called Theurgy, 6.

Elliot, Captain Joseph, first Junior Grand Warden, 201.

Engineer, 71.

England, Grand Lodge of, established by four London Lodges, 201. Anthony Sayer, George Payne, John Theophilus Desaguliers, 202. Noble Grand Masters, the Dukes of Montagu and Wharton, 202-3. First Book of Constitutions, 204. Summary of, 205. Recognizes two Degrees, 206. Founders of, 207. Innovations, 207. The Gormogons, 209. Hogarth's Plate, 211. Attacks on the Freemasons, 212. Repeal of O.R. XIII forbidding the making of Masters by private Lodges, 213. Precedency of the Lodges, 214. Act of Constituting a Lodge, 215. Irregularities, Spurious Rituals, 216. Counterblast by Martin Clare, 218. The first Royal Freemason, 219. The Freemasons' *Pocket Companion*, 220. Oration of Martin Clare, Initiation of Frederick, Prince of Wales, New Edition of Book of Constitutions, 221. A Digression on Degrees, 221-41. Alterations in the Constitutions, 242. Organized Rebellion against the authority of the Grand Lodge, 243. The Craft falls into disfavour, 244. The first English Military Lodge, the Manningham Letters, 245. The Great Division, 252. Ancients and Moderns, Laurence Dermott, and Henry Sadler, 252. Constitutions of the Ancients, a proposal to amalgamate with the Moderns, 257. Ancients assume the title of York Masons, Royal Freemasons among the Moderns, 258. Unsuccessful attempt at a fusion with the Ancients, 259. Negotiations resumed, 260. Articles of Union, Recognition of the Royal Arch and Past Master's Degrees, 261-2. United Grand Lodge, 263. Prince of Wales Grand Master, and suc-ceeded by the Duke of Connaught, 263. Crowe Collection of documents acquired in 1913, 263. Action of the Grand Lodge with respect to the rejection of a belief in the Deity by the G. Orient of France, 281-2.

Entered Apprentice, 173-4, 181, 186, 190, 191, 206, 207, 219, 226, 234, 261.

Epoch of Transition, the, 230.

Errol, the tenth Earl of, a member of the Lodge of Aberdeen in 1670, 186.

Essay, or Masterpiece, 171-3, 181.

Essenes, origin and customs of the, 8. Other theories with regard to, 9-10.

Euclid, 129, 132, 134, 135, 137, 154. Letter from, 218, 231.

Europe, alleged Scots Degrees spread like a pestilence throughout, 241. Freemasonry on the Continent of, 277-316.

Evelyn, John, the term Gothic Architecture introduced by, 57.

Exter, Dr. J. G. von, 287.

F

Fama Fraternitatis, the, 45, 50, 51.

Fan Tracery, 63.

Far East, the, Java, the Straits Settlements, Siam, China, and Japan, 320. The Triad Society, 320.

Fellow Craft, 173, 174, 189, 191, 205-7, 219, 226, 229, 234, 261.

Fencing the Lodge, 180.

Fergusson, James, 61.

Fiji Archipelago, the, 349.

Findel, J. G., 225, 247.

Fischer, Robert, 292.

Fludd, Robert, philosopher and physician, the central figure of Rosicrucian literature, 48, 51.

Folkmoot, the, 89.

Forest Law, the, 86, 87, 89.

Fortitude and Old Cumberland Lodge, 243. See Lodges, English, the Four Old.

Four Crowned Martyrs, the, 20. See Quatuor Coronati.

France, 78, English Lodges constituted in, 219. Traditional Masonry of, 238. Persecutions, 243. Early Grand Masters, 277-8. Multiplication of degrees, 278. Grand Lodge and Grand Orient, 279. Ancient and Accepted Scottish Rite, 280, 329. The Buonapartes, 280-1. Belief in a Deity expunged from Constitutions, 281. See also Companionage and Guilds.

Francken, H. A., 327.

Frank Mason, 75.

Franklin, Benjamin, 217, 332-4.

Frankpledge, the system of, 81, 88, 89, 91, 97. Pledge day, 66. View of, 72, 153.

Frederick II, King of Prussia, made a Freemason, 283. Protector of the Craft, 285. Alleged founder of the Ancient and Accepted Scottish Rite, 328.

Frederick II, German Emperor, 285.

Frederick Leopold, Prince, Protector of the three Prussian Grand Lodges, 285.

Free Carpenters, Lodge of, 297.

Freemasonry, origin of, genealogical proofs extend to 14th century, 1. Whether influenced by the customs of the Druses, Ansariyeh, Begtaschi, and Yesidis, 2. Soofees of Persia, 3. Symbolism of the mason's art in China, 3. Theories of Origin, the Ancient Mysteries, 4. The Essenes, 8. The Roman Colleges, 10. The Culdees, 13. The Vehm-Gerichte, 15. The Steinmetzen, 16. The Craft Guilds of France, 25. The Companionage, 31. The Rosicrucians, 44. Fraternity of Architects, 58. Masonry formerly Geometry, 62. Mediæval Masons, agree not to work unless *Free*, 68. Order of the Temple of Sion, 107. Continental perversions of, 237. Did Masonry pursue two paths, one to the East, the other to the West? 322.

Freemasons, the, early use of term, 68, 77, 95, 109, 111, 113, 115, 118, 120, 124, 142, 145. Oxford Company of, 77. London Company of, 108. Of Staffordshire, Dr. Plot on, 119, Travelling, 99, 102.

Free Stone, 74, 77.

French Operative Terms, 30.

Fylfot, or Swastika, 168.

G

Gagarin, Prince, 309.

Geminiani, F. X., 228-9.

General Head-Meeting Day, at Alnwick, 1701, 122.

General Regulations, the, of 1720, compiled by Grand Master Payne, 206, 223, 226.

George V, H.M. King, 263.

Germany, 78, 128, 240. English Lodges constituted in, 219. Frederick the Great initiated in the first German Lodge, 283. Grand Lodges, the Three Globes, 283. The Grand National, 284. Royal York, 286. Hamburg, 286. Saxony, 287. The Sun, Bayreuth, 288. The Eclectic Union, Frankfort, 289. Concord, Darmstadt, 290. Independent Lodges, 290-3. Union of German Freemasons, the High Degrees, 293. The St. John's Degrees, 296. See Constitutions, Degrees and Steinmetzen.

Giles, Herbert A., on Chinese Symbolism, 322.

Girdlers of London, the, extensive powers of, 118.

Gloves, the custom of giving, 66, 74, 181.

Gnostics, the, 104, 160.

Godwin, George, 61.

Gogel, J. P., 289.

Goodric, Sir H., 120.

Gormogons, Ancient Order of the, 208-12, 238-9.

Grandidier, the Abbé, 24.

Grand Orient System, a French invention, 330. In theory and in practice, 330.

Grant of Arms to Grand Lodge of England, 351.

Greece, Freemasonry in, of French origin, Grand Orient and Supreme Council, 315.

Greeting, the, of the Steinmetzen, 21-2.

Greeven, R., 238, 241.

Gridley, Jeremy, 334.

Grips, cited in connection with the Steinmetzen, 21, 22. The Companionage, 36. The Freemasons, 183, 189. The Triad Society, 321.

Grotesques of the British Masons, 71. See Wahrzeichen.

Guatemala, 330.

Guiana, 331.

Guilbrette or Accolade, the, 35.

Guilds, compared with the Roman Colleges, 11. The German, 16. The French Craft, at the close of the Imperial rule, 25. Guilds succeeded the Roman Colleges, 26. Attempt to suppress them, 27. Usages of, tabulated, by Etienne Boileau, 1258; the "Tour of France"— Germ of the Companionage, 27-8. The greater and lesser masterpiece; Ceremonial at the Reception of Masters; the "Fraternities," 28-9. *Prud'hommes*, 29. Charles Martel and the Stonemasons, 30. Masonic, 68. Supreme Guild, 69, 118. Frith Guilds, 89, 96. Social, Merchant, Craft, 84, 97, 103. Travelling, 99. Weavers', 104. Mediæval, 104. Of London, 105. Become Companies, 106. Suppression of, 109. Company of ffreemasons, 111. Masons' Company, 113. Girdlers, tailors, 118-9. Alnwick Company, 121. Cathedral Builders, not a separate organization, 156. Marks common to, 162. In Scotland, form Incorporations, 171.

Gulston, W., 228.

H

Hacquet, Germain, 327-8.

Halberstadt, the Ordinances of, in 1693, refer to a word, 22-3.

Hamburg, the first German Lodge established at, 219. Grand Lodge of, 286.

Hamilton, Gen. Alexander, 185.

Harnett, C., 336.

Harrison, George, 335.

Head Lodges, in Germany, 18, 23. In Scotland, 174, 179.

Healths in Lodge, 250.

Henry III, the time of, assigned as the date when Papal Bulls were given to travelling Freemasons, 99, 103.

Henry VI, a legendary patron of the Masons, 94, 120, 138, 158.

Hermes, 139.

Hermetic (or Egyptian) Art, the, called Theurgy, 6.

Hermetic Mystery, the, 55.

Hermetical Philosophers, the, 160.

Hertzveld, L. H., 247.

Hexapla or Hexalpha, the, 53, 168.

High Degrees. See Additional Degrees and Rites.

Hiram Abif, 33, 42, 43, 142, 159.

Hiram, King of Tyre, 139, 324.

Hogarth, William, his plate, "The Mystery of Masonry brought to light by the Gormogons," 211.

Holland, the Craft persecuted in, 243. High degrees, 246-50. Early Lodges, a Grand Lodge, united with Belgium in a Grand Orient, 306. Red Masonry, Division of the Master's degree, 307.

Holme, Randle, herald and antiquary, 114-15.

Honduras, 330.

Hour Glass Form, the, 168.

House of Call, its use to the French companions, 33, 40.

Howling, the custom of, 34.

Hughan, W. J., 114, 117, 127, 146, 156, 182, 233, 258.

Hund, the Baron von, a leading figure in the Strict Observance, 239-40.

Hungary, 297.

I

Incorporations, 171-2.

India, early Lodges in, Ancients and Moderns, Lodge for Native Gentlemen, 318. Architect Caste, 319. Indian Customs reappear in Masonic Lodges, 320. East India Islands, 320.

Ingeniator, 71, 103.

Innovations, in 1723 three striking, 207. Continental, 248.

Installed Master, degree of, 235-6, 260, 266.

Institutions, the three English Benevolent, 259-60, 263-4.

Intender, 181.

Ireland, early Freemasonry in, 124, 187. Grand Lodge of Ireland, 1725, of Munster, 1726, 190-1. Constitutions, 1730, merger of the two Grand Lodges, 1731, 192. Letter from the Grand Mistress of the Freemasons, 193. First Military Lodge, 192. Regulations of 1741, Royal Arch, 1743, 198-9. Constitutions, 1751, the alleged Lady Free-

mason, 199, 200. The *Pocket Companion*, 1735, 220, 232. Three steps of Masonry, 236. New Regulations, 1768, 266. Schismatic Grand Lodge of Ulster, 267.
Irregular Makings, 184.
Italy, Architects of, 78-9. The Craft persecuted, 243. Lord George Sackville, the Roman Lodge, Papal Bulls, Grand Orient, 312

J

Jackson, Gen. Andrew, 341.
Jacobites, the, their influence on Masonry, 208, 238, 239, 277.
Jacques, Maître, 31. Sons of, 31.
James VI, of Scotland, 178.
Janisch, J. G., 286.
Japan, 320.
Java, 320.
Jesuits, supposed influence of the, 238.
Jewels of the Craft, the method of wearing, 250.
Johnson, Sir John, 338.
Journeyman, the travelling, in France, 28. In Germany, 22.
Judicia Civitatis Lundoniæ, 29.
Justice Seat, the Court of, 86.

K

Keith, Gen. James, 300, 308.
Kellerman, Marshal, 280.
Kent, Duke of, 261, 311.
Ker, Rev. W. L., 179, 180.
Kerwin, William, Free Mason, 1594, 109
Kilmarnock, the Earl of, 197, 239.
King, Rev. C. W., 160.
Kingston, James, the fourth Lord, 192, 214.
Klein, S. T., 323.
Kloss, Dr. G., 238, 241.
Knights, of St. John of Jerusalem, 193, 196. Templar, 39, 239-41, 257, 274, 285, 335. See Rites.
Knipe, Dr., 100.
Komosô, the, of Japan, challenged by Signs, 3.
Krause, Dr., K.C.F., 10.

L

Lalande, J. J. de, 277.
Lamball, Jacob, first Senior Grand Warden, 201, 221.
Lane, John, 233.

Latomus, 74.
Law Day, 91.
Laws (English) of the Middle Ages, and the Freemasons, 80. Frankpledge or *Frith Borh*, 81. The Assembly, 81. Referred to in the Regius and Cooke MSS., 84. Held every year or third year, 85. Assembly at York, 86. Annual Assembly and Sheriff's Turn, 88. Traditionary Assemblies, 89. Athelstan, a Guild Patron, 90; Unlawful Assemblies, 91. Statutes of Labourers, 91. 3 Henry VI, c. i, 93. The Mystery of Maconrye, 94. Signs and tokens, 95.
Leet, the Court, 72, 91, 92, 97.
Legends of the Craft, 14, 67, 80, 81, 87, 93, 94, 109, 120, 125, 142, 156-9, 237. The Companionage, 37, 42. Hiramic, 44, 142. The Guild, 96. The Quatuor Coronati, 150. The Scottish Lodges, 176. The Irish Lady Freemason, 199. Prehistoric Grand Masters, 241.
Leigh, Sir Egerton, 338.
Lewis, Professor T. Hayter, 59, 61, 161, 163, 164.
Liberia, 324.
Liebnitz, G. W., the Baron von, 45.
Little, R. W., well-known mystic, 276.
Livre des Métiers, 27, 29.
Lodge, early references to the, 66-9.
Lodges, the principal cited, *American*, 332, 334-7. *Australian*, 348. *Austrian*, 296. Free Carpenters, 22. *English*, Alnwick, 121. Bradford, 123. The "Four Old," founders of the first Grand Lodge, 121, 201, 207, 214, 216, 243, 258, 262. Masons' Company, 111, 116. Promulgation, 260. Quatuor Coronati, 219. Reconciliation, 262. Stewards, 221, 262. York, 122. *French*, 277, 279-80. *German*, the first three, 283. The five Independent, 290. *Indian*, 318. *Irish*, Cork, Dublin, 190-1. *Italian*, 312. *Portuguese*, 314. *Scottish*, Aberdeen, 172, 176, 181, 183, 186, 188, 264. Atcheson's Haven, 173, 175, 182, 194. Brechin, 195. Canongate Kilwinning, 193-4. Dumfries, 176, 181, 195. Dunblane, 176, 181, 182, 186, 189, 195. Dundee, 175, 177, 178, 195. Dunfermline, 175. Edinburgh (Mary's

Chapel), 110, 112, 162, 172, 174-6, 179, 181-2, 184-5, 189, 193, 195, 265. Glasgow, 175-7, 186, 194. Haddington, 175, 181. Haughfoot, 188, 194. Jedburgh, 195. Kelso, 181, 195. Kilwinning, 162, 172-4, 176, 179, 180-2, 184, 186, 189, 193, 195-8, 265, 273. Melrose, 176, 181, 194. St. Andrew's, 175, 178. Scoon and Perth, 77, 176, 178, 181, 195, 196, 265. Stirling, 174-8, 181. *Swedish*, St. Jean Auxiliare, 301. Lodge of the Swedish Army, 301.

Lorraine, Francis of, the first Royal Freemason, 219, 221, 296, 306.

Louis Napoleon, the Emperor, 281.

Lovell, Lord, 219.

Lully, Raymond, 56.

Lüttmann, M. A., Provincial Grand Master of Hamburg and Lower Saxony, 283, 286.

Luxembourg, the Duc de, 279.

Luxemburg, the Grand Duchy of, 308.

Lyon, David Murray, 173, 175, 180, 182, 184, 185, 190, 193-4, 273.

M

Mackenzie, K. R. H., well-known mystic, 276.

Maclean, J. H., traditional Grand Master of France, 278, 300.

Maçonrye, the Mystery of, said to have been written by Henry VI, 94.

Madagascar, 325.

Magellan, Ferdinand de, ratifies a treaty in the Philippines by blood brotherhood, 321.

Magistri Comacini, or Masters of Como, the, 65, 79, 101.

Magnan, Marshal, 281.

Maier, Michael, 49.

Mainwaring, Colonel H., 112.

Maisterstick, 171. See Essay.

Maistre de Pierra, 30.

Malta, Knights of, 193, 316, 342. Lodge in, Napoleon Buonaparte said to have been initiated in the island, 316.

Manichæans, the, 104.

Manitoba, 348.

Manningham, Dr. T., Deputy Grand Master, 1752-56, Letters of, in regard to the "Scots degrees" manufactured on the Continent, 245-51.

Manuscript Constitutions of the British Freemasons, the, 62, 67, 72, 77. Variously described, 125. The two earliest, 126. The oldest dated form, 126. Divided into groups or families, 128. Dr. Begemann on, 129-46. Regius MS., 129. Cooke, 133. T. W. Tew, 138. Ordinary versions, 140. Genealogy, 141. Roberts family, 143. The New Articles, 144. MSS. divisible into three clusters, 146, 154. The "booke of urbanitie," 148. Quatuor Coronati, legend of the, 150. Patrons of the building trades, 150. Church of the Four at Canterbury, 152. Edwin and Athelstan in Masonic fable, 153. Geometry the handmaid of Symbolism, 154. Speculative Masonry in the 14th century, 155. The Constitutions not a monopoly of the Church builders, 156. Written traditions possessed in Britain by the Masons' Craft only, 157. The Masons' Creed, 158. Dr. Begemann's conclusions examined, 158. Scottish versions, 181. English copies of, burned by scrupulous brothers, 202. Gothic constitutions, the, James Anderson ordered to digest, 202. His Book approved, 203. Versions or Families of the, cited. Aberdeen, 181. Atcheson's Haven, 139, 141, 143, 182. Buchanan, 141, 143. Beaumont, 141, 143. Cama, 141, Cole, 141. Cooke, 81, 84-7, 89, 126, 127, 130, 131, 133, 134, 136, 137, 140, 146, 153, 155, 164. Dodd, 141. Dumfries, 181. Grand Lodge, 82, 89, 126, 139, 140, 141, 143, 146, 155, 158. Harleian, 77, 114, 115, 143, 145. Hope, 83. Inigo Jones, 141, 142. Kilwinning, 181. Melrose, 77, 181. Masons' Company, 114. Macnab, 143, 145. Plot, 141. Regius, 67, 80, 81, 84-9, 126, 127, 129, 133, 141, 146, 153, 155, 164. Roberts, 81, 117, 141, 143, 159. Rawlinson, 143. Sloane, 77, 112, 140, 141, 146. Spencer, 141-2. Stirling, 181. T. W. Tew, 138, 140, 141, 143. William Watson, 136, 140, 158. York, 77, 83, 122.

Maria Theresa, the Empress, 296.

Mark Degree, the, 262, 342. See Rites.

Marriot, H. P. F., on the Secret Societies of West Africa, 325.

Marshall, Thomas, 228-9.

Martel, Charles, 14, 30, 126, 140, 143.

Mary, H.M. Queen, 263.

Mason Word, the, 182-3, 186, 189, 237.

Masonic Homes and Institutions, 259-60, 263-4, 343.

Masonic Signs. See Signs.

Masonry, as a Speculative Science declined into an Operative Art, 155.

Masons' Company of London, the, 68, 69, 76, 105, 108-18, 159, 160, 162.

Masons' Creed, the, in ancient times, 158. Under the Grand Lodge of England, 206, 207, 210, 235, 242, 245, 262. Negation of, in France, 281. Scope of, in Germany, 288. In Hungary, 299. In India, 318.

Masons' Marks, their resemblance to the Symbols of the Gnostics, Hermeticists, Rosicrucians, and Phœnicians, 53, 160-1. May reveal the origin of the Pointed Style, 61. Similar emblems used by other trades, also by Guilds and Lodges, 110, 161-2. Said to be hereditary, 162. Opinions of eminent authorities upon, 163-6. Principal types, 167-9. Originally developed in the East, 169.

Masons, Trade Secrets of the, 70.

Massena, Marshal, 280.

Master, or Fellow Craft, 173, 206, 226, 229, 231, 232, 234.

Master Law, the, 71.

Master Mason, 74, 103, 104, 111, 118, 174, 191, 193, 203, 206, 220, 226, 233, 261.

Master Masons, the services of, not confined to ecclesiastical buildings, 103-5.

Master of Work, 73, 173, 176, 185.

Masterpiece, 28, 36, 181. See Essay.

Masters' Lodges, 220, 233, 243, 333.

Master's Part, the, 206, 207, 213, 220, 223, 224, 229-30, 233, 234.

Mauritius, 326.

Mediæval Operative Masonry, 57. Gothic Architecture, 57. Fraternity of Architects, Papal Bulls, 58. Eleventh century, demand for more ecclesiastical buildings, 58. Influence of the Crusaders, 59. Masons' Marks, 61. English Gothic, 62. Scottish Style, 64. Magistri Coma-cini, 65. York Fabric Rolls, 65-7. The Lodge, 66. Masonic Guilds, 68. Secrets of the Trade, 70. Grotesques, 71. Superintendents of English Buildings in the Middle Ages, how described, 71. Masons, titles of, 71-9. References to, in the Manuscript Constitutions, and Lodge Records, 77. Freemason, earliest use of term, 77. Mediæval Builders, three distinct methods of, 78. Continental Builders, their titles, 78. The Tracing Board in Oriental Masonry, 318.

Mellinet, Gen., the last Grand Master of France, 281.

Mexico, 330.

Military Lodges, 197, 245, 257, 264, 301, 334, 335, 337-42, 346, 348.

Millstone Makers, the French, their singular method of admitting a Master, 28.

Milman, Dr., 101.

Mitchell, William, 273-4.

Moderns, or Regular English Masons, the, 252-60, 318, 337-40.

Moira, Earl of, 258, 265, 317-18.

Montagu, Duke of, the first noble Grand Master, 203, 215, 307.

Montague, Viscount, 219.

Montaleau, A. L. R. de, 279-80.

Montfort, Simon, Comte de, 30.

Moray, Sir R., 50, 112.

Morgan, William, abduction of, 340.

Morin, Stephen, 327.

Morocco, 324.

Moszynski, Count A., 309.

Motto of the Masons and Freemasons, 108-9.

Mozambique, 326.

Munster, G. Lodge of, 191, 192.

Murat, Prince Lucien, 281.

Murray, James, 228-9.

Myrc, John, Canon of Lillieshall, 132.

Mysteries, the Ancient, Earliest, 4. Most widely diffused, Eleusinian Conformity between death and initiation, 4. Common features, the Hermetic Art, 6. Philosophy, signs of recognition, 6. Mithras, the Sun-God, 6. Mithraic Mysteries under the Romans, 7. Survived in Gaul, 44. The Masons said to have derived a body of tradition from, 157.

N

Naymus Grecus, 126, 139, 143.
Negro Grand Lodges, 346.
New Articles, the, 114, 117, 144, 147, 159, 160.
New Brunswick, 348.
New Caledonia, 349.
Newfoundland, 348.
New Zealand, 349.
Nicaragua, 330.
Nicolai, C. F., 50.
Non-Operative Masons, Scottish terms for, 185-6.
Norfolk, the Duke of, 215, 282, 332.
Norway, 289, 305.
Nova Scotia, 346, 348.

O

Oaths, 2, 8, 12, 32, 40, 70, 77, 92, 99, 115, 123, 145, 153, 171, 181, 182, 192, 240, 259, 290, 321.
Oceania, 348-9.
Œcumenical Volgi, the, 208, 238.
Old Regulation XIII, 206, 226, 234, 251.
Order of the Temple, 270.
Orders, the Three, of Masonry, E.A., F.C., and M.M., 249, 265.
Outfield Lodge, 184, 188.
Oxnard, Thomas, 333.

P

Paisley, Lord, 213, 215.
Palgrave, Sir F., 90.
Papworth, Wyatt, 68, 70, 73, 102, 163.
Paracelsus, Theosophist, Physician, and Chemist. 45,
Paraguay, 330.
Parentalia, or Memoirs of the Family of Wren, 57, 100.
Passed Masters, 229.
Pass Words. See Words.
Paston, John, 106. Margaret, 108, 110. Letters, 106.
Payne, George, the Second Grand Master, 134, 202, 205-7, 215, 220, 223, 225-7, 236, 244, 249, 251.
Pays, a term used in the Companion-age, 34.
Pennell, John, 192.
Pentalpha, the, 168.
Perdiguier, Agricol, author of Livre du Compagnonnage, 32, 43.
Persecutions, Masonic, 243, 313.

Persia, natives of, made Masons, 317. Master builders in, tracing boards, 319.
Peru, 331.
Philippe le Bel, 30.
Philippine Islands, the, Lodges in, the Katapunan Society, 320. Blood Brotherhood, 322.
Phillips, Erasmus J., 346.
Philo-Musicæ et Architecturæ Societas, London, 227, 230.
Philosopher's Stone, the, 50, 56.
Philosophers, the Hermetic, 53-4.
Picus de Mirandola, Scholar and Philosopher, 56.
Pike, Albert, 52, 54, 154, 159.
Plot, Dr. R., his account of the Freemasons, 119. Cited, 93, 94, 142, 158, 225.
Pocket Companion, the, 218, 220, 221, 232, 236.
Poggio Bracciolini, 45, 127.
Poland, Freemasonry in, early Lodges, a Grand Lodge, dormancy, 309. Various Rites, Ukase closing the Lodges, 310.
Portugal, early Lodges in, the Craft persecuted on land seeks refuge in the shipping, 314. United Grand Orient of Lusitania, 314. Ancient and Accepted Scottish Rite, 329.
Posse, Count K. C., 301.
Preston, William, 225, 258.
Price, Henry, Prov. G.M. New England, 333, 346.
Prichard, Samuel, 216, 231, 235, 237, 253.
Prince Edward Island, 348.
Promulgation, the Lodge of, 260.
Prussia, Grand Lodges of, 283-6.
Pyramid, the, 167.
Pythagoras, 53, 56, 135, 139.

Q

Quatuor Coronati, or Four Crowned Martyrs, mentioned in the Constitutions of the Steinmetzen, 20. In the Regius MS., 132. Legend of the, 150. Their vogue in Germany and France, 151. Holland and Britain, 151. Patron Saints of the Building Trades, 153. Lodge of the, 59, 146, 219, 227.
Quebec, 346-8.

R

Radcliffe, James and Charles, 238, 277, 300.
Ramsay, the Chevalier, 193. His famous Oration, 195, 196, 237-9, 278.
Rawlinson, Dr. R., 99, 100.
Reconciliation, the Lodge of, 261-2.
Réunion (or Bourbon), 325.
Ribbons worn by Freemasons, 250.
Richmond, Duke of, 213, 215, 228, 230.
Riego, Rafael de, 313.
Rites, Orders, and Side Degrees, Academie des vrais Maçons, Contrat Social, Elus Coens, Philadelphians, Philalethes, Rît Egyptien, Rît Moderne, Rose-Croix, Scots Philosophic, 279. American, 342. Ancient and Accepted Scottish (q.v.). Draskovich, 297. Clermont, Emperors of the East and West, 240, 278, 280, 327. Helvetic, 311. Knights of the East, 240, 278; Eagle, Holy Land, 248; Malta, 249, 342; Red Cross, 294, 342; St. John of Jerusalem, 240 ; Sword, 248, 307; Templars (q.v.). Mark (q.v.). Melisino, 308. Memphis, 316. Perfection or Herdom, Princes of the Royal Secret 327. Red Masonry, 307. Roya Arch (q.v.). Royal Order of Scotland, 237. St. Andrew's (q.v.). Scots' Degrees (q.v.). Scottish Master, 278. Strict Observance (q.v.). Swedenborgian, 316. Swedish, 285, 299, 304, 308. Temple of Syon, 107-8. York Rite, 343. See Additional Degrees, and Digression.
Robert the Bruce, 272-3.
Rose and Cross, 46, 48.
Rosenkreuz, Christian, 45-7, 276.
Roses, Wars of the, 106.
Rosicrucians, the, origin of, 44. Prophecy of Paracelsus, 45. The Fama Fraternitatis, 45, J. V. Andrea, 48, 276. Symbolism of the Rose and Cross, 48. Robert Fludd, 48. Michael Maier, 49. Supposed Influence on Masonry, 50. Opinions of Albert Pike, 52. Of Woodford, 52. Egypt the Cradle of the Hermetic Art, 56. Marks or Symbols of the, 160. The Rosicrucian Society, 275. The Study of Occult

Science taught by the Siri Society of Egypt, and prevalent in West Africa, 325.
Rosicrucians, Society of, in Anglia, founded A.D. 1866, 276.
Roslin, the Laird of, and the Mason Word, 183. Cited, 194.
Rosse, Earl of, the first Irish Grand Master, 190, 192.
Roumania, Profusion of Rites in, 316.
Rowe, John, 334, 335, 337.
Royal Arch, the, 199, 235, 257, 259, 261-3, 269, 293, 316, 336, 342.
Royal Freemasons, the First, Francis of Lorraine, 219, 221. Danish, 304-5. Dutch, 306. English, 221, 258, 261, 263-4. French, 278, 279, 281. German, 283, 285, 288, 292. Scottish, 178. Swedish, 301-4.
Royal Somerset House and Inverness Lodge, 243. See Lodges, English, the Four Old.
Russia, Freemasonry in, Melisino, Strict Observance, and Swedish Rites, 308. Grand Lodges, the Craft Suppressed, 309.
Rutowsky, Count, 287.
Rylands, W. H., 38, 109, 112, 162-6.

S

Sacrist, 73.
Sadler, Henry, 188, 252-6.
Sandwich or Hawaiian Islands, 349.
Sankey, Edward and Richard, 112-3.
San Salvador, 330.
Sarry, Charles, Master of the first German Lodge, 283.
Satirical and Impure Figures in Churches, 71.
Saxony, Grand Lodge of, 287.
Sayer, Anthony, the first Grand Master of Masons, 201, 207, 214-16, 226.
St. Alban, the Proto-Martyr, 126, 134, 137, 153.
St. Amphibal, 135, 137, 153.
St. Amphibalus, 153.
St. Andrew's Degrees, 237, 294, 301.
St. Andrew's Lodges, 285, 294, 297, 302, 305, 334.
St. Blaise, the Banner of, 29.
St. Clair Charters, 68, 175-6.
St. Clair, Sir William, 64, 175. William of Roslin, 194, 198.
St. Helena, Island of, 324.

St. John, the Ancient Order of, 265.
St. John the Baptist, Day of, 201, 204, 226.
St. John the Evangelist, Festival of, 122, 181.
St. John of Jerusalem. See Knights.
St. John's Lodges, 196, 265, 285, 286, 294, 298, 300, 301, 302, 305.
Scald Miserables, the, 244.
Schaw, William, General Warden, 173, 175, 179, 184.
Schaw Statutes, the, 162, 173, 178-9, 181, 195, 265.
Scheffer, Count C. F., first Grand Master of Sweden, 300-1.
Schisms (Masonic), Kilwinning, 197, 265. Edinburgh, 265. Ulster, 267. See Divisions.
Schlegel, Gustave, author of Thian-ti-hwi, or Heaven-Earth League, 322.
Schroeder, F. L., 287.
Scotland, early Masonry of, 170. Incorporations, 171-2. Companies, 172. Schaw Statutes, 173. Head Lodges, 174. St. Clair Charters, 175. Old Records, 176. Ancient Lodges, 177. Masonic Convention at St. Andrew's, 178. King James VI reputed a Freemason, 178. Customs, 180. Fencing the Lodge, Festival of St. John, Banquets, Oaths, Essays, 180-1. Initiation, a simple ceremony, 182. The Mason Word, 182. Irregular Makings, 184. Commissions or Dispensations, 184. Speculative Masons, 185. Geomatics and Domatics, 186. Degrees, 188. A Plurality of, 188. Earliest Minute of Third Degree, 193. Grand Lodge formed, 1736, 194. Mary's Chapel given the first place on the Roll, 195. Ramsay's Oration, 195. Secession of "Mother Kilwinning," 197. So-called Scots Degrees on Continent, 237, 246, 248. Diplomas issued, 264. Lodge of Kilwinning rejoins the Grand Lodge, 265. Past Master Ceremonial recognized, 266.
Scots Degrees, 237-40, 246-50, 278, 300, 311. See Rites.
Scots Grand Lodge, 280.
Secret Tribal Societies of West Africa, 325.
Senegal, 324.
Servia, Lodges in, 316.

Seton, Alexander, 267.
Siam, 320.
Signs, exchanged by travellers with native tribes, used by Komosô of Japan, 3. By initiates in the Ancient Mysteries, 6. The Essenes, 8. The Vehm-Gerichte, 15. The Arabians, 225. Mediæval Masons, 68. Signs and tokens, named in Stat. 11, Henry VII, 95; otherwise cited, 68, 123, 246, 248, 323-4. By Aubrey and Dugdale, 99. Randle Holme, 115. Dr. Plot, 119. By Sir Richard Steele, 123. Associated with the Mason Word, 182. Named in Ramsay's Oration, 196. By Dr. Manningham, 247, 248. Continental, 248. Used by the Secret Societies, of China, 321.
Siri Society of Egypt, the, formed for the study of Occult Science, and flourishes in the Soudan and Senegambia, 325. A Key to the African religion, and the practices of the Secret Societies of Africa, 325.
Smith, Rev. Haskett, on the Druses of Mount Lebanon, 324.
Smith, D. Crawford, 178.
Society of Freemasons, 115, 119.
Solomon, a founder of the Companionage, 31. The Sons of, 31. The Wise King, 161, 183, 241. The Seal of, 53, 168.
Soofees of Persia, the, 3.
Soubise, Maître (or Père), 31. The Sons of, 31.
Spain, Lodge founded by the Duke of Wharton at Madrid, 214. Persecutions of the Craft, the patriot Riego, 313. Grand Orients and Grand Lodges, 313-4. Ancient and Accepted Scottish Rite, 329.
Speculative (or Symbolic) Masonry, 108, 110, 113, 117, 121, 122, 124, 149, 172, 180, 183, 184, 189, 190, 194. The Ornaments of, derived from the customs of Oriental builders, 320.
Speth, G. W., 147, 156.
Spratt, Edward, Irish G. Secretary, 200.
Spurious Rituals, 216-9, 231-2, 235-7, 256.
Squire, Edmund, 228.
Statutes, the English, 75-6, 92-5, 109. Jud. Civ. Lund., 29. Of Labourers, 30, 84, 91. 3 Hen. VI, 93, 106, 120. 15 Hen. VI, c. vi, 138.

Steinmetzen, origin of the, 16. Formed about the 12th century, 17. Statutes of 1459, 1462, and 1563, 18. Four Head Lodges, 18. A Fraternity established, 20. Differed from other Crafts in not having journeymen associations, 20. Admission of passed apprentice—method of greeting, 21. Travelling journeymen, 22. A *word*, but no *sign*, 22. Chief Lodge at Strasburg, 23. German writers, errors of, with regard to, 24. Compared with the French Companions, 33.

Stewards, the Grand, 244, 250, 262.

Sthael, Peter, Rosicrucian, 50.

Stone, Nicholas, the King's Master Mason, 111.

Stonemasons, the French, 31. See Steinmetzen.

Story of the Guild, 96, 125.

Straits Settlements, the, 320.

Strasburg Constitutions of 1459, 18, 20, 23, 78.

Strathallan, Viscount, President of the L. of Dunblane, 1696, 186.

Strathmore, the Earl of, 219, 232, 283.

Strict Observance, the, 237-41, 284, 285-9, 291, 297, 299, 303, 304, 308, 310-12.

Strong, the Family of, 113, 118.

Stuart, Charles Edward, the Young Pretender, 238-41.

Stubbs, Dr. W., 85, 90, 91.

Stukeley, Dr. W., 54, 134, 223, 226.

Sumatra, 320.

Sun, Grand Lodge of the, at Bayreuth, 288.

Superintendents of English Buildings in the Middle Ages, 71-9.

Supervisor, 72.

Supreme Councils, 33°, all trace their descent directly or indirectly from Charleston, S.C., members of (S.G.I.G.), their supposed powers, 329. Relation towards Grand Orients. Cited, 271, 276.

Sussex, Duke of, 261, 262.

Swastika, or Fylfot, 168.

Sweden, Freemasonry in, of French Origin, 300. St. Jean Auxiliare, Sweden's Mother Lodge, 301. King Adolf Fredrik, Protector of the Craft, the Lodge of the Swedish Army, the Swedish Rite, 301. A Grand Lodge, Royal Freemasons,

302. Templarism, its two branches, the Strict Observance and the Swedish Rite, 303.

Switzerland, the Craft persecuted, 243. Early Lodges, an English Prov. G. Lodge, 310. Strict Observance, Helvetic Rite, Grand Lodge Alpina, 311.

Symbolism, of the Mason's Art, referred to in the earliest of the Chinese Classics, 4. Of the Ancient Mysteries, 6. Of the Essenes, 8. Of the Collegia, 12. Of the Vehm-Gerichte, 15. Of the Steinmetzen, 21, 22. Of the French Craft Guilds, 28. Of the Companionage, 35, 39. Of the Rosicrucians, 53. The Freemasons, 53. Originated during the splendour of Mediæval Operative Masonry and not in its decay, 79. Remarks of Sir W. Dugdale, Randle Holme, and Dr. Plot, 100, 115, 120. Of Sir Richard Steele, 123. Of Dr. Begemann, 142. Of Albert Pike, 154, 159. Communicated with the Mason Word, 182. Adopted by the Crusaders, 195-6. Digression on, 222. Of the Mason's Art, became forgotten, 224. Inherited by the 1st Grand Lodge, 227. Figuratively applied to human conduct by the earliest ancestors of the Chinese people, 323.

T

Tailors of Exeter, the, extensive powers of, 119.

Tasmania, 349.

Tau, the, 167.

Templarism in Masonry, 238-41, 291, 299, 303.

Temple of Syon, Order of the, 108.

Tilers, Parliament of the, forbidden, 98.

Tokens. See Signs.

Tomlinson, R., 333.

Topage, or Challenge, the, 34.

Torgau, Ordinances of, 1462, 18, 23.

Tour of France, the, 28, 31, 33, 35.

Tracing Board, the, in Modern, Oriental and Mediæval Operative Masonry, 318.

Tradition, Community of, between the Masons of Britain and France, 30.

Travelling Journeymen, of France, 28. Of Germany, 22.
Triad Society, or Heaven and Earth Alliance, Symbols and Customs, 320-1. Blood Sacrifice, Ritual, 321. Architectural Symbolism, 322.
Trisula, or Trident, 169.
True Mason, 77.
Tullman, Charles, 302.
Tunis, 324.
Turkey, Lodges formed in, by foreign Masonic Powers, 315.
Turn, or Tourn, the Sheriff's, 88, 91.

U

Union, Articles of (1813) between the two Grand Lodges of England, 261.
Uruguay, 331.

V

Vaughan, Thomas, 50.
Vehm-Gerichte, the, Customs and History, 15. Suppression of, 16.
Venezuela, 331.
Vesica Piscis, 169.
Viollet le Duc, 78.
Viswacarma, the Heavenly Architect, 319.

W

Wahrzeichen, or Signs of a Mason, 71.
Waite, A. E., 44, 48.
Wales, Princes of, made Masons, 221, 263, 264.
Walpole, Horace, 244.
Wardens General, 173, 175, 179, 182, 185.
Ware, Samuel, 30.
Warrant, or Charter, the first, 192; not to be confused with a Deputation, 215.
Warren, General Sir Charles, 7. General Joseph, 335, 337-8.
Washington, General George, 338.
Webb, Joseph, 338.
West Indies, the Barbadoes, Bermuda, Cuba, Guadeloupe, Jamaica, Trinidad, Martinique, 326. Porto Rico, 326. Hispaniola, Hayti, or San Domingo, the Cradle of the Ancient and Accepted Scottish Rite, 327. Transformation of the Rite of Perfection into a System of 33 Degrees, 328. Constitutions of the new Rite, Supreme Councils formed at Port-au-Prince and Paris, 328.
Weymouth, Viscount, 220.
Wharton, Philip Duke of, 203, 204, 211-2, 214, 215, 238, 313.
Whymper, H. J., 242.
Wilhelmsbad, Convention of, 241, 284.
William I, German Emperor, 285.
Winton, Earl of, 238, 312.
Women in Masonry, 199, 200, 330.
Woodford, Rev. A. F. A., 52, 128, 166.
Words (or Passwords), Secret, referred to, 15, 23, 34, 36, 40, 49, 77, 99, 115, 182-4, 189, 196, 224, 237, 246, 249, 260, 285, 307, 323. See Mason Word.
Works, Clerk of the, 73. Master of the, 73, 78.
Wray, Sir Cecil, D.G.M., 231.
Wrede-Sparre, Count A. E., 299, 301.
Wren, Sir Christopher, 50, 57, 58, 100, 101, 118, 120, 242, 249, 251.
Wursburg Cathedral, two famous pillars in, 24.
Wykeham, William of, 68, 72.

Y

Yelaguin, General, 308.
Yesidis of Armenia, the, 2, 323.
York, the Culdees of, King Athelstan, Prince Edwin, the Assembly, 14. Fabric Rolls, 65, 67. Lodge Warden, 67. Master Mason, 74. Forest Law, 86, 87. Lodge at A.D. 1705, 122. Presidents and Deputy Presidents, 122. King Edwin, 138, 191. Grand Lodge of All England at, Speech of the Junior Grand Warden, 191. Reference to, in the Constitutions of 1738, 197. Royal Arch in, 199. Ancient York Lodges organized by the "Ancients," 256. Title of York Masons, assumed by the "Ancients," not justified, 258. Grand Lodge of, recognized five Degrees, 257. York Rite, 343.
York, Edward, Duke of, 286.
Young, Brigham, expelled from Masonry, 342.

Z

Zetland, Earl of, 262-3.
Zinnendorf, J. W. von, German Grand Master, 284, 289.

A CATALOG OF SELECTED
DOVER BOOKS
IN ALL FIELDS OF INTEREST

A CATALOG OF SELECTED DOVER
BOOKS IN ALL FIELDS OF INTEREST

CONCERNING THE SPIRITUAL IN ART, Wassily Kandinsky. Pioneering work by father of abstract art. Thoughts on color theory, nature of art. Analysis of earlier masters. 12 illustrations. 80pp. of text. 5⅜ x 8½.   0-486-23411-8

CELTIC ART: The Methods of Construction, George Bain. Simple geometric techniques for making Celtic interlacements, spirals, Kells-type initials, animals, humans, etc. Over 500 illustrations. 160pp. 9 x 12. (Available in U.S. only.)   0-486-22923-8

AN ATLAS OF ANATOMY FOR ARTISTS, Fritz Schider. Most thorough reference work on art anatomy in the world. Hundreds of illustrations, including selections from works by Vesalius, Leonardo, Goya, Ingres, Michelangelo, others. 593 illustrations. 192pp. 7⅞ x 10¼.   0-486-20241-0

CELTIC HAND STROKE-BY-STROKE (Irish Half-Uncial from "The Book of Kells"): An Arthur Baker Calligraphy Manual, Arthur Baker. Complete guide to creating each letter of the alphabet in distinctive Celtic manner. Covers hand position, strokes, pens, inks, paper, more. Illustrated. 48pp. 8¼ x 11.   0-486-24336-2

EASY ORIGAMI, John Montroll. Charming collection of 32 projects (hat, cup, pelican, piano, swan, many more) specially designed for the novice origami hobbyist. Clearly illustrated easy-to-follow instructions insure that even beginning papercrafters will achieve successful results. 48pp. 8¼ x 11.   0-486-27298-2

BLOOMINGDALE'S ILLUSTRATED 1886 CATALOG: Fashions, Dry Goods and Housewares, Bloomingdale Brothers. Famed merchants' extremely rare catalog depicting about 1,700 products: clothing, housewares, firearms, dry goods, jewelry, more. Invaluable for dating, identifying vintage items. Also, copyright-free graphics for artists, designers. Co-published with Henry Ford Museum & Greenfield Village. 160pp. 8¼ x 11.   0-486-25780-0

THE ART OF WORLDLY WISDOM, Baltasar Gracian. "Think with the few and speak with the many," "Friends are a second existence," and "Be able to forget" are among this 1637 volume's 300 pithy maxims. A perfect source of mental and spiritual refreshment, it can be opened at random and appreciated either in brief or at length. 128pp. 5⅜ x 8½.   0-486-44034-6

JOHNSON'S DICTIONARY: A Modern Selection, Samuel Johnson (E. L. McAdam and George Milne, eds.). This modern version reduces the original 1755 edition's 2,300 pages of definitions and literary examples to a more manageable length, retaining the verbal pleasure and historical curiosity of the original. 480pp. 5³⁄₁₆ x 8¼.   0-486-44089-3

ADVENTURES OF HUCKLEBERRY FINN, Mark Twain, Illustrated by E. W. Kemble. A work of eternal richness and complexity, a source of ongoing critical debate, and a literary landmark, Twain's 1885 masterpiece about a barefoot boy's journey of self-discovery has enthralled readers around the world. This handsome clothbound reproduction of the first edition features all 174 of the original black-and-white illustrations. 368pp. 5⅜ x 8½.   0-486-44322-1

STICKLEY CRAFTSMAN FURNITURE CATALOGS, Gustav Stickley and L. & J. G. Stickley. Beautiful, functional furniture in two authentic catalogs from 1910. 594 illustrations, including 277 photos, show settles, rockers, armchairs, reclining chairs, bookcases, desks, tables. 183pp. 6½ x 9¼. 0-486-23838-5

AMERICAN LOCOMOTIVES IN HISTORIC PHOTOGRAPHS: 1858 to 1949, Ron Ziel (ed.). A rare collection of 126 meticulously detailed official photographs, called "builder portraits," of American locomotives that majestically chronicle the rise of steam locomotive power in America. Introduction. Detailed captions. xi+ 129pp. 9 x 12. 0-486-27393-8

AMERICA'S LIGHTHOUSES: An Illustrated History, Francis Ross Holland, Jr. Delightfully written, profusely illustrated fact-filled survey of over 200 American lighthouses since 1716. History, anecdotes, technological advances, more. 240pp. 8 x 10¾. 0-486-25576-X

TOWARDS A NEW ARCHITECTURE, Le Corbusier. Pioneering manifesto by founder of "International School." Technical and aesthetic theories, views of industry, economics, relation of form to function, "mass-production split" and much more. Profusely illustrated. 320pp. 6⅛ x 9¼. (Available in U.S. only.) 0-486-25023-7

HOW THE OTHER HALF LIVES, Jacob Riis. Famous journalistic record, exposing poverty and degradation of New York slums around 1900, by major social reformer. 100 striking and influential photographs. 233pp. 10 x 7⅞. 0-486-22012-5

FRUIT KEY AND TWIG KEY TO TREES AND SHRUBS, William M. Harlow. One of the handiest and most widely used identification aids. Fruit key covers 120 deciduous and evergreen species; twig key 160 deciduous species. Easily used. Over 300 photographs. 126pp. 5⅜ x 8½. 0-486-20511-8

COMMON BIRD SONGS, Dr. Donald J. Borror. Songs of 60 most common U.S. birds: robins, sparrows, cardinals, bluejays, finches, more–arranged in order of increasing complexity. Up to 9 variations of songs of each species. Cassette and manual 0-486-99911-4

ORCHIDS AS HOUSE PLANTS, Rebecca Tyson Northen. Grow cattleyas and many other kinds of orchids–in a window, in a case, or under artificial light. 63 illustrations. 148pp. 5⅜ x 8½. 0-486-23261-1

MONSTER MAZES, Dave Phillips. Masterful mazes at four levels of difficulty. Avoid deadly perils and evil creatures to find magical treasures. Solutions for all 32 exciting illustrated puzzles. 48pp. 8¼ x 11. 0-486-26005-4

MOZART'S DON GIOVANNI (DOVER OPERA LIBRETTO SERIES), Wolfgang Amadeus Mozart. Introduced and translated by Ellen H. Bleiler. Standard Italian libretto, with complete English translation. Convenient and thoroughly portable–an ideal companion for reading along with a recording or the performance itself. Introduction. List of characters. Plot summary. 121pp. 5¼ x 8½. 0-486-24944-1

FRANK LLOYD WRIGHT'S DANA HOUSE, Donald Hoffmann. Pictorial essay of residential masterpiece with over 160 interior and exterior photos, plans, elevations, sketches and studies. 128pp. 9¼ x 10¾. 0-486-29120-0

THE CLARINET AND CLARINET PLAYING, David Pino. Lively, comprehensive work features suggestions about technique, musicianship, and musical interpretation, as well as guidelines for teaching, making your own reeds, and preparing for public performance. Includes an intriguing look at clarinet history. "A godsend," *The Clarinet,* Journal of the International Clarinet Society. Appendixes. 7 illus. 320pp. 5⅜ x 8½. 0-486-40270-3

HOLLYWOOD GLAMOR PORTRAITS, John Kobal (ed.). 145 photos from 1926-49. Harlow, Gable, Bogart, Bacall; 94 stars in all. Full background on photographers, technical aspects. 160pp. 8⅜ x 11¼. 0-486-23352-9

THE RAVEN AND OTHER FAVORITE POEMS, Edgar Allan Poe. Over 40 of the author's most memorable poems: "The Bells," "Ulalume," "Israfel," "To Helen," "The Conqueror Worm," "Eldorado," "Annabel Lee," many more. Alphabetic lists of titles and first lines. 64pp. 5$\frac{3}{16}$ x 8¼. 0-486-26685-0

PERSONAL MEMOIRS OF U. S. GRANT, Ulysses Simpson Grant. Intelligent, deeply moving firsthand account of Civil War campaigns, considered by many the finest military memoirs ever written. Includes letters, historic photographs, maps and more. 528pp. 6⅛ x 9¼. 0-486-28587-1

ANCIENT EGYPTIAN MATERIALS AND INDUSTRIES, A. Lucas and J. Harris. Fascinating, comprehensive, thoroughly documented text describes this ancient civilization's vast resources and the processes that incorporated them in daily life, including the use of animal products, building materials, cosmetics, perfumes and incense, fibers, glazed ware, glass and its manufacture, materials used in the mummification process, and much more. 544pp. 6⅛ x 9¼. (Available in U.S. only.) 0-486-40446-3

RUSSIAN STORIES/RUSSKIE RASSKAZY: A Dual-Language Book, edited by Gleb Struve. Twelve tales by such masters as Chekhov, Tolstoy, Dostoevsky, Pushkin, others. Excellent word-for-word English translations on facing pages, plus teaching and study aids, Russian/English vocabulary, biographical/critical introductions, more. 416pp. 5⅜ x 8½. 0-486-26244-8

PHILADELPHIA THEN AND NOW: 60 Sites Photographed in the Past and Present, Kenneth Finkel and Susan Oyama. Rare photographs of City Hall, Logan Square, Independence Hall, Betsy Ross House, other landmarks juxtaposed with contemporary views. Captures changing face of historic city. Introduction. Captions. 128pp. 8¼ x 11. 0-486-25790-8

NORTH AMERICAN INDIAN LIFE: Customs and Traditions of 23 Tribes, Elsie Clews Parsons (ed.). 27 fictionalized essays by noted anthropologists examine religion, customs, government, additional facets of life among the Winnebago, Crow, Zuni, Eskimo, other tribes. 480pp. 6⅛ x 9¼. 0-486-27377-6

TECHNICAL MANUAL AND DICTIONARY OF CLASSICAL BALLET, Gail Grant. Defines, explains, comments on steps, movements, poses and concepts. 15-page pictorial section. Basic book for student, viewer. 127pp. 5⅜ x 8½. 0-486-21843-0

THE MALE AND FEMALE FIGURE IN MOTION: 60 Classic Photographic Sequences, Eadweard Muybridge. 60 true-action photographs of men and women walking, running, climbing, bending, turning, etc., reproduced from rare 19th-century masterpiece. vi + 121pp. 9 x 12. 0-486-24745-7

CATALOG OF DOVER BOOKS

ANIMALS: 1,419 Copyright-Free Illustrations of Mammals, Birds, Fish, Insects, etc., Jim Harter (ed.). Clear wood engravings present, in extremely lifelike poses, over 1,000 species of animals. One of the most extensive pictorial sourcebooks of its kind. Captions. Index. 284pp. 9 x 12. 0-486-23766-4

1001 QUESTIONS ANSWERED ABOUT THE SEASHORE, N. J. Berrill and Jacquelyn Berrill. Queries answered about dolphins, sea snails, sponges, starfish, fishes, shore birds, many others. Covers appearance, breeding, growth, feeding, much more. 305pp. 5¼ x 8¼. 0-486-23366-9

ATTRACTING BIRDS TO YOUR YARD, William J. Weber. Easy-to-follow guide offers advice on how to attract the greatest diversity of birds: birdhouses, feeders, water and waterers, much more. 96pp. 5³⁄₁₆ x 8¼. 0-486-28927-3

MEDICINAL AND OTHER USES OF NORTH AMERICAN PLANTS: A Historical Survey with Special Reference to the Eastern Indian Tribes, Charlotte Erichsen-Brown. Chronological historical citations document 500 years of usage of plants, trees, shrubs native to eastern Canada, northeastern U.S. Also complete identifying information. 343 illustrations. 544pp. 6½ x 9¼. 0-486-25951-X

STORYBOOK MAZES, Dave Phillips. 23 stories and mazes on two-page spreads: Wizard of Oz, Treasure Island, Robin Hood, etc. Solutions. 64pp. 8¼ x 11. 0-486-23628-5

AMERICAN NEGRO SONGS: 230 Folk Songs and Spirituals, Religious and Secular, John W. Work. This authoritative study traces the African influences of songs sung and played by black Americans at work, in church, and as entertainment. The author discusses the lyric significance of such songs as "Swing Low, Sweet Chariot," "John Henry," and others and offers the words and music for 230 songs. Bibliography. Index of Song Titles. 272pp. 6½ x 9¼. 0-486-40271-1

MOVIE-STAR PORTRAITS OF THE FORTIES, John Kobal (ed.). 163 glamor, studio photos of 106 stars of the 1940s: Rita Hayworth, Ava Gardner, Marlon Brando, Clark Gable, many more. 176pp. 8⅜ x 11¼. 0-486-23546-7

YEKL and THE IMPORTED BRIDEGROOM AND OTHER STORIES OF YIDDISH NEW YORK, Abraham Cahan. Film Hester Street based on *Yekl* (1896). Novel, other stories among first about Jewish immigrants on N.Y.'s East Side. 240pp. 5⅜ x 8½. 0-486-22427-9

SELECTED POEMS, Walt Whitman. Generous sampling from *Leaves of Grass*. Twenty-four poems include "I Hear America Singing," "Song of the Open Road," "I Sing the Body Electric," "When Lilacs Last in the Dooryard Bloom'd," "O Captain! My Captain!"—all reprinted from an authoritative edition. Lists of titles and first lines. 128pp. 5³⁄₁₆ x 8¼. 0-486-26878-0

SONGS OF EXPERIENCE: Facsimile Reproduction with 26 Plates in Full Color, William Blake. 26 full-color plates from a rare 1826 edition. Includes "The Tyger," "London," "Holy Thursday," and other poems. Printed text of poems. 48pp. 5¼ x 7. 0-486-24636-1

THE BEST TALES OF HOFFMANN, E. T. A. Hoffmann. 10 of Hoffmann's most important stories: "Nutcracker and the King of Mice," "The Golden Flowerpot," etc. 458pp. 5⅜ x 8½. 0-486-21793-0

THE BOOK OF TEA, Kakuzo Okakura. Minor classic of the Orient: entertaining, charming explanation, interpretation of traditional Japanese culture in terms of tea ceremony. 94pp. 5⅜ x 8½. 0-486-20070-1

FRENCH STORIES/CONTES FRANÇAIS: A Dual-Language Book, Wallace Fowlie. Ten stories by French masters, Voltaire to Camus: "Micromegas" by Voltaire; "The Atheist's Mass" by Balzac; "Minuet" by de Maupassant; "The Guest" by Camus, six more. Excellent English translations on facing pages. Also French-English vocabulary list, exercises, more. 352pp. 5⅜ x 8½. 0-486-26443-2

CHICAGO AT THE TURN OF THE CENTURY IN PHOTOGRAPHS: 122 Historic Views from the Collections of the Chicago Historical Society, Larry A. Viskochil. Rare large-format prints offer detailed views of City Hall, State Street, the Loop, Hull House, Union Station, many other landmarks, circa 1904-1913. Introduction. Captions. Maps. 144pp. 9⅜ x 12¼. 0-486-24656-6

OLD BROOKLYN IN EARLY PHOTOGRAPHS, 1865-1929, William Lee Younger. Luna Park, Gravesend race track, construction of Grand Army Plaza, moving of Hotel Brighton, etc. 157 previously unpublished photographs. 165pp. 8⅞ x 11¾. 0-486-23587-4

THE MYTHS OF THE NORTH AMERICAN INDIANS, Lewis Spence. Rich anthology of the myths and legends of the Algonquins, Iroquois, Pawnees and Sioux, prefaced by an extensive historical and ethnological commentary. 36 illustrations. 480pp. 5⅜ x 8½. 0-486-25967-6

AN ENCYCLOPEDIA OF BATTLES: Accounts of Over 1,560 Battles from 1479 B.C. to the Present, David Eggenberger. Essential details of every major battle in recorded history from the first battle of Megiddo in 1479 B.C. to Grenada in 1984. List of Battle Maps. New Appendix covering the years 1967-1984. Index. 99 illustrations. 544pp. 6½ x 9¼. 0-486-24913-1

SAILING ALONE AROUND THE WORLD, Captain Joshua Slocum. First man to sail around the world, alone, in small boat. One of great feats of seamanship told in delightful manner. 67 illustrations. 294pp. 5⅜ x 8½. 0-486-20326-3

ANARCHISM AND OTHER ESSAYS, Emma Goldman. Powerful, penetrating, prophetic essays on direct action, role of minorities, prison reform, puritan hypocrisy, violence, etc. 271pp. 5⅜ x 8½. 0-486-22484-8

MYTHS OF THE HINDUS AND BUDDHISTS, Ananda K. Coomaraswamy and Sister Nivedita. Great stories of the epics; deeds of Krishna, Shiva, taken from puranas, Vedas, folk tales; etc. 32 illustrations. 400pp. 5⅜ x 8½. 0-486-21759-0

MY BONDAGE AND MY FREEDOM, Frederick Douglass. Born a slave, Douglass became outspoken force in antislavery movement. The best of Douglass' autobiographies. Graphic description of slave life. 464pp. 5⅜ x 8½. 0-486-22457-0

FOLLOWING THE EQUATOR: A Journey Around the World, Mark Twain. Fascinating humorous account of 1897 voyage to Hawaii, Australia, India, New Zealand, etc. Ironic, bemused reports on peoples, customs, climate, flora and fauna, politics, much more. 197 illustrations. 720pp. 5⅜ x 8½. 0-486-26113-1

THE PEOPLE CALLED SHAKERS, Edward D. Andrews. Definitive study of Shakers: origins, beliefs, practices, dances, social organization, furniture and crafts, etc. 33 illustrations. 351pp. 5⅜ x 8½. 0-486-21081-2

THE MYTHS OF GREECE AND ROME, H. A. Guerber. A classic of mythology, generously illustrated, long prized for its simple, graphic, accurate retelling of the principal myths of Greece and Rome, and for its commentary on their origins and significance. With 64 illustrations by Michelangelo, Raphael, Titian, Rubens, Canova, Bernini and others. 480pp. 5⅜ x 8½. 0-486-27584-1

PSYCHOLOGY OF MUSIC, Carl E. Seashore. Classic work discusses music as a medium from psychological viewpoint. Clear treatment of physical acoustics, auditory apparatus, sound perception, development of musical skills, nature of musical feeling, host of other topics. 88 figures. 408pp. 5⅜ x 8½.　　　0-486-21851-1

LIFE IN ANCIENT EGYPT, Adolf Erman. Fullest, most thorough, detailed older account with much not in more recent books, domestic life, religion, magic, medicine, commerce, much more. Many illustrations reproduce tomb paintings, carvings, hieroglyphs, etc. 597pp. 5⅜ x 8½.　　　0-486-22632-8

SUNDIALS, Their Theory and Construction, Albert Waugh. Far and away the best, most thorough coverage of ideas, mathematics concerned, types, construction, adjusting anywhere. Simple, nontechnical treatment allows even children to build several of these dials. Over 100 illustrations. 230pp. 5⅜ x 8½.　　　0-486-22947-5

THEORETICAL HYDRODYNAMICS, L. M. Milne-Thomson. Classic exposition of the mathematical theory of fluid motion, applicable to both hydrodynamics and aerodynamics. Over 600 exercises. 768pp. 6⅛ x 9¼.　　　0-486-68970-0

OLD-TIME VIGNETTES IN FULL COLOR, Carol Belanger Grafton (ed.). Over 390 charming, often sentimental illustrations, selected from archives of Victorian graphics—pretty women posing, children playing, food, flowers, kittens and puppies, smiling cherubs, birds and butterflies, much more. All copyright-free. 48pp. 9¼ x 12¼.
　　　0-486-27269-9

PERSPECTIVE FOR ARTISTS, Rex Vicat Cole. Depth, perspective of sky and sea, shadows, much more, not usually covered. 391 diagrams, 81 reproductions of drawings and paintings. 279pp. 5⅜ x 8½.　　　0-486-22487-2

DRAWING THE LIVING FIGURE, Joseph Sheppard. Innovative approach to artistic anatomy focuses on specifics of surface anatomy, rather than muscles and bones. Over 170 drawings of live models in front, back and side views, and in widely varying poses. Accompanying diagrams. 177 illustrations. Introduction. Index. 144pp. 8⅜ x11¼.　　　0-486-26723-7

GOTHIC AND OLD ENGLISH ALPHABETS: 100 Complete Fonts, Dan X. Solo. Add power, elegance to posters, signs, other graphics with 100 stunning copyright-free alphabets: Blackstone, Dolbey, Germania, 97 more—including many lower-case, numerals, punctuation marks. 104pp. 8⅛ x 11.　　　0-486-24695-7

THE BOOK OF WOOD CARVING, Charles Marshall Sayers. Finest book for beginners discusses fundamentals and offers 34 designs. "Absolutely first rate . . . well thought out and well executed."—E. J. Tangerman. 118pp. 7¾ x 10⅝.　　0-486-23654-4

ILLUSTRATED CATALOG OF CIVIL WAR MILITARY GOODS: Union Army Weapons, Insignia, Uniform Accessories, and Other Equipment, Schuyler, Hartley, and Graham. Rare, profusely illustrated 1846 catalog includes Union Army uniform and dress regulations, arms and ammunition, coats, insignia, flags, swords, rifles, etc. 226 illustrations. 160pp. 9 x 12.　　　0-486-24939-5

WOMEN'S FASHIONS OF THE EARLY 1900s: An Unabridged Republication of "New York Fashions, 1909," National Cloak & Suit Co. Rare catalog of mail-order fashions documents women's and children's clothing styles shortly after the turn of the century. Captions offer full descriptions, prices. Invaluable resource for fashion, costume historians. Approximately 725 illustrations. 128pp. 8⅜ x 11¼.
　　　0-486-27276-1

HOW TO DO BEADWORK, Mary White. Fundamental book on craft from simple projects to five-bead chains and woven works. 106 illustrations. 142pp. 5⅜ x 8. 0-486-20697-1

THE 1912 AND 1915 GUSTAV STICKLEY FURNITURE CATALOGS, Gustav Stickley. With over 200 detailed illustrations and descriptions, these two catalogs are essential reading and reference materials and identification guides for Stickley furniture. Captions cite materials, dimensions and prices. 112pp. 6½ x 9¼. 0-486-26676-1

EARLY AMERICAN LOCOMOTIVES, John H. White, Jr. Finest locomotive engravings from early 19th century: historical (1804–74), main-line (after 1870), special, foreign, etc. 147 plates. 142pp. 11⅜ x 8¼. 0-486-22772-3

LITTLE BOOK OF EARLY AMERICAN CRAFTS AND TRADES, Peter Stockham (ed.). 1807 children's book explains crafts and trades: baker, hatter, cooper, potter, and many others. 23 copperplate illustrations. 140pp. 4⅝ x 6. 0-486-23336-7

VICTORIAN FASHIONS AND COSTUMES FROM HARPER'S BAZAR, 1867–1898, Stella Blum (ed.). Day costumes, evening wear, sports clothes, shoes, hats, other accessories in over 1,000 detailed engravings. 320pp. 9⅜ x 12¼. 0-486-22990-4

THE LONG ISLAND RAIL ROAD IN EARLY PHOTOGRAPHS, Ron Ziel. Over 220 rare photos, informative text document origin (1844) and development of rail service on Long Island. Vintage views of early trains, locomotives, stations, passengers, crews, much more. Captions. 8⅞ x 11¾. 0-486-26301-0

VOYAGE OF THE LIBERDADE, Joshua Slocum. Great 19th-century mariner's thrilling, first-hand account of the wreck of his ship off South America, the 35-foot boat he built from the wreckage, and its remarkable voyage home. 128pp. 5⅜ x 8½. 0-486-40022-0

TEN BOOKS ON ARCHITECTURE, Vitruvius. The most important book ever written on architecture. Early Roman aesthetics, technology, classical orders, site selection, all other aspects. Morgan translation. 331pp. 5⅜ x 8½. 0-486-20645-9

THE HUMAN FIGURE IN MOTION, Eadweard Muybridge. More than 4,500 stopped-action photos, in action series, showing undraped men, women, children jumping, lying down, throwing, sitting, wrestling, carrying, etc. 390pp. 7⅞ x 10⅝. 0-486-20204-6 Clothbd.

TREES OF THE EASTERN AND CENTRAL UNITED STATES AND CANADA, William M. Harlow. Best one-volume guide to 140 trees. Full descriptions, woodlore, range, etc. Over 600 illustrations. Handy size. 288pp. 4½ x 6⅜. 0-486-20395-6

GROWING AND USING HERBS AND SPICES, Milo Miloradovich. Versatile handbook provides all the information needed for cultivation and use of all the herbs and spices available in North America. 4 illustrations. Index. Glossary. 236pp. 5⅜ x 8½. 0-486-25058-X

BIG BOOK OF MAZES AND LABYRINTHS, Walter Shepherd. 50 mazes and labyrinths in all–classical, solid, ripple, and more–in one great volume. Perfect inexpensive puzzler for clever youngsters. Full solutions. 112pp. 8⅛ x 11. 0-486-22951-3

PIANO TUNING, J. Cree Fischer. Clearest, best book for beginner, amateur. Simple repairs, raising dropped notes, tuning by easy method of flattened fifths. No previous skills needed. 4 illustrations. 201pp. 5⅜ x 8½. 0-486-23267-0

HINTS TO SINGERS, Lillian Nordica. Selecting the right teacher, developing confidence, overcoming stage fright, and many other important skills receive thoughtful discussion in this indispensible guide, written by a world-famous diva of four decades' experience. 96pp. 5⅜ x 8½. 0-486-40094-8

THE COMPLETE NONSENSE OF EDWARD LEAR, Edward Lear. All nonsense limericks, zany alphabets, Owl and Pussycat, songs, nonsense botany, etc., illustrated by Lear. Total of 320pp. 5⅜ x 8½. (Available in U.S. only.) 0-486-20167-8

VICTORIAN PARLOUR POETRY: An Annotated Anthology, Michael R. Turner. 117 gems by Longfellow, Tennyson, Browning, many lesser-known poets. "The Village Blacksmith," "Curfew Must Not Ring Tonight," "Only a Baby Small," dozens more, often difficult to find elsewhere. Index of poets, titles, first lines. xxiii + 325pp. 5⅝ x 8¼. 0-486-27044-0

DUBLINERS, James Joyce. Fifteen stories offer vivid, tightly focused observations of the lives of Dublin's poorer classes. At least one, "The Dead," is considered a masterpiece. Reprinted complete and unabridged from standard edition. 160pp. 5$\frac{3}{16}$ x 8¼. 0-486-26870-5

GREAT WEIRD TALES: 14 Stories by Lovecraft, Blackwood, Machen and Others, S. T. Joshi (ed.). 14 spellbinding tales, including "The Sin Eater," by Fiona McLeod, "The Eye Above the Mantel," by Frank Belknap Long, as well as renowned works by R. H. Barlow, Lord Dunsany, Arthur Machen, W. C. Morrow and eight other masters of the genre. 256pp. 5⅜ x 8½. (Available in U.S. only.) 0-486-40436-6

THE BOOK OF THE SACRED MAGIC OF ABRAMELIN THE MAGE, translated by S. MacGregor Mathers. Medieval manuscript of ceremonial magic. Basic document in Aleister Crowley, Golden Dawn groups. 268pp. 5⅜ x 8½. 0-486-23211-5

THE BATTLES THAT CHANGED HISTORY, Fletcher Pratt. Eminent historian profiles 16 crucial conflicts, ancient to modern, that changed the course of civilization. 352pp. 5⅜ x 8½. 0-486-41129-X

NEW RUSSIAN-ENGLISH AND ENGLISH-RUSSIAN DICTIONARY, M. A. O'Brien. This is a remarkably handy Russian dictionary, containing a surprising amount of information, including over 70,000 entries. 366pp. 4½ x 6⅛. 0-486-20208-9

NEW YORK IN THE FORTIES, Andreas Feininger. 162 brilliant photographs by the well-known photographer, formerly with *Life* magazine. Commuters, shoppers, Times Square at night, much else from city at its peak. Captions by John von Hartz. 181pp. 9¼ x 10¾. 0-486-23585-8

INDIAN SIGN LANGUAGE, William Tomkins. Over 525 signs developed by Sioux and other tribes. Written instructions and diagrams. Also 290 pictographs. 111pp. 6⅛ x 9¼. 0-486-22029-X

ANATOMY: A Complete Guide for Artists, Joseph Sheppard. A master of figure drawing shows artists how to render human anatomy convincingly. Over 460 illustrations. 224pp. 8⅜ x 11¼. 0-486-27279-6

MEDIEVAL CALLIGRAPHY: Its History and Technique, Marc Drogin. Spirited history, comprehensive instruction manual covers 13 styles (ca. 4th century through 15th). Excellent photographs; directions for duplicating medieval techniques with modern tools. 224pp. 8⅜ x 11¼. 0-486-26142-5

CATALOG OF DOVER BOOKS

DRIED FLOWERS: How to Prepare Them, Sarah Whitlock and Martha Rankin. Complete instructions on how to use silica gel, meal and borax, perlite aggregate, sand and borax, glycerine and water to create attractive permanent flower arrangements. 12 illustrations. 32pp. 5⅜ x 8½.　　　　　0-486-21802-3

EASY-TO-MAKE BIRD FEEDERS FOR WOODWORKERS, Scott D. Campbell. Detailed, simple-to-use guide for designing, constructing, caring for and using feeders. Text, illustrations for 12 classic and contemporary designs. 96pp. 5⅜ x 8½.
0-486-25847-5

THE COMPLETE BOOK OF BIRDHOUSE CONSTRUCTION FOR WOOD-WORKERS, Scott D. Campbell. Detailed instructions, illustrations, tables. Also data on bird habitat and instinct patterns. Bibliography. 3 tables. 63 illustrations in 15 figures. 48pp. 5¼ x 8½.　　　　　0-486-24407-5

SCOTTISH WONDER TALES FROM MYTH AND LEGEND, Donald A. Mackenzie. 16 lively tales tell of giants rumbling down mountainsides, of a magic wand that turns stone pillars into warriors, of gods and goddesses, evil hags, powerful forces and more. 240pp. 5⅜ x 8½.　　　　　0-486-29677-6

THE HISTORY OF UNDERCLOTHES, C. Willett Cunnington and Phyllis Cunnington. Fascinating, well-documented survey covering six centuries of English undergarments, enhanced with over 100 illustrations: 12th-century laced-up bodice, footed long drawers (1795), 19th-century bustles, 19th-century corsets for men, Victorian "bust improvers," much more. 272pp. 5⅜ x 8¼.　　0-486-27124-2

ARTS AND CRAFTS FURNITURE: The Complete Brooks Catalog of 1912, Brooks Manufacturing Co. Photos and detailed descriptions of more than 150 now very collectible furniture designs from the Arts and Crafts movement depict davenports, settees, buffets, desks, tables, chairs, bedsteads, dressers and more, all built of solid, quarter-sawed oak. Invaluable for students and enthusiasts of antiques, Americana and the decorative arts. 80pp. 6½ x 9¼.　　0-486-27471-3

WILBUR AND ORVILLE: A Biography of the Wright Brothers, Fred Howard. Definitive, crisply written study tells the full story of the brothers' lives and work. A vividly written biography, unparalleled in scope and color, that also captures the spirit of an extraordinary era. 560pp. 6⅛ x 9¼.　　0-486-40297-5

THE ARTS OF THE SAILOR: Knotting, Splicing and Ropework, Hervey Garrett Smith. Indispensable shipboard reference covers tools, basic knots and useful hitches; handsewing and canvas work, more. Over 100 illustrations. Delightful reading for sea lovers. 256pp. 5⅜ x 8½.　　　　　0-486-26440-8

FRANK LLOYD WRIGHT'S FALLINGWATER: The House and Its History, Second, Revised Edition, Donald Hoffmann. A total revision—both in text and illustrations—of the standard document on Fallingwater, the boldest, most personal architectural statement of Wright's mature years, updated with valuable new material from the recently opened Frank Lloyd Wright Archives. "Fascinating"—*The New York Times*. 116 illustrations. 128pp. 9¼ x 10¾.　　0-486-27430-6

PHOTOGRAPHIC SKETCHBOOK OF THE CIVIL WAR, Alexander Gardner. 100 photos taken on field during the Civil War. Famous shots of Manassas Harper's Ferry, Lincoln, Richmond, slave pens, etc. 244pp. 10⅝ x 8¼.　0-486-22731-6

FIVE ACRES AND INDEPENDENCE, Maurice G. Kains. Great back-to-the-land classic explains basics of self-sufficient farming. The one book to get. 95 illustrations. 397pp. 5⅜ x 8½.　　　　　0-486-20974-1

CATALOG OF DOVER BOOKS

A MODERN HERBAL, Margaret Grieve. Much the fullest, most exact, most useful compilation of herbal material. Gigantic alphabetical encyclopedia, from aconite to zedoary, gives botanical information, medical properties, folklore, economic uses, much else. Indispensable to serious reader. 161 illustrations. 888pp. 6½ x 9¼. 2-vol. set. (Available in U.S. only.)   Vol. I: 0-486-22798-7   Vol. II: 0-486-22799-5

HIDDEN TREASURE MAZE BOOK, Dave Phillips. Solve 34 challenging mazes accompanied by heroic tales of adventure. Evil dragons, people-eating plants, bloodthirsty giants, many more dangerous adversaries lurk at every twist and turn. 34 mazes, stories, solutions. 48pp. 8¼ x 11.   0-486-24566-7

LETTERS OF W. A. MOZART, Wolfgang A. Mozart. Remarkable letters show bawdy wit, humor, imagination, musical insights, contemporary musical world; includes some letters from Leopold Mozart. 276pp. 5⅜ x 8½.   0-486-22859-2

BASIC PRINCIPLES OF CLASSICAL BALLET, Agrippina Vaganova. Great Russian theoretician, teacher explains methods for teaching classical ballet. 118 illustrations. 175pp. 5⅜ x 8½.   0-486-22036-2

THE JUMPING FROG, Mark Twain. Revenge edition. The original story of The Celebrated Jumping Frog of Calaveras County, a hapless French translation, and Twain's hilarious "retranslation" from the French. 12 illustrations. 66pp. 5⅜ x 8½.
0-486-22686-7

BEST REMEMBERED POEMS, Martin Gardner (ed.). The 126 poems in this superb collection of 19th- and 20th-century British and American verse range from Shelley's "To a Skylark" to the impassioned "Renascence" of Edna St. Vincent Millay and to Edward Lear's whimsical "The Owl and the Pussycat." 224pp. 5⅜ x 8½.
0-486-27165-X

COMPLETE SONNETS, William Shakespeare. Over 150 exquisite poems deal with love, friendship, the tyranny of time, beauty's evanescence, death and other themes in language of remarkable power, precision and beauty. Glossary of archaic terms. 80pp. 5³⁄₁₆ x 8¼.   0-486-26686-9

HISTORIC HOMES OF THE AMERICAN PRESIDENTS, Second, Revised Edition, Irvin Haas. A traveler's guide to American Presidential homes, most open to the public, depicting and describing homes occupied by every American President from George Washington to George Bush. With visiting hours, admission charges, travel routes. 175 photographs. Index. 160pp. 8¼ x 11.   0-486-26751-2

THE WIT AND HUMOR OF OSCAR WILDE, Alvin Redman (ed.). More than 1,000 ripostes, paradoxes, wisecracks: Work is the curse of the drinking classes; I can resist everything except temptation; etc. 258pp. 5⅜ x 8½.   0-486-20602-5

SHAKESPEARE LEXICON AND QUOTATION DICTIONARY, Alexander Schmidt. Full definitions, locations, shades of meaning in every word in plays and poems. More than 50,000 exact quotations. 1,485pp. 6½ x 9¼. 2-vol. set.
Vol. 1: 0-486-22726-X   Vol. 2: 0-486-22727-8

SELECTED POEMS, Emily Dickinson. Over 100 best-known, best-loved poems by one of America's foremost poets, reprinted from authoritative early editions. No comparable edition at this price. Index of first lines. 64pp. 5³⁄₁₆ x 8¼.   0-486-26466-1

THE INSIDIOUS DR. FU-MANCHU, Sax Rohmer. The first of the popular mystery series introduces a pair of English detectives to their archnemesis, the diabolical Dr. Fu-Manchu. Flavorful atmosphere, fast-paced action, and colorful characters enliven this classic of the genre. 208pp. 5³⁄₁₆ x 8¼.   0-486-29898-1

THE MALLEUS MALEFICARUM OF KRAMER AND SPRENGER, translated by Montague Summers. Full text of most important witchhunter's "bible," used by both Catholics and Protestants. 278pp. 6⅝ x 10. 0-486-22802-9

SPANISH STORIES/CUENTOS ESPAÑOLES: A Dual-Language Book, Angel Flores (ed.). Unique format offers 13 great stories in Spanish by Cervantes, Borges, others. Faithful English translations on facing pages. 352pp. 5⅜ x 8½. 0-486-25399-6

GARDEN CITY, LONG ISLAND, IN EARLY PHOTOGRAPHS, 1869–1919, Mildred H. Smith. Handsome treasury of 118 vintage pictures, accompanied by carefully researched captions, document the Garden City Hotel fire (1899), the Vanderbilt Cup Race (1908), the first airmail flight departing from the Nassau Boulevard Aerodrome (1911), and much more. 96pp. 8⅞ x 11¾. 0-486-40669-5

OLD QUEENS, N.Y., IN EARLY PHOTOGRAPHS, Vincent F. Seyfried and William Asadorian. Over 160 rare photographs of Maspeth, Jamaica, Jackson Heights, and other areas. Vintage views of DeWitt Clinton mansion, 1939 World's Fair and more. Captions. 192pp. 8⅞ x 11. 0-486-26358-4

CAPTURED BY THE INDIANS: 15 Firsthand Accounts, 1750-1870, Frederick Drimmer. Astounding true historical accounts of grisly torture, bloody conflicts, relentless pursuits, miraculous escapes and more, by people who lived to tell the tale. 384pp. 5⅜ x 8½. 0-486-24901-8

THE WORLD'S GREAT SPEECHES (Fourth Enlarged Edition), Lewis Copeland, Lawrence W. Lamm, and Stephen J. McKenna. Nearly 300 speeches provide public speakers with a wealth of updated quotes and inspiration–from Pericles' funeral oration and William Jennings Bryan's "Cross of Gold Speech" to Malcolm X's powerful words on the Black Revolution and Earl of Spenser's tribute to his sister, Diana, Princess of Wales. 944pp. 5⅜ x 8⅜. 0-486-40903-1

THE BOOK OF THE SWORD, Sir Richard F. Burton. Great Victorian scholar/adventurer's eloquent, erudite history of the "queen of weapons"–from prehistory to early Roman Empire. Evolution and development of early swords, variations (sabre, broadsword, cutlass, scimitar, etc.), much more. 336pp. 6⅛ x 9¼. 0-486-25434-8

AUTOBIOGRAPHY: The Story of My Experiments with Truth, Mohandas K. Gandhi. Boyhood, legal studies, purification, the growth of the Satyagraha (nonviolent protest) movement. Critical, inspiring work of the man responsible for the freedom of India. 480pp. 5⅜ x 8½. (Available in U.S. only.) 0-486-24593-4

CELTIC MYTHS AND LEGENDS, T. W. Rolleston. Masterful retelling of Irish and Welsh stories and tales. Cuchulain, King Arthur, Deirdre, the Grail, many more. First paperback edition. 58 full-page illustrations. 512pp. 5⅜ x 8½. 0-486-26507-2

THE PRINCIPLES OF PSYCHOLOGY, William James. Famous long course complete, unabridged. Stream of thought, time perception, memory, experimental methods; great work decades ahead of its time. 94 figures. 1,391pp. 5⅜ x 8½. 2-vol. set. Vol. I: 0-486-20381-6 Vol. II: 0-486-20382-4

THE WORLD AS WILL AND REPRESENTATION, Arthur Schopenhauer. Definitive English translation of Schopenhauer's life work, correcting more than 1,000 errors, omissions in earlier translations. Translated by E. F. J. Payne. Total of 1,269pp. 5⅜ x 8½. 2-vol. set. Vol. 1: 0-486-21761-2 Vol. 2: 0-486-21762-0

MAGIC AND MYSTERY IN TIBET, Madame Alexandra David-Neel. Experiences among lamas, magicians, sages, sorcerers, Bonpa wizards. A true psychic discovery. 32 illustrations. 321pp. 5⅜ x 8½. (Available in U.S. only.) 0-486-22682-4

THE EGYPTIAN BOOK OF THE DEAD, E. A. Wallis Budge. Complete reproduction of Ani's papyrus, finest ever found. Full hieroglyphic text, interlinear transliteration, word-for-word translation, smooth translation. 533pp. 6½ x 9¼. 0-486-21866-X

HISTORIC COSTUME IN PICTURES, Braun & Schneider. Over 1,450 costumed figures in clearly detailed engravings–from dawn of civilization to end of 19th century. Captions. Many folk costumes. 256pp. 8⅜ x 11¾. 0-486-23150-X

MATHEMATICS FOR THE NONMATHEMATICIAN, Morris Kline. Detailed, college-level treatment of mathematics in cultural and historical context, with numerous exercises. Recommended Reading Lists. Tables. Numerous figures. 641pp. 5⅜ x 8½. 0-486-24823-2

PROBABILISTIC METHODS IN THE THEORY OF STRUCTURES, Isaac Elishakoff. Well-written introduction covers the elements of the theory of probability from two or more random variables, the reliability of such multivariable structures, the theory of random function, Monte Carlo methods of treating problems incapable of exact solution, and more. Examples. 502pp. 5⅜ x 8½. 0-486-40691-1

THE RIME OF THE ANCIENT MARINER, Gustave Doré, S. T. Coleridge. Doré's finest work; 34 plates capture moods, subtleties of poem. Flawless full-size reproductions printed on facing pages with authoritative text of poem. "Beautiful. Simply beautiful."–*Publisher's Weekly.* 77pp. 9¼ x 12. 0-486-22305-1

SCULPTURE: Principles and Practice, Louis Slobodkin. Step-by-step approach to clay, plaster, metals, stone; classical and modern. 253 drawings, photos. 255pp. 8⅛ x 11. 0-486-22960-2

THE INFLUENCE OF SEA POWER UPON HISTORY, 1660–1783, A. T. Mahan. Influential classic of naval history and tactics still used as text in war colleges. First paperback edition. 4 maps. 24 battle plans. 640pp. 5⅜ x 8½. 0-486-25509-3

THE STORY OF THE TITANIC AS TOLD BY ITS SURVIVORS, Jack Winocour (ed.). What it was really like. Panic, despair, shocking inefficiency, and a little heroism. More thrilling than any fictional account. 26 illustrations. 320pp. 5⅜ x 8½. 0-486-20610-6

ONE TWO THREE . . . INFINITY: Facts and Speculations of Science, George Gamow. Great physicist's fascinating, readable overview of contemporary science: number theory, relativity, fourth dimension, entropy, genes, atomic structure, much more. 128 illustrations. Index. 352pp. 5⅜ x 8½. 0-486-25664-2

DALÍ ON MODERN ART: The Cuckolds of Antiquated Modern Art, Salvador Dalí. Influential painter skewers modern art and its practitioners. Outrageous evaluations of Picasso, Cézanne, Turner, more. 15 renderings of paintings discussed. 44 calligraphic decorations by Dalí. 96pp. 5⅜ x 8½. (Available in U.S. only.) 0-486-29220-7

ANTIQUE PLAYING CARDS: A Pictorial History, Henry René D'Allemagne. Over 900 elaborate, decorative images from rare playing cards (14th–20th centuries): Bacchus, death, dancing dogs, hunting scenes, royal coats of arms, players cheating, much more. 96pp. 9¼ x 12¼. 0-486-29265-7

MAKING FURNITURE MASTERPIECES: 30 Projects with Measured Drawings, Franklin H. Gottshall. Step-by-step instructions, illustrations for constructing handsome, useful pieces, among them a Sheraton desk, Chippendale chair, Spanish desk, Queen Anne table and a William and Mary dressing mirror. 224pp. 8⅛ x 11¼.
0-486-29338-6

NORTH AMERICAN INDIAN DESIGNS FOR ARTISTS AND CRAFTSPEOPLE, Eva Wilson. Over 360 authentic copyright-free designs adapted from Navajo blankets, Hopi pottery, Sioux buffalo hides, more. Geometrics, symbolic figures, plant and animal motifs, etc. 128pp. 8⅜ x 11. (Not for sale in the United Kingdom.)   0-486-25341-4

THE FOSSIL BOOK: A Record of Prehistoric Life, Patricia V. Rich et al. Profusely illustrated definitive guide covers everything from single-celled organisms and dinosaurs to birds and mammals and the interplay between climate and man. Over 1,500 illustrations. 760pp. 7½ x 10⅛.   0-486-29371-8

VICTORIAN ARCHITECTURAL DETAILS: Designs for Over 700 Stairs, Mantels, Doors, Windows, Cornices, Porches, and Other Decorative Elements, A. J. Bicknell & Company. Everything from dormer windows and piazzas to balconies and gable ornaments. Also includes elevations and floor plans for handsome, private residences and commercial structures. 80pp. 9⅜ x 12¼.   0-486-44015-X

WESTERN ISLAMIC ARCHITECTURE: A Concise Introduction, John D. Hoag. Profusely illustrated critical appraisal compares and contrasts Islamic mosques and palaces—from Spain and Egypt to other areas in the Middle East. 139 illustrations. 128pp. 6 x 9.   0-486-43760-4

CHINESE ARCHITECTURE: A Pictorial History, Liang Ssu-ch'eng. More than 240 rare photographs and drawings depict temples, pagodas, tombs, bridges, and imperial palaces comprising much of China's architectural heritage. 152 halftones, 94 diagrams. 232pp. 10¾ x 9⅞.   0-486-43999-2

THE RENAISSANCE: Studies in Art and Poetry, Walter Pater. One of the most talked-about books of the 19th century, *The Renaissance* combines scholarship and philosophy in an innovative work of cultural criticism that examines the achievements of Botticelli, Leonardo, Michelangelo, and other artists. "The holy writ of beauty."–Oscar Wilde. 160pp. 5⅜ x 8½.   0-486-44025-7

A TREATISE ON PAINTING, Leonardo da Vinci. The great Renaissance artist's practical advice on drawing and painting techniques covers anatomy, perspective, composition, light and shadow, and color. A classic of art instruction, it features 48 drawings by Nicholas Poussin and Leon Battista Alberti. 192pp. 5⅜ x 8½.
0-486-44155-5

THE MIND OF LEONARDO DA VINCI, Edward McCurdy. More than just a biography, this classic study by a distinguished historian draws upon Leonardo's extensive writings to offer numerous demonstrations of the Renaissance master's achievements, not only in sculpture and painting, but also in music, engineering, and even experimental aviation. 384pp. 5⅜ x 8½.   0-486-44142-3

WASHINGTON IRVING'S RIP VAN WINKLE, Illustrated by Arthur Rackham. Lovely prints that established artist as a leading illustrator of the time and forever etched into the popular imagination a classic of Catskill lore. 51 full-color plates. 80pp. 8⅜ x 11.   0-486-44242-X

HENSCHE ON PAINTING, John W. Robichaux. Basic painting philosophy and methodology of a great teacher, as expounded in his famous classes and workshops on Cape Cod. 7 illustrations in color on covers. 80pp. 5⅜ x 8½.   0-486-43728-0

LIGHT AND SHADE: A Classic Approach to Three-Dimensional Drawing, Mrs. Mary P. Merrifield. Handy reference clearly demonstrates principles of light and shade by revealing effects of common daylight, sunshine, and candle or artificial light on geometrical solids. 13 plates. 64pp. 5⅜ x 8½. 0-486-44143-1

ASTROLOGY AND ASTRONOMY: A Pictorial Archive of Signs and Symbols, Ernst and Johanna Lehner. Treasure trove of stories, lore, and myth, accompanied by more than 300 rare illustrations of planets, the Milky Way, signs of the zodiac, comets, meteors, and other astronomical phenomena. 192pp. 8⅜ x 11. 0-486-43981-X

JEWELRY MAKING: Techniques for Metal, Tim McCreight. Easy-to-follow instructions and carefully executed illustrations describe tools and techniques, use of gems and enamels, wire inlay, casting, and other topics. 72 line illustrations and diagrams. 176pp. 8¼ x 10⅞. 0-486-44043-5

MAKING BIRDHOUSES: Easy and Advanced Projects, Gladstone Califf. Easy-to-follow instructions include diagrams for everything from a one-room house for bluebirds to a forty-two-room structure for purple martins. 56 plates; 4 figures. 80pp. 8¾ x 6⅜. 0-486-44183-0

LITTLE BOOK OF LOG CABINS: How to Build and Furnish Them, William S. Wicks. Handy how-to manual, with instructions and illustrations for building cabins in the Adirondack style, fireplaces, stairways, furniture, beamed ceilings, and more. 102 line drawings. 96pp. 8¾ x 6⅜. 0-486-44259-4

THE SEASONS OF AMERICA PAST, Eric Sloane. From "sugaring time" and strawberry picking to Indian summer and fall harvest, a whole year's activities described in charming prose and enhanced with 79 of the author's own illustrations. 160pp. 8¼ x 11. 0-486-44220-9

THE METROPOLIS OF TOMORROW, Hugh Ferriss. Generous, prophetic vision of the metropolis of the future, as perceived in 1929. Powerful illustrations of towering structures, wide avenues, and rooftop parks–all features in many of today's modern cities. 59 illustrations. 144pp. 8¼ x 11. 0-486-43727-2

THE PATH TO ROME, Hilaire Belloc. This 1902 memoir abounds in lively vignettes from a vanished time, recounting a pilgrimage on foot across the Alps and Apennines in order to "see all Europe which the Christian Faith has saved." 77 of the author's original line drawings complement his sparkling prose. 272pp. 5⅜ x 8½. 0-486-44001-X

THE HISTORY OF RASSELAS: Prince of Abissinia, Samuel Johnson. Distinguished English writer attacks eighteenth-century optimism and man's unrealistic estimates of what life has to offer. 112pp. 5⅜ x 8½. 0-486-44094-X

A VOYAGE TO ARCTURUS, David Lindsay. A brilliant flight of pure fancy, where wild creatures crowd the fantastic landscape and demented torturers dominate victims with their bizarre mental powers. 272pp. 5⅜ x 8½. 0-486-44198-9

Paperbound unless otherwise indicated. Available at your book dealer, online at **www.doverpublications.com**, or by writing to Dept. GI, Dover Publications, Inc., 31 East 2nd Street, Mineola, NY 11501. For current price information or for free catalogs (please indicate field of interest), write to Dover Publications or log on to **www.doverpublications.com** and see every Dover book in print. Dover publishes more than 500 books each year on science, elementary and advanced mathematics, biology, music, art, literary history, social sciences, and other areas.